MUSIC LIBRARIANSHIP IN THE UNITED KINGDOM

Music Librarianship in the United Kingdom

Fifty Years of the United Kingdom Branch of the International Association of Music Libraries, Archives and Documentation Centres

Edited by
RICHARD TURBET

ASHGATE

Published by
Ashgate Publishing Limited
Gower House
Croft Road
Aldershot
Hants GU11 3HR
England

Ashgate Publishing Company
Suite 420
101 Cherry Street
Burlington
VT 05401-4405
USA

Ashgate website: http://www.ashgate.com

British Library Cataloguing in Publication Data
Music librarianship in the United Kingdom : fifty years of the UK branch of the
    International Association of Music Libraries
    1.International Association of Music Libraries 2.Music librarianship - Great
    Britain - History
    I.Turbet, R. B. (Richard Beaumont)
    026.7'8'0941

Library of Congress Cataloging-in-Publication Data
Music librarianship in the United Kingdom : fifty years of the UK Branch of the
International Association of Music Libraries / edited by Richard Turbet.
        p. cm.
    Includes bibliographical references.
    ISBN 0-7546-0572-8 (hardback : alk. paper)
        1. Music librarianship--Great Britain. I. Turbet, Richard. II. International
Association of Music Libraries, Archives, and Documentation Centres.
United Kingdom Branch.

ML111 .M758 2002
026'.78'0941--dc21

2002028119

ISBN 0 7546 0572 8

Typeset by Bournemouth Colour Press, Parkstone and printed and bound in Great Britain by MPG Books Ltd., Bodmin, Cornwall.

Contents

A note on the contributors   vii

Foreword   x
Susi Woodhouse

Introduction   xii
Richard Turbet

Acknowledgements   xv

Abbreviations   xvi

1 Fifty years of IAML(UK)   1
   Brian Redfern and Ruth Hellen

2 'Shrouded in mystery': the development of music provision in public
   libraries in Great Britain, 1850–1950   17
   Malcolm Lewis

3 Music information skills at the University of Reading   57
   Christopher Cipkin

4 'The turning wheel': training for music librarianship over 50 years   74
   Ian Ledsham

5 *Musaurus* and *MusBib*   84
   Ann Harrold and Graham Lea

6 'The most intricate bibliographical enigma': understanding George
   Thomson (1757–1851) and his collections of national airs   99
   Kirsteen McCue

7 Con *Brio:* a history of the Branch journal   120
   Malcolm Jones

8 Making a library for IAML(UK)   127
   John Wagstaff

9 The unique first edition of Byrd's *Gradualia* in York Minster Library   137
   Richard Turbet

10 Information technology and music libraries   141
   Julie Crawley

11 Larks ascending: co-operation in music libraries – the last 50 years   172
    Pamela Thompson

12 Cecilia: towards a map of the music resource of the UK and Ireland   200
    Paul Andrews

13 Greater than the sum of its parts: towards a national service for music
    performance material   209
    Malcolm Jones and John Gough

14 International outreach: fireworks of the 1990s?   220
    Roger Taylor

15 Things to come – or, ignorance is not Bliss so don't shoot the messenger! 236
    Eric Cooper

Index   245

A note on the contributors

Paul Andrews took his PhD at the University of Wales, Aberystwyth, with work on the composer Herbert Howells. He also holds a Diploma in Theology from the University of Oxford. He was Music Librarian at Bedford Central Library and the Royal College of Music, and is now Project Manager for Cecilia and is an ordained priest in the Church of England.

Christopher Cipkin is Liaison Librarian for Music, Film and Drama at the University of Reading. He has a particular interest in training both library users and staff. Recently, he has published articles on music skills for librarians and on professional mentoring. Christopher is also a Member of the Institute for Learning and Teaching (ILT).

Eric Cooper moved from industry to librarianship in 1949 where he specialized in music and sound recording. His lifelong interest in non-print media and technology continues to this day. He says, to quote Bronowky, 'My regret is I will not be around to see how it turns out'.

Julie Crawley is Deputy Librarian at the Faculty of Music Library, University of Oxford. She has previously worked as Assistant Librarian at the University of Exeter. Julie studied musicology at King's College, London, and Library and Information Science at the University of Illinois, Urbana-Champaign. She has been a member of IAML(UK) since the late 1980s and was General Secretary from 1991 to 1995.

John Gough has worked with music for most of his professional life. An active musician, he has practical experience of the problems surrounding the provision of performance materials. Music librarian for Sutton Coldfield for 20 years, he is now Head of Music Services for Birmingham Libraries. John has served IAML in various capacities over many years and is at present a member of the IAML Executive.

Ann Harrold has been a music librarian at the Central Music Library, Westminster, an information officer at the Library Association, and Publicity Manager for Library Association Publishing. She was the founder of Music Press. Ann has an MLS from Loughborough, her dissertation being on music iconography in seventeenth-century Dutch art. She has been a member of IAML and the RMA.

Ruth Hellen has always worked in public libraries, becoming Audio Visual Librarian with the London Borough of Enfield in 1989 and subsequently Library Resources Unit Manager. She became involved with IAML(UK) as Conference Secretary, later joining the Executive Committee and serving as Press and PR Officer. Ruth was IAML(UK) President from 1998 to 2001 and is currently a Vice President of IAML.

Malcolm Jones, after gaining a degree in Music and English Literature at Southampton, joined Birmingham Public Libraries as a graduate trainee. Shortly after qualifying, he was appointed Birmingham's first Music Librarian, with a brief to create the department. He is a past President and Honorary Member of IAML(UK). He took early retirement in 1995 and now works in the area of music bibliography and information technology, having been project manager for Encore! In 2002 he received the Chartered Institute of Library and Information Professionals' Tony Kent Strix Award for outstanding practical innovation or achievement in the field of information retrieval. Malcolm has been Reader in the Church of England for over 30 years, and in spare time he and his wife, Frances, take to the canals in the narrowboat, Encore!

Graham Lea combined the chairmanship of the school Gramophone Society with the presidency of the Jazz Club. After reading philosophy, then geology, he became an information management consultant and computer scientist. Graham is a specialist in knowledge systems, and served as Chairman of the Association of Database Producers. He participated in a London University course on Medieval and Renaissance music.

Ian Ledsham is a professional musician and qualified librarian. He was Librarian of the Barber Institute of Fine Arts and Music at the University of Birmingham, England, before deciding to pursue a freelance career. He now works as a choir trainer, organist and accompanist, runs the Music Information Consultancy providing freelance research and is a partner in Allegro Training, which provides information skills and management training. He is an honorary Research Fellow in the Department of Music at the University of Birmingham and University Organist there.

Malcolm Lewis is Senior Librarian: Music and Multi-Media with Nottingham City Libraries. He has worked in public libraries since 1966 and before his current appointment worked as music librarian with Croydon, Norwich, Norfolk and Nottinghamshire Libraries. Actively involved in IAML(UK) since the 1970s Malcolm was a member of the Executive Committee from 1985 to 2002 and served as Branch President from 1992 to 1995.

Kirsteen McCue is a lecturer in the department of Scottish Literature at the University of Glasgow. She was formerly director of the Scottish Music Information Centre, and works regularly as a presenter for the British Broadcasting Corporation (BBC).

Brian Redfern was appointed lecturer at North Western Polytechnic Library School (later Polytechnic of North London) in 1961. He retired in 1981 and became editor of MPA's *Music in Print* catalogue until 1997. His posts held with IAML have included President IAML(UK), international President and *Fontes* editor.

Roger Taylor is Performing Arts Librarian at Somerset Libraries Arts and Information. He has worked in public libraries since 1971. Roger served as President of IAML(UK) from 1995 to 1998, and in 1998 was awarded a Library Association Royal Charter Centenary Medal. From 1994 he undertook many professional outreach visits, including Albania (seven times), Bulgaria, Croatia, Hungary, Macedonia and Slovenia. In 1997 he worked as a consultant for the Council of Europe in Vukovar, Croatia.

Pamela Thompson studied Russian at Leeds University, taught English in Czechoslovakia and worked for seven years at Blackwell's Music Shop before moving to the Royal College of Music, where she remains Chief Librarian. She has been involved in IAML work since 1981 as Treasurer and President of both the UK Branch and the international association. She directed the project to produce a Library Information Plan for music and was a founder trustee of the Music Libraries Trust. She translated some 500 articles for the sixth edition of The New Grove Dictionary of Music and contributed articles to the seventh edition. She is a regular speaker at conferences in the UK and abroad.

Richard Turbet is head of Arts and Humanities in Aberdeen University Library, where he is also the Music Librarian. Richard has held posts at the University of Dundee, the University of Calgary, the National Central Library and the Prison Service College. His many publications include *Tudor Music: A Research and Information Guide* (1994) which won the Oldman Prize.

John Wagstaff was born in Kidderminster, Worcestershire. After graduating in music from the universities of Reading and London he was appointed Assistant Librarian in charge of music at King's College London in 1985. Since 1988 he has been Librarian at the Faculty of Music at Oxford University. His activities within IAML(UK) include editorship of *Brio* (1990–94) and of the second edition of the *British Union Catalogue of Music Periodicals* (1998). Since 2001 he has been editor of IAML's international journal, *Fontes artis musicae*.

Susi Woodhouse is currently President of IAML(UK & Irl) and has served on the Executive Committee for a number of years. She undertook the research for the Music Library and Information Plan published by IAML(UK) in 1993, has contributed to the Encore! project, and is project director for Cecilia, the collection map of music resources in the UK and Ireland.

Foreword

Susi Woodhouse

A golden jubilee is a significant milestone providing not only an occasion to celebrate but also to honour people, to remember times past, to take stock, to assess changes that have taken place, to reaffirm a sense of purpose and to look ahead at what the future may hold. It is, therefore, a privilege and a pleasure to provide this short foreword to whet the appetite for what follows. If, in doing so, I anticipate others, I make no apology as I believe repetition simply serves to underpin the message and helps build the platform from which the train to the future departs.

What will immediately be evident from even the briefest of perusals of the broad-ranging chapters which follow is that they reflect, despite their varied topics, common themes: commitment, a keen sense of purpose, a wealth of expertise and a shared passion and delight in music. It does not seem to matter what kind of library or institution we work in, it is the subject which drives us and which motivates our activities. For me, this is what characterizes the Branch and is what is embodied in this Golden Jubilee. I have always felt that being a part of the Branch is rather like belonging to an extended family: we are all somehow related through our shared love of music and our wish to share that pleasure with as many people as possible. (As an aside, it is interesting to note that many of us practise what we preach in that we sing, play, conduct, compose and undertake research in our lives away from our work – I wonder how many other subject specialists can claim the same? Do art librarians paint? Are law librarians closet barristers?)

We are lucky, of course, to be working with a subject which is so much more than that. No one but the most diehard of philistines could not agree that music and its performance are vital elements in our cultural heritage and traditions, offering a rich outlet for creativity and personal fulfilment (and, by the by, form a significant component of the UK cultural industries). What is available in our libraries, archives, museums and other specialist institutions – whether unique heritage items, special collections or core materials – not only underpins much of this activity but also ensures its continuation. Further, it is the people who are responsible for the management and development of those collections who are key to that continuity, people whose knowledge and expertise of both music and their particular communities of users brings the two together to maximum, and sometimes magical, effect. Who are these people? Music librarians and archivists – special people doing a special job. Sadly, there are nowhere near as many of them as there could be: all too often specialist staff have fallen victim to the inexorable march of cutbacks over the years. It is my hope, however, that the greater general understanding of the importance of libraries we are now seeing will bring a turn in the tide and that such expertise will once again be a valued asset.

It is this expertise upon which the Branch has drawn during its 50-year life, and which, coupled with the sense of purpose and commitment I have already highlighted, has led to the many notable achievements set out in the pages which follow. For me – as one who has been involved in only the past decade of Branch life – highlights must include the work on the International Standard Music Number (ISMN), and the inspiration leading to the development of the Music Library and Information Plan: truly the foundation stones of the future, upon which the Branch has already begun to build.

Having mentioned the future, it seems appropriate to end with a quick glimpse in that direction. We live in changing times – one could say that the only certainty for the future is the continuity of change, as indeed it is true to say that change has driven the past. In the past 50 years the language of music has advanced and diversified, as have the ways in which it is performed, published and listened to. The onward march of technology has been the catalyst for much of this and has had a direct effect on the way in which we work. At a day-to-day level it allows us to communicate and develop ideas far more quickly and easily, and a great deal of the administrative business of the Branch now relies on email. More importantly, information and communication technology (ICT) allows us to share our expertise with others, to pool our ideas and create access to music in new ways, opening up to new audiences. Typically, the Branch has already turned the opportunity brought by technology to its advantage through projects such as Encore! and Cecilia, and is busy developing even more ambitious strategies to unlock the potential of ICT to good effect. It is this spirit of adventure which lies at the heart of the Branch and which will launch the journey of discovery for the next 50 years. I wish all on board bon voyage!

Introduction

Richard Turbet

My text for this Golden Jubilee is taken from Imogen Holst, 'Gustav Holst's manuscripts', in *Brio,* volume 4, part 2, 1967, pages 2–4, beginning to read at the fourth page: 'Music librarians are, without any doubt, the most helpful people on earth.'

This observation by a musician of such standing is of course a compliment, but it is also a challenge. It was good to have reached a point to justify such praise in 1967, but it requires effort to remain at that point, in order to sustain that opinion. Imogen Holst made her comment 15 years after the foundation of IAML(UK). I hope these succeeding chapters confirm that the same could be said today, 35 years later, and that the momentum of the Branch's activities suggest that similar sentiments would be justified 15, 35 and 50 years hence.

It will be seen from the contents of this book that the Branch is not only at the forefront of developments in music librarianship, but is often the creator of those developments. One reason for its confidence in its future is its knowledge of, and respect for, its past. So the sequence of chapters begins with the account by two past presidents of the Branch's first 50 years. The Branch has been blessed with a succession of outstanding presidents and two of them, Brian Redfern and Ruth Hellen, have been ideally placed to observe its earlier and more recent progress.

Another of the Branch's strengths has been its ability to embrace music librarians from all types of library. Malcolm Lewis, another past president, provides a definitive account of the history of music within public libraries. Britain's libraries have taken their educational role seriously, and throughout this book there are examples of music librarians enabling readers to learn and discover more about the subject. Christopher Cipkin tells of how he teaches information skills to students of music at the University of Reading. People also need educating for music librarianship itself. Ian Ledsham, formerly a music librarian and now a professional trainer and educator, outlines its fortunes as a taught subject, and describes the steps taken by the Branch to create courses and hold conferences that help all sorts and conditions of music librarians, from the very new and intimidated, to the experienced and harassed. A dozen years ago Ann Harrold and Graham Lea launched *Musaurus,* a musical thesaurus and much more, with its companion *MusBib,* a bi-monthly current awareness facility. Here they give an account of the impetus behind these initiatives, and describe subsequent developments. The Branch has always shown interest in, supported and, where possible, initiated scholarly research in music bibliography and music librarianship. At IAML's international conference in Edinburgh during 2000 Kirsteen McCue contributed to a presentation about the Scottish publisher, George Thomson, and she now shares with us some of the fruits of her research into this 'most intricate bibliographical enigma'.

Once people achieve a post in music librarianship, or have it thrust upon them, it is essential that they receive support. Besides the courses and conference noted by Ian, the Branch provides two further significant means of keeping sometimes isolated colleagues in touch with their fellows elsewhere: first, through its bi-annual journal *Brio* and, more recently, with the establishment of the IAML(UK) Library. Few periodicals as subject specific as *Brio* can have maintained such a high standard of relevant and interesting professional and scholarly content throughout their existence. Credit goes to the contributors, but also to the succession of excellent editors. As one of these, Malcolm Jones is well placed to take us through the history of *Brio* and of its much appreciated offspring the *Newsletter.* Meanwhile the library, another practical and valuable initiative, is described by its founding, and still current, librarian John Wagstaff. My own minute contribution celebrates a bibliographical jewel which resided in its library for many years undetected and then, even when detected, unappreciated.

Information technology (IT) has become essential not only to research and education, but also to the practicalities of music librarianship. Julie Crawley provides a comprehensive chronological account of IT as it has been relevant to music libraries. In many instances IT has been used in order to further co-operation. Indeed, underlying nearly every function and initiative of the Branch is the need and desire to co-operate. Having been president of both the International Association and the UK Branch, Pam Thompson is in a unique position to provide an overview. The three chapters that follow focus on specific aspects. Paul Andrews writes about the Cecilia project of which he is the manager. John Gough and Malcolm Jones consider all aspects of the provision of performance sets. Then, a globetrotting Roger Taylor investigates the implications of a policy of outreach: music librarianship has never been so adventurous.

Our book concludes, as it began, with a doyen of British music librarianship. Eric Cooper has, like Brian Redfern, made a unique and indelible mark, and as Brian took us back to the Branch's origins, so Eric ponders the sort of future in which it might find itself. His chapter is only a conclusion in that it comes at the end of this book. Otherwise it is provocative and stimulating, with that elusive combination of energy and wisdom that becomes visionary.

Each chapter is a separate item, and care has been taken to preserve individual voices and idiosyncrasies. The contents of some chapters overlap, but it is important to see certain topics from different perspectives, and such occasional overlaps have been left to take their places in the respective narratives. Certain concerns occur, some of them more than once. Music librarianship is rigorously democratic and egalitarian, yet there is frustration and despair at those who see it as elitist, inconvenient, irrelevant, incomprehensible or a threat. Money is short. Where there should be ideals there is often a vacuum. What carries music librarians through, and what makes most of them want to remain music librarians, is love and knowledge of music, and the evangelistic desire to provide whatever kind of music and information is required for whoever wants it. Add to this the projects and initiatives that have come into being and succeeded through the sheer diligence and determination of the membership, and it is clear that Imogen Holst's fine compliment from 1967 holds good in 2003, and looks good for many years to come.

Acknowledgements

The Editor thanks the following for their support and encouragement: Ruth Hellen, Susi Woodhouse and the members of the Festschrift Project Group – Kathy Adamson, Geoff Thomason and Professor John Tyrrell. At Ashgate Publishing we were in the care of Rachel Lynch, who could not have been more helpful, constructive and, when appropriate, reassuring. At Aberdeen University Library I thank my colleague Caroline Craig for her photographic skills.

Abbreviations

AACR	*Anglo-American Cataloguing Rules*
AACR2	*Anglo-American Cataloguing Rules 2*
ACE	Automatic Computing Engine
AGM	annual general meeting
AHCI	*Arts and Humanities Citation Index*
AHDS	Arts and Humanities Data Service
AHRB	Arts and Humanities Research Board
ALA	Associate of the Library Association
AMIA	Albanian Music Information Agency
ARPANET	Advanced Research Projects Agency Network
Aslib	Association of Special Libraries and Information Bureaux
AVG	Audio Visual Group
BARM	Building a Regional Music Resource
BBC	British Broadcasting Corporation
BCM	*British Catalogue of Music*
BIDS	Bath Information Data Service
BITNET	Because It's Time Network
BL	British Library
BLCMP	Birmingham Libraries Co-operative Mechanisation Project
BLCPP	British Library Co-operation and Partnership Programme
BLDSC	British Library Document Supply Centre
BLISS	British Library Information Sciences Service
BLLAL	British Library Library Association Library
BNB	British National Bibliography
BPI	British Phonographic Industry
BRS	Bibliographic Retrieval System
BUBL	Bulletin Board for Libraries
BUCOMP	*British Union Catalogue of Music Periodicals*
BUCOS	*British Union Catalogue of Orchestral Sets*
CALIM	Consortium of Academic Libraries in Manchester
CANTATE	Computer Access to Notation and Text in Music Libraries
CD	compact disc
CD-ROM	compact disc – read only memory
CERN	Centre européenne pour la recherche nucléaire
CONARLS	Circle of Officers of National, Academic and Regional Library Systems

CURL	Consortium of University Research Libraries
DARMS	Digital-Alternate Representation of Music Scores
DAT	digital audio tapes
DDC	Dewey Decimal Classification
DILS	Department of Information and Library Studies
DNER	Distributed National Electronic Resource
DVD	digital versatile disc
EAD	Encoded Archival Description
EARL	Electronic Access to Resources in Libraries
EDINA	Edinburgh Data and Information Access
EEC	European Economic Community
EEVL	Edinburgh Engineering Virtual Library
eLib	Electronic Libraries Programme
EM	East Midlands
EMRLS	East Midlands Regional Library Service
ERIC	Educational Resources Information Center
ERMULI	Education and Research in Music Libraries
EU	European Union
FID	Fédération international de documentation
FIGIT	Follett Implementation Group of Information Technology
FTP	File Transfer Protocol
GLASS	Greater London Audio Specialization Scheme
HEFCE	Higher Education Funding Council for England
HILT	High Level Thesaurus
HTML	HyperText Markup Language
HTTP	HyperText Transfer Protocol
IAMIC	International Association of Music Information Centres
IAML	International Association of Music Libraries
IAML(UK)	International Association of Music Libraries, Archives and Documentation Centres, United Kingdom Branch
IAML(UK & Irl)	International Association of Music Libraries, Archives and Documentation Centres, United Kingdom and Ireland Branch
IASA	International Association of Sound Archives
ICT	information and communication technology
IFLA	International Federation of Library Associations
IIB	Institut international de bibliographie
IIMP	International Index to Music Periodicals
IN	Information North
ISAD(G)	General International Standard for Archival Description
ISCM	International Society for Contemporary Music
ISDN	Integrated Services Digital Network
ISI	Institute for Scientific Information
ISMN	International Standard Music Number
ISO	International Standards Organization

ISTP	*Index to Science and Technical Proceedings*
IT	information technology
JANET	Joint Academic Network
JISC	Joint Information Systems Committee
LA	Library Association
LAHQ	Library Association headquarters
LAR	*Library Association Record*
LASER	London and South East Region
LC	Library of Congress
LEA	local education authority
LIB	Library and Information Bureau
LINC	Library and Information Co-operation Council
LIP	Library and Information Plan
LIP Music	Libraries and Information Plan for Music
LISA	*Library and Information Abstracts*
LISC	Library and Information Services Council
LP	long-playing record
MARC	machine readable cataloguing
MIC	Music Information Centre
MILDRED	Music in Libraries: a Directory for Resource Discovery
MIMAS	Manchester InforMation and Associated Services
MLO	Music Libraries Online
MLT	Music Libraries Trust
MPA	Music Publishers' Association
MP3	Motion Picture Expert Group audio layer III
MPEG	Motion Picture Expert Group
MuSe	Music Search
NBLC	Nederlands Bibliotheek en Lektuur Centrum
NLS	National Library of Scotland
NW	North West
NWP	North Western Polytechnic
NWRLS	North Western Regional Library System
OCLC	Online Computer Library Center
OLU	Open Learning Unit
OMNI	Organizing Medical Networked Information
OPAC	online public access catalogue
OSTI	Office for Scientific and Technical Information
PADS	Performing Arts Data Service
PC	personal computer
RDN	Resource Discovery Network
RidIM	Répertoire international d'iconographie musicale
RILM	Répertoire international de littérature musicale
RIPM	Répertoire international de la presse musicale

RISM	Répertoire international des sources musicales [International Inventory of Musical Sources]
RNCM	Royal Northern College of Music
RSLP	Research Support Libraries Programme
SCI	*Science Citation Index*
SMDL	Standard Music Description Language
SOSIG	Social Science Information Gateway
SRG	Sound Recordings Group
SRO	Scottish Record Office
SSCI	*Social Science Citation Index*
SWALCAP	South West Academic Libraries Co-operative Automation Project
SWOT	strengths/weaknesses/opportunities/threats
SWRLS	South Western Regional Library System
SWULSCP	South West University Libraries Systems Co-operation Project
TCP/IP	Transmission Control Protocol/Internet Protocol
TML-L	Thesaurus Musicarum Latinarum
UDC	Universal Decimal Classification
UKOLN	UK Office for Library Networking
UN	United Nations
UNESCO	United Nations Educational, Scientific, and Cultural Organization
URL	Universal Resource Locator
UUK	UniversitiesUK
VERONICA	Very Easy Rodent Oriented Internet-wide Computer Archive
VLE	virtual learning environment
WAIS	Wide Area Information Servers
WM	West Midlands
WMRLS	West Midlands Regional Library Service
WWW	World Wide Web
XML	Extensible Markup Language

Chapter 1

Fifty years of IAML(UK)

Brian Redfern and Ruth Hellen

The history of IAML(UK), 1953–1980

Brian Redfern

Since the dawn of the twentieth century change has been so rapid that to look back 50 years is to look at another world. The International Association of Music Libraries was founded over a period of two years at meetings at Basel and Florence (both in 1949), Luneburg (1950) and Paris (1951), the last named being under the auspices of United Nations Educational, Scientific, and Cultural Organization (UNESCO). The United Nations has as its main aim the establishment of peace between nations. One way of helping this ideal to be achieved was in the creation of international organizations such as IAML. Europe particularly had suffered greatly in the two World Wars (1914-18 and 1939-45) and many of its cities came near to total destruction. Germany, so much associated with the history of music, had been crushed in the drive for total surrender, only four years before the meetings in Basel and Florence. The people were weary. Not only that, when IAML(UK) was founded in 1953 some wartime rationing still continued in the UK and ended only in 1954. Armed forces were involved in another international conflict in Korea leading to the loss of many more lives and yet more loss of the nation's wealth. Those in power in academic institutions and local authorities had an immediate excuse for not spending money on libraries.

However, there was a sense of change in the air; the Festival of Britain in 1951 and the Coronation in 1953 had both helped to lift people's spirits. Strangely, it was the returning ex-servicemen who had injected a sense of hope. Library schools had been established originally to help the librarians among them to catch up on the lost years. Music was the Cinderella in most public libraries. Very few local authorities had special music libraries and many relied upon subscriptions to the Henry Watson Music Library in Manchester and Liverpool Central Music Library, while in London the opening of the Central Music Library by Westminster in the late 1940s offered a service to anyone with a ticket from any other library. Some other authorities provided a good service, such as Bournemouth, Burnley, Enfield and the West Riding of Yorkshire, but music was limited frequently to a few shelves, sometimes with no allowance for the larger size of music, which made it difficult to shelve and keep in any sort of order. Stock was limited to the popular piano classics, a few items for other instruments, and vocal scores were mostly Gilbert and Sullivan items. Miniature scores were sometimes provided and a service of orchestral scores and parts was available in some county libraries. Librarians with very little or no understanding of music and how it was performed had to provide what service there was. This led to some oddities. For example, in some libraries chamber music parts were provided by binding all the first violin parts for a composer's string quartets in one volume, second violin parts in another and so on. The final irony was that only three volumes could be borrowed at any one time! Qualified staff were the exception rather than the rule. If a member of staff wanted to develop existing stock he or she might be allowed to do so but, if that person left, a replacement with a similar interest in music might not be sought. Music was regarded by some librarians as a nuisance. It needed special suppliers, came in a variety of different sizes, there were lots of books about it and readers kept on demanding gramophone records. Library committees in those days had much greater control over selection of material and could not see that there was a parallel between printed texts of Shakespeare's plays and scores or records of Beethoven's symphonies. Music was seen as ephemeral and frivolous.

There was, therefore, a need for an association of librarians who believed profoundly in the importance of music, some of whom might feel that Beethoven was possibly as significant as Shakespeare. Why, then, did it take two years for British music librarians to come together to form the UK Branch? Probably the very situation which made the development of a branch so necessary. There was a certain aloofness in the British Museum Library and in academic libraries, which made public librarians rather suspicious. Whatever the reason, it was not until 23 March 1953 that the UK Branch of IAML was formally set up with Alec Hyatt King (Keeper of the Music Room, British Museum) as its first President, John Davies (BBC Music Librarian) as Chairman and Walter Stock (Librarian, Royal Academy of Music) as Secretary and Treasurer. I suspect that this event would not have occurred without the essential groundwork of those three. They were to remain in post until 1967. No provision was made in the constitution for their replacement by the vote of the membership at large; only by the Committee. Nowadays this would be regarded as a bad idea, but their groundwork was sound and they created a firm basis for the future.

The Branch developed a structure, and several highly successful events occurred in their period of office. A number of subcommittees were formed in the first year. In addition to the Officers the Committee included Jean Allen (representing Scottish Libraries), Barbara Banner (Teaching Institutions), Charles Cudworth (Universities), Cecil Hopkinson (Associated Members), Dom Anselm Hughes (Musicologists), Lionel R. McColvin (Public Libraries), R.C.W. Collinson (Association of Special Libraries and Information Bureaux – Aslib) and Leonard Duck (the Library Association). Both the Aslib and the Library Association committee representations subsequently ceased, but IAML(UK) members worked hard to continue to develop relationships with the Library Association with some measure of success.

Subcommittees were established to deal with Finance and Membership, Arrangements and Constitution. King, Davies and Stock were on all subcommittees. Indeed, the only other person involved was Hopkinson on the Arrangements Subcommittee. I first became involved in IAML in 1961 and it soon became apparent to me that, while King had many ideas on the way IAML should develop, it was Stock who was the driving force in making them happen and who was responsible for much of the work and success of the Association during his period in office, working particularly hard after his wife died in 1958, and it is fair to describe him as IAML(UK)'s 'nuts and bolts' man. Everything he touched was managed with finesse and a cheerful, almost apologetic smile. Stock retired in 1970, having been one of the real characters in IAML(UK). Dapper could have been a word invented to describe him as he was always smartly dressed. Even during a heatwave at the Brussels conference in 1982 he always wore a lounge suit and tie, and carried an umbrella!

By the second year of its existence the Branch had advertised quite extensively. For example, a brochure, 'An Open Letter to Librarians, Musicologists and All Interested in Music Libraries', had been produced. The membership increased during 1954 by 20 to 106, but how much that increase resulted from publicity is not known. Additional subcommittees were set up:

- Publications and journal of librarianship
- Music exhibitions
- Gramophone records
- Classification and cataloguing
- Bibliography
- An ad hoc committee for a standard music catalogue (with representation from the Library Association [LA], British National Bibliography [BNB], British Museum and Cramer's Public Libraries Department).
- Special subcommittees, one with the Music Publishers' Association (MPA) and one on symbols of music with the British Standards Institute.

Of all those subcommittees the most encouraging were Gramophone records and Symbols of music because they involved other members.

The third annual report for 1955-56 shows the Association gathering strength. The British Council provided funds for Stock to represent the UK at the Brussels International Conference, where King was elected President of the International body for 1955-59. There was a good attendance of UK members. This was the first occasion on which the UK Branch raised the matter of the crippling effect of the annual dues which had to be sent to the International body.

Back home the first attempt to persuade the MPA to co-operate in the production of a list of music currently available in print met with failure. The first weekend conference was held at Bristol and was deemed a success. The year 1956 saw the first publication of the *British Catalogue of Music (BCM)* and further attempts with the MPA to start a list of music in print to supplement the *BCM* were unsuccessfully made. A proposal to publish a UK Branch bulletin met with more success. However, optimism was too soon and the next annual report (1957-58) announced a delay. Another delay was the Branch's inability to support an annual conference. Only 17 members applied for the 1957 Edinburgh conference and it was cancelled. Plans for the international conference in Cambridge in 1959 were already being drawn up and it was decided to delay another national conference until after that.

An important step was the submission of a memorandum in February 1958 to a committee on public libraries in England and Wales set up by the Ministry of Education under the chairmanship of Sir S.C. Roberts. The membership as a whole was involved by asking for submission of ideas, and the response was good. Attention was drawn to the severe limitations of music services in public libraries in many areas, so poor indeed, in some areas, as to be described as non-existent. The same adjective could be used to describe attendance at the Branch's winter meetings. A visit to libraries in Oxford had to be abandoned through lack of support. The Cambridge conference was, however, very successful. The papers can be seen in a fully bound publication, *Music Libraries and Instruments,* published by Hinrichsen (Sherrington and Oldham, 1959). Max Hinrichsen had himself become an enthusiastic member of IAML(UK). The reference to instruments signifies that this was a joint conference held with the Galpin Society, which seems to have been a rather silent partner in the organization of the conference. The most forward-looking paper was that by Eric Coates of the BNB, who had formulated the *BCM* Classification, a faceted scheme which was used to arrange the entries in the catalogue. King and Davies were on the *BCM* committee and both subsequently confessed to me that they did not understand the scheme. It says much for their generosity of spirit that they accepted the scheme for the bibliography in spite of their misgivings. Nevertheless, faceted classification did divide the membership at times, reflecting a pattern all too apparent in the wider world of librarianship.

In 1965 a proposal from the Gramophone Libraries subcommittee to publish a textbook on gramophone libraries was approved. The delayed weekend conference in Edinburgh was held in April 1961, still with only 17 members in attendance. Perhaps for that period there was too much emphasis on Scottish music collections to attract members from the South. With the help of a generous grant from Aslib, the subcommittee on the catalogue of miniature and full scores proposed that A. Dennis Walker should compile a catalogue of these items. It was hoped that the cards containing the catalogue would be deposited in the Henry Watson Music Library.

In April 1969 a successful weekend conference was held at Birmingham University on the theme of music library services in the 1960s, some 50 members attending. There was a wide range of papers, such as County Library services to music and drama, photo-duplication of music and consequent problems of conservation and copyright, music collections in libraries of the West Midlands and their development, and sources of Shakespeare's songs. A day visit to libraries in Oxford was a part of the conference, as was a morning visit to Birmingham University music library and the Barber Institute of Fine Arts.

The first issue of *Brio* with Ruzena Wood (National Library of Scotland) as its first editor, appeared in 1964 and established a reputation as the best periodical issued by a Branch. Wood resigned in 1973, after setting a very high standard. *Brio* almost ceased at the time of the international conference that year, but a personal plea by Harald Heckmann (then Secretary General of the International body) that we should keep producing the journal because it was so good and could serve as an example to other branches, made the *Brio* subcommittee change its mind, especially when Clifford Bartlett (BBC Music Library) and Malcolm Jones (Music Librarian, Birmingham Public Libraries) volunteered to work jointly as editors.

Major changes occurred in the Committee in 1968. King was a charming man with a great love of music, particularly that of Mozart. He had a wide knowledge of many things and loved to go fishing at Southwold in his spare time. As Keeper of the Music Room, he made a major contribution to music in this country. In 1968 he resigned as President and the committee elected Davies in his place. I became Chairman. Stock remained as Secretary, but Alan Sopher (Librarian Central Music Library, Westminster) became Treasurer. The position of Immediate Past President was created and King became its first holder. He remained as the 'power behind the throne' until the mid-1970s. Davies received the MBE in 1968: the first honour to be awarded to an IAML(UK) member, essentially for services to the BBC and the musical life of the country. It was well deserved. He had an encyclopedic knowledge of music, which he put at the service of the wider music public. He was an incisive and humorous speaker. No one present at the Bristol conference in 1972 will ever forget his hilarious account of his travels throughout the world visiting music libraries. Sadly, he died only a few months later.

The 1969 conference was held in Cambridge at Magdalene College in bitterly cold weather, but it was a most enjoyable occasion as were all the conferences organized with increasing efficiency by Stock. Work on the International Inventory of Musical Sources (RISM) had been gathering pace and the British Museum was the obvious place on which the work in this country should be centred, although many other libraries contributed catalogue entries of their holdings. During the rest of the year the Committee had to face disappointment on two projects. First, the proposed miniature scores catalogue, by this time completed by Walker, was returned to the compiler. He and the committee failed to agree on cataloguing standards. A proposed union catalogue of music periodicals being compiled by Ernest Sheard and Morris Garratt had to be abandoned through pressure of work on both of them.

Michael Short (Lambeth Public Libraries) became Secretary both to IAML(UK) and to the committee responsible for the 1973 London international conference. He was also asked to investigate the possibilities of creating an exhibition in honour of Holst whose centenary would occur in 1974: this was very successful. Two information leaflets were produced, one on the work of the Branch, the other on music librarianship as a career.

For me 1972 was a difficult year. My first wife died suddenly in July and then Davies died equally suddenly in August. At this time a certain John May was making himself known to IAML(UK). In response he was nominated to represent

Associate Members as Freddie Dymond (Blackwell) wished to retire. I do not, however, think we can claim any credit for what turned out to be a very astute decision, made for the wrong reasons!

This was also the year in which the Library Association published the Long Report (Long, 1972). In 1965 I gave the students at North Western Polytechnic (NWP) a project to investigate the library services of the London colleges of music. What they discovered was that the service was very patchy and in some colleges almost non-existent. By the end of the decade, research into libraries had become big business and I managed to persuade the NWP Library School to support our investigation of music library services generally. The NWP, the Vaughan Williams Trust and the Library Association financed the project and Maureen Long was appointed. She had been a recent student at the NWP Library School and had a joint degree in Music and Mathematics from Exeter. The skills acquired in completing the latter proved invaluable and she produced an excellent report. More than one foreign member of IAML told me that other countries were envious of IAML(UK) for its *Brio* and then the Long Report. IAML(UK)'s contribution was very important as various members of the Branch, particularly those on the Committee, were 'guinea pigs' being asked to comment on the various draft questionnaires Long produced. Their contributions were invaluable and considerably influenced the final form. Like many such ventures, this report did not have a great effect, but the ideas are still there to be implemented and it gives a very clear picture of music librarianship in the early 1970s.

The 1970s for the UK Branch were a period of development and consolidation. Membership by 1980 was 238. Most annual conferences were held jointly with the Sound Recordings Group (SRG), which by 1974 had become the Audio Visual Group (AVG): 1972 Bristol; 1974 York (the revised constitution was approved); 1975 Aberystwyth; 1976 Oxford (first attempt at independence from IAML defeated); 1977 Manchester; 1978 Canterbury; 1979 Edinburgh. There was a natural mixture of members. Some local authorities (for example, Westminster) had two completely independent departments for music and records, but most combined them with the result that staff were likely to be members of both, with some conflict of interest. The *Gramophone Record Libraries* handbook (Currall, 1970) was IAML(UK)'s 'baby', but its two editors, Harry Currall and Eric Cooper, both played important roles in the SRG/AVG. The latter was also President of the Public Libraries Commission of IAML International for a number of years.

There was growing dissatisfaction in the UK with the excessive dues demanded by the IAML secretariat from branches. A typical year (1974) saw UK receipts of £1148 and dues to the International body of £1009. This led a group of members at the Oxford conference in 1976 to propose independence for the UK. So important was this seen to be, that Anders Lönn (Secretary General) came to the conference and successfully persuaded the UK branch to continue in membership.

Catalogues were important features of life in those days. Both E.T. 'Bill' Bryant and I were members of the UK committee on the *Anglo-American Cataloguing Rules (AACR)* published in the mid-1960s, but not as music specialists. Progress in the use of computers made a revision of these rules imperative. The revision committee invited the Branch to submit evidence on the draft rules for music. A subcommittee was set up in 1973 with myself as Chairman and Richard Andrewes (Cambridge University) as Secretary. Other members were Bartlett, Jones, Miriam Miller (BBC) and Patrick Mills (British Library). The revision committee kept a very tight schedule and we found it a hard task. Andrewes in particular worked very hard to produce our draft comments. *AACR2* appeared in 1978.

Talks on a national discography led nowhere, but a joint committee with the SRG was set up to consider the interloan and co-operative purchase of multiple copies of vocal scores and orchestral parts, with myself as convenor and Jones as secretary. It was decided that work on vocal scores would be best done on a regional basis. Ken Anderson (Loughborough Library School) edited such a catalogue for the East Midlands which would serve as a model. The *British Union Catalogue of Orchestral Sets (BUCOS)* (Reed, 1989) was established with financial backing from the NWP, the British Library and the Vaughan Williams Trust, and Sheila Cotton was appointed as Research Assistant. The work was so successfully completed that the BBC subsequently appointed her to complete their orchestral catalogue for publication. A second edition of *BUCOS* appeared in 1989. Tony Hodges (Royal Northern College of Music – RNCM) was authorized to produce a union list of music periodicals in 1975, although he had already been working on it for some time. Miller in her presidential report for 1978/79 anticipated publication within the year.

Another activity engaging the Branch at this time was a memorial concert for McColvin at St John's Smith Square in 1977, with a new work commissioned from Short. McColvin was City Librarian of Westminster and a doughty supporter of music librarians. Finally, the Branch began to co-operate more closely with the MPA through meetings of the Music Bibliography Group. Presidents in this period were myself until 1976, Miller until 1979 and May from 1979 to 1983. Short resigned as Secretary in 1973 to concentrate on composition. Elizabeth Hart (Enfield Public Libraries) was elected in his place. She followed in the tradition of first-class secretaries to the Branch, as did Susan Clegg (Birmingham School of Music) who succeeded her in 1979. Sopher continued as Treasurer until 1977. He worked very unobtrusively but very determinedly and handled our relationship with IAML at Kassel with quiet and impeccable resolve. He was succeeded by Julian Hodgson (Lambeth Public Libraries) until 1978 when Ruth Davies (Cambridge College of Arts and Technology) took over. The second Cambridge international conference in 1980 was a fitting climax to this first period of nearly 30 years in the Branch's history.

IAML(UK) 1980 – IAML(UK & Irl) 2003

Ruth Hellen

At the 1980 IAML Congress in Cambridge the name of the Association was changed to the long, but inclusive, International Association of Music Libraries, Archives and Documentation Centres. Brian Redfern was now IAML President and, at home, John May had become IAML(UK) President, an appointment that was to revolutionize the way in which Branch affairs were organized. Two initiatives, which continue to the time of writing, were the systematic monitoring of cuts in music library services, and the first official meeting with a government Minister. In the minefield of copyright, the first edition of the MPA's *Code of Fair Practice* (MPA, 1992) was published and provided much needed guidance to librarians and musicians. This was to be revised during subsequent years and, despite its imperfections, stands as a testimony to the cordial relationship between music librarians and music publishers in the UK.

The results of John May's reorganization were announced at the annual general meeting (AGM) in the following year: the work of the Executive Committee would now be complemented by a number of specific committees and working groups, with the intention of involving more members and, crucially, enabling the Branch to carry out more work. The result has been that, over the years, an average of 30 per cent of the membership has been actively involved in Branch work, a statistic viewed with envy by some of our colleagues in other countries. A valuable addition to the Branch publications programme was made when Bob Stevens became the first *Newsletter* Editor. The *Newsletter* was intended to complement *Brio,* to provide a more informal forum for news exchange and to ensure that members received more regular mailings. A succession of editors has ensured that it remains lively and relevant.

The IAML(UK) and the Library Association have always had members in common and the Branch now became an 'Organisation in Liaison' with the LA. Whether this status conveys any particular benefits on the Branch has, from time to time, been the subject of discussion; the amount of co-operation has always depended largely on the individual people involved at any one time, but it is surely a good thing for professional bodies to be seen as partners in the wider world. This relationship continues with the Association, which became the Chartered Institute of Library and Information Professionals in 2002.

The Branch name change was finally agreed in 1982, the initial proposal having been defeated at the previous year's AGM. The official version was now the International Association of Music Libraries, Archives and Documentation Centres, United Kingdom Branch, which was abbreviated to IAML(UK). At this point subscriptions were raised by 40 per cent; this excited a good deal of comment but was reluctantly agreed to be necessary owing to escalating costs. An initiative which met with universal approval was the announcement of the formation of the

ERMULI Trust, another brainchild of John May, which was formed to support education and research in the field of music librarianship. Over the next few years much groundwork was completed and the Trust became fully operational in 1986 with an impressive list of patrons. It has since supported the attendance of delegates at Annual Study Weekends and has contributed funding to a number of Branch initiatives. In 1994 it was re-launched as the Music Libraries Trust and has benefited from the continued appointment of dedicated and talented chairmen and trustees.

Following a long gestation period, *BUCOS* was published to great acclaim. This co-production with the Polytechnic of North London was to make life so much easier for staff dealing with performance sets and showed that a national union catalogue was possible. The importance of the catalogue was demonstrated by the demand for the second edition, published by the British Library in co-operation with IAML(UK), in 1989 and a supplementary edition in 1995.

After an outstanding presidency, in 1983 John May handed over to Roger Crudge, of Avon County Libraries. Over the years the Branch has been blessed with a series of excellent presidents, all different in their approach and expertise, but all totally committed to music library services.

The need for comparative statistics was addressed by the first *Annual Survey of Music Libraries,* compiled in 1984 by Roger Taylor (Somerset County Libraries). This was produced for the next 15 years by a series of hard-working editors but was suspended from 2000, owing largely to the lack of responses from an increasing number of libraries without music specialists. The *British Union Catalogue of Music Periodicals* (Wagstaff, 1998) appeared during the same year, edited by Tony Hodges. It is in the nature of this kind of publication that it becomes out of date very quickly and work started on the second edition just a few years later. After quietly progressing under the leadership of John Wagstaff, the new edition was finally published in 1998.

In 1985 the committee monitoring cuts in music library services came up with the idea of an 'Action Pack' to assist music librarians whose services were under threat. This was co-ordinated by Liz Hart and served as a guide to action for several years. This principle carries on to the present day with involvement in campaigns against cuts or closure, and personal support and advice for anxious librarians. While deploring the loss of expertise, Branch members as usual took a practical course of action and initiated a training course for library staff who were thrown in at the deep end; this was entitled 'Everything you wanted to know about music but were afraid to ask' and the course retained its popularity for several years until the commitment became too heavy for the course leaders.

The first rumblings of the possibility of a standard numbering scheme for music to complement the well-established International Standard Book Number had been heard two years previously and during 1986 a long campaign for an International Standard Music Number began with the submission of proposals to IAML, the MPA and other interested parties.

All was not well with relations with IAML International, as Roger Crudge handed over the Branch and its constitutional deliberations to Malcolm Jones (Birmingham City Libraries). The international constitution was being re-examined and the UK Branch had put forward a set of proposed amendments. At the same time, some Branch members were unhappy with the relationship with the parent body and were proposing the formation of a separate UK association. The following year, serious discussions concerning the relationship with IAML International came to a head with a Special General Meeting in October. Here it was proposed that a two-tier membership should be set up: members could decide whether to opt for full international membership or for UK membership only. After much discussion, some of it passionate, the proposal was carried, partly thanks to the possibility that more funds would be available for work within the UK. In subsequent years it could be seen that this decision had been the right one, as it enabled many people to stay in membership but at a lower cost. It remains, however, obligatory for key officers to be personal international members, and many UK members continue to be active in the work of international committees and working groups.

Agreement was reached to establish a prize in honour of C.B. Oldman, Principal Keeper of Printed Books at the British Museum from 1948 to 1959. This is awarded for the best work of music librarianship, bibliography or reference published each year and, with only one exception, has been awarded every year to date. In most cases, the authors have received their prizes at the relevant AGM and have spoken warmly of the help given to them by music librarians.

The publications programme continued with two titles in 1988 and 1989: *The Availability of Printed Music: A Report* (IAML[UK], 1988) published with the aid of a grant from the Arts Council of Great Britain, and *Sets of Vocal Music: A Librarian's Guide to Interlending Practice,* edited by Malcolm Lewis (1989). The list of Branch publications over the years has been carefully chosen according to need and the availability of resources for production. Most remain in print for several years, bringing in welcome additional income, providing tangible proof of members' expertise and adding to the literature on what is seen as a very specialized subject.

A threat to the time-honoured lending of recordings in libraries appeared in the guise of statements by the recording industry that libraries were, in effect, reducing sales of recordings to the public. Home taping was seen as a major cause for concern, although librarians expressed the view that the production and sale of pirate recordings from overseas posed a far greater threat than library users making single copies. Discussions between the LA and the British Phonographic Industry (BPI), in consultation with IAML(UK), began in earnest. It was proposed that a cost-free licence would be granted to libraries, who would have to agree to impose a 'hold-back' on new issues and to limit the number of copies of each recording purchased. An agreement was reached the following year, ostensibly for implementation during 1990.

The 1989 international conference, in partnership with IASA, was held in Oxford. The UK Branch Annual Study Weekend was timed to follow on immediately afterwards, giving IAML(UK) members a rare opportunity to experience at least part of this international event. It has always been difficult for UK music librarians, particularly those in public libraries, to obtain funding for international conferences. For some, this problem has even been experienced when applying to attend UK study weekends, a shameful state of affairs given the relevance of the topics covered and the theoretical obligation of managers to support continuing professional development.

Following the ISMN proposals in 1986, a project group was set up to see through the implementation of the scheme. This was to prove a long, hard struggle for the three main protagonists, Malcolm Jones, Malcolm Lewis and Alan Pope, who were rumoured to have spent nights under canvas on French soil to keep Branch expenses for meetings on this initiative to a minimum. The persistence and hard work of the ISMN Project Group were finally vindicated with the establishment of the ISMN Agency in 1993.

The 1990s were remarkable both for the continuation and, in some cases culmination, of established projects and for the sudden mushrooming of opportunities for funding and research. In 1992 a new service for members was begun with the agreement to establish an IAML(UK) Library. This would be a collection of books and journals which could assist members with their day-to-day jobs, their work for the Branch and personal professional development. It was set up under the management of John Wagstaff at the Music Faculty Library of Oxford University. Use of the library over the next few years was patchy, but this facility is of immense help to those who turn to it.

An opportunity to carry out research into music library provision arose when the Library and Information Commission established Library and Information Plans (LIPs). Under the leadership of Pam Thompson, IAML(UK) bid for, and was granted, funding to survey the current situation in the UK and Republic of Ireland; this was one of very few subject LIPs and was seen as a potential model for future projects. The Music LIP statement, compiled by Susi Woodhouse, was published in 1993 under the patronage of Julian Lloyd Webber. For the first time, here was a national picture of music services which showed the extremely varied nature of provision around the country. The report contained 53 recommendations which, while eventually unable to be funded by the Library and Information Commission, continue to be achieved as part of other projects. The LIP research established links with libraries in the Republic of Ireland which have continued to the present day, with proposals agreed in 2002 for a joint branch of IAML.

As any organization gets older, it inevitably loses links with its founders. Walter Stock,[1] the first Branch Secretary and Treasurer, died in 1993 and most Annual Reports for a number of years have contained tributes to members who have recently died. We owe a great deal to the organization's pioneers, many of whom have continued to work for the Branch long after retirement.

In spite of IAML's commitment to working internationally, some aspects of political life in a wider sphere have presented problems. Having worked hard to achieve a great deal of expertise in copyright matters, music librarians now had to cope with the fact that copyright in Europe was to be extended to 70 years after the death of the author. This meant that several major composers in effect went back into copyright after having spent a brief period in the public domain, causing practical problems for music libraries, which now held officially unavailable material.

In January 1994, after several years of discussions, the BPI and the LA finally signed a rental agreement which prevented libraries from lending BPI members' recordings for the first three months after issue and limited the number of copies of each title to be held in individual libraries. This had a serious impact on issue figures (and, of course, on income) and caused librarians to look again at what they were buying.

Most music librarians have never been afraid to get to grips with new technology and the now familiar phenomenon of email was introduced to IAML(UK) members by Julie Crawley, in the form of a Branch bulletin board. This eventually became the IAML(UK) discussion list, which revolutionized communication between Branch members and which continues to provide an efficient method of solving enquiries.

The Annual Study Weekend organizers took a leap of faith in arranging Belfast as this year's venue. In spite of prophecies of doom, the weekend was an outstanding success which built on the links already made between the Republic of Ireland, Northern Ireland and the rest of the UK. At the time there were glimmerings of peace in Northern Ireland and it was felt that, in some small way, IAML(UK) was part of the process. After all, music knows no boundaries. IAML(UK) influence began to reach even further with the first visit to Albania by Roger Taylor. This was the start of a period of intense outreach activity, chronicled elsewhere in this book, which did a great deal for the international profile of the Branch.

Another prize was established, this time in honour of Bill Bryant,[2] who had been a driving force in music and audiovisual librarianship for many years, and was well known for his encouragement of students and young librarians. The E.T. Bryant Memorial Prize is awarded for a significant contribution to the literature of music librarianship, produced by a student or a music librarian new to the profession.

Delegates at the 1995 Ormskirk Annual Study Weekend saw special achievement awards presented to the ISMN trio. This weekend was notable for its record attendance which included ten delegates from overseas, in particular two intrepid Albanian ladies who took part in the traditional midnight walk. It has been standard practice since this time to invite colleagues from overseas to attend Study Weekends; they gain from the experience and UK members have the opportunity to learn about music libraries in a wide range of countries.

At this time the Branch became involved in a campaign to save the National Music and Disability Information Service (then housed at Dartington College) after funding became unavailable. Unfortunately this was to no avail and the service was disbanded the following year. The information service continued, however, under the auspices of Sound Sense, the organization devoted to community music.

Members were saddened to hear of the death of Alec Hyatt King,[3] the noted music scholar and former Deputy Keeper of Printed Books at the British Museum and the first President of IAML(UK). He was a prime example of the way in which IAML members across the world are well known and respected for their work in music.

Following the success of the email list, the IAML(UK) internet home page was established, again by Julie Crawley, and was to become a major aspect of Branch publicity and communication. Once established, the Internet became a major source of music information and the Branch ran several very popular courses dealing with on-line music resources.

Music librarians had, for several years, witnessed with dismay the abandonment of specialist teaching in university departments of information science. In partial answer to the problem, a distance learning module for music librarianship was drawn up by Ian Ledsham, whose account of his work is included in this book.

In the history of co-operation 1997 was a landmark year, as Music Libraries Online was established to provide conservatoire and university music libraries with access to each others' catalogues. Librarians outside music were beginning to see the value of working with colleagues in other sectors, but library co-operation has always been a part of the lives of music librarians and Pam Thompson has written about this and other co-operative ventures in a separate chapter. One long-established aspect of co-operation has been the interlending of performance sets between libraries and an important survey of the use of performance sets in libraries was carried out by Roger Taylor. This showed that over 6000 people were performing *Messiah* over a period of two months, with Faure's *Requiem* in second place with 3500 performers. The findings were presented at a high-profile seminar in Birmingham, with an audience composed of librarians, library users and publishers' representatives. This event was a good example of the inclusiveness of the Branch, which represents not just librarians, but also their clients and suppliers.

British Library staff have always been deeply involved with the work of IAML, both nationally and worldwide. In 1998 the British Library made its long-awaited move into the new library in St Pancras; Branch members were able to admire the results in a series of visits and during the many committee meetings kindly hosted by British Library staff.

The Courses and Education Committee began a new chapter in its existence this year with the resurrection of the basic music course for library staff. The content was completely overhauled and the course was re-named 'Music for the Terrified'. Since the re-launch the course has been run at least three times each year and is regularly oversubscribed. This is, in a way, an indictment on library authorities which have allowed specialist knowledge to be run down, and reflects the need for staff to feel comfortable with a subject which is very popular but intimidating to the untrained. The Committee, at the time of writing, under the leadership of Liz Hart, has since initiated several new courses covering different aspects of music provision which have proved just as popular.

The end of the year was shadowed by the sudden death of John May.[4] He had been a towering figure in the affairs of IAML(UK), continuing to be involved and committed until the end of his life, and the Branch owes him an enormous debt of gratitude.

The following year, 1999, was truly remarkable. The first good news was that the Surrey Performing Arts Library, a major collection of performance materials, was not, as previously proposed, to be dispersed but had been found a new home in a local winery. The inevitable jokes masked feelings of relief that this vital resource was to be maintained. This success was due in large part to the establishment of an active user group, which put forward practical proposals and provided much needed support for the library staff. It is a matter of regret that other threatened services were not able to call upon this level of support.

The subject of performance sets is never far from the minds of music librarians and there had been, for many years, an overwhelming need for a national union catalogue of vocal sets. Regional catalogues became quickly outdated and searching for locations was time-consuming. The establishment of the British Library Co-operation and Partnership Programme provided the ideal opportunity to build on the work begun by Malcolm Jones on the West Midlands Vocal Sets Catalogue; grants were received this year and in 2000 for two phases of the Encore! catalogue, an online catalogue of performance sets in UK libraries and something which had been high on the wish list of music librarians for many years. Funding from the higher education sector was granted to a consortium of conservatoire and university libraries for a collaborative retrospective cataloguing project known as Ensemble. This was notable for the willingness of the participants to share catalogue records, something which had previously been considered unthinkable.

The main event of 2000 was the international IAML conference in Edinburgh, the culmination of years of planning by Roger Taylor and his team. This was agreed by participants from all over the world to have been a vintage conference, enhanced by the wonderful location and by the active participation of its patron, Sir Peter Maxwell Davies.

Copyright has always been a talking point with IAML and the end of the year saw an intense period of lobbying to ensure that the new European copyright legislation did not leave libraries with fewer rights than before. At the time of writing, discussions are taking place with the MPA and other interested parties to find the best way forward for both rights holders and users.

During 2001 the Branch continued the tradition of meeting Members of Parliament and government officials, and impressing on them the value of music library services. This was partly achieved through membership of the National Music Council, which initiated a series of meetings with government ministers to discuss issues concerning music and to increase the profile of music within government. Closer to home, the Minister for the Arts, Baroness Tessa Blackstone, was the guest speaker at the official launch of Encore! at the British Library.

The future looks exciting – the success of Encore! reminds us of the need to take advantage of funding opportunities as they arrive and there is no doubt that IAML(UK & Irl) will continue to use the skills of its members to bring music services to the people of the UK and Ireland. Most music librarians are, by nature, modest people who do their utmost to get music to the people who need it. This seems as good a place as any to applaud the hard work, dedication and astounding level of expertise of past and present members of the United Kingdom and Ireland Branch of IAML – long may the work continue.

IAML(UK) Presidents, 1953-2003

1953–68	Alec Hyatt King	British Museum
1968–72	John H. Davies	BBC Music Library
1972–76	Brian Redfern	Polytechnic of North London
1976–79	Miriam Miller	BBC Music Library
1979–83	John May	May & May
1983–86	Roger Crudge	Avon County Libraries
1986–89	Malcolm Jones	Birmingham City Libraries
1989–92	Pamela Thompson	Royal College of Music Library
1992–95	Malcolm Lewis	Nottingham County Libraries
1995–98	Roger Taylor	Somerset County Libraries
1998–2001	Ruth Hellen	Enfield Libraries
2001	Susi Woodhouse	Resource

Notes

1 Obituary: *Brio,* **30** (2).
2 Obituaries: *Library Association Record,* **92** (8) and **92** (9); *Brio,* **27** (2).
3 *Brio,* **32** (2); *Library Association Record,* **97** (5).
4 *Brio,* **36** (1); *Guardian,* 19 March 1999; *Library Association Record,* **101** (3).

Bibliography

Currall, Henry H.J. (1970), *Gramophone Record Libraries: Their Organisation and Practice,* 2nd edn (first published 1963), London: Crosby Lockwood.
Davies, R.R. (1983), 'The International Association of Music Libraries, Archives and Documentation Centres, United Kingdom Branch IAML(UK): a comparative study', unpublished MLS dissertation, Loughborough University of Technology.
IAML(UK) (1988), *The Availability of Printed Music in the UK: A Report,* Boston Spa: IAML(UK).
IAML(UK) (1997), *IAML(UK) Sets Survey.* London: IAML(UK).
Lewis, M. (ed.) (1989), *Sets of Vocal Music: A Librarian's Guide,* Boston Spa: IAML(UK).
Long, M.M. (1972), *Musicians and Libraries in the United Kingdom* (Long Report), London: Library Association.
Music Publishers' Association (1992), *Code of Fair Practice,* revd edn, London: MPA.
Reed, A. (ed.) (1989), *British Union Catalogue of Orchestral Sets,* 2nd edn, Boston Spa: British Library Document Supply Centre. (First edn, 1982, comp. S. Compton.)

Sherrington, U. and Oldham, G. (eds) (1959), *Music Libraries and Instruments: Papers Read at the Joint Congress of the International Association of Music Libraries and the Galpin Society,* London: Hinrichsen.

Wagstaff, J. (ed.) (1998), *The British Union Catalogue of Music Periodicals,* 2nd edn, Aldershot: Ashgate. (First edn, 1985, comp. A. Hodges.)

Woodhouse, S. (1993), *Library and Information Plan for Music: Written Statement,* London: IAML(UK).

Chapter 2

'Shrouded in mystery': the development of music provision in public libraries in Great Britain, 1850–1950

Malcolm Lewis

after careful examination of the early works on Public Libraries, it would appear that the origin of the Music Department, as such, is shrouded in mystery. (T.S.M., 1935)

Although the modern public library movement in Great Britain can be said to have begun with the passing of the 1850 Public Libraries Act, the national network of publicly funded, freely accessible public libraries developed painfully slowly, and the provision of music collections and services in libraries was even slower. Indeed, it is easy to argue that it took well over 100 years before most public libraries provided music services that could satisfy even the basic needs of musicians and music lovers in the areas they served.

However, this does not mean that the development of music services in public libraries since the mid-nineteenth century lacks interest or incident. Coal merchants, grocers and opticians are among the many individuals who played their part in helping British public libraries develop music services during their first 100 years; and there were a number of enlightened librarians and library authorities who in a variety of ways developed and extended the provision of music in their libraries having recognized, to a greater or lesser extent, the importance of music in the lives of the people in their local communities.

While the 1850 Act is usually seen as the starting point for modern public library provision, three towns, Canterbury, Warrington and Salford, established libraries under the 1845 Museums Act and before the 1850 Act came into force. However, Canterbury was not a public library in the true sense of the word (it charged admission to its museum and hence its library). Although Warrington restricted borrowing to subscribers until 1891 (Kelly, 1977, p. 10; County Borough of Warrington, Museum Committee, 1906, p. 11), it holds a significant place in the history of music in public libraries as it was the first to have a collection of music and the first to print a catalogue of its collection.

The collection was owned by John Fitchett Marsh, the Town Clerk of Warrington, who had already proved to be a supporter of public libraries having given evidence in 1849 to the Select Committee of the House of Commons whose work led directly to the 1850 Public Libraries Act. In 1849 Warrington Museum's annual report noted:

> your Committee ... have accepted the deposit, by way of loan, of a valuable collection of books of Standard Music [that is, scores], which are accessible to the public at the Museum, or may be borrowed by Subscribers under proper regulations. The collection contains at present 55 volumes, to which a considerable addition will be made shortly. (Warrington, 1849, p. 5)

In the following year it was reported:

> Mr Marsh's collection of Music, alluded to in their last report, has been completed, and now numbers 123 volumes ... your Committee invite attention to the collection, as tending to advance the public taste by giving access to standard works of the most eminent composers of the present and past ages. (Warrington, 1850a, p. 5)

This last comment was somewhat of an exaggeration (there were, for instance, no works by J.S. Bach or original works by Beethoven) but it certainly was an interesting and in some ways a notable collection, and its contents were published as a *Catalogue of Standard Music deposited, by way of loan, in the Warrington Museum & Library, by Mr Marsh* and printed in the museum's first book catalogue which was published in 1850 (Warrington, 1850b, pp. 125–31).

In the same year that the catalogue of Marsh's collection was published, the first Public Libraries Act was passed. While this was a landmark event for librarianship in this country, the legislation did have severe limitations the legacy of which in many ways crippled public library development for at least the next 100 years and which, more pertinently, had the effect of hindering the widespread provision of music in the country's libraries. The 1850 Act was limited to towns in England and Wales with a population of 10 000 or more; its provisions were not obligatory and it limited the amount that could be levied on local ratepayers to ½d in the pound. Even so, the money raised could only be spent on buying or renting land or buildings and on management and maintenance costs. This only highlighted the major practical weakness of the Act which was that it did not permit any money to be spent on the provision of stock: 'Donations will abundantly supply the books' was the optimistic assumption of the Parliamentary Select Committee which had examined the public library question in 1849 (Kelly, 1977, pp. 14–15; Munford, 1951, p. 28).

Following the passing of the 1850 Act, there was hardly a rush to make public libraries available. Only eight were opened in the first five years following the Act, but two of these, at Manchester and Liverpool, were to play a major part in public library music provision throughout the next 100 years. Manchester opened its first library on 2 September 1852 but was quickly followed by Liverpool, which opened its reference library just over six weeks later on 18 October. Both libraries may have started with some examples of music in their reference collections, but it was Liverpool that became the first public library to lend music scores to the public free of charge.

In October and November 1853 Liverpool opened two branch lending libraries, the first to be established by any library authority in the country. These branches operated from schools in the north and south of the city, and an assistant master from each school was appointed as lending librarian. Although at first the libraries were only open to the public for two hours on two evenings a week, the library committee soon appointed Robert William Roulston, sub-librarian at the Liverpool Lyceum Library, as Superintendent of Lending Libraries to be responsible directly to the committee for the efficient management of these branches (Cowell, 1903, pp. 48–9; Malbon, 1982, pp. 99–100).

Roulston is important as he was responsible for two innovations in British library practice. In 1857 he started a book service for the blind by putting into circulation ten volumes in Moon embossed type (Malbon, 1982, p. 108) and in 1859 he introduced the first free lending collection of music scores in any British library (Cowell, 1903, p. 52). Liverpool's annual report for 1858–59 describes this collection:

> The Committee, being desirous to encourage the growing taste for music, ordered, a few months ago, a number of standard musical works, comprising the most popular oratorios and a complete set (as far as published) of the 'Standard Lyric drama' being a series of operas, with English and French words, together with some other books bearing on the general science. (Carr, 1938, p. 598)

Peter Cowell, who in his youth had worked in one of the original branch libraries and was latterly Chief Librarian of Liverpool, described the service at the Second International Library Conference in 1897: 'It is just forty years since we sought to popularise our lending libraries by circulating vocal and instrumental music. This gave great satisfaction to a number of persons, and the circulation of music has formed a feature of the work of all our libraries ever since' (Cowell, 1898, p. 101). The success of this new service was immediate, 2000 volumes being issued in the first year (Carr, 1938, p. 598).

It is worth recording that Roulston, despite these pioneering innovations and the fact that he 'discharged his duties with assiduity and tact', became so frustrated by the library committee's lack of sympathy with the need for improvement and enlargement of the lending libraries, that he resigned in December 1863 and died 33 years later having pursued a second career as a highly successful and prosperous coal merchant (Malbon, 1982, pp. 203, 317).

It is not clear when Manchester first started lending music scores on a systematic basis but we know that music books, at least, were available at the Hulme Branch Library in 1864 and that 135 volumes of music were available when the new Cheetham Branch Library was opened in 1872 (Credland, 1899, pp. 62, 102–3). However, it is certain that scores were generally available by about the middle of the 1870s as Charles W. Sutton the Chief Librarian reported at the Library Association's Thirty-Sixth Annual Meeting in 1913 that 'For forty years all the twenty-four Manchester Lending Libraries had supplied very good selections of music, which were among their most popular collections' (Music, 1913, p. 647) and in 1877 William Axon observed:

One pleasing feature should not go unnamed. The musical taste of the Lancashire people has long been a matter of note. The managers of the [Manchester] lending libraries have therefore done well in providing a liberal supply of the best musical compositions. The works of Bach, Beethoven, Handel, Haydn, Mozart, Meyerbeer, and others of more recent date will help to keep alive and elevate this taste. (Axon, 1877, p. 114)

Between 1853 and 1867 a number of legislative changes took place that in a limited way improved the potential for public library development. The 1850 Act was extended to royal and parliamentary burghs in Scotland in 1853, and in 1854 in Scotland and 1855 in England and Wales laws were passed which enabled library authorities to levy a penny rate for the provision of libraries as well as giving them the power to buy materials to stock them. Subsequent legislation in 1866 extended library powers to even the smallest town or parish (Aitken, 1971, pp. 53–5; Kelly, 1977, pp. 20–22). From 1850 until 1879, 79 libraries were established under the Public Libraries Acts or local Acts of Parliament (Kelly, 1977, pp. 494–6) and, although most of these libraries had little or no printed music, musical literature was provided, especially in the larger libraries. For example, in Birmingham in 1867, Hullah's *Rudiments of Music* and Turle and Taylor's *Singing at Sight* were noted as being 'Among the books most in request' in the Lending Department (Edwards, 1869, pp. 145, 147–8); indeed out of 11 662 volumes in the Lending Library, only 22 other titles exceeded the *Rudiments of Music*'s 37 issues that year (Borough of Birmingham, 1867, pp. 17–21).

The 1880s saw some improvement in the provision of music in public libraries. This was especially true in the West Midlands where several music collections were being created, including two whose importance has been long forgotten. Birmingham Public Libraries started its first music collection at its Constitution Hill Branch Library in June 1880 and the next month started another in the Central Lending Library. The collections were modest. That at Constitution Hill consisted of 67 volumes, while that at the Lending Library had only 57. However, the popularity of the Constitution Hill collection was remarkable, attracting 839 issues by the end of the year, an average of more than 12 issues for each title in only seven months. Issues of scores at the Central Lending Library were a more modest 309 by the end of December (Borough of Birmingham, 1880, pp. 16–19), but the obvious demand for music demonstrated by these collections was such that by the end of the following year music scores were available in all five of Birmingham's lending libraries. At the end of December 1881, the first full year of operation of the music collections in each of its lending libraries, Birmingham had a collection of 512 scores producing a total annual issue of 3984 volumes, nearly eight issues per score per year (Borough of Birmingham, 1883, pp. 81–2). The annual reports for 1883 and 1884 noted that 'A special feature of the Lending Libraries has been the purchase of a collection of Music, with the most encouraging results. There are in the Libraries nearly 800 volumes of the works of the best Masters and Composers, and the issues in 1884 were nearly 7000' (Borough of Birmingham, 1885, p. 3).

The number of public libraries in the Birmingham area in 1880 was quite remarkable with 16 independent library authorities issuing a total of 1.5 million volumes a year. The Birmingham annual report for 1880 noted:

> It is worthy of remark in this report that the success of the Free Libraries at Birmingham cannot be justly estimated unless account is taken of the number of Free Libraries which have arisen in its neighbourhood. No town in England is so surrounded with Free Libraries, which no doubt owe their establishment to the example and success of Birmingham. (Borough of Birmingham, 1880, p. 3)

This was certainly true of Handsworth, a small town just over 2 miles north-west of the centre of Birmingham, which operated an independent library service until 1911 when it was amalgamated with Birmingham. Less than two years after opening its library in May 1880, Handsworth's library committee decided to expand its collections by providing 'a selection of standard musical works' in the lending library. 'The advantages of the Public Libraries in Birmingham have been extended in this direction with marked success, and the Committee have no doubt that a similar satisfactory result will follow the addition of a good selection of musical works to the Handsworth Library' (Handsworth Public Library, 1882, pp. 6–7).

Two members of the library committee selected Handsworth's music collection and 187 volumes were purchased:

> and placed at the service of the ratepayers on July 24th, 1882. The selection, as in the other departments of your Library, is a thoroughly comprehensive one, intended to meet the most diverse tastes, and to illustrate every school of musical thought. The works of Beethoven, Handel, Cherubini, Sullivan, Mozart, representative names in Oratorio, Opera, Mass, Song or Study, are now on your shelves. The issue in this section of your Committee's work for the eight months during which it has been opened has been 1877 volumes, a sufficient number to justify the step taken in this direction. (Handsworth Public Library, 1883, pp. 6–7)

Over the next few decades whenever libraries established what for their time were significant music collections, comments on the extraordinary popularity of music scores in libraries were to be found in reports by individual librarians and their committees. In 1882–83 the music scores in Handsworth Library issued an average of 15 times a year in only eight months while the comparative issues for 'Juvenile Literature' (201 volumes) were just under 12 times a year and for 'Poetry and Drama' (254 volumes) two per year (Handsworth Public Library, 1883, pp. 11–12). This high level of demand for music scores was mirrored at Aston Manor, another independent library authority on the outskirts of Birmingham. Aston Free Library opened in February 1878 in temporary premises and moved to permanent accommodation four years later. A music collection was added in January 1886, the annual report noting that:

> the privileges of borrowers have been extended by the establishment of a Musical Section, comprising the principal Oratorios, Operas, Cantatas, and Chamber Music. Although at present only a small number of volumes have been provided in this section, they have

been largely used and highly appreciated by the borrowers, and the Committee hope, by continual additions, to render this department fully equal to the requirements of readers. (Aston, 1886, pp. 3, 8)

In 1886–87, its first full year of operation, the collection of 135 music scores attracted 1486 issues, comfortably outperforming in terms of issues per volume every other category of book in the central lending library with the exception of fiction and juvenile literature, something the music collection continued to do for the next 24 years until Aston ceased to be an independent library authority in 1911 (Aston, 1887–1911). In tracing the development of music collections in the first 50 years of the public library movement, those at Handsworth and Aston libraries are interesting as the quality and relevance of their collections provides a useful benchmark against which the growth of music provision in other libraries in the country, with the notable exceptions of Manchester and Liverpool, can be measured. Handsworth's annual report noted in 1887:

> our Musical Library is acknowledged to be of special and almost unique excellence among Free Public Libraries. It has been noticed in the various publications interested in Libraries, and enquiries are now being received by your Librarian from other towns for information that may assist in establishing similar Musical Sections.

This despite Handsworth having a population of less than 33 000 (Handsworth Public Library, 1887, p. 9; Ogle, 1897, p. 323).

Even though there were lending collections of music in libraries in the West Midlands as well as in Liverpool, Manchester, Nottingham, Sheffield and a handful of other places, there is little evidence that the provision of music played much part in the thinking of most librarians and their committees until the 1890s. In an address to the Library Association in 1888, J. Potter Briscoe, Chief Librarian of Nottingham, remarked that although the supply of printed music for circulation 'has got beyond the range of experiment', 'The provision of printed music has been too often overlooked by the management of Free Public Libraries … . It is to be hoped, however, that when the matter is brought to their notice, there will be a liberal supply provided at no distant date. The advantages offered will be quickly appreciated … ' (Briscoe, 1888, p. 146).

But if few music collections were established between 1850 and 1890, several libraries supplemented their income by means of profits from musical entertainments. The earliest recorded instance of this appears to be at Oxford where from 1854 to 1860 the library committee organized lectures and concerts during the autumn and winter seasons. In the first year these events showed a profit of £43.16s.0d. and in the first two years at least, they were attended by more than 500 people on average (Kelly, 1977, pp. 37, 57, 95). Airdrie Library, which opened in 1856, was so poorly funded that it was not until it started receiving the profits from a series of concerts in 1878 that it was able to open during the daytime (Kelly, 1977,

p. 64). Five years later in Wandsworth, 'a concert was given at the Town Hall by Miss Lilian Greville, and the sum of £26 was handed over by her towards the library funds' (Davis, 1891, p. 186). If this seems unremarkable, it was two and a half times the amount Clerkenwell Library received as a gift from the Worshipful Company of Skinners, which apparently enabled James Duff Brown to buy over 120 music scores for his library in 1895 (Clerkenwell Public Library, 1895b, p. 7).

But using income, whether raised from concerts or, more conventionally, from the rates, was not the only way that libraries were able to add to their collections. Donations and bequests were common, even though in many cases they were 'the unsaleable debris of mid-Victorian private collections, hastily dumped by the rising generation under the mistaken idea that they were conferring a benefit on the public at the same time that they were ridding their shelves of useless lumber ... ' (Myres, 1963, p. 285). At one extreme, donations could provide the bulk of a library's stock; 'The Cottesmore Village Library ... possesses 523 works; 428 having been presented, 79 purchased out of the library rate, and 16 obtained from the proceeds of a concert' (Anon., 1903, p. 246). At the other extreme donations could be of exceptional importance, the two most significant gifts of music coming under the direct control of public libraries in the nineteenth century being those of James Walker at Aberdeen and Andrew Wighton at Dundee.

James Walker of Aberdeen spent many years building up a collection of several hundred volumes relating to the history, theory and practice of music, and in 1891 he presented his collection to Aberdeen Public Library 'as the nucleus of a musical department, to be created therein'. The collection, to which Walker continued to add after it was given to the library, is especially strong in Scottish music and contains nearly 400 items of music printed before 1801 including some which are unique (Cooper, 1978, pp. 3, 6; Robertson, 1894, p. 10).

In 1884 Andrew Wighton's collection of music scores and manuscripts became the property of Dundee Public Libraries, having been in the custody of the Town Council since his death in 1866. Wighton was born in Perthshire in 1804 and as a young man had opened a grocer's business in Dundee. Despite this rather unlikely background 'Wighton travelled widely in Europe to collect his music ... . He paid special attention to works of Scottish origin or association, and made copies of early manuscripts and of a number of rare printed works which are now lost' (King, 1963, pp. 56, 145). Wighton's collection, due to be rehoused in the specially built Wighton Heritage Centre for the Study and Appreciation of Scottish Music in Dundee, contains 620 bound volumes and several unique items. Music in the collection includes early editions of Playford's *Dancing Master* and D'Urfeys's *Pills to Purge Melancholy,* the Bunting Collection of Irish music and several books of Welsh music, although the main strength of the collection is in the hundreds of volumes of vocal and instrumental music of Scottish origin or association, including Wighton's own copies of manuscripts such as the unique Blaikie Manuscript (Wighton, 2002).

With a few notable exceptions, there was a general apathy towards the provision of printed music in public libraries up to the end of the 1880s, but from 1890 there is increasing evidence from the number of catalogues, reading lists and articles in the professional press that music was being seen as having a legitimate place on library shelves, even though 'the music stock of some places consisted largely of material provided freely by advertising agents – bound in cases begilt with the announcements of local butchers and bakers, and with the pages interleaved with further advertisements' (McColvin, 1937, p. 3).

Public libraries in 1890 were quite different from anything that exists today. There were hardly any professionally qualified staff (the Library Association's certificate scheme had only started in 1885); money to buy books and other materials was pitifully scarce; only a minority of libraries were housed in purpose-built accommodation; electric lighting was almost unknown; and the public had no direct access to the lending stock and had to rely on indicators or printed catalogues to find which books were available for loan (Kelly, 1977, pp. 66–74, 89–91, 103–4).

It is interesting that the man who revolutionized public libraries in Great Britain by successfully introducing open access in public lending libraries and who was the most radical, innovative and controversial public librarian of the late nineteenth and early twentieth centuries should also be the most influential propagandist for music librarianship in the country. James Duff Brown was born in Edinburgh in 1862. The son of musical parents, he started work in the book trade when he was 12 and three years later, in 1878, started work as a junior library assistant at the Mitchell Library in Glasgow. In 1884, while still at the Mitchell, Brown became the Glasgow correspondent of the London *Musical Standard;* in 1886 he published his *Biographical Dictionary of Musicians* which contained a 'Bibliographical Subject-Index' which he modestly subtitled 'A tentative index of the principal subjects and works in the English literature of music' (Brown, 1886); and in September 1888 he was appointed Librarian of Clerkenwell Free Public Library in London (Munford, 1968, pp. 2–12).

In September 1892 Brown attended the Library Association's annual conference in Paris and reported to his library committee:

> The visits to the Parisian municipal Libraries were of very great interest … . In every one of the 65 libraries provided by the municipality there are large collections of Music and works on art manufacturers, which are lent out to borrowers without much restriction. I trust the Commissioners will feel disposed to gradually build up both music and Art libraries on lines somewhat similar to those followed in Paris. (Clerkenwell Vestry, 1892, pp. 227–8)

It is not clear when Brown first added music scores to his library's collection, but by 1894, the same year that Brown transformed public librarianship by introducing a sustainable system of open access to the lending stock for the first time in any British public library, Clerkenwell's annual report noted:

> The classes which show the greatest increase [in issues] are Sciences and Arts and Miscellaneous Literature. The large increase in the former, nearly 35 per cent, is mostly due to the circulation of *Music* from the Fine Arts section. Works for the pianoforte, popular operas and violin music are most in demand, and I would urge that in future more

attention be given to this class, especially by the provision of music for pianoforte solo and combinations of various instruments. It is my belief that a well-equipped music section will do much to reduce the demand for *Fiction* in Public Lending Libraries and add greatly to their practical value. (Clerkenwell Public Library, 1894, pp. 12–13)

There are two things worth noting in this passage, leitmotifs that echo through British public library history down to the present day. The first is an implicit plea for a larger book fund; the second is that of the public librarian despairing at the public's insatiable demand for popular fiction and their relative lack of interest in 'improving' literature. As already mentioned, Brown was able to expand his library's music collection following a gift by the Skinners' Company of 10 guineas (Clerkenwell Public Library, 1895b, p. 7) which apparently enabled him to buy over 120 scores but, even so, the music collection was 'so much used and appreciated' that his committee requested that:

any Reader who may have spare copies of oratorios, operas, cantatas or collections of songs, bound or unbound, to give to the Library, should place them in the hands of the librarian as soon as possible. The Commissioners will be glad to accept gifts of this nature from Borrowers, as the funds available for the purchase of music are somewhat scanty. (Clerkenwell Public Library, 1895a, p. 62)

Less than three years after his appointment at Clerkenwell, Brown published a subject list of music books which was designed to help other librarians build up music collections in a systematic way:

In many libraries some of the most important subjects are so shabbily treated as to suggest the thought that they are represented at all only as the outcome of accidental gifts or purchases made in error. Music especially seems to be a subject entirely left to the chances of haphazard gifts and purchases. With very few exceptions this subject is left in most libraries to take care of itself, and any books which may be found catalogued are either part of a series or rudimentary books of no authority. (Brown, 1891, p. 147)

At the end of this article, Brown gave a list of over 100 recommended titles, the forerunner of the much more substantial list of over 700 works which appeared in his pamphlet of 1893, *Guide to the Formation of a Music Library,* number 4 in a series of subject lists published by the Library Association. In this, Brown observed that:

As most librarians are aware, the presence of music in libraries established under the Acts has only recently been generally recognised as desirable, and though a few – certainly not more than half-a-dozen – libraries formed collections many years ago, the great majority still ignore the matter. There are still librarians who deny the claims of music in any form to representation in public libraries, though they admit with readiness any kind of picture-book; but these will doubtless be speedily brought to reason and consistency as the public demand for music becomes more emphatic ... . It is the main object of this series of subject-lists to rectify what has in many instances been simply library formation on the happy-go-lucky principle of selection by instinct instead of knowledge; and if this brief tract does anything to remedy the haphazard method of collecting music its only object will have been accomplished. (Brown, 1893, pp. 1–2)

The provision of music in libraries was indeed becoming more widespread. In 1891 Birkenhead, Chelsea and Norwich published lists of music in their collections and at Camberwell the Library Commissioners agreed 'That the sum of sixty pounds ... be expended for Books of Music [that is, music scores] to be placed in the Peckham, Livesey and Dulwich Libraries such sum to include binding in stiff covers with pigskin backs' (St Giles Camberwell. Commissioners of Free Public Libraries, 1891, p. 274). In 1892 E.R. Norris Mathews, City Librarian of Bristol, observed in a paper delivered at the Library Association's Paris conference:

> One might hesitate to connect so closely music with libraries, were it not that many members of the Library Association are devoted to the science of music, and are amongst its most ardent students ... . We find that already many of the principal towns in Great Britain, including Birmingham, Manchester, Nottingham, Sheffield, Derby, Cardiff, not to mention several of the Metropolitan free libraries, have been circulating musical works amongst their readers for some years with the best possible results. (Mathews, 1893, p. 190)

However, the provision of music by public libraries was still very patchy. Even at Leeds, which had the third largest book stock in the country, it was reported that in 1894 'there was an outcry for a musical library', a demand that could not be satisfied because of a totally inadequate book fund (Hand, 1904, p. 26; Ogle, 1897, pp. 306–7). But in some of the more progressive authorities, librarians and their committees were trying out a number of ideas designed to stimulate music appreciation and library use. In 1893 Chelsea introduced a duplicate ticket for music 'to allow readers who may wish to borrow music from the lending library, to do so without interfering with their ordinary reading... ' (Anon., 1893, p. 335). Harmony, theory, singing and violin classes were organized by the Wolverhampton Free Library Committee (Wolverhampton Free Library, 1891) while at Derby, 'Picture exhibitions and Promenade Concerts in the art gallery do much to popularise the work of the committee and their librarian' (Ogle, 1897, p. 224). More commonly, library lectures were provided 'not only as valuable aids in making known the contents of a library on particular subjects, but as tending to foster a closer relationship between the institution and its frequenters' (Haxby, 1911, p. 123). A good example which illustrates how these aims could be achieved were the talks on music given as part of the lecture series inaugurated by Handsworth Public Library in the winter of 1886–87. In the first series, John Bragg, a member of the library committee, gave a lecture on '"The Sacred Music in the Handsworth Public Library, with some notices of the Composers." Illustrated by Vocal and Instrumental Music by the Choir and Organist of the Wretham Road Church, Handsworth' (Handsworth Public Library, 1887, p. 23). In the following year he gave another, this time on '"Madrigals, Glees, and Part Songs, with Remarks on the Practice of Vocal Part

Music in the Home," ... with Illustrative Selections from the Music in our Library',
this time by the 'Ladies and Gentlemen of the Wretham Road Church Choir'
(Handsworth Public Library, 1888, p. 23).

By 1899, in proportion to the total number of library authorities in the country,
there were still relatively few public libraries where the provision of music was
taken seriously and where collections were being built up purposively. Liverpool
was evidently still one of these because although overall it lost nearly 3000
borrowers and over 40 500 issues from the lending libraries between 1898 and 1899,
it was able to report that in the same year '18,096 volumes of music were issued for
home recreation and study, showing an increase of 2,281' (Anon., 1900, p. 322).
Peter Cowell, the Chief Librarian, writing four years later, noted that:

> The large amount of standard music – the compositions of the great masters – provided in
> both of the lending branches; but more particularly in the Reference Library is much used
> and appreciated, and the valuable aid in its selection given by the late Mr. Best, organist
> of St George's Hall, and later by Dr. Peace, his successor, deserves to be thankfully
> recorded. (Cowell, 1903, pp. 52–3)

Equally valuable work was being achieved in far smaller places. Aston Manor,
the product of whose penny rate was one twentieth that of Liverpool's (Ogle, 1897,
pp. 306, 320), was able to publish a 24-page music catalogue in 1899 and in the
same year add to its music collection a selection of scores which included:

> The Meistersinger, Parsifal, and Der Ring de [sic] Nibelungen (4 vols.), by R. Wagner;
> Beethoven's Sonatas; Mozart's Sonatas; ... Te Deum (Berlioz); ... Nineteenth Century
> Pieces for the Pianoforte, Augener's Edition, 9 vols.; ... The Grand Duke (Sullivan); ...
> Pagliacci (Leoncavallo); L'Amico Fritz (Mascagni); Hansel and Gretel (Humperdinck);
> The Geisha, A Gaiety Girl, A Greek Slave, *and* An Artist's Model (Sidney Jones); The
> Belle of New York (Kerker); ... The Circus Girl, The Shop Girl, The Gay Parisienne, and
> A Runaway Girl (Ivan Caryll) ...

as well as about 25 other works (Aston, 1899, p. 14). In London, Hampstead opened
a lending department in January 1899 which contained 13 000 volumes including 'a
special collection of 500 works of music, principally operatic scores' (Anon., 1899,
p. 83).

Meanwhile in Manchester, the Deputy Chief Librarian noted that in each of the
12 lending libraries 'there is a special collection of music' (Credland, 1899, pp.
270–71), but the important news in Manchester libraries in 1899 was that Dr Henry
Watson had offered to transfer the ownership of his collection of musical works to
the Public Free Libraries Committee. Henry Watson was born in Burnley in 1846
and as a musician was largely self-taught. His enthusiasm for choral singing led him
to be associated with many choral societies. 'So great were his activities that at one
time he was conductor of no fewer than eight different vocal societies.' In later years
he was Professor of the choral department of the Manchester Royal College of
Music and afterwards Dean of the Faculty of Music of the Victoria University. 'It

was noteworthy that he did not care for the work of modern composers, and that his love was for old-fashioned music on which he was a recognized authority' (Manchester Library Fellowship, 1915, p. 261).

According to Watson he had always hoped to make his collection available to his 'fellow-citizens' and in his letter offering the collection to the library, he gave his reasons for doing so:

> First, the want which in my earlier years, as a student, I felt on account of the difficulty of obtaining access to important and necessary works of reference. Secondly, the hope of benefiting the younger members of the profession who are similarly situated. Thirdly, the desire to assist societies engaged in the study of vocal and instrumental music, who find the constant purchase of scores and parts a heavy and often fatal drain on their resources. (Watson, 1899, p. 793)

In 1899 the collection consisted of 'about 5000 volumes – bound and unbound – many of them rare, and extremely valuable for purposes of reference, besides a large quantity of separate vocal and instrumental scores and parts … '. Watson acknowledged that 'aware of my aim, many generous friends, sympathising with my design have passed over to me valuable additions to my library' and his hope was:

> that the collection … may become the nucleus of a really important musical section of the free library, and that such further additions, by gift or purchase, may be made to it as will ultimately result in the possession by the citizens of a Free Reference and Lending Library of Music worthy [of] the musical reputation of Greater Manchester. (Watson, 1899, p. 793)

According to Leonard Duck the collection at this time contained over 16 000 items, including 2500 books about music (Duck, 1961b, pp. 55–6). The offer was subject to the custody and control of the library being left in the hands of Dr Watson during his lifetime 'or until such time as my engagement in the active duties of my profession may cease … '. The libraries committee accepted Watson's offer and agreed to allow him to continue in charge of the collection as honorary music librarian on the understanding that any student of music could have access to the collection on making an application to the chief librarian. F. Bentley Nicholson, described as 'the Music Librarian' in 1915, observed:

> On the death of Dr. Watson the library came under the direct control of the Libraries Committees [sic], and the following year (1912) saw its removal to its present quarters in the Temporary Reference Library. Since then large additions have been made to the stock on the shelves, and the dearth of the works of modern composers has been largely counteracted by recent purchases. As proof of the increased usefulness of the library it was announced that there were now about 4000 borrower's cards in use as against 290 in the doctor's time. (Manchester Library Fellowship, 1915, p. 261)

The period from 1900 to 1910 saw other significant additions to public library collections. The Henry Watson Music Library was augmented by several gifts including the donation in 1900 of Dr C.J. Hall's music library of some 500 volumes (City of Manchester, 1900, p. 6) and by the transfer in 1904 of the collection of music books belonging to the Hargreaves Trust (City of Manchester, 1904, p. 7). In 1905 Leeds Public Library purchased 123 lots at the sale of the Taphouse collection of printed music (King, 1963, p. 71) and in 1907 Robert A. Marr's collection of 481 volumes of musical literature and manuscripts was presented to Edinburgh Public Libraries by his sister following his death. 'This was a timely donation, since a Musical Section had been formed in the same year within the Central Library lending department … .' This new collection included 557 volumes of vocal and instrumental music, and its establishment had been recommended by a deputation of library committee members who had seen similar collections when visiting a number of English public libraries in the spring of 1906. A catalogue of the Marr Collection was issued as an appendix to the *Catalogue of Music and Musical Literature* produced in November 1907 (White, 1975, pp. 107–8, 110–11). However, apart from the Henry Watson Library, the most important acquisition during this period was that of the John B.M. Camm Music Library which was presented to Bournemouth Public Library in 1910. Charles Riddle, the Chief Librarian, described the background to this gift:

> Mr. Camm was for twenty-two years rector of a remote parish in Dorsetshire … and about five hours' distance from London. Passionately fond of music, the only orchestral music Mr. Camm would hear in those days were the Saturday Concerts in the winter at the Crystal Palace. Owing to his parish duties it was impossible for him to be present at the Concerts, so the directors and Sir August Manns gave him permission to attend the rehearsals … . Having in mind the struggles and hardships of some of the great musicians … he decided to part with his wonderful library in order that the musicians of the district, unable to purchase the expensive scores, should be able to have access to his collection of music … (Riddle, 1914a, p. 8)

The collection contained about 4000 items including 180 books and 775 orchestral full scores (Riddle, 1914b, pp. 114–15) and apart from some solo music 'issued to bona-fide students for home study at the discretion of the Chief Librarian', was for reference only. Riddle again: 'It is believed to be the finest collection of modern orchestral scores in the possession of any library authority in the United Kingdom' (Riddle, 1914b, p. 115) and:

> Some day Bournemouth will be considered a great music centre, and much has been done towards that by the continuous maintenance of the Municipal Orchestra for twenty years, but the correlative adjunct to that has been supplied by Mr Camm's munificence, enabling the Council and the Library Committee to make Bournemouth's speciality MUSIC. (Riddle, 1914a, p. 7)

Riddle was immensely proud of this collection and housed it in a purpose-built

'Music Room' at the new Central Library, opened in March 1913. John Warner described this room in 1928:

> The Music Room itself, 30 feet by 30 feet, is furnished with a carpet, busts of composers on pedestals, framed portraits of musical celebrities and other amenities of a music room ... . The room is unique for there is at present no other public library in the country with a separate room devoted to an open access Music Library and containing so much orchestral music. (Warner, 1928, p. 208)

Music library provision developed steadily between 1900 and 1918, reflected by the increasing number of music catalogues published during the period. Leeds now had its music collection and published a catalogue of its holdings in 1902; Warrington published a 16-page catalogue in 1906 ('including large additions to the sets of Orchestral Scores and Parts' [County Borough of Warrington, Museum Committee, 1907, p. 11]); Cardiff's 1908 catalogue (75 pages) was in two parts, music literature and music scores, its value being 'enhanced by the exhaustive index which gives references to every subject, title, author, composer, and librettist in the catalogue' (Anon., 1908, p. 300). Finsbury (1911) and Hampstead (1912) published music catalogues in their respective 'Quarterly Guides' for readers; Bolton (1913) published a 114-page catalogue, 'Class list No.4 – "Music and domestic economy"' (!); and in 1915 Manchester prepared a catalogue of the 200 or so music scores and books in Braille type held in the Henry Watson Music Library (City of Manchester, 1915, p. 13).

C. Zanetti writing in 1942 recalled his time as a youth working in a large city library, almost certainly Newcastle upon Tyne, just before the turn of the nineteenth century:

> in the days when city councillors were known to remark that anyone who was able to weigh a pound of sugar could be a librarian ... . The decision to introduce musical scores into the lending department was the cause of much argument. Opinion seemed to be fairly evenly divided, one half being in favour of the new move, and the other declaring that music wasn't books and had, therefore, no legitimate place on the shelves of a public library. However, the innovation proved to be particularly popular with our readers, and the music section became only second in public favour to the fiction section. (Zanetti, 1942, pp. 65–6)

James Duff Brown echoed this finding in 1907 when he wrote 'Nearly every public library of any importance has now established a music collection, and the general experience is that it is one of the most popular and appreciated sections in the library' (Brown, 1907, p. 155). The following year A. Cecil Piper of Brighton observed:

> The English people are undoubtedly a music-loving nation ... . This being so, the study

of music should be encouraged by all possible means; and what better method of encouraging the love of music is there than that of circulating it by means of Public Libraries? There are now few Public Libraries of any size that have not yet started a music collection; but it is indeed hard to understand why there should be even one Public Library, large or small, without a music section. Is not music as much a necessity of life as are books? (Piper, 1908, p. 78)

This was not, however, a view universally shared. In an address to the Library Assistants' Association in 1913 Mr R.T.L. Parr, a Local Government Board auditor declared: 'The English people not only lack desire for reading, but they are also deficient in taste for music, and he held that it was no place of the public library to provide musical scores for amateur drawing-room entertainments' (G.R.B., 1913, p. 706). Even Piper, like a number of librarians who wanted to encourage music in libraries, warned against providing popular music scores:

They are not music in the same sense as the works of the great musicians, and ... works of this type have an effect similar to what a popular but indifferent work of fiction would have on a person of high intellectual calibre, and it is a wise thing, as well as the duty, [of] Public Libraries to supply only the best. (Piper, 1908, p. 78)

Fortunately for the public, others were less high-minded. In 1913 Herbert Jones of Kensington stated: 'Beyond the more important books and scores for the student in the reference library, they must also have, if they were to make this popular to the ratepayers generally, popular music that the man and woman of to-day required' (Music, 1913, p. 646). Bailie Hoey, Chairman of the Glasgow Libraries Committee, agreed:

In the sixteen branch libraries of Glasgow there were something like 4000 volumes of music, and any or all of these books could be taken to the homes of the people. That, of course, was very desirable. The piano and violin were to-day in the artizan communities almost in every house, so far as his city of Glasgow was concerned at any rate, and it was a considerable saving to the working people to be able to get from the library current popular music which otherwise would cost them a shilling or half a crown. By such means they could approach the ratepayer and tell him he had good value for his money ... (Music, 1913, p. 647)

By 1918 public library provision had expanded considerably. There were now 423 library authorities in England, 61 in Wales and 82 in Scotland and many of these had been persuaded to open libraries because of the grants made available by Andrew Carnegie who between 1879 and 1913 donated £1.75 million towards the establishment of public libraries in the United Kingdom (Kelly, 1977, pp. 116, 123). In 1913 Carnegie set up the Carnegie United Kingdom Trust to carry on his philanthropic work and the Trustees commissioned Professor W.G. S. Adams to prepare a report 'regarding the provision of Free Public Libraries in the United Kingdom'. *A Report on Library Provision & Policy,* was published in 1915 and concluded that although there was still scope for library development in urban areas, 'the question of the small towns and country districts and of the large population which is scattered through them deserves first consideration. A great advance is here required ...' (Adams, 1915, p. 15).

There had been considerable interest in the 'rural library problem' for many years but little had been achieved. Speaking in 1906, Henry Farr, Deputy Librarian of Cardiff, noted that 'Ten years ago the extension of the Acts to counties was said to be the pressing library problem of the hour; but ... the solution is little, if any, nearer than it was a decade ago' (Farr, 1906, p. 175), and in 1913 John McKillop observed, 'We have in this country a system under which access to collections of literature is the civic right of 79 per cent of our urban population and of 2.4 per cent of our rural population' (McKillop, 1914, p. 48).

The Carnegie Trust assisted several library schemes in rural areas and legislative support for the establishment of county libraries came in the 1918 Education (Scotland) Act and the 1919 Public Libraries Act. The 1919 Act was of seminal importance as it removed the penny rate limitation in England and Wales (this did not happen in Scotland until 1920, and then only in a limited way) and allowed county councils to extend library provision to any areas they served which did not already have a library service. However it also 'placed the English [and Welsh] county libraries, like those of Scotland, firmly within the ambit of the education service, and thereby marked them off sharply from their urban counterparts' (Kelly, 1977, p. 217). The establishment of county library services after 1919 is important in the history of music library provision as county libraries developed distinctive forms of library provision which influenced music librarianship until the 1990s, not least through the formation of many of the 'music and drama' collections which exist in county libraries and in some city libraries to this day.

Adoption of the 1918 and 1919 Acts began slowly but by the end of 1927 only seven authorities in England, Wales and Scotland had not adopted powers under the Acts, even though in general 'The scale of provision was ... pitifully inadequate' (Kelly, 1977, pp. 219–20). Even so, many of the new library authorities had librarians whose energy and ingenuity made up for the meagre resources with which they had to work. The county librarian's duty was not just to create a library service, but also was to create a demand for the services they were trying to provide. Music collections were started in some of the earliest county libraries, but Duncan Gray, County Librarian of Warwickshire, was of the opinion that this was not enough:

> The public library, as an agency for the promotion of general culture, should not confine its activities solely to the provision of literature, but by providing the means, should assist in the promotion of a more general appreciation of good music. There is a particular need for assistance in this field in rural communities as, though townspeople usually can, if they wish, learn to appreciate good music by taking advantage of the opportunities afforded them of attending the general concerts, chamber concerts, and organ recitals which form part of the musical activities of most towns, these opportunities are but seldom afforded to village people. The result is that the same backward state exists in connection with musical appreciation as that which exists in connection with the reading of good books ... to teach musical appreciation, demonstration by means of recitals is absolutely essential, and the provision of volumes of musical scores only embraces half the problem. (Gray, 1922, pp. 175–6)

The Carnegie Trustees supported this need by helping to subsidize The Village and Country Town Concerts Fund which in 1921 for example arranged 'good concerts by expert performers … and three tours, each of a week in duration, were given by this association in different counties … '. Initiatives such as this were supplemented by concerts put on by county libraries themselves, Warwickshire being one of the first to do this (Gray, 1922, pp. 175–80). Kent also had ambitions for music: 'It is proposed to add a music section to the library in the near future. As, however, it is impossible to shelve more stock in the present quarters of the County Library, only music definitely asked for has been purchased' (Carnegie United Kingdom Trust, 1925, p. 33).

'Adult education' was seen by county libraries as one of their major functions and local organizations started to take advantage of the new music collections, as in Cumberland where 'The newly established sections on music and drama have achieved a rapid popularity, largely through the activities of women's institutes and dramatic societies' and in Middlesex, where 'In response to requests from the Women's Institutes, the Committee are providing copies of glees and songs in sufficient quantities for the use of Choral Societies' (Carnegie United Kingdom Trust, 1925, pp. 29, 41). The provision of sets of music for use by choirs had by the beginning of the 1920s, as far as is known, only been provided by the Henry Watson Music Library in Manchester, although a national scheme for collecting 'copies of oratorios which had been used by members of various societies throughout the country and lending them to other societies who might want them' had been proposed by H. Tapley-Soper of Exeter Public Library as far back as 1913. This, he suggested, 'would be a source of income, and a very great benefit to small societies in the country' (Music, 1913, p. 648). Kate Fearnside, the Librarian of Waterloo-with-Seaforth in 1918, advocated closer co-operation with local church choirs who could be 'directed to the music shelves of the town's library by being informed from time to time of the resources of that section' (Fearnside, 1918, pp. 146–7). Burnley devised what appears to have been a novel approach to building a collection of vocal sets. Its Massey Music Library had been donated by Edward Stocks Massey and had opened in 1924. In 1927 it was reported that the library committee was 'collecting from all the churches and chapels of the town sets of music no longer in current use, and large collections have been "pooled" in their hands, thus producing a very considerable common stock. It is proposed to complete each set up to thirty copies, and to issue a catalogue', which it did in 1929 (A.E., J.V.S. and E.G.T., 1927, p. 309; Burnley Libraries Department, 1929). Nearby Bury also formed a 'Choir Music Library', 'several choirs "pooling" their volumes to form a nucleus stock' (McColvin, 1930, p. 124).

The idea that the provision of music was a legitimate core activity of the public library grew steadily during the 1920s. In 1922 Sir Henry Walford Davies, then professor of music at Aberystwyth and latterly a well-known broadcaster and successor to Elgar as Master of the King's Musick, appealed for the development of music libraries in an address to the Library Association's annual conference in Cardiff (Davies, 1923, pp. 19–20) and in 1924 Lionel McColvin, who was to become the pre-eminent advocate of music libraries in later decades, published *Music in Public Libraries,* the first book on the subject by a British librarian (McColvin, 1924). McColvin, who wrote the book when Chief Assistant Librarian at Wigan, was at this stage of his career rather conservative and dogmatic about music provision:

> The first principle by which we should be guided in selecting music for the public library is this: concentrate first of all upon the classics. Beethoven and Chopin and Mozart are and will always prove to be the most popular composers in any collection. Before going any further, before even venturing into the more debateable realms of modern and native music, see that the bulk, if not all, of the works of Beethoven, Chopin, Schumann, Mozart, and then Schubert, Bach, Mendelssohn and some of Brahms, are – not on your shelves, but in the homes of your readers. (McColvin, 1923, p. 154)

McColvin goes on to say that most of the music provided should be for the pianist, and should, in the main, be within the capability of 'the average competent amateur'. Chamber parts should be provided sparingly and orchestral scores not at all: 'A piano score of a symphony is one hundred times more useful than a full score' (McColvin, 1923, pp. 154–6). Only a small selection of organ music should be provided as organists and their churches ought to have their own collections; church music should be excluded completely as it should be 'provided by those who require it – the church authorities'; and music for choirs was totally unsuitable for libraries 'because not only would the library loan period be useless, but also because the range is so large that selection would be invidious' (McColvin, 1924, pp. 19–20). To be fair to McColvin, he wanted music to be used and not sit on the shelves ('saving in a few large towns, the student of any of the arts must be considered *after* and not *before* the amateur' [McColvin, 1923, p. 155]); he was not totally against providing popular music ('but the 'light' music should be the best of its kind' [McColvin, 1924, p. 13]); and he was very conscious that smaller libraries had limited funds to spend on music and therefore had to be very selective. But one thing to which he was implacably opposed was the prospect of gramophone records in libraries.

The earliest recorded use of a gramophone in public libraries appears to have been at Waterloo-with-Seaforth in 1915 when music was used to entertain a group of young women from the Girls' Evening School who attended the library to learn more about 'the uses and pleasures of a Public Library' (Anon., 1915, p. 379), but the earliest serious advocacy for the provision of gramophone records in libraries seems to have been by William Law, Clerk to the Brighton Public Library, Museum and Art Gallery, at a meeting of the Library Assistants' Association in October 1911. Law argued that although public library services were limited by the penny rate 'too much is often made of the rate limitation, and it would almost appear that many library committees make it the excuse for neglecting to keep their libraries up-to-date'. Law said that libraries should be actively helping teachers and school libraries, should make proper provision for young people and even think of extending their services to working men's clubs, missions, Sunday schools and similar institutions:

Indeed they might even go further and supplement the reading by the provision of gramophone records, and music rolls for the piano player. Music is already provided for the piano in most libraries. Why not also supply the best pieces of the great masters of music in the form of music rolls and records of the best quality? Some may object to this on the score that it is not quite within the scope or function of a public library to distribute these, but, in recent years, library author[i]ties have been called upon to perform duties which would have surprised the founders of the public library movement. Besides it will be readily admitted that the issuing of these rolls and records is much more in harmony with the idea of a public library than the distributing of sterilized milk, which is done in Battersea. (Law, 1911, p. 227)

In January 1918 the North London Gramophone and Phonograph Society became the first gramophone society to meet in a public library when 'commodious and comfortable quarters' were secured for its members at Islington Central Library. The society moved location to Islington's North Branch at the end of 1921 and this was to remain the society's permanent headquarters for the rest of its existence even though 'there seems to have been no inherent link between society and library' (Bryant, 1972, pp. 22–3, 35). An article in *Sound Wave* in 1924 noted that there had recently been a letter in the press proposing that in public libraries:

rooms should be set apart where the best music could be rendered free by gramophone. This is a really sound proposition – our libraries, municipal and privately conducted, are depressing and awe-inspiring institutions ... [and a] practical scheme like that suggested by Mr. Collins would attract the custom they undoubtedly deserve, and materially assist in the development of the knowledge of good music ... . We venture to think that the establishment of music centres at the Libraries will not only widen the circles of musical appreciation, but by so doing, will materially help the Gramophone Companies with the sale of their records. (Bryant, 1972, pp. 52–3)

Two years before this, in his address to the Library Association conference in 1922, Walford Davies had argued strongly for the availability of recorded music in libraries:

you should get a little sound-proof room in which a boy who reads about Bach could come and listen to a record of one of his works. There is an idea that music belongs to experts. Music is the mother tongue of the ordinary people. That boy who comes to hear that gramophone record will never see the pinnacle with his eye by the nature of things, but he can only look at it with his ears; and the library of music will remain a barren fact unless you use the practical means. (Davies, 1923, p. 20)

McColvin, however, would have none of this:

Our function is to supply literature – that is to say, books for people to read, music for people to play, pictures for them to look at; and until we have given our readers all the musical scores they can wish to interpret themselves, it is not our duty to provide the interpretation. (McColvin, 1923, p. 156)

He seems to have changed his attitude somewhat by 1926 and recognized that libraries were doing useful work by playing music in libraries:

> In the *Gateshead Library Record*, No.32, an appeal is made for a gramophone especially in order that the poor children may have the opportunity to hear good music. May I suggest that, if the appeal has not yet been answered, the librarian communicates with the Gramophone Company, which has assisted many libraries in this work? (McColvin, 1926, p. 169)

Although the lending of records to individual borrowers does not appear to have started until 1940, records were already being used by libraries, especially in conjunction with extension activities and in fulfilling their educational role. As early as 1923, and during its first year of operation, Selkirk County Library 'possessed a gramophone and records which were lent for use in connection with lectures on music and other activities at the [library] centres ... ' (Carnell, 1938, p. 104). Five years later, Stanley Snaith of Islington Central Library was arguing that where libraries provided educational talks on music, the use of gramophone records was essential if the talks were to be effective:

> The gramophone, like the cinema, has suffered a good deal of unmerited obloquy. But the time has come when none but pedants and prejudiced judges will refuse it that appreciation and understanding which it deserves ... . Every library, in my opinion, should attempt to educate its public in literature and music concurrently. In this work the gramophone is an indispensable tool ... . I can think of no work more germane, more significant, more valuable, more likely to be appreciated, than education by music. The tool is in our hands, perfected, simple to use, and absurdly inexpensive; and none are better qualified to use it than we, whose aim should be nothing less than to raise the culture of the nation and to give people something really worth living for. (Snaith, 1928, pp. 6, 9)

'Extension work' such as Snaith's music talks, had long been a feature of public library work. Harold Jolliffe defined 'extension work' as 'seeking by any means to increase the usefulness and the use made of public libraries ... ' (Jolliffe, 1968, p. 22) and this definition embraces the wide range of activities organized or encouraged by libraries in their efforts to promote the public's appreciation and knowledge of music and, hopefully, the use of their library's collections. In the 1920s examples of such activities included 'first-class chamber music concerts' in Northampton 'given from time to time under the auspices of the libraries committee' (McColvin, 1924, p. 69); the series of wireless concerts established in 1923 at Hoxton Library in Shoreditch which ran until at least 1930 (C.M.J., 1953, p. 422; E.E.P., 1931, p. 283); municipal concerts and music lectures at Ipswich, where 'concert-lectures are held in the Court-yard in suitable weather'; and the continuing provision at Llanelli library of a Music Room which possessed 'a grand piano and violin ... [and where] Students are allowed to play any of the music which is in stock at the Library' (Warner, 1928, pp. 212–13).

Notable donations and bequests in the decade following the end of the First World War included the gift by Richard Bonner Morgan, a Cardiff optician prominent in local musical life, of the important Mackworth Collection of some 500 items of printed music and 60 or so volumes of music manuscripts to Cardiff Public Library in 1919 (Boyd, 1973, pp. 135–6; King, 1963, p. 89); Huddersfield's music library which was 'inaugurated by a gift from Mr Samuel Firth' in 1924 (A.E. and E.G.T., 1924, p. 253) and where, by 1928, 3407 borrowers held 'extra Music tickets' (McColvin, 1928, p. 203); the bequest by the composer Archdeacon George Gardner of his 600–volume musical library to Cheltenham Library in 1925 (Gloucestershire, 1925, p. 6); and in 1929 the presentation to Bristol City Library by George Riseley, a former organist of Bristol Cathedral, of his collection of 2000 volumes of music which he had collected over a period of 60 years (Anon., 1929, p. 276).

The Kenyon Committee was set up in 1924 to investigate the adequacy of library provision in England and Wales and how it could be extended and completed. It reported in 1927 having found that 'Music collections naturally represent a common feature of local library provision; we have a note of 157 urban library authorities which maintain collections, and several of the new county libraries are adopting the same policy' even though 'Most of these are very small in extent and cannot hope to meet fully the needs of choral and orchestral societies'. Kenyon recognized that 'A music library naturally offers very special problems in regard to classification, cataloguing and binding' but the major difficulty was that 'very few libraries can maintain adequate music collections on their own account, and that every argument for co-operation and for some form of central library as regards the provision of books applies with equal force to the provision of music scores' (Board of Education, Public Libraries Committee, 1927, p. 140). The co-operative provision of music was very slow in developing, but in general the Kenyon Report appears to have stimulated a gradual improvement in public library music provision in the 1930s despite the severe economic depression which affected the country in the first half of the decade and the continuing problem of 'the small institution with a very restricted income, an untrained staff, and an inadequate stock of books' (Nowell, 1930, p. 88).

In 1927, Glasgow nearly became the first urban public library service in the country to operate a record library, or, as it was described, a 'system of gramophone record exchange'. This was one of two ideas concerning the development of music services in Glasgow made at the time, but it was only the second, that a Music Reference Library be established, that was finally implemented (Barr, 1977, p. 79). The Music Room, which was the first of the special subject departments in the Mitchell Library, opened in 1930 with a stock of 12 000 items, supplemented in the same year by the purchase of the major portion of Frank Kidson's library, part of which had already been bequeathed to Leeds Public Library (King, 1963, p. 73). Kidson was a recognized authority on early English music and folk song and the Mitchell's collection of his manuscript and printed volumes, which was supplemented by further additions made in 1948 and 1949, numbered some 9000 separate items in 1977 of which nearly 700 were unique or unrecorded in the *British Union-Catalogue of Early Music* (Schnapper, 1957). The collection is particularly rich in folk songs and dances of Great Britain and Ireland, early operas and ballad operas and popular vocal music of the eighteenth and nineteenth centuries, but it also contains over 150 early hymnals and psalters, 200 volumes each of string and flute music and over 500 volumes of keyboard music (Barr, 1977, pp. 80–85; Rolland, 1961, pp. 95–8). Other significant bequests and gifts to public libraries in the 1930s included the Moody Manners Collection of opera and song to the Mitchell Library in 1934 (Barr, 1977, pp. 85–6), J.A. Fuller Maitland's collection of books, music and English church music manuscripts bequeathed to Lancaster Library in 1936 (King, 1963, pp. 76–7, 146) and the acceptance in 1938 by Perth's Sandeman Public Library of Lady Dorothea Stewart Murray's Atholl Collection. The latter is an important collection of around 600 books and manuscripts, especially strong in Scottish music, which includes all the great song and music collections of the eighteenth and nineteenth centuries as well as the manuscript of William Dixon's Tune Book of 1734, the earliest known manuscript of bagpipe music in Britain (Aitken, 1971, p. 199; Douglas, 1999, pp. 5–6).

There were several interesting developments relating to music provision in public libraries during the 1930s. Liverpool concentrated the musical stores of its 16 branch libraries at the Central Lending Library in 1930 to form a music section of some 5000 volumes (Anon., 1930, p. 223) and shortly afterwards 'this section was enriched by the deposit of the music collections of the Liverpool Philharmonic Society which were saved when the Philharmonic Hall was destroyed by fire in 1933' (Liverpool Public Libraries, 1954, preface). Bradford bought the scores of the works that had been performed at the Bradford Festival of Chamber Music, the Northern Promenade Concerts and the Bradford Philharmonic Concerts, and in 1930 these produced 4699 issues (McColvin, 1931, p. 58). In 1934 the Henry Watson Music Library moved into the new Manchester Central Library ('the most notable public library building in Britain during the inter-war years' [Kelly, 1977, p. 275]) thus ending 20 years of being housed in temporary accommodation (Duck, 1961a, p. 133), and in the same year Middlesex County Library started operating a record library for schools on behalf of the education committee, and used the recordings for record recitals and music appreciation classes in its branch libraries (Bryant, 1985, p. 265).

In Nottingham a new music and drama library was opened in December 1936:

> Its success was immediate, and it now takes an important place in the music activities of the City. Many students and executants have in the past experienced difficulty in obtaining works now available, and they are taking full advantage of the increased facilities. Works of difficulty for which there might have been thought to be little call are being well used, e.g. Stravinsky's *Le sacre du printemps* miniature orchestral score was borrowed five times in three months, and his *Pétrouchka* four times ... (City of Nottingham, 1937, p. 4)

Jean Allan understood why surprise was expressed at the popularity of music that was not normally found in libraries:

the trouble runs in a vicious circle – public libraries on the whole (there are honourable exceptions, and we bow to Birmingham) are not bold enough in their policy regarding music, and the public, consequently, do not learn to expect with confidence the best and finest from their public library, so that we librarians ourselves discourage those who would be our best readers. Conversely, not expecting, they fail to seek, or ask, too often simply coming to the conclusion: 'Oh, they wouldn't have that in the library'; so that pessimistic librarians speak, in a certain sense, correctly when they say 'there is no demand' for this or that great work, old or new … music provision in public libraries needs a much wider view than (generally speaking) it has had hitherto. (Allan, 1937, pp. 40–41)

Jean Allan's music library in Edinburgh was the scene of a hitherto untried development in British public librarianship. Ernest Savage became Chief Librarian of Edinburgh in February 1922 and after devoting his first few years there to the conversion of the libraries to open access and the classification of the book stock by the Library of Congress Classification, he began to turn his attention to other ways of making the book stock 'productive'. In Savage's view the only way to achieve this in a large central library was to scrap the artificial division of libraries into reference and lending departments and to introduce specialist subject departments. 'Grouping into subject departments resuscitates moribund books, saves good books from being buried alive … progress demands planning for reference and home reading books in departments by subject, with each department in charge of special librarians' (Savage, 1937b, pp. 615, 621). Savage had been much impressed by the intensive subject specialization practised in some of the large public libraries in the USA when he visited that country in 1926. 'The plan of putting each class of books, throughout the service, in the care of special librarians has not been tried [in the United Kingdom]; until it is, the charges that librarianship is superficial and libraries chance-assorted are unanswerable' (Savage, 1937a, p. 573). The choice of staff for these subject departments would, however, have to be right. Writing in 1937 Savage noted:

> The longer I live the more certain I am that every keeper of books, whether special or not, must be a librarian. His knowledge should be of the bibliography of a subject rather than of the subject. An art librarian who daubs, or a music librarian who wears long hair, fools around with a fiddle and spoils good paper with slapdash semi-breves and crotchets, is no true librarian unless he can class, catalogue and bring books to the point of use. (Savage, 1937a, p. 574)

Following these principles Savage set up four special departments between 1932 and 1936, including the music library which opened in December 1934. The basic collection was formed from 'the books on music and musical scores … from the Reference and Central Home Reading Libraries' of the Central Library supplemented by items in branch libraries that were not already held in the Central Library. 'A library of over 10,000 items was thus put together, and rapidly became a focal point of Edinburgh's musical life' (Edinburgh Public Libraries, 1936, p. 5; White, 1975, p. 157).

The Central Music Library thus became a master collection, containing a copy or copies of every book and score in the service. Books for reference and current periodicals on music are used only in the room. Home reading books are issued as before, but when on the shelves they are at hand to reinforce the reference books. The centre of musical interest so formed is cared for by librarians who have a good knowledge, rapidly growing, of the history and bibliography of music. ... Use increased. Enquiries multiplied. ... The music library, while retaining former users, was reaching a wider circle of better-informed, more critical musicians and music-lovers who required crack service. The librarians took greater interest in work which was responsible, won for them more respect, and satisfied them because it was profitable to readers and to themselves ... . In brief, the librarianship was of a high value ... (Savage, 1937b, pp. 616–17)

Savage wrote interestingly about music libraries and music librarians. In 'One way to form a music library' he was scathing about the 'dominant Dewey':

The Decimal Classification of music, in truth, vivisects composers and outrages common sense. What are we to think of divisions which are named Dramatic or theatre music, Church or sacred music, Vocal music, Orchestral and chamber music, Keyboard instrumental music, String instrumental music, and so on? No fewer than three of the above groups are Orchestral, three are Vocal, and all Instrumental. ... The sub-divisions of these headings increase the confusion, so that by the most crafty prestidigitation the scores in which a violinist is interested, and the works of a composer, are shuffled into bo-peep places all over the collection; Beethoven being strewn about to help executants who are presumed not to know that he composed sonatas unless they blunder upon them among a bunch of sonatas. (Savage, 1935, pp. 103–4)

About music librarians he was somewhat kinder:

A music librarianship is one of the most interesting jobs in our profession: it attracts young librarians with musical tastes; and if we choose practical men who love music, who appreciate order and good business methods (the first laws in any library), and if we avoid those who wear long hair, sashes for ties, and other advertisements of self-esteem we ought to be sure of good service. (Savage, 1935, p. 107)

One month after the appearance of 'One way to form a music library', Lionel McColvin, who called Savage's article 'quite the best survey of the field that has ever appeared in this country' (McColvin, 1935, p. 232), published a brief but important article in *Library World*. In 'Music in public libraries' he admitted that in the ten years since he wrote his book of the same title:

I have been increasingly conscious of its shortcomings, especially its sins of omission; moreover, conditions have changed considerably since then ... . The years since 1924 have seen an upheaval in the musical world – in the conditions under which we listen and perform. In 1924 broadcasting and the gramophone were new; we could not judge what effect they would have upon the use of music collections. (McColvin, 1935, pp. 229–30)

McColvin's change of mind concerning the type of provision of music in public libraries was set out more fully in the second edition of his book *Music Libraries: their organisation and contents*, which was published in 1937 and written with the help of Harold Reeves. In this completely revised version of his earlier book, which included an expansion of his classification scheme for music that had first appeared in the 1924 edition, he recognized that the demands of music library users had transformed the use of music collections in public libraries:

> To-day we cater not only for practitioners but also for an ever-growing body of listeners, who, with their wireless sets can hear, from all parts of Europe and beyond, a bewildering range of music … . Wireless is the factor which to-day influences most aspects of musical provision in libraries … . Music now appeals to large numbers who have had no musical education whatever, and, who cannot, often, read the simplest scores. These people will read about music but will not use music itself … (McColvin and Reeves, 1937, p. 5)

McColvin believed that because of this a wider range of books needed to be provided although there also had to be a broader range of scores, not just for musicians and others who could read music well, but for the novice and for 'those who can follow a line or two and gradually learn more about the content, form and instrumentation of the work … ' (McColvin and Reeves, 1937, p. 6). Provision also needed to be made for 'the professional musician, the advanced student and the scholar. This is particularly necessary in the larger centres, but here, as in other branches of the library service, co-operation and specialisation should be developed to enable us to serve advanced and limited needs even in the smallest places' (McColvin and Reeves, 1937, p. 8). The provision of popular music as we now call it – 'this lower stratum of popular songs, dance music, song and skip shows, and pretty-pretty pieces' as McColvin described it – was still frowned upon (McColvin and Reeves, 1937, pp. 8–9).

Extension activities continued to flourish in the 1930s. Leonard Chubb, who succeeded McColvin as Chief Librarian of Ipswich, described cultural activities provided in the library of a medium-sized provincial town in 1933. The library supported two 'study groups'. The first studied drama, gave public readings and produced plays, while the second group 'known as the Library Singers … meet weekly during the winter months for rehearsal and have become an excellent choir. A work for performance is chosen at the commencement of each session and public concerts are given in the Library Lecture Hall in early December and April'. An amateur operatic society and orchestra also rehearsed on library premises, and music lectures and concerts were arranged on alternate weekends (Chubb, 1934, p. 8). In Coventry, E. Austin Hinton, the City Librarian, was the 'Founder, moving spirit and first secretary' of the Coventry Libraries Music Circle which began in 1935 and 'indulged in' 'lectures, song-recitals, chamber music, and concert-going … as well as recorded music'. For the first two years of its existence it met in the Gulson (Central) Library Lecture Room and Bryant describes the society as 'an outstanding example of the public library being used to extend musical culture in the city … ' (Bryant, 1972, pp. 78–9). One of the most interesting and innovative examples of extension work was at Surbiton where in

1936 the District Council established an orchestral centre in the public library. The object of the centre was:

> to provide facilities for orchestral practice more particularly, but not exclusively, for young people who, when at school, were members of their school orchestras. The main idea is clear – it is to prevent these young folk from dropping what should be an interesting and valuable leisure time pursuit. Subsidiary advantages are that, so encouraged, these folk would take further lessons which would be of value to local teachers, buy more music which would benefit local music sellers, and enable school orchestras to be augmented by old scholars on big occasions. (Dommett, 1936, p. 154)

An honorary conductor was appointed, letters were sent to local schools and music teachers, publicity was distributed and an article about the proposed centre appeared in the local newspaper. The response was so enthusiastic that in addition to the creation of three orchestral groups of differing abilities, plans were made to organize chamber ensembles 'such groups practising at home and playing their pieces at the centre for the enjoyment of their fellow members … ' (ibid.).

'Owing to war conditions and latterly to lack of space in the Library, the Music Room was closed from the outbreak of war in September, 1939 until April, 1953.' Thus the Second World War came to Glasgow's music libraries (Barr, 1977, p. 79). Writing at the end of 1940 Edmund Corbett, Acting Borough Librarian of Mitcham in south London, looked back on the first months of the war:

> Early last year I had the privilege of giving a survey in this journal of the public library service after three months of war. The outlook in that period of quiescent warfare was bright; after a landslide in issues on the outbreak of war most libraries made a rapid recovery and issues frequently exceeded those of the pre-war period; staffs were little affected except in instances where members were seconded to A.R.P. [air raid precautions], food control and other governmental duties; hours of opening were affected to a minor degree only and book funds were still normal. (Corbett, 1941, p. 4)

This was the beginning of the 'phoney war' which lasted until April 1940, before the effects of the war really began to bite. It can hardly be said that work in public libraries carried on without disruption during the first couple of years of the war, but not all musical activities in libraries were allowed to come to a halt. 'The normal course of winter lectures and meetings of the Library Club and W.E.A. [Workers' Educational Association] have been maintained at Mitcham and have met with increased response; a new venture, the Gramophone Club, at which systematically arranged programmes of gramophone records are given, is exceedingly popular' (Corbett, 1940, p. 13). In Surbiton the orchestra continued to meet in the library (Stevenson, 1940, p. 56) and in Kent, the Erith Libraries Committee established a Municipal Musical Society 'to help and encourage amateur music talent' in the town. The society was supported by the committee through generous financial grants and the supply of music from the public library, and an average of 140 musicians met weekly throughout the winter of 1939–40 before giving a public concert in the spring that was attended by an audience of over 800 people and which was reviewed by *The Times* the following day (Berry, 1940, pp. 29–31). At Rugby 'a gramophone recital of Edith Sitwell's poems read by Constant Lambert to William Walton's music' [that is, *Façade*] prompted the local newspaper to suggest 'that the establishment of a lending library of gramophone records may well be a legitimate extension of Rugby's activities' (Collison, 1940b, p. 252). If this suggestion had been taken up, Rugby would have been the first library in the country to lend records to individuals. As it was, that distinction seems to belong to Herefordshire County Library, 'the result of a gift of 300 discs to the library in 1940. This was the personal collection of a local resident who stipulated that, after her death, the records were to be offered to the library … ' (Bryant, 1985, p. 266). The library accepted the offer of the collection, which included some spoken-word recordings and a gramophone, and the service started in November 1940 (Sydney and Shaw, 1949, pp. 212–13). In 1941 Herefordshire Library's annual report noted that 'although the scope is at present limited very considerably by lack of necessary funds for its maintenance, this service of the library is regularly used' (Beattie, 1941, p. 149) and in April 1944 A. Shaw Wright, the County Librarian, wrote:

> I would recommend any librarian who has a similar gramophone records collection in his care to extend its use to members of the general public. Our own collection, now in the fourth year of existence, has been so used. Only 15 records (out of an issue of more than 1,500 during this period) have had to be withdrawn owing to excessive wear or other damage. (Wright, 1944, p. 148)

New music library services continued to be provided in 1940. In St Marylebone's new central library 'the neat and sensible accommodation for miniature scores and sheet music is particularly noteworthy' (Collison, 1940a, p. 231); the new extension to Ealing's Central Library included a music room 'specially shelved for some 1,200 scores and books on music' (Hope, 1940, p. 285), and at Hove a 'Music and Fine Arts Annexe' was opened in the late autumn (Collison, 1940c, p. 305).

From 1941 until the end of the war in 1945, there are, understandably, few recorded instances of developments in music library services. Even though in August 1940 the Government issued a memorandum recognizing 'the importance of maintaining and, where necessary, extending the Public Library service', libraries began to suffer from constraints on their activities and use that were outside their control. These included a severe shortage of qualified staff; restricted access to libraries caused by daytime air raids, the blackout and disrupted transport services; a sharp increase in the cost of books and binding; the cessation of new library building; paper and other shortages which restricted book supply; and the destruction of books and buildings by enemy action (Corbett, 1941, pp. 4–6; Kelly, 1977, pp. 327–9).

The intensive bombing raids of the winter of 1940–41 damaged and destroyed many libraries including the central libraries of Coventry and Plymouth, but the greatest loss of music was in May 1941 when Liverpool's music library was completely destroyed following the bombing of the Central Lending Library, a disaster in which 200 000 books were lost (Anon., 1945b, p. 90). A number of important music collections were destroyed including the Booth collection of plainsong and Dr J D. Hayward's collection of chamber music (Liverpool Public Libraries, 1954, preface). Fortunately a temporary service was successfully improvised, the collection began to be rebuilt and by 1954 issues had reached 71 387 a year, rising to 314 091 issues and a stock of nearly 50 000 volumes when the new Music Library suite was opened in 1959 (Anderson, 1961, p. 60; Chandler, 1959, p. 162).

But not all was gloom and doom. Arthur Henry Mann's important collection of music and manuscripts by William Crotch was presented to Norwich Public Library by Bayford Stone in 1941, Mann's collection of manuscript notes on East Anglian musicians having already been donated to the same library following his death in 1929 (King, 1963, pp. 84, 146). In the same year West Riding County Library's music collection was made freely available to all the county library's borrowers after having been available since the early 1930s only to evening institute classes and groups organized by the education committee (Moore, 1949, pp. 45–6). Some libraries continued to organize concerts, as at Brighton and Chorley (Collison, 1941, p. 170; 1942, p. 59), and at Bradford where a long-running series of weekly lunchtime concerts was inaugurated in August 1943 (Jolliffe, 1968, p. 283). Record recitals continued to be encouraged, as at Beckenham where in 1943 the borough librarian started a 'Library Gramophone Circle' (Bryant, 1972, p. 101) and at Swindon where a Gramophone Society was started by one of the very few local authorities to establish a new library service during the war years ('Borderer', 1944, pp. 123–4). In autumn 1943 Lindsey and Holland County Library started a collection of gramophone records of classical music for the use of tutors of musical appreciation classes. Although the service had only been in operation for six months, the County Librarian wrote in March 1944 that 'it is proving so popular that it is now being extended to Service personnel and to schools, and we confidently anticipate that the formation of a separate department for this work will soon be necessary' (Curtis, 1944, p. 132). In March 1944 West Ham became the first non-county library in the country to operate a record lending library, even though the service was restricted to use by groups and all costs except salaries were paid for by the education committee (Sydney and Shaw, 1949, pp. 212–14), and early in the same year, Edinburgh restored its music library in the Central Library after the collection had been temporarily housed elsewhere to avoid the risk of damage ('Borderer', 1944, p. 67).

Planning for the post-war public library service began as early as 1941 when Lionel McColvin, by now the City Librarian of Westminster, was commissioned by the Library Association, of which he was also honorary secretary, to undertake a survey of the current condition and future needs of the public library service in Great Britain. McColvin's work was completed in 1942 and, not surprisingly in such a wide-ranging report, music is scarcely mentioned. However, he did recommend that large central libraries should have subject departments whereby 'the whole wide field of library provision … is broken down into a number of more manageable components, each embracing a main division of knowledge', one of which would be a music department:

> Without Departmentalization the large central lending library becomes unwieldy, unattractive and confusing to the reader and prevents any sound assistance from a staff which cannot operate effectively over such a large field. In such conditions assistance to individual readers becomes almost impossible yet it is in just such an overgrown jungle that assistance is particularly needed. (McColvin, 1942, p. 67)

This is a timeless argument and a fundamental principle of effective central library management, taken up by many librarians in the 1960s and 1970s but seemingly ignored by many senior library managers at the beginning of the twenty-first century.

The five years from 1945 to 1950 'were occupied mainly in the tasks of renovation and recovery, and were hampered by persisting shortages of books, staff, building materials, even at times fuel. Replacement of damaged or worn-out stock proceeded only slowly, and new buildings, however desperately needed, were hard to come by' (Kelly, 1977, p. 350).

The most significant development in music librarianship in the immediate post-war period was the relatively rapid growth of gramophone record libraries, notably in London and the south-east of England. The first public library to set up a record lending service for individual library users after the end of the war appears to have been at Chingford in Essex, which started its service in January 1946. In October the same year, Holborn started a record library exclusively for use by groups in the borough and a similar service began in St Pancras the following month. In 1947, record libraries from which individuals could borrow were started in Walthamstow and Penge on the outskirts of London, at Hornchurch in Essex and at Sutton Coldfield in the West Midlands (Swift, 1949, pp. 205–6; Sydney and Shaw, 1949, pp. 212–13) and these presaged a dramatic expansion in provision so that by October 1948, 29 authorities in the London area were maintaining gramophone record libraries (Horrocks, 1949, p. 85). One of the largest of these was that at Westminster which obtained funding to start the service in January 1947 and opened a record library in July 1948 at its new central lending library with an initial stock of 5000 discs (Hickling, 1949, p. 208). The records were available to both individuals and societies, and the service 'from the outset proved a great – even an embarrassing – success', so much so that by the end of March 1949, just over eight months after the service started, nearly 81 000 records had been issued (City of Westminster, 1949, p. 5). Justification for the provision of record libraries came early. In 1947 C.D. Overton described the gramophone record library which had recently been set up in Walthamstow:

It has proved to be extremely popular and has served to fill a growing need in the community. During the war years, as a result of C.E.M.A. [Council for the Encouragement of Music and the Arts] concerts and other orchestral concerts arranged in the Borough ... there had been a considerable increase in the number of residents interested in serious music. The gramophone record library thus comes at a time when there is a growing demand for music by the best artists. It has often been maintained that the true musical appreciator will always prefer to hear and watch a concert than listen to a recording of the work. In reply to this it can be said that even in the largest towns concerts are comparatively few and it is seldom possible to hear other than on records the greatest exponents of individual composers. Again, owing to the present high price of records, it is just as impossible for the ordinary citizen to buy all the records he wants to hear as it is for him to buy all his books. We have been providing the latter as fully as we are allowed, and now has come the time to cater also for the music lover. (Overton, 1947, p. 224)

There were of course some librarians who viewed the provision of records as an unnecessary luxury:

The appeal of the record library is necessarily restricted, since comparatively few people possess gramophones. Furthermore, the most popular type of music is as ephemeral as that light fiction we so rightly scorn, and record purchase, restricted to the classics, therefore caters for an even smaller minority. What other rate-supported amenity is provided for so few users? (Bateman, 1949, p. 118)

There were also other genuine concerns. *The Library Association Record* devoted its July 1949 issue to the 'comparatively new departure' of gramophone record librarianship but its editor warned:

Librarians seem to have got on with this new job in a typical business-like fashion. Anyone who has talked with users of gramophone records will soon find himself in a strange new world, where scratch-filters, thorns, and fifty cycle hums compete in importance with the merits of Beecham and Van Beinum, Welitsch and Schwarzkopf. It is to be hoped that we will continue to give our borrowers the best available in the easiest way we can, and will not be involved in any way in the arcana of a sect that may easily become fanatics ... . One final matter may be emphasized. No library should embark on the formation of a gramophone record collection unless it has already an adequate book-fund. The administration costs of a gramophone record collection are high: replacement charges are higher, if the records are to be worth using. Let us not neglect our primary purpose of providing recorded learning in the pursuit of recorded music. (Stevenson, 1949, p. 203)

There were of course considerable extra costs in opening and maintaining a record library. Apart from the start-up costs of buying the initial collection which were exacerbated by libraries having to pay 'full purchase tax, at an iniquitous rate' (Callander, 1949, p. 206), special stationery, storage units, a gramophone to test damaged records, carrying boxes and a visible index for use as an indicator for the public to know which records were currently available all had to be provided. On top of this there were staff costs. The London and Home Counties Branch of the Library Association had formulated some standards for staffing record libraries (Hunt et al., 1949, p. 217) but none had the problems experienced at Westminster where Jean Hickling reported that 'Originally a staff of one was provided, but by the time the service had been in operation for six weeks, this was increased to two, and the work now done by the department occupies the full time of three assistants' (Hickling, 1949, p. 211). However, some interesting ways of reducing running costs were being found, one of the most innovative being that devised at Lambeth and described by T.E. Callander the Chief Librarian:

> Some time and effort was wasted at Lambeth in compiling a typescript sheaf catalogue before it was realized that a printed catalogue was essential. At the same time when this idea penetrated, it was realized also that any two public library collections of roughly equal size and scope must overlap to a very large extent, and that there was a case for combining with another library similarly placed. Accordingly, Finsbury and Lambeth joined forces to print a combined catalogue of their record collections, each library issuing a local edition under its own distinctive cover. The considerable saving in typesetting costs has enabled each library to sell a well-produced catalogue at 1s. per copy and to cover its production costs at this price. (Callander, 1949, p. 208)

As has been noted, some record libraries would only lend records to local societies and not to individuals. The obvious justification for this was that more people would obtain value from the records if they were used by private groups and societies who arranged their own recitals. By March 1947 ten societies were registered at Holborn Central Library who between them borrowed approximately 150 records each month (Swift, 1947, p. 66), while at Westminster in July 1949, 39 societies were registered, mainly representing 'music groups attached to business houses and departments of the Civil Service' but also schools and youth clubs (Hickling, 1949, p. 210).

Whether or not a library had its own gramophone record lending service, many libraries continued to help to arrange record recitals for the public as at Fulham where it was reported that in 1946 the 'Gramophone Society recitals are attended each week by about 90 people … ' (Horrocks, 1947, p. 74); at Swindon where at its new Arts Centre there were library gramophone groups for both adults and juniors (Jolliffe, 1947, p. 124); and at Stepney where 'The list of extension activities, with gramophone club, play reading group and adult lectures, is indeed impressive. It is doubtful, however, whether it is within the library's province to organize park entertainments, concert parties, open-air and old-tyme dancing' (Horrocks, 1949, p. 284). While Stepney had a splendidly individual approach to providing musical 'extension activities', Holborn was more conservative but, as described by L.H. Sidwell in 1949, it provided 'public recitals of gramophone records on … a scale unique in this country and possibly anywhere'. Weekly recitals were started in October 1947 and were given at the East Holborn library each Monday evening and Friday lunchtime, and at midday at Holborn Town Hall every Wednesday. The programmes were quite varied and included numerous listeners' requests which were included in the programmes wherever possible. Winter attendances at the Town Hall recitals averaged over 100 and an interesting feature of the lunchtime recitals was that they ran from 12.15 p.m. to 2 p.m., thus allowing workers to drop in as and when they were able. 'Some listeners, no doubt following National Gallery wartime habits, bring sandwiches. This is encouraged since only by doing so can many find time to hear the recitals' (Sidwell, 1949, p. 110). One interesting activity at East Holborn library was a Children's Music Club which met once a month in the Music Room. 'Music quizzes are the most popular of the varying forms of entertainment for its members and some of the quite young children have proved surprisingly knowledgeable' (ibid.).

In terms of music librarianship 1948 was Westminster Public Libraries' year. A room devoted entirely to music and musical literature and including a new gramophone record library was opened in July in the new Central Lending Library (McColvin, 1948a, p. 240) but of even more significance, the Central Music Library was opened on 21 October. Ralph Vaughan Williams recognized the regional and national significance of this library at the opening ceremony:

> To-day we have made a real start in placing music in its proper position by giving it a home of its own ... . Of course there are a few music libraries and if you go into the British Museum you can find most music ... . But you cannot take it away. This is a lending library here and you will be able to take the music home and study it, which is the whole difference between this library and the British Museum. (Westminster, 1948, p. 7)

The concept of a central music lending library had first been considered in the late 1920s when a committee under the chairmanship of Sir William Henry Hadow had been set up to assess the viability of such a scheme, although Lionel McColvin reported in 1932 that the work of the committee had 'been temporarily suspended as the economic conditions have been such as to make any appeal for support untimely ... ' (Library Association, 1932, p. 21R; McColvin, 1948b, p. 335). The idea was revived during the Second World War when Mrs Winifred Christie Moor, a former concert pianist, was using the music section of the New York Public Library and had the idea of creating a similar large collection in London where practising musicians could borrow scores for study and performance. In 1946 Mrs Christie Moor gave the substantial sum of £10 000 to fund a 'London music library' and a company was set up to bring about the scheme. By 1947 the Central Music Library Company had secured the private library of the music critic Edwin Evans Junior which was later augmented by the major portion of Gerald M. Cooper's music library which was presented by Professor E.J. Dent to whom it had been bequeathed (King, 1963, p. 75; Pemberton, 1962, p. 318). The Arts Council promised funding to help with 'the expenses of cataloguing and making the library available for general use' (Central Music Library, 1948, p. 2) and all the collection now lacked was a home. It was Lionel McColvin, now Chief Librarian of Westminster, who offered to house the collection in the Buckingham Palace Road Library and undertook to administer it alongside Westminster's own music collection even though the Central Music Library was, and remains to this day, the property of a separate limited company and is only deposited at Westminster on long-term loan.

The library opened with approximately 25 000 items of music and musical literature which McColvin described as

> a widely representative collection, covering music for solo instruments, chamber music, songs, operas, choral works, etc., with an extensive range of miniature scores, several full orchestral scores and sets of parts for some 200 orchestral works (the Charles Woodhouse Collection), together with books on musical history, biography and practice and a quantity of miscellanea including many libretti. (McColvin, 1948b, p. 334)

By the following year the collection had grown and 'now includes nearly 30,000 items of music and books on music [which] will be a very valuable asset not only to Westminster but to the nation as the stock is freely available for loan to music lovers and libraries throughout the country' (City of Westminster, 1949, p. 9). The music collection at Westminster, comprising both that library's own music collection along with that of the Central Music Library, made the Buckingham Palace Road Library one of the most significant public music lending libraries in the country. As Westminster had been allocated responsibility for music in the Metropolitan Special Collections Scheme (Leggatt, 1949, p. 186) and was a major supplier of music requests sent to the National Central Library, it was for many years, including the formative years of the British Library Lending Division, probably the most important music lending library in the country (Line, 1975, pp. 1–6; Pemberton, 1962, p. 320; Reed, 1983, p. 48).

In 1950 the Library Association and many individual library authorities celebrated the anniversary of the passing of the 1850 Public Libraries Act. Some libraries took this as an opportunity to look forward and invest in the future as, for example, at Castleford where the local authority decided 'The Centenary will be celebrated by the formation of a gramophone record library for which £250 has been allocated in this year's estimates … ' (Anon., 1950, p. 197) and at Colne which 'increased its book fund by 50 per cent as a result of a report to the Committee based upon the booklet, *A Century of public library service*. In addition to this increase, £150 is to be spent on music (but not on gramophone records)' (Anon., 1950, p. 164). But 100 years after the passing of the first Public Libraries Act, how far had the provision of music been accepted by British public libraries?

The opportunity for librarians to specialize in music librarianship had already started with 'The Literature of Music' being introduced as a separate study option in the new Library Association examination syllabus which was introduced in January 1946 (Anon., 1945a, pp. 12–13). Even so, the chance of being employed as a professionally qualified music librarian was fairly limited for many years, as is shown by the fact that of 387 English, Welsh and Scottish public libraries that responded to a survey of music libraries in 1973 only 152 employed music or music sound recordings librarians, and of these only 100 were credited with a Library Association professional qualification (Long, 1974). Nevertheless there were by now several distinguished and mature collections which had a regional and sometimes national significance well beyond that of their local community, examples being the music libraries at Edinburgh, Glasgow, Liverpool, Manchester, Birmingham and Westminster. Record libraries were beginning to be established, albeit slowly, and even though the years of heated debate in the professional press over the merits of mono or stereo long-playing record (LP) provision, open access versus closed access, and whether there should be loan charges were still some way off, the argument as to whether libraries should stock popular music recordings had already begun. The provision of sets of orchestral and vocal music was still very patchy, the wide-scale interlending of music scores was still in its infancy and it was to be many years before the music publishing industry in this country produced popular music scores in formats that were considered appropriate for addition to most library collections.

By 1950, therefore, it can be seen that some progress had been made in the provision of music in British public libraries but, as Ralph Vaughan Williams pointed out in a centenary message to the Library Association: 'I am very glad to see that in late years the public libraries have woken up to the importance of music as part of our general culture. Many libraries have now a good collection of music scores, but, as you yourselves know, much remains to be done' (Vaughan Williams, 1950, p. 111).

Bibliography

A.E. and E.G.T. (1924), 'At home and abroad', *Library Association Record,* **2** (New Series), 251–7.

A.E., J.V.S. and E.G.T. (1927), 'At home and abroad', *Library Association Record,* **5** (New Series), 307–21.

Adams, W.G.S. (1915), *A Report on Library Provision & Policy by Professor W.G.S. Adams to the Carnegie United Kingdom Trustees,* Edinburgh: Neill and Company.

Aitken, W.R. (1971), *A History of the Public Library Movement in Scotland to 1955,* Glasgow: Scottish Library Association.

Allan, J. (1937), 'Music collections', *Library Association Record,* **39**, 40–41.

Anderson, K. (1961), 'Public Service for Music: The Use of Standard Methods in Liverpool's New Music Library', in Sherrington, U. and Oldham, G. (eds), *Music, Libraries and Instruments: Papers Read at the Joint Congress, Cambridge, 1959, of the IAML and the Galpin Society,* London: Hinrichsen, pp. 60–61.

Anon. (1893), 'Library notes and news', *The Library,* **5**, 331–41.

Anon. (1899), 'Library notes and news', *Library Association Record,* **1** (Part 1), 78–92.

Anon. (1900), ' Library notes and news', *Library Association Record,* **2**, (Part 1), 319–27.

Anon. (1903), 'Notes and news. Library practice. Cottesmore: exemplary work in a village', *Library Association Record,* **5**, 246–7.

Anon. (1908), 'Recent library publications', *Library Association Record,* **10**, 300–304.

Anon. (1915), 'Notes and news', *Library Association Record,* **17**, 374–80.

Anon. (1929), 'At home and abroad', *Library Association Record*, **7** (New Series), 275–81.

Anon. (1930), 'At home and abroad', *Library Association Record*, **8** (New Series), 221–5.

Anon. (1945a), 'An outline of the examinations syllabus and some points from the regulations', *Library Association Record*, **47**, 12–13.

Anon. (1945b), 'Liverpool Public Libraries: reconstructed central lending library', *Library Association Record*, **47**, 90.

Anon. (1950), 'Centenary notes', *Library Association Record*, **52**, 163–4, 197–8.

Aston (1886), Manor of Aston Local Board. *The eighth annual report of the Free Libraries Committee. March 26th, 1885, to March 25th, 1886*.

Aston (1887–1911):

Manor of Aston Local Board. Free Libraries Committee. Annual reports, 1886–90.

Aston Manor Public Library. Free Libraries Committee. Annual reports, 1890–94.

Aston Manor Urban District Council. Free Libraries Committee. Annual reports, 1894–1903.

Borough of Aston Manor. Free Libraries Committee. Annual reports, 1903–11.

Aston (1899), Aston Manor Urban District Council. *the twenty-first annual report of the Free Libraries Committee. April 1st, 1898, to March 31st, 1899*.

Axon, W.E.A. (1877), *Handbook of the public libraries of Manchester and Salford*, Manchester: Abel Heywood and Son.

Barr, G.R. (1977), 'The Music Room', in *The Mitchell Library Glasgow 1877–1977*, Glasgow District Libraries, pp. 79–88.

Bateman, R. (1949), 'Gramophone record libraries', *Library Association Record*, **51**, 118.

Beattie, M. (1941), 'County library notes', *Library Association Record*, **43**, 148–50.

Berry, G. (1940), 'A municipal musical society', *Library World*, **43**, 29–31.

Board of Education, Public Libraries Committee (1927), *Report on Public Libraries in England and Wales* (Kenyon Report) (Cmd. 2868, 1927).

'Borderer' (1944), 'Municipal library notes', *Library Association Record*, **46**, 67–8, 123–4.

Borough of Birmingham (1867), *The sixth annual report of the Free Libraries Committee. 1867*, Birmingham: Borough of Birmingham.

Borough of Birmingham (1880), *The nineteenth annual report of the Free Libraries Committee. 1880*, Birmingham: Borough of Birmingham.

Borough of Birmingham (1883), *The twentieth and twenty-first annual reports of the Free Libraries Committee. On the years 1881 and 1882*, Birmingham: Borough of Birmingham.

Borough of Birmingham (1885), *The twenty-second & twenty-third annual reports of the Free Libraries Committee. On the years 1883 and 1884*, Birmingham: Borough of Birmingham.

Boyd, M. (1973), 'Music manuscripts in the Mackworth Collection at Cardiff', *Music and Letters*, **54**, 133–41.

Briscoe, J.P. (1888), 'Book music in public libraries', *Library Chronicle*, **5**, 146–7.

Brown, J.D. (1886), *Biographical dictionary of musicians: with a bibliography of English writings on music*. Paisley and London: Alexander Gardner.

Brown, J.D. (1891), 'Subject lists I – music', *The Library*, **3**, 147–51.

Brown, J.D. (1893), *Guide to the formation of a music library*, London: Simpkin, Marshall, Hamilton, Kent and Co.

Brown, J.D. (1907), *Manual of Library Economy*, revd edn, London: Library Supply Co.

Bryant, E.T. (1972), 'The Gramophone Society movement: a history of the gramophone societies in Britain, including their links with public libraries', unpublished MA thesis, Queen's University of Belfast.

Bryant, E.T. (1985), *Music Librarianship : A Practical Guide*, 2nd edn, Metuchen and London: Scarecrow Press.

Burnley Libraries Department (1929), *Catalogues of the stock in the Edwards Stocks Massey Music Library, Burnley,* Burnley: Veevers and Hensman.

Callander, T.E. (1949), 'Lambeth', in 'Gramophone record collections: a symposium', *Library Association Record,* **51**, 204–11.

Carnegie United Kingdom Trust (1925), *County Libraries in Great Britain and Ireland: Report, 1925,* Edinburgh : Carnegie United Kingdom Trust.

Carnell, E.J. (1938), *County Libraries: Retrospect and Forecast,* London: Grafton.

Carr, J.A. (1938), 'Music and libraries', *Library Association Record,* **40**, 595–9.

Chandler, G. (1959), 'Liverpool Music Library suite', *Library Association Record,* **61**, 160–62.

Central Music Library (1948), *Order of proceedings* [of the opening ceremony].

Chubb, L. (1934), 'The activities of a public library in a provincial town of medium extent', *Library Association Record,* **1** (Fourth Series), 6–14.

City of Manchester (1900), *Forty-Eighth Annual Report of the Public Free Libraries Committee. 1899–1900.*

City of Manchester (1904), *Fifty-Second Annual Report of the Public Free Libraries Committee. 1903–1904.*

City of Manchester (1915), *Sixty-Third Annual Report of the Public Libraries Committee. 1914–1915.*

City of Nottingham (1937), *Annual Report of the Public Libraries and Museum Committee, 1936–37.*

City of Westminster (1949), *Report of the Public Libraries Committee. 1948–1949.*

Clerkenwell Vestry (1892), 'Minutes of the meeting of the Library Commissioners', *Report of J.D. Brown to the Commissioners,* 26 September, 224–9.

Clerkenwell Public Library (1894), *Seventh annual report of the Commissioners. 1894.*

Clerkenwell Public Library (1895a), *Quarterly guide for readers,* 1 (4), April, 66–70.

Clerkenwell Public Library (1895b), *Eighth annual report of the Commissioners. 1895.*

C.M.J. (1953), Obituary of Thomas Green, Library Association Record, **55**, 422.

Collison, R.L.W. (1940a), 'Municipal library notes', *Library Association Record,* **42**, 231–2.

Collison, R.L.W. (1940b), 'Municipal library notes', *Library Association Record,* **42**, 252–3.

Collison, R.L.W. (1940c), 'Municipal library notes', *Library Association Record,* **42**, 305–6.

Collison, R.L.W. (1941), 'Municipal library notes', *Library Association Record,* **43**, 170–72.

Collison, R.L.W. (1942), 'Municipal library notes', *Library Association Record,* **44**, 58–9.

Cooper, B.A.R. (1978), 'Catalogue of early printed music in Aberdeen libraries', R*oyal Musical Association Research Chronicle,* **14**, 2–138.

Corbett, E.V. (1940), 'War: the first three months', *Library Association Record,* **42**, 11–14.

Corbett, E.V. (1941), '1940 and after: a review of the public library service after fifteen months of war', *Library Association Record,* **43**, 4–6.

County Borough of Warrington, Museum Committee (1906), *Report of the Director and Librarian for the Year Ending 30th June 1906.*

County Borough of Warrington, Museum Committee (1907), *Report of the Director and Librarian for the Year Ending 30th June 1907.*

Cowell, P. (1898), 'Reminiscences of library work in Liverpool during forty years', in *Transactions and proceedings of the Second International Library Conference held in London July 13–16, 1897,* 99–102.

Cowell, P. (1903), *Liverpool Public Libraries: A History Of Fifty Years,* Liverpool: Free Public Library.

Credland, W.R. (1899), *The Manchester Public Free Libraries,* Manchester: Public Free Libraries Committee.

Curtis, A.C. (1944), Letter to the editor, *Library World*, **46**, 132.

Davies, H.W. (1923), 'On music libraries' *Library Association Record*, **1** (New Series), 19–20.

Davis, C.T. (1891), 'The Free Public Library, Wandsworth', *The Library*, **3**, 186.

Dommett, W.E. (1936), 'Orchestral centres at public libraries', *Library Association Record*, **38**, 154.

Douglas, S.M. (1999), *The Atholl Collection Catalogue: 300 Years of Scottish Music and Poetry*, Perth and Kinross Libraries.

Duck, L.W. (1961a), 'The Henry Watson Music Library', *Library World*, **63**, 132–6.

Duck, L.W. (1961b), 'The public provision of music for choirs and orchestras', in Sherrington, U. and Oldham, G. (eds), *Music, Libraries and Instruments: Papers Read at the Joint Congress, Cambridge, 1959, of the IAML and the Galpin Society*, London: Hinrichsen, pp. 53–60.

E.E.P. (1931), 'Municipal library notes', *Library Association Record*, **1** (Third Series), 282–4.

Edinburgh Public Libraries (1936), *Report of the Librarian for the Years 1934 and 1935*.

Edwards, E. (1869), *Free own libraries*, London: Trübner and Co.

Farr, H. (1906), 'The libraries and the counties', *Library Association Record*, **8**, 169–77.

Fearnside, K. (1918), 'Co-operation between a town library and local societies and bodies', *Library Association Record*, **20**, 140–49.

Gloucestershire (1925), 'Valuable gift to the public library', *Gloucestershire Echo*, 9 October, 6. [N.B. a note by A.E. in the *Library Association Record*, **(3)** (New Series), p. 331 is apparently wrong in describing the collection as containing 6000 volumes.]

Gray, D. (1922), *County Library Systems. Their History, Organisation and Administration*, London: Grafton.

G.R.B. (1913), 'Library Assistant's Association. November meeting', report on a paper, 'The public library movement from the ratepayers' point of view', given by R.T.L. Parr, Local Government Board Auditor, *Library Association Record*, **15**, 706–7.

Hand, T.W. (1904), 'The Leeds Public Free Libraries', *Library Association Record*, **6**, 1–28.

Handsworth Public Library (1882), *Report of committee for year ended 25th March, 1882*.

Handsworth Public Library (1883), *Report of committee for year ended 25th March, 1883*.

Handsworth Public Library (1887), *Report of committee for year ended 25th March, 1887*.

Handsworth Public Library (1888), *Report of committee for year ended 25th March, 1888*.

Haxby, R. (1911), 'The history, organization, and educational value of municipal library lectures', *Library Association Record*, **13**, 123–32.

Hickling, J. (1949), 'Westminster', in 'Gramophone record collections. A symposium', *Library Association Record*, **51**, 204–11.

Hope, C. (1940), 'Extension to Ealing Central Library', *Library Association Record*, **42**, 285–6.

Horrocks, S.H. (1947), 'Municipal library notes', *Library Association Record*, **49**, 73–4.

Horrocks, S.H. (1949), 'Municipal library notes', *Library Association Record*, **51**, 85–6, 283–4.

Hunt, K.G., Harrod, L.M., Stevenson, W.B. and Richards, F.A. (1949), 'Gramophone record libraries', *Library Association Record*, **51**, 215–17.

Jolliffe, H. (1947), 'Swindon's Arts Centre and Junior Library', *Library Association Record*, **49**, 123–4.

Jolliffe, H. (1968), *Public Library Extension Activities*, 2nd edn, London: Library Association.

Kelly, T. (1977), *A History of Public Libraries in Great Britain 1845–1975*, 2nd edn (revised), London: Library Association.

King, A.H. (1963), *Some British Collectors of Music c.1600–1960*, Cambridge: Cambridge University Press.

Law, W. (1911), 'The influence of the public library', *Library Assistant*, **8**, 227–9.

Leggatt, D. (1949), 'The Metropolitan special collections scheme', *Library Association Record*, **51**, 186.

Library Association (1932), Annual report, *Library Association Record*, **2** (New Series), 3R–29R.

Line, M.B. (1975), 'The British Library and the provision of music on interlibrary loan', *Brio*, **12** (1), 1–6.

Liverpool Public Libraries (1954), *Catalogue of the Music Library*, Liverpool: Central Public Libraries.

Long, M.W. (1974), *Music in British Libraries. A Directory of Resources*, 2nd edn, London: Library Association.

Malbon, R. (1982), 'Liverpool Public Libraries 1850–1899: a study of the development of a municipal library service', unpublished MA thesis, University of Sheffield.

Manchester Library Fellowship (1915), Report on an address delivered by F. Bentley Nicholson on 'The Henry Watson Music Library and its founder', *Library Association Record*, **17**, 260–61.

Mathews, E.R. N. (1893), 'Libraries and music', *The Library*, **5**, 190–92.

McColvin, L.R. (1923), 'Libraries and the fine arts', *Library Association Record*, **1** (New Series), 150–56.

McColvin, L.R. (1924), *Music in Public Libraries*, London: Grafton.

McColvin, L.R. (1926), 'Municipal libraries: reports and notes', *Library Association Record*, **4** (New Series), 165–70.

McColvin, L.R. (1928), ' Municipal libraries: reports and notes', *Library Association Record*, **6** (New Series), 201–5.

McColvin, L.R. (1930), 'Municipal library notes', *Library Association Record*, **8** (New Series), 123–9.

McColvin, L.R. (1931), 'Municipal library notes', *Library Association Record*, **1** (Third Series), 57–9.

McColvin, L.R. (1935), 'Music in public libraries', *Library World*, **37**, 229–32.

McColvin, L.R. (1942), *The Public Library System of Great Britain: A Report on Its Present Condition with Proposals for Post-War Reorganization*. London: Library Association.

McColvin, L.R. (1948), 'New Central Lending Library, Westminster', *Library Association Record*, **50**, 240–43.

McColvin, L.R. (1948), 'Central Music Library', *Library Association Record*, **50**, 334–5.

McColvin, L.R. and Reeves, H. (1937), *Music Libraries: Their Organisation and Contents, with a Bibliography of Music and Musical Literature, Vol. 1*, London: Grafton.

McKillop, J. (1914), 'The rural library problem', *Library Association Record*, **16**, 48–56.

Moore, G. (1949), 'A library of music scores', *Library Association Record*, **51**, 45–8.

Munford, W.A. (1951), *Penny Rate: Aspects of British Public Library History 1850–1950*, London: Library Association.

Munford, W.A. (1968), *James Duff Brown 1862–1914, Portrait of a Library Pioneer*, London: Library Association.

Music (1913), 'Music in public libraries: with special notes on the John B.M. Camm Music Reference Library, and a comparison of the classification of orchestral music', discussion following the presentation of the paper by Charles Riddle, *Library Association Record*, **15**, 645–8.

Myres, J. N. L. (1963), 'Presidential address', *Library Association Record*, **65**, 282–9.

Nowell, C. (1930), 'Broadcasting and public libraries, *Library Association Record*, **8** (New Series), 81–92.

Ogle, J.J. (1897), *The free library: its history and present condition*, London: George Allen.

Overton, C.D. (1947), 'A gramophone record library service', *Library Association Record*, **49**, 224–5.

Pemberton, J. (1962), 'The Central Music Library', *Library World*, **63**, 318–22.

Piper, A. C. (1908), 'Music in public libraries', *Library World*, **11**, 78–9.

Reed, T. (1983), 'Making music available: the problems of provision and interlending of music scores', *Brio*, **20** (2), 45–52.

Riddle, C. (1914a), 'Music in public libraries, with special notes on the "John B. M. Camm Music Reference Library," and a comparison of the classifications of music', *Library Association Record*, **16**, 1–10.

Riddle, C. (1914b), 'The library movement in Bournemouth', *Library Association Record*, **16**, 109–18.

Robertson, A.W. (1894), 'The public libraries of Aberdeen', *The Library*, **6**, 1–12.

Rolland, G.H. (1961), 'The music collection in the Mitchell Library', in Sherrington, U. and Oldham, G. (eds), *Music, Libraries and Instruments: Papers Read at the Joint Congress, Cambridge, 1959, of the IAML and the Galpin Society*, London: Hinrichsen, pp. 95–9.

St Giles Camberwell. Commissioners of Free Public Libraries (1891), *Minute book*, 14 October, 273–7.

Savage, E.A. (1935), 'One way to form a music library', *Library Association Record*, **2** (Fourth Series), 100–107.

Savage, E.A. (1937a), 'Special librarianship in general libraries: 1. The capital difficulty in book selection', *Library Association Record*, **39**, 570–74.

Savage, E.A. (1937b), 'Special librarianship in general libraries: 2. Subject departments in public libraries', *Library Association Record*, **39**, 615–21.

Schnapper, E.B. (ed.) (1957), *The British Union-Catalogue of Early Music, Printed before the Year 1801: A Record of Holdings of Over One Hundred Libraries throughout the British Isles*, London: Butterworth.`

Sidwell, L.H. (1949), 'The gramophone and the local authority', *The Gramophone*, **27**, 109–10.

Snaith, S. (1928), 'The gramophone in public libraries', *Library World*, **31**, 6–9.

Stevenson, W.B. (1940), 'Municipal library notes', *Library Association Record*, **42**, 55–6.

Stevenson, W.B. (1949), 'Discophily', *Library Association Record*, **51**, 203.

Swift, J. (1947), 'Holborn Public Library', *Library Association Record*, **49**, 64–6.

Swift, J. (1949), 'Holborn', in 'Gramophone record collections. A symposium', *Library Association Record*, **51**, 204–11.

Sydney, E. and Shaw, L.J. (1949), 'Gramophone record libraries: a tabulation', *Library Association Record*, **51**, 212–14.

T.S.M. (1935), 'Notes on the development of music sections in public libraries', *Library World*, **37**, pp. 232, 234.

Vaughan Williams, R. (1950), 'A responsibility to music', *Library Assistant*, **43**, 111.

Warner, J. (1928), *Reference Library Methods*, London: Grafton.

Warrington (1849), *The report of the Museum Committee, to the Council of the Borough of Warrington for the year ending 1st November, 1849*.

Warrington (1850a), *Third annual report of the Museum Committee to the Council of the Borough of Warrington, being for the year ending 1st Nov. 1850*.

Warrington (1850b), *Catalogue of Standard Music deposited, by way of loan, in the Warrington Museum & Library, by Mr Marsh in Catalogue of the books in the Warrington*

Museum and Library. Warrington: Printed for the Committee by Haddock and Son, pp. 125–31.

Watson, H. (1899), Letter to Alderman Southern, chairman of the [Manchester] Free Libraries Committee, in 'Library notes and news', *Library Association Record,* **1** (Part 2), 787–97.

Westminster (1948), 'Westminster's new music library', *Westminster & Pimlico News,* 29 October, 7.

White, A.G.D. (1975), 'The public libraries of Edinburgh 1800–1970: an historical survey', unpublished FLA thesis, Library Association.

Wighton (2002), The Wighton Collection of Dundee. Available from: URL http://www.dundeecity.gov.uk/centlib/wighton/wighton.htm

Wolverhampton Free Library (1891), *Programme for session 1891–2.*

Wright, A. S. (1944), Letter to the editor, *Library World,* **46**, 148.

Zanetti, C. (1942), 'Retrospect. A mental flash-back', *Library Association Record,* **44**, 65–7.

Chapter 3

Music information skills at the University of Reading

Christopher Cipkin

A range of approaches is being taken towards developing music information skills at the University of Reading. This chapter will explore planning of teaching, formal delivery of sessions at different academic levels and informal methods of developing information skills.

There has been much debate about whether classroom-based teaching is the best way to impart information skills, including whether classroom-based instruction is really the librarian's responsibility at all. On the one hand, librarians have been accused of regarding teaching such skills as an end in itself, rather than integrating their teaching fully within the academic curriculum. On the other hand, as student numbers increase, basic information skills can be imparted most easily within a classroom situation, especially during the early stages of their course. The best approach is to regard classroom teaching as an important part of the user education portfolio, but also to concentrate on a range of other methods (Bluck, Hilton and Noon, 1994, p. 13). This combined approach has been adopted at the University of Reading Music Library and, therefore, what follows covers both formal and informal methods of user education.

The University of Reading Music Library is situated within the Department of Music. It serves a client population of about 100 full-time and part-time students, eight members of teaching staff and a range of users from across the university and beyond who are involved in musical activities. The undergraduate programme is divided into three 'parts', relating to the three years of their course. The Music Library has one full-time Music Liaison Librarian who is also responsible for information skills delivery.

At the micro-level, many of the teaching techniques used within the Music Library have been adapted from techniques used across the university. This said, account has to be taken of the subject norms of music. As Bluck has argued, humanities users tend to 'muddle along with no systematic approach, often browsing instead of using bibliographies or even library catalogues' (Bluck, Hilton and Noon, 1994, p. 27). Music students need to be aware of the landscape of information searching and the particular problems it poses. Music libraries are among the most 'hybrid' in terms of the range of printed, audiovisual and electronic resources they provide. Students need to be able to isolate the two sound recordings from the twenty hits they might get by searching the online public access catalogue (OPAC) for Beethoven's Ninth Symphony. They need to recognize that the online version of Grove's dictionary is more up to date than the printed version and they should be able to distinguish between 'good' and 'bad' editions of published scores. These are just a few examples of the information skills specific to music users. Students cannot be expected simply to acquire these skills by using the library. A systematic approach that aims to make students think about the information they are looking for, question how they obtain it and evaluate the suitability of the material they retrieve is essential. Some understanding of the different types of information skills is necessary, among both students and academic staff. Individual students will have specific information skills needs, strengths and weaknesses. Academic staff may interpret information skills as library skills or as IT skills. In reality, information skills are built on both basic library and IT skills and it is for this reason that SCONUL developed the Seven Pillars Model (SCONUL, 2000, p. 6). This model revises previous information skills models in recognizing that skills develop iteratively and in parallel, rather than sequentially. In individual students, there may be a need to focus on developing one or more 'pillars' of the model at different stages of a student's information skills development, such as how to compare and evaluate information or how to synthesize information.

The relatively small size of the Music Library user population, compared with the other Reading University Library sites, means that innovative methods can be explored more easily because the Music Liaison Librarian knows each individual user. Even in this situation, staff and students can fail to recognize the importance of music information skills. The key to a successful information skills strategy is to stress the relevance of information skills. The way to make sessions relevant is to integrate them as fully as possible – not just into the course, but as part of the holistic learning process offered by the institution. This means focusing very clearly on the users' needs. For example, the timing of sessions is crucial. An hour-long session on using the library is of little value to freshers in week one of their course. By week five, however, a session is particularly timely, especially when they have just received their first assignments and they have begun to overcome the information overload which they invariably suffer at the start of their university careers. Moreover, holding the session during a timetabled slot rather than as an optional extra gives it further validity, especially if the tutor can be persuaded to attend. In order to be fully integrated, the formal class assignment might be used as the means of assessing information skills development, with feedback obtained from academics. For example, it may be specified that students are expected to cite a wide range of monograph, periodical and electronic sources in their bibliography. At the extreme end of a continuum ranging from isolated library sessions to integrated information skills education lies problem-based learning, in which specific problems related to the course become catalysts for learning. Students are then encouraged to identify learning objectives, define the problem, clarify terms, collect, analyse and synthesize information before providing a solution. Academic tutors and library staff work together within the context of a class-session to support the student (Corrall and Hathaway, 2000, p. 27). Problem-based learning is something that Reading University Library is aiming towards and it can be seen to some extent in the programme for Part I students. The problem-based approach also helps to shift the focus away from the numbers and types of sessions delivered to the outcomes of sessions.

Planning information skills delivery

Strategic planning at the macro-level

Planning is vitally important at the strategic level. Like most academic institutions, the University of Reading has an information skills group which was initially set up to examine the range of information skills activities across the library, promote best practice, share ideas and resources, and plan new approaches to information skills delivery. The Seven Pillars Model, mentioned above, may be adopted by such a strategic group to ensure that all aspects of skills development are being addressed within an institution (Corrall and Hathaway, 2000, p. 19). Another reason that this group is important is that it can identify other aspects of the service which have an impact on information skills: for example, the promotion of resources or the quality of signs and guides. The Music Liaison Librarian is an active member of the Information Skills Group at Reading University Library and contributes to meetings by suggesting new ideas and taking back to the Music Library ideas on teaching which have been adapted elsewhere within the university.

Planning at the micro-level

Each formal information session, from freshers' induction to detailed seminars for postgraduates, is also planned out. The planning process can take up to three times the length of the actual session, especially if it has not been taught before. The exact details of what is required from the session, the number of students attending, the length of the session and assessment details are discussed with the academic tutor. Out of this discussion, a 'session plan' is devised, based on the needs of the students. This matching of the session to the needs of the students is critical. Maple (Maple, Christensen and Abromeit, 1996) has identified a number of questions to ask when determining the content of a session. The planning document forms a useful tool when discussing the session in more detail with colleagues, and it acts as an aide-memoire when it comes to delivering the session. The plan can also be useful to academic colleagues – at the University of Reading it has been incorporated into the course documentation retained for Quality Assessment Audit inspection. It can also be kept and revised for future sessions, to save having to reinvent the wheel.

   Typically, a plan has the following headings (see Appendix 1 for an example):

- Aim: a broad outcome, such as 'familiarizing students with the Library catalogues'.
- Objectives: these should be clear and should consist of a maximum of three or four measurable outcomes. In order that the outcomes should be measurable, it is normal for objectives to begin with a verb, such as 'Search for known items using the OPAC' or 'Write down the call number of a sound recording located in the card catalogue'. The objectives, or learning outcomes, can be given to students at the start of a session to give them an idea of what they are expected to achieve and to help them (as well as the deliverer of the session) evaluate how well they have achieved the objectives.
- Method: this section of the plan is the one of most use during the actual delivery of the class. It is best set out as a step-by-step breakdown of the order of the session, in as much detail as is needed, perhaps with an indication of the time to be taken on each activity: demonstration of different search screens [5 minutes]; ask students to search for Apel, *Notation of Polyphonic Music* (Apel, 1953) [2 minutes], for example.
- Assessment: this section is directly related to the objectives section because assessment is only achievable if the objectives are measurable. For example, if the objective specifies that by the end of the session students will be able to write down a call number from using the catalogue (note the verb), a quiz would be a suitable method of assessment. If the objective is too vague and not easily measured (for example, students will be able to perform a subject search), assessment is increasingly difficult. Assessment can take many forms and these are outlined in more detail below under the descriptions of the specific formal and informal teaching methods.
- Feedback: this section is optional, but potentially very important if the quality of the teaching is to be constantly monitored and improved. The section is used to record what methods are going to be used to evaluate the quality of teaching in order to improve the session for next time. This may take the form of an evaluation sheet, verbal feedback, the success with which students attempt a library exercise or even comments from a focus group.
- Resources: this section can be used as a checklist before the session to ensure all the materials are available. A note of the number of students expected to attend is useful in order to gauge the quantity of materials required, such as handouts, printed guides, bookmarks, overhead transparencies, assignment sheets and evaluation forms.

Summary of planning information skills delivery

Planning seems like common sense, but the importance of this stage cannot be overestimated. The main consideration is how the session can be made relevant to the user. The key to this is integration within the curriculum.

Delivery of formal sessions to different user groups

This section outlines some of the different approaches adopted towards delivering information skills sessions to various different parts of the user population. This breakdown demonstrates how Reading University Library's approach is progressive: trying to match the needs of students at different stages of their course and also the different ways in which sessions are made timely and relevant. Students' information skills should develop hand-in-hand with their subject knowledge.

Freshers' lectures

During Freshers' Week, all new students in the university have the option of attending a joint presentation given by the Library and Information Technology Services staff. These presentations, which are not subject specific, but which are given by the faculty, are held in large lecture theatres rather than in the library. The aim of the presentation is simply to alert students to the range of services available, to encourage them to use the services and to reassure them that there is lots of help available. As a member of the Information Skills Group, the Music Liaison Librarian is involved in both the planning and delivery of these presentations. As a result, the Music Liaison Librarian is also fully aware of the information new students have already received prior to any music-specific sessions.

Freshers' induction at the Music Library

At the end of Freshers' Week, at the request of tutors, students are introduced to the Music Library as part of a wider induction to the department. The decision was made to keep this session as short and basic as possible because of the information overload students tend to be suffering by this time in the first week at university. There is also little need for them to use the library in the first few weeks of term and, so, any detailed information is likely to have been forgotten by the time they come to use the library in earnest a few weeks later. The session is restricted to 15–20 minutes with the aim being simply to introduce students to the library and its staff. An introductory *Getting Started Guide* is distributed, which explains basics such as finding a book on a reading list and how to find a sound recording. Students can read the guide at their own pace. As part of the induction, the five rooms of the library are visited and the layout is explained. Students are reassured that they will receive a more detailed session in week five of the autumn term, just after they have received details of their first assignment.

Initial information skills session

The first full session for new students takes place in week five of the autumn term as an integral part of the Musicology course. The tutor is, therefore, usually present and this helps to stress the importance attached to developing information skills. There are two aims to the session: assessing information and its uses, and general tips on using the Music Library.

Immediately prior to the information skills session, students are given their first assignment by their tutor. They are required to prepare a programme note, with an annotated bibliography, for a work composed within the past 40 years. The aim of the assignment is really to encourage them to find out about contemporary composers, on whom there are relatively few published monographs. The assignment therefore requires students to look critically at alternative sources of information. These include using scores, recordings, dictionaries, periodicals and the World Wide Web (WWW) to answer questions such as how a piece is scored, how long it lasts, what critics have said about it and when the composer was born. Thus, a potential information problem (lack of monographs on a topic) becomes the focus during the information skills session for developing a conceptual framework with students on how information is produced and how it can be accessed (card catalogues, OPACS, WWW, and so on). These are two of the concepts identified by Maple (Maple, Christensen and Abromeit, 1996). The problem-based information skills session focuses on how music libraries are among the most 'hybrid' in terms of their provision of a mix of printed, audiovisual and electronic formats. The session then covers how alternative formats can be used as information sources and how these alternative formats can be located.

The second part of the session highlights some 'useful tips for music students' and attempts to convey how the information skills session is subject specific and relevant to them. There is a particular focus on the catalogues and how to limit searches to sound recording or score, and how to search for uniform, genre and distinctive titles. An informal quiz, completed in groups, is distributed in class to get students thinking of search terms they would use.

All the above activities take place in a Department of Music lecture room (with tables arranged in a circle to aid interactivity). The final part of the session takes place in the library and aims to reinforce what has been covered in the session by giving students the opportunity to make a start searching for materials relating to their first assignment. Thus the direct link between library skills and meeting the students' immediate information needs is made. Library staff and the academic tutor are also on hand to support learning and address individual problems and concerns. The assessment is the programme note assignment, submitted to and marked by the tutor. Feedback on the quality of the sessions comes in the form of a visual 'smiley' chart, completed by students after the class. The tutor is also asked for informal feedback about how students performed and how the session might be altered in future.

'Studying Music' course

As with many undergraduate courses, the first year tends to be based on a limited number of core texts and standard dictionaries. In the final term of the first year, all music students are required to attend a course entitled 'Studying music', which aims to develop a range of analytical, musicological and more general study skills. As part of the course, library sessions entitled 'Developing information skills' focus on taking students beyond relying on reading lists and local monograph sources. The sessions also aim at encouraging their ability to locate printed music and sound recordings. The sessions are promoted as relevant to students in that they are designed to encourage them to start preparing for the Part II (that is, second year) courses, which form part of their split finals. Objectives of the session include:

- identifying search terms (including broader, narrower, related terms and synonyms)
- locating periodical articles using the Library's own periodicals index
- recognizing and registering for the online musical abstracting service Réperetoire international de littérature musicale (RILM)
- performing subject searches on the library's OPAC
- locating scores and sound recordings effectively using genre and uniform titles
- citing references.

The class takes the form of interactive discussions followed by a practical exercise in which students are divided into groups and required to analyse a past examination question before going on to identify suitable sources using a range of printed and electronic tools. The feedback session includes a discussion on citing the references retrieved. Self-paced worksheets on searching for printed music and sound recordings are given out as a homework assignment.

Currently, assessment does not contribute towards the degree mark, which has meant, in the past, that students tended not to attend sessions nor to complete the exercise. These problems have been overcome by:

- a well publicized register
- requesting students to hand in work to their tutor to reinforce that the work is regarded as important
- integrating the library assignment with the assignment for other units taught by academics and including it on the same handout
- a comment on the student's record concerning non-completion of the library exercise.

The Music Liaison Librarian marks the part of the assignment relating to the library sessions and individual feedback is given to allow the librarian the opportunity to address individual student problems. After the first use of the assignment, many things were learnt about assessment. In particular, it is important to make it clear how many marks are available for each question so that total equality is achieved across all pieces of work. Students will compare answers!

Part II and Part III students

During the second and third years of their studies, Music Department students receive fewer formal, class-based information skills sessions. As their information needs become more individual and specialized, there is a need for them to receive more individual attention. The exception to this is a lecture to Part III Musicology students at the stage of planning their extended essays and dissertations. For example, as part of the recent course on British Music 1875–1918, the Music Liaison Librarian delivered a lecture on the Music Library's special Finzi Collection. This collection contains the printed music and books which belonged to Gerald Finzi, and it is rich in sources for anyone studying late nineteenth-century and early twentieth-century English music. The class was supported with an exhibition of items from the collection, an explanation of how to obtain the material and information about accessing materials held at other libraries using interlibrary loans services.

Taught postgraduate students

It cannot be assumed that taught postgraduates are *de facto* expert library users. They will have come from a variety of institutions with varied library systems. Mature students, especially those returning to study after many years, may have forgotten the skills they had adopted and such skills, even if remembered, will almost certainly be out of date. In order to ensure the sessions are pitched at the right level and are relevant to taught postgraduates, a number of issues need to be addressed. These include the proportion of taught postgraduates who were previously undergraduates at the same institution and who have, therefore, already familiarized themselves with many aspects of using the library service. It may be that the session will need to divide a class up in order to provide extra sessions to bring students from other institutions up to speed. Alternatively, and perhaps not so discriminatingly, less experienced students can be paired with more experienced ones. Another way of addressing this problem is to offer self-paced worksheets to the less experienced for them to attempt before the main session. The level of IT skills, among mature students in particular, might need to be addressed, perhaps by advising a course run by staff from the university's Information Technology Service. (This said, technophobia is becoming less prevalent. Increasingly, it is the case that all types of student have IT skills, though the level of these skills still needs to be carefully assessed.) A final consideration is the nature of the course. If it is part-time, or includes several students who only travel in once a week, the session needs to be timed to coincide with when students are in the university. Reading overcomes this problem by ensuring that sessions are fully integrated in a research skills course, which is a compulsory unit taken by all taught postgraduates in the first term of their course. The library contributes two sessions to the course. The first session examines how to identify and locate material held at the University of Reading. At the end of the first session, a library search exercise is distributed to check that all students have reached the same level. The exercise involves using manual and online catalogues, printed indexes and bibliographies. Individual feedback is then given. The second session looks at how to identify, locate and obtain material held outside the University of Reading. Objectives include introducing a range of online databases such as RILM and the British Library OPAC. Guided searching of the WWW by using subject gateways is covered, as well as interlibrary loan services and access to other libraries. The assignment is set by the Music Liaison Librarian in conjunction with the tutor and must be completed in order to fulfil the requirements of the taught postgraduate programme. It takes the form of preparing a bibliography on a single work, listing manuscript sources, relevant secondary material, a published version of the work and details of a sound recording. Assessment (undertaken by the tutor) takes into account both the quality of the referencing (bibliography is another element of the research skills course taught by other tutors) and the range of databases and other sources consulted to obtain the information.

Research postgraduates

For research students without a regular timetable and with very individual research needs, the library offers individual sessions, based on accessing online databases and demonstrating the transferability of searching techniques. These would normally take the form of an afternoon one-to-one appointment with the Music Liaison Librarian. Increasingly, these sessions focus on electronic sources. As Barry has argued, researchers require new skills at all stages of the information process, although she uses a sequential rather than a consecutive model such as the Seven Pillars approach mentioned above (Barry, 1997, p. 225).

Academic staff

The key to a successful information skills programme for students lies in convincing academic colleagues of the importance of information skills. In effect, academics need to become the agents who will champion the information skills work of the library. Ideally, they will be beneficiaries of training and trainees themselves (Levant and Cleeton, 1993, p. 34). This can be an uphill struggle. Staff are often too busy to learn about new library services, they may fear being exposed as poorly equipped to handle information and, sad but true, many continue to rely on the same sources they consulted when they were students. Some staff will be expert users of IT while others will only use a computer reluctantly. At the University of Reading, it was found that an individual approach to each academic was best. The benefits of online information were promoted to them through a glossy information pack, a range of email communications and personal invitations to a training session, with the aim of tempting them into training by the benefits rather than intimidating them because of their ignorance. One-to-one surgeries were held, with all but one member of staff choosing to attend. Examples relating to the academics' own specialisms were used to demonstrate databases. Self-paced worksheets were also given out, to which staff could refer. At the University of Reading, the Music Liaison Librarian also set up a departmental email list for academics to discuss library issues. Electronic services updates (such as changes to password access or the OPAC interface), new services and feedback (including comments from the IAML[UK] list) can be sent to all academics and make them feel more in touch with what is happening in the library. The result is also that the library appears to be at the forefront of electronic developments and library staff are promoted as experts in this field. Professional trust is developed and academics feel confident inviting the Music Liaison Librarian to run sessions which are an integrated part of the academic programme. As mentioned earlier, professional course documentation increases this image, which is not about trying to persuade colleagues that librarians are academics, but that librarians are professionals with a distinctive service to offer.

Having been convinced of the benefits of the services offered and the ability of the staff to know what they are talking about, staff will both support the information skills programme and actively promote services to students. Another benefit is that library issues can become more prominent on the Music Department's staff meeting agenda, to the extent that at the University of Reading, the library is now a standing item on this agenda. Such meetings can be used as a forum for information and promotion, but also to discuss new approaches to information skills delivery.

Informal approaches to information skills development

So far, this chapter has focused on formal sessions delivered to a whole class. Of equal importance in the process of teaching and learning, however, are the strategic learning methods adopted away from the classroom, which provide students with opportunities to develop their skills at the point of need. Students have a wide variety of ways of learning. For many, an individual approach is best, or the ability to learn at their own pace. For some, a practical approach rather than one grounded in theory may be preferred. Furthermore, while the classroom-based approach is useful early in a student's career (when it is necessary to communicate a few key points to large groups of people), as the student progresses, the information needs become more individual and so the class-based approach becomes less appropriate. Outlined below are some of the informal methods adopted at the University of Reading.

Individual tutorials and surgeries

Drop-in sessions and tutorials, if adequately promoted, are a proactive way of ensuring students with information skills needs have an alternative to the classroom-based learning which 'user education' has traditionally been about. As part of an initiative to increase and improve use of electronic resources, especially for final year students and postgraduates, each Wednesday afternoon in term is set aside by the Music Liaison Librarian for one-to-one tuition, there being no lectures on Wednesday afternoons in the department. The initiative was launched at the start of an academic year, as students began to select special subjects and dissertation topics. Publicity through posters, the library newsletter and via tutors ensured a stream of students seeking advice. Although individual tutorials are the most time-consuming approach, they can be the most rewarding, both for the user and for the librarian. In the long run, this approach also ensures that pay-per-search databases (which at Reading includes RILM online) are being used more cost-effectively. Students are encouraged to arrange an appointment with the Music Liaison Librarian, although if the librarian is available, students are free to drop in. Students may also book an alternative time if Wednesday afternoon is not convenient. The benefit of stressing one afternoon a week is that students become familiar with a service being offered at a particular time. At the time the student books an appointment, it is worth finding out which topic the student is particularly interested in researching, perhaps gauging which databases, if any, they have already investigated and also registering them in advance for any passwords they may need. Such preliminary investigations allow the Music Liaison Librarian to prepare more fully for the session and to think in advance of useful resources (printed as well as electronic) that may be used or mentioned. There is little point in drawing up a formal 'lesson plan', but planning is still of great benefit. Knowing as much as you can about the student's course can also help. For example, if the student is taking a Musicology specialism, the information they will require will be very different from, say, a student writing a performance practice essay, even if the subject is ostensibly the same ('I'm looking for stuff about Prokofiev').

Printed teaching aids

One of the advantages of being a member of Reading University Library's Information Skills Group is that the Music Liaison Librarian is aware of, and has access to, a wide range of teaching resources, including worksheets. These have been made available electronically on the WWW and can be easily tailored to the needs of music students. Sheets have been prepared for music students using OCLC databases (including RILM) and also more general databases, including the library OPAC and the Arts and Humanities Citation Index. Sheets are graded from basic level to advanced searching. Tailoring means that useful tips on searches involving genre and distinctive titles can be included, as well as how to limit searches to score or sound recording as well as monographs.

For students who, for whatever reason, do not approach a member of Library staff for help, a number of other printed and electronic guides have been produced. As with the tailored worksheets, the current approach to subject guides is to grade them. Currently, the Music Library offers a *Getting Started Guide,* an *Advanced Guide to Finding Information* and an *Internet Resources Guide* (available at: www.library.rdg.ac.uk/Lib/Subj/music.html). The *Getting Started Guide* (mentioned above as the one handed out to students during their initial welcome to the library) includes basics such as searching for items on a reading list and a breakdown of the call number sequence for Music. The *Advanced Guide to Finding Information* (usually offered to final-year and postgraduate students) covers using periodicals and indexes, finding theses, using online databases, access to special collections and inter-library loans. The *Internet Resources Guide* is only made available online because links change so frequently. It primarily refers users to gateways or hubs rather than individual sites, and includes IAML(UK and Irl)'s list of useful web sites. All these guides are updated annually and can be given out as summaries of both classroom-based sessions and individual tutorials.

Enquiry work

The value of using an enquiry to develop a user's information skills should not be forgotten. Enquiry work can become a vital part of the information skills package if the attitude adopted is that it is about showing users how to find the answer rather than about giving them the answer. For many, experiential learning will be remembered far more easily than a classroom lecture. The moment the student asks a question is the moment that the student has expressed an information need. It is at this point that some guidance on locating or using information is most relevant. After assessing what the user actually needs (such as a score rather than a recording or information about Copland and not just about American music) it is worth assessing whether the user is likely to benefit from being shown how to find the answer rather than simply being given the answer. It may be inappropriate to give a lengthy demonstration of how to use the OPAC if the enquirer is a one-off visitor or appears to be particularly pushed for time. If the user is going to benefit from learning how to find the answer, encourage an active approach. Get the user to do the work, to sit at the computer and perform the search or to select the relevant index volume.

Conclusion

A recent email from the head of department warning staff about a sudden increase in interlibrary loan applications was one indication that the combination of approaches taken at Reading was beginning to have some impact. The key to this success lay in a number of factors:

- a strategic as well as operational view of information skills provision
- close co-operation with academic colleagues (information skills is the responsibility of both parties!) allied to an attempt to integrate information skills provision within the academic programme
- availability of a portfolio of different ways in which students can develop their information skills.

The approach taken at the University of Reading, however, is also a cyclical one, and student feedback can be useful in showing areas for improvement. A number of initiatives are planned to improve and build on the work described above. As a way of embedding information skills even more firmly into the academic programme, the Music Liaison Librarian has compiled a paper of exercises and tasks which academics could set students as part of the teaching of a course (Appendix 2). These ideas have been presented to academics to help them plan a new undergraduate syllabus. At the strategic level, the university is also re-examining the guides it produces. The Music Liaison Librarian has suggested to the Information Skills Group a layout that follows more closely the way users acquire information skills. Recently, a range of possible guide structures were put to a focus group for discussion as well as to obtain their comments about the level and content of existing guides. As a result of another focus group, there is a plan to change the interface of the OPAC screen for users who log in as Music Library clients. This change will mean the screen defaults to a form that allows users to search by item type more easily and extra text on searching for genre and distinctive titles may be included.

The most exciting change currently being planned is the use of Blackboard™ – a virtual learning environment (VLE) accessed via the Internet. The use of Blackboard™ is being encouraged at a strategic level within the university to integrate the use of information technology into teaching and learning. Virtual learning environments are also particularly useful for supporting the development of information skills because so much information is now available online. The proposal, which has been planned in detail with an academic in the Department of Music, is that Blackboard™ will supplement the formal class sessions described above. These class sessions will provide the structure for an online course, comprising four graded units, which undergraduate students will be required to complete at different stages during their degree programme. Resources to support classroom teaching and information skills assignments (integrated fully into the degree programme) will only be made available online. Students will be required to access and submit work in this online environment, developing both their information and information technology skills in the process. Discussion boards, special notices and quizzes may also be used.

Other ideas for improving information skills teaching are likely to emerge over time. The cyclical nature of planning and improving teaching has proved to be one of the problems of preparing this chapter because of the ever-changing nature of information skills provision. This said, it is also one of the strengths of Reading University Music Library that the process is cyclical and based on constant improvement.

Appendix 1: Session plan

Department of Music postgraduate seminars

Library and information skills part 1: information at Reading

Aim:
To introduce students to information contained within the library and the services offered

Objectives:
By end of session students will be able to locate library materials using both online and manual catalogues and indexes

Method:
Welcome
Distribution of library map and *Getting Started Guide*
Overview and tour of the library
Explanation of the card catalogues, including the periodicals index
RISM
Self-paced introduction to Unicorn
Get students to register for RILM/WorldCat in preparation for following week

Assessment:
Worksheet: answers to be prepared for the following week's session

Feedback:
Self-assessment of worksheet

Resources:
Library map
Getting Started Guide
Exercise
OPAC worksheets (levels 1 and 2)

Appendix 2: List of ideas presented to academics for incorporation into the new syllabus

Integrating information skills more effectively into Music Department courses

This paper is an outcome of a recent focus group which allowed students to give feedback on library services. It also ties in with the library's wider work to promote information skills. The focus group highlighted that even third-year students lack some fundamentally important information skills. This is particularly evident when it comes to locating music in collected works and also when performing some searches on Unicorn.

The Library is keen to take an approach to developing information and study skills which is integrated into the curriculum rather than seen by students as an optional extra. Such an approach will be far more successful and will be a particular credit to the department during the subject review inspection.

Here are a few ideas which colleagues may like to consider when planning courses to encourage them to explore the materials available in the library. I have suggested some of the skills which students might develop by these methods of teaching. Some of the ideas are already being put into practice by individual staff, but I thought it would be useful to share these ideas further. The list is not exhaustive and you may have other ideas you would like to share with colleagues:

One seminar within the programme of a module could be held in the library with an explanation of some of the standard works, complete editions etc. in the field.
Skills developed: awareness of literature and layout of library.

Assignment details could stipulate that at least one journal article or review should be included in the bibliography (other than ones given on the reading list!).
Skills developed: use of indexes, referencing.

Credit could be given for work using facsimile sources.
Skills developed: searching for different forms of score, use of primary material.

More comparative assignment could be set: compare old and new Grove articles, LP and CD versions of a work, different arrangements or editions of a piece of music, for example.
Skills developed: locating information, locating non-print materials, comparative skills.

Students could be asked to watch an opera video or listen to a recording in a group and comment on it before making a presentation.
Skills developed: group work, critical ability, locating non-print formats.

Students could be asked to *identify* the most recent literature written about a topic, rather than simply being told what has been written.
Skills developed: information finding, use of catalogues and indexes, current awareness.

Students could be asked to locate materials in the Finzi Collection.
Skills developed: awareness of research collections, use of printed and online catalogues.

Students could be pointed to Internet subject gateways and be asked to use them to identify relevant material.
Skills developed: IT skills, critical ability.

Details of useful web sites for specific courses could be posted on the library's *Internet Resources Guide* for Music. Students could then be asked to view these sites before a class. (The Open University has an advanced approach similar to this.)
Skills developed: IT skills.

In preparing presentations for seminars, students could also be asked to prepare an assessed bibliography on the topic for the benefit of other students when they come to write their essays.
Skills developed: information searching and selection, citation.

Students could be set the task of comparing and contrasting two polemic writers or an outdated and contemporary writer and be asked to refer to a selection of their writings.
Skills developed: information searching, evaluation and comparison.

Students could be referred to a range of sources and be asked to evaluate them for usefulness, relevance, authority, and so on, in the study of a particular issue.
Skills developed: use of catalogues, evaluative skills.

Students could be asked to recommend the best recording the library has of a certain work, with an explanation as to why they have made that choice.
Skills developed: use of printed and online catalogues, evaluative skills.

Students could be asked to identify for themselves two texts that show a shift in musical thought on a particular issue.
Skills developed: information searching, comparative and evaluative skills.

Students could be asked to annotate their bibliography and say what use the item was – one way of demonstrating they have done some reading!
Skills developed: bibliographic skills, evaluative skills.

Each student in a group could be allocated a different text and be asked to read it and prepare an abstract for the benefit of the rest of the group.
Skills developed: summarizing and synthesizing information.

Students could be asked to write a Grove-like dictionary entry.
Skills developed: research skills, bibliographic skills, writing and editing skills.

Students could be asked to identify for themselves contemporary issues in music by scanning appropriate journals.

Skills developed: literature scanning and current awareness.

Registering for RILM/WorldCat could be one of the stated learning outcomes of the module.
Skills developed: use of information technology and access to electronic databases.

Bibliography

Apel, W. (1953), *The Notation of Polyphonic Music, 900–1600*, Cambridge, MA: Medieval Academy of America.

Barry, C. (1997), 'Information skills for an electronic world: training doctoral research students', *Journal of Information Science*, **23** (3), 225–38.

Bluck, R., Hilton, A. and Noon, P. (1994), *Information Skills in Academic Libraries: A Teaching and Learning Role in Higher Education*. SEDA paper 82, Birmingham: Staff and Educational Development Association.

Corrall, S. and Hathaway, H. (eds) (2000), *Seven Pillars of Wisdom? Good Practice in Information Skills Development*, London: SCONUL.

Levant, J. and Cleeton, D. (1993), *Marketing the Training Function*, London: Kogan Page.

Maple, A., Christensen, B. and Abromeit, K. (1996), 'Information literacy for undergraduate music students: a conceptual framework', Notes, **52** (3), 744–53.

SCONUL (2000), *Information Skills in Higher Education: A SCONUL Position Paper*, London: SCONUL. Available online at: http://www.sconul.ac.uk/publications/ publications.htm#2. (Accessed 18 April 2002.)

Chapter 4

'The turning wheel': training for music librarianship over 50 years

Ian Ledsham

1953. The beginning of IAML(UK). My friend Maxwell – now long retired – is beginning his career as a chartered librarian. He is employed by a large north-western borough council proud of its library, its night-school classes, and its cultural life – centred around a repertory theatre, several choral societies, an opera club, a gramophone record society and an amateur orchestra – not to mention the numerous church and chapel choirs in the town.

Maxwell's training has been similar to that of many of his colleagues in the public library service. After National Service, he joined the local library and was awarded a traineeship. He is given time off to attend library classes at the Manchester Technical College – what today we would call day release. Alongside the core subjects (today's terminology) he specializes in English Literature, and especially in the nineteenth century and the novels of Dickens. Examinations are set and moderated by the Library Association. After successfully completing the examinations, he becomes an Associate of the Library Association (ALA) and is promoted to Assistant Lending Librarian. In this role he develops his staff management skills (rostering sentry duties in the army has given him a head start here), acts as Readers' Adviser, assists in the Reference Library when necessary, and keeps an eye on the tramps using the Newspaper Reading Room as a bolthole on cold winter days.

His wife, Claudine, is also a librarian. She is some years younger, but, as she has not had to do National Service, she is taking her examinations at about the same time. She is a pianist and singer, and her interest in music lands her the job of music librarian. The borough has a substantial collection of performance materials, sponsored by the local brewery. Her training for the job is purely that of an interest in music, and an ability to read a score, and thus to talk on equal terms with her users.

By the mid-1950s, Maxwell had submitted a thesis in order to upgrade his ALA to a Fellowship of the Library Association (FLA) and obtained a promotion to a neighbouring borough where he became Lending Librarian. This borough had no performance sets, and borrowed what it required from other libraries in the area. It did have a collection of music scores (mainly classical with some musical comedies and the occasional music hall collection or light music anthology) and music books

– especially those needed by local grammar schools for teaching O and A levels. As Lending Librarian, Maxwell was responsible for this collection and for recommending purchases to add to it. As there was no post for a music librarian, his wife moved into children's librarianship and never worked in music libraries again.

Though the names are changed, the circumstances are real. The training could have been done as a one-year, full-time course, but in practice many librarians opted to remain in employment and go down the part-time route. Correspondence courses were also offered for those not within travelling distance of a library school. These qualification routes would have been the norm for librarians in provincial public libraries. Some of the larger public libraries – Westminster in London, Liverpool, Manchester – had music librarians with more formal musical qualifications, but there was no specific music librarianship training.

In the academic sector, things were not that different. There were far fewer universities than today, and situations would have varied depending on the size of the collection. Where a professional post (in today's terms) existed – and this would be at the oldest universities and the conservatoires, and at the BBC Music Library – a music qualification was the prerequisite. Library qualifications were a bonus but not a necessity. In other universities with music departments, the library may well have been managed by the music department, possibly even by the departmental secretary, with academic staff making purchases as required.

The 1960s saw both a growth in universities – with a consequent rise in demand for librarians – and the start of the move towards librarianship as a university subject. In 1933 the Library Association had announced a revised syllabus for its professional examinations which included Music as an option. In 1964, the Association began to allow universities to set their own examinations, based on the LA syllabus. The number of library schools also continued to increase, and three-year undergraduate courses were developed. These needed to have other subject content to make them a full undergraduate course. This meant that some schools were able to offer music librarianship as an option within the three-year course. Brian Redfern's course at the Polytechnic of North London was the most renowned of these – but courses were also offered for a time at the College of Librarianship Wales, in Aberystwyth, and at Ealing Polytechnic and Leeds College of Commerce (later Leeds Polytechnic).

In 1966 the Library Association authorized a graduate diploma, allowing those with a degree in another subject to obtain a recognized librarianship qualification. By the mid-1970s, most of the universities had replaced the LA syllabus and examinations with their own examinations, and the LA had become an accrediting body rather than a professional examination body.

In the early 1970s, Maxwell was still Lending Librarian, but moves were now afoot to lend sound recordings (long-playing records in those days!) as part of the library service. The skills needed to handle these esoteric (at least they were esoteric in northern libraries in the 1970s) media meant that Maxwell was relieved of responsibility for the music collection and a music librarian was appointed. Similar developments had been occurring in public libraries across the UK throughout the mid-1960s and up to the mid-1970s. At the same time, university music courses were proliferating and academic collections were being developed to service these courses. These were also times of substantial public expenditure, and staffing and stock levels rose accordingly.

So, between 1960 and 1980 librarianship training had moved from its apprenticeship-based roots – frequently part-time and often by correspondence course (distance learning in today's jargon) – examined by professional association examinations (which restricted career options to one sphere), to being a graduate profession (with a greater range of transferability) which could be entered either by an undergraduate course in librarianship or through another degree with a postgraduate qualification in librarianship. At the same time, the number and range of music libraries had led to a substantial increase in those with specific responsibility for music collections and able to call themselves 'music librarian'.

To put this in context, I began my professional career in 1978, exactly halfway through the period under discussion. My first post was in a public library authority very near to that in which Maxwell had begun his career in the 1950s. When Maxwell's wife was music librarian in the 1950s she was one of only two music librarians in the entire county (which comprised a large county authority and about a dozen independent borough authorities). When I began work in 1978, all the library authorities had been combined into a single, county-wide authority, and I was one of six music librarians – three of whom boasted music degrees.

The rise of the graduate diploma offered a career route for music graduates – and a rising number entered the profession in the 1970s and 1980s. As many were to realize, a degree in music and a diploma in librarianship does not automatically lead to a knowledge of music librarianship. Because of the isolated working conditions of many music librarians, occasional day courses continued to flourish – sometimes in quite rarefied subjects. One of the first I attended was regularly offered by Eric Cooper and covered the care and handling of audiovisual media. It offered advice in repairing broken cassette tapes, and how to identify a badly worn record stylus – both skills now as outmoded as handloom weaving!

And it was not solely recorded music that presented challenges. Uniform titles, vocal scores and lost clarinet parts, compact discs (CDs) and 78s, music hire, complex intellectual property rights, specialist supply chains, unique binding requirements – all these are aspects of music librarianship which set it apart from mainstream library work, and which require some unique skills and an understanding of the subject.

In the 1980s a view began to emerge that subject specialists were not necessary in librarianship. This view was not restricted to music librarianship, but music seems to have suffered more than most subjects. Music came to be regarded as difficult or elitist – especially classical music. In addition, the pressures on public expenditure (which had been less substantial in the 1960s and 1970s) began to increase considerably after the election of a Conservative government in 1978. Music (for which read, especially, CDs) came to be seen as a prime income generator – for which you need sales staff and accountants, not specialists! Thus, in

1981, when I was running a public authority collection in the north-east Midlands of England, I had £6000 with which to buy sound recordings. The charges on the lending of recorded material generated £15 000 per year. Not a lot in today's terms, but when I left a large university music library some 15 years later, my total annual purchasing budget for all types of material (except periodicals) was only £15 000.

The music librarianship option offered by Brian Redfern at the Polytechnic of North London ceased in 1981. The limited number of other courses which had sprung up in the previous 15 years had already withered by then. The option of a degree followed by a graduate diploma had become increasingly popular. The reduction to one year of librarianship study meant refining the syllabus, and one obvious method was to remove all subject specialization, whether it be music librarianship or children's librarianship. Library schools and university Information Studies departments were merely responding to demands from potential students, who did not want to spend another three years training after a first degree, and employers, who increasingly wanted library managers. Management studies, information technology and statistics all began to inveigle their way into the syllabus, and more traditional subject knowledge was inevitably edged out. Of course, the increasing prevalence of recordings in music libraries did not mean that there was no need for music librarianship skills. But such skills were not going to be provided by the library schools.

By the 1980s, IAML(UK) had appointed an Education Officer to its Executive Committee. However, it was not initially the role of that officer to address gaps in professional education. Although the preceding analysis seems to indicate a clear-cut change in librarianship education over a given number of years, such change is more easily seen through the binoculars of hindsight. In the 1980s, awareness of the changes that had taken, and were still taking, place in professional training filtered through in a less coherent and perceptible way. Although the appointment was possibly initiated by the demise of the Polytechnic of North London's Music Librarianship course, the Education Officer's role was initially directed more to the perceived need for training for library assistants and to a review of the opportunities for working in a music library (professional and non-professional). This work resulted in a guide to working in a music library (recently issued in a revised version) and to moves towards developing a course for library assistants with no musical knowledge who, perforce, found themselves working with music.

During the 1980s, IAML(UK)'s subcommittee structure had thrown together conferences and courses in a single, hard-worked committee. Inevitably, much of the committee's time and work was devoted to organizing and running the annual conference – by the late 1980s an Annual Study Weekend, a name change which itself drew attention to the educational concern of IAML(UK). But a voluntary committee, no matter how hard-working, charged with organizing an annual, residential conference which generally added to IAML(UK)'s coffers was never going to be able to devote sufficient attention to other courses, and in the early 1990s the Courses and Education Sub-committee was put in place, leaving the Conferences Sub-committee with a sole, focused responsibility.

The work on developing a course for library assistants now bore fruit in the shape of a portable, one-day course – Music for the Terrified – which could be mounted in any region of the country and for which a team of regional trainers was developed, thus helping to minimize the cost of the course. This remains one of IAML(UK)'s most successful training ventures.

By the early 1990s, IAML(UK) was increasingly aware of and concerned about the lack of professional training in music librarianship. It expressed this concern – but without much effect or suggestion for development – for several years. This is not to criticize its apparent inaction. A voluntary body, IAML(UK) had an increasing number of projects to co-ordinate at this time, among them development of the International Standard Music Number, negotiation of the sound recordings lending licence which the 1988 Copyright Act had brought in and promotion of its new library assistant's training course.

In 1995, the newly re-launched Music Libraries Trust (MLT) suggested to the IAML(UK) Executive Committee that it might be willing to fund a lectureship in music librarianship. The trust's suggestion was passed by the Executive Committee to its Courses and Education Subcommittee, of which I was, at that time, acting Chair. The suggestion was taken up by the committee who devised a questionnaire to be sent to all UK Information Studies departments. It sought to establish whether a number of departments (up to ten) would be willing to have a visiting lecturer give a single lecture on music librarianship or, alternatively, whether one department was willing to host a series of lectures forming a ten-week course in music librarianship.

The responses to that questionnaire – and I still have them – were uniformly depressing. Comments such as 'Insufficient demand from students' and 'Too specialist' seemed to confirm our worst fears But among the negative responses were some which – perhaps scenting money on offer – indicated willingness to consider a lecture or lecture series. But, the most exciting suggestion came from the University of Wales, Aberystwyth, that, rather than a lecture course, we should consider developing a module in Music Librarianship to be included in the distance learning BSc offered by the Open Learning Unit (OLU) at Aberystwyth's Department of Information and Library Studies (DILS), the largest distance learning course for librarianship in the country.

This seemed an imaginative suggestion, and early in 1996 I met with Clare Thomas, Director of the OLU, and Nancy Kenny, Secretary of the MLT. As a former dancer, Clare Thomas had an innate feeling for the importance of the performing arts and the need for adequate education. Both Nancy Kenny and Michael Freegard, Chairman of the trustees, were convinced of the importance of this project and determined it should succeed. The conviction and enthusiasm of these three was to prove essential to the project, and I have placed on record elsewhere the gratitude of IAML(UK) to them for their support and enablement.

As discussions proceeded it became clear that preparing a module was going to be a bigger project than originally envisaged. The OLU advised that the project would require three to four months' full-time work. A costing was drawn up. This was much more than was then available for the project. The MLT, however, had already begun to appreciate that its role in many of the projects it wanted to pursue should be that of facilitator, and its members started to find ways of funding the project. The Britten-Pears Foundation was eventually persuaded to support the project. This was in no small way due to the support of one its trustees, the British Library's Music Librarian, Hugh Cobbe, and the then Librarian of the Britten-Pears Library, Professor Paul Banks.

In the mid-1990s, academic libraries were beginning to undergo considerable change. Successive governments had increased substantially the number of students in higher education. Whereas in the 1960s less than 2 per cent of the population attended university – a figure still well under 10 per cent in the 1970s – government targets in the mid-1990s were reaching 30 per cent and upwards. On the other hand, funding for universities had not increased by anything like that amount. Pressures on staffing were considerable, and ways to increase efficiency were constantly being sought. One way was to reduce the level of specialization even further. This began to happen across the board: posts which had previously been full-time music librarian posts (already few in number) became music plus other responsibilities, such as history or fine art or drama and dance; previously shared posts, such as English and Music were now redefined to cover the entire humanities. (As will become clear, this was to open a new training front.)

My own post as a full-time academic music librarian was one of the first to disappear under the inevitable structural changes required by the expansion of the universities. Instead of moving over to become a humanities information officer, I opted to move into freelance work.

To return to the MLT initiative: the IAML(UK) Executive Committee invited me – in my comparatively new freelance capacity – to undertake the work of researching and writing the proposed module. A contract was agreed between myself, the MLT and the OLU in the autumn of 1996. As part of that agreement, I was to attend a course in writing Open Learning materials at Aberystwyth in December 1996. I well remember that first visit, since I drove through heavy snowstorms across the peaks of the Welsh mountains to get there.

Money was finally secured at the beginning of 1997, and work began in earnest with a thorough review of music librarianship literature. It soon became clear that librarianship had changed so much since the mid-1980s that the bulk of literature to be surveyed would be post-1990. (That said, the oldest article included in the module dates from 1937.) By October 1996, following discussions with the UK music library community, including members of IAML(UK), a proposed syllabus had been drawn up. We had not progressed very far into the work when the OLU suggested that what had been proposed as a ten-credit module should become a 20–credit one. I was assured that this would not mean twice the work. In fact, it did increase the workload from what was originally proposed, but it ultimately allowed a more flexible product.

'Open learning' aims to remove barriers for access to education which traditional courses often impose. Many open learning students have worked as library assistants and are seeking to improve their qualifications. In some cases, this practical experience is counted in place of the A level qualifications that traditional courses require. In many cases, students will be undertaking their study while holding down a job. They also have to work in isolation – removed from their fellow students and lecturers – apart from the Annual Study Week which takes place in January or July, depending on when students begin the course. This means that course materials must be structured in a particular way. It also means that everything required for the course, including any reading material, has to be included with the course material.

The course is modular. Subjects are taught in discrete, self-contained packages called modules. Each 'chapter' of a module is called a unit. Modules carry a given number of credits, and a stated number of credits must be earned to obtain a degree. Some modules are compulsory (core modules), others are optional (electives). Music Librarianship is offered as two elective modules, each of five units, with each module being worth ten credits. Module 1, 'An Introduction to Music Librarianship', is designed to give a taste of music librarianship, to prepare students who may have to manage a music collection within a wider responsibility. It explains basic concepts which must be grasped when dealing with music in libraries. Module 2, 'Advanced Music Librarianship', looks in more detail at the tasks of the music librarian. Module 1 can be taken on its own – which is attractive to students who may not want to be music librarians but have an interest in music. It should also mean that, as more students take this option, a wider range of professional staff have some knowledge of the requirements of music librarianship. Given the changes in staffing structure in libraries, and the increasing prevalence of shared responsibility posts, this is an attractive option. Module 2 can only be taken after completion of Module 1, and is aimed at those who see themselves seeking a professional career in music libraries.

Looking back at pre-1960 training, this 'new' approach has a very old-fashioned ring to it. The correspondence course, and training while continuing in employment, were the method of choice for many seeking to gain librarianship qualifications for most of the first six decades of the twentieth century. While the aims of open learning may be more student-friendly than the traditional correspondence course, and new technologies such as email and CD-ROM can supplement the educational process, the fundamental approach of learning in one's own environment and at a speed to suit one's lifestyle (within certain minimum and maximum constraints) remains popular, and is increasingly common in other areas of vocational training such as nursing and management studies.

The methods of assessing student work are also intended to be 'student-friendly', while still demanding a high level of work. For open learning students, who may have been out of formal education for many years, traditional essay-writing can be a formidable barrier. The first module provides two assignments: a taped radio documentary presentation of about 15 minutes' duration describing and evaluating music library provision and requirements in a chosen location (often the one in which the student works), and a written report to the library authority recommending developments and improvements in the service provision. Module 2 also has two assignments: a set of music cataloguing exercises, and a choice of reports/essays ranging from preparing a disaster plan for the music library to writing an article about the work and role of music libraries intended for publication in a general library journal.

As work progressed it became clear that there were two areas which were going to be difficult to teach 'off the page': the description of various printed and recorded music formats, and the study of reference sources. The original idea was to use a video presentation to describe formats and, for teaching reference sources, to develop an interactive disc or CD-ROM. As we explored these possibilities it became obvious that the time and expertise needed was greater than the funding available would allow. As an interim measure, I wrote a section describing formats, which, while somewhat heavy, imparts the information. The reference sources section of the module is supplemented by a half-day teaching session at the Annual Study Weeks which all students must attend once a year.

The first module was available for students in January 1998, and the second some months later. In the past four years, over 50 students have completed one of the modules – about a dozen students have opted to undertake both modules. In the context of replies to our questionnaire that there was 'insufficient demand from students' this is a particularly rewarding response.

The assignments produced by students have in many cases been of a very high standard. They have ranged from descriptions of the music libraries at Canterbury Cathedral and the BBC, to discussions of music-making and library provision in Cardiff, a history of the oldest public music library in Wales, and a review of provision in music libraries south of Dublin. The most rewarding accolades have come from the students themselves, who, above all, appear to have enjoyed completing the modules.

When funding for the research work was obtained, the Britten-Pears Foundation stipulated that the module must eventually be made available on a 'stand-alone' basis as part of a professional development option for librarians. This recognized the fact that there had been no comprehensive music library training in the UK for nearly two decades, and also that those with responsibility for music libraries may not have originally seen themselves in that role. A stand-alone training package would allow them to supplement their general librarianship training with specific music library knowledge – a real example of lifelong learning.

This was a new departure for the University of Wales, since the option carried no degree element. Work commenced on the stand-alone version in 1999. It was originally envisaged as a multimedia disc containing all the material required. Finance and possible access problems led to a change in design. The bulk of the material is in printed form, adapted from the undergraduate modules but condensed into a single volume. Supplementary material on an interactive CD-ROM covers especially the formats and reference source elements (including Internet sources) of the course which in the undergraduate modules are taught during the study week. The course was published in 2000.

This project broke new and exciting ground. For the MLT, it was the first time that it had acted as 'broker', obtaining external funding rather than using its own limited financial resources. For the OLU, it was the first time that an external tutor had been used to develop a course. Given the natural conservatism of academic institutions in the UK, the positive and outgoing attitude of the OLU was essential in persuading the university authorities to accept this approach. It is interesting that several other specialist areas of librarianship in the UK have begun to follow the same route. The OLU is well advanced in preparing a module on rare book librarianship, and the UK Art Librarians have also expressed interest in working with OLU.

Though this was undoubtedly a major development in music librarianship training in the UK in the 1990s, it has not been the only development. The changes in academic library staffing alluded to previously have been matched by developments in public libraries, where entire music departments have been closed, or where previously separate music sections have been merged (or re-merged) into lending divisions, and where staffing responsibilities have been redefined. The rise of para-professional staff has seen an increase in the range of staff having to deal with music materials in their everyday work.

In many cases, such staff have had little or no opportunity for training in dealing with music materials, and the past five years has witnessed an increase in the number and range of training courses available to library staff. IAML(UK) has itself participated in this expansion of training. Alongside its regular Music for the Terrified course it has developed training in areas such as music reference skills, and dealing with performance sets.

The private sector has also moved into this area. The Chartered Institute of Library and Information Professionals (formerly the Library Association) runs a course on Internet resources for music, and my own company, Allegro Training, has developed a range of music librarianship training courses alongside information skills training for other professions.

Looking back over the past 50 years of training for music librarians, it may seem that we have come full circle. Once again, distance learning and part-time study have become popular methods of acquiring music library skills, formerly separate music libraries have been reintegrated into cultural centres and music departments that sprang up in the 1960s have disappeared or been merged and their library collections 'frozen' or transferred. But look again! The training provided in 1953 equipped librarians for a single career. Employment norms at that time meant it was quite probable that librarians would remain in one career for 40 years. Now, students look for transferable skills; they expect – want – to experience more than one career during their lifetime. The portable, modular structure of today's training allows a wider range of people to receive the training they need at the time in their career that they need it. Training emphasizes the information skills that librarianship has always had but repackages them in a way which makes them transferable to many other areas in what has rightly been called the Information Age. The burgeoning of in-service training – geared both to professional and non-professional staff – provides a richer, more varied, more flexible training than was available 50 years ago: a training that can respond more rapidly to the changing needs of the profession and of the public it serves.

As for Maxwell and Claudine, they enjoy a happy retirement. But I rather imagine that, were they starting again, they would relish the range and variety of training and opportunities available to them today.

Chapter 5

Musaurus and *MusBib*

Ann Harrold and Graham Lea

Music Press was set up in 1990 as a specialist music publisher. It was thought that the existing indexes and thesauri did not enable librarians and music scholars to find the information they needed, and also were published in some cases several years after the period they covered. It cannot be said that the ground was well covered. Probably we authors saw ourselves in the role of reformers, but we hoped at the time that we did not sound like an ill-tempered Klavier. The products were *Musaurus* and *MusBib.* We initially introduced *MusDoc,* but we discovered that three products were one too many for a small organization to manage.

Both Music Press products were produced on an Archimedes. None of it could have been done with a personal computer (PC); the advantage of an Acorn is that all the systems software is on a chip, leaving the whole of the hard disk for whatever is needed. Unfortunately, Archie (the Archimedes) has recently died on us, being the ripe old age of ten.

Musaurus

Musaurus is a guide to the structure of musical knowledge, and has three parts: a scholarly introduction; a comprehensive hierarchical thesaurus, with some 4000 terms covering the scholarly professional and business aspects of music; an alphabetical, fully rotated index of some 9000 terms which includes every significant word in *Musaurus.*

Introduction to Musaurus

This is a concise version of the Introduction to *Musaurus* from the 1991 edition.

Nature and principles of thesauri   In our view, a music thesaurus should permit the inclusion of music scores and all scholarly, professional and business aspects of music – for the music profession and industry, as well as for information professionals such as music librarians, information scientists and records managers.

The word thesaurus is used in two distinct senses. It is a source of considerable aggravation for scholars who prefer its *sensu stricto* usage (as a structured system for organizing information) when the ignorami produce a *senso lato* thesaurus (an alphabetically arranged list of words) in the belief that they have reached Valhalla.

There are international standards for thesauri (for example, BSI, 1987), but they are committee products where vested interests in defending alphabetical thesauri have prevented a recommendation being made that a systematic display should be the first essential. Of course, it is much more difficult to produce a structured thesaurus, as the British Standard admits. Nor are standards always sensible, as RILM has found in its use of the International Standards Organization (ISO) recommendation for Russian transliteration (which differs from the British Standard): rendering Tchaikovsky as Cajovskij is absurd.

The situation is further confused by the dictionary producers who have developed synonym (and sometimes antonym) dictionaries and called them thesauri. Censure, contempt, disapprobation, disgrace and opprobrium to the likes of Collins and Chambers for their misleading plaints ('more recently there has emerged the type of thesaurus … ') and failure to admit that the word thesaurus is better for sales purposes than synonym dictionary, although perhaps it is understandable if their word-locked users do not know the meaning of synonym. This may be another peculiarly Scottish practice, since Aberdeen University Press published in 1990 a Scots thesaurus.

But it is not only the synonym dictionary producers who produce alphabetical listings dressed up as thesauri. Most thesauri, particularly if developed in the USA, are also alphabetical lists of terms, with perhaps a broader term, some narrower terms and the odd cross-reference. There is no possibility in such lists of discovering a real structure for the body of information they purport to cover, because there is no hidden structure. The result is that there is no proper synonym control, since similar terms are not brought together – indeed, the alphabetical sorting acts as a highly effective randomizing technique. The consequence of the lack of synonym control is that there will be a high incidence of cross-correlation.

Such 'thesauri' have come about for two reasons: they are often in effect a list of headings for the production of poorly designed abstracting and indexing publications; and they are an admission of the defeat at the task of producing a structured scheme, which is an intellectually demanding and labour-intensive task. They are not a work of scholarship. Furthermore, alphabetical thesauri require users to have prior knowledge of what exists and what they want.

The process of distinguishing the subclasses of a class is logical division, while the reverse process is called classification. A sound classification system must be produced by the logical division of the whole of the particular universe of knowledge, so as to avoid absent classes. The process of differentiating co-ordinate classes is known as *fundamentum divisionis,* for which there are three fundamental rules: there must be only one *fundamentum divisionis* at each step; the co-ordinate classes must be collectively exhaustive for the superclass; and the successive steps of the division must proceed by gradual stages. The result of violating the first rule is to have overlapping classes: the fallacy of cross-division, which is a corollary of cross-correlation.

Alphabetical and chronological arrangements for information obviate the need for value judgements about the relative importance of various subjects. It is, in effect, intellectual egalitarianism, founded presumably on the subconscious belief that words and ideas have feelings and deserve the right to equal treatment. If this is not the case, the alternative hypotheses involve a presumption of a lack of understanding of indexing theory, a lack of intellect and laziness. The fact that Indo-Germanic languages have alphabets that allow alphabetical sorting is a bonus for an index, for other languages that do not have alphabets must therefore rely on structured systems. But to rely on alphabetical arrangements for information in a thesaurus is either an anti-intellectual activity or an abrogation of intelligence.

A good thesaurus should consist of two parts: a subject listing with a hierarchical arrangement, and an alphabetical index. With the development of online databases over the last 35 years, it has become clear that those that did not adopt a hierarchical system with a coding scheme are failing seriously. Too many references of low relevance are produced in response to a search request, with the result that users often give up rather than face the task of tackling a poor retrieval.

Completeness is also an important requirement in information retrieval. A coding system is essential for efficient and effective information retrieval, as well as for convenience in database creation.

A library catalogue is a device designed to indicate what was once in the library. It is generally unhelpful about works on loan, works that have been stolen and works that have been mis-shelved. At best it only gives information about what a particular library, or sometimes a group of libraries, contains. There is a disjunction between catalogue and union list systems that provide access to library holdings, and bibliographical systems that provide access to what exists. The intelligent researcher and library user is likely to want access to all that exists. This is the role for the bibliographical services: the library catalogue is unhelpful, because it is the housekeeper and not a proper index to what exists in the library, or elsewhere.

Cataloguing is an aspect of indexing, which is concerned with the wider universe of what exists. Even fully online catalogues that do allow access to title words in combination are primitive, mostly because of the inadequate classification systems that are used, with the forced reliance on natural language searching.

It is remarkable that, in 1886, the Cooperation Committee of the American Library Association issued a circular (*Library Notes*), drawing attention to a scheme for producing catalogue cards for current books and proposing cards for articles in the periodical literature. Yet more than 100 years later, despite the availability of computers, databases and communication networks, libraries are still obsessed with cataloguing their own monograph holdings rather than helping access to what actually exists, with the consequence that cataloguing is often considered to be more important than bibliography. Thus books are given obsessive attention, even to the extent of having their dimensions recorded, while papers in journals are largely ignored, because the journal is deemed to have been processed when publication details for one issue have been recorded. This has resulted in a decline in scholarship. But readers, scholars and customers for library services need to know what exists, and in which libraries the material may be seen. Furthermore, it is most desirable that such information be made available within days of its publication, rather than many years later, as is the case at present. It is for these reasons *inter alia* that Music Press decided to produce a music bibliography that is based on the indexing system elaborated as *Musaurus.*

Musaurus is intended to act as a guide for the organization of all kinds of music information collections; it is more fully developed than any other system. Understandably, there is some conservatism about changing shelving systems, since the effort required to re-shelve a collection is considerable.

Musaurus can also be used for indexing music books and journals, as well as specialist bibliographies. There is also significant potential in the field of records management. A thesaurus provides a guide to the structure of music knowledge for authors and those who wish to benefit from its pedagogical qualities.

Review of existing systems   The literature of music librarianship, which is not extensive, is disproportionately concerned with the problem of shelving scores. This seems to have distracted attention from the greater problem of an adequate classification system of music as a whole. There have been some brave attempts to devise better systems, but the amount of work involved, particularly for a full-time music librarian, and the frequent lack of aids like a powerful computer, have made this a very difficult task.

Music librarians have had to make do with inadequate classification schemes, rearranging their libraries as slightly better classifications become available or existing schemes are abandoned.

There is a sense with some complex schemes, such as Dewey, that it should be possible for a non-specialist to use them. This may be a worthy objective, but the result is a scheme that can be of only limited value to those whom it is primarily intended to serve – the end users, not the librarians or cataloguers. There is a serious lack of scholarship in existing schemes, mostly caused by design deficiencies.

The ghost of Cutter continues to haunt present-day schemes: the solution offered at the end of a short (usually alphabetical, and partially analysed) list, is often to arrange other material by A-Z. It would seem that not even the prolific Anonymous can escape being Cuttered, or Gregorian chants attributed to Gregory and put under 'G' in a composer index. Another ghostly but unhelpful presence is the British Museum's 91 rules of cataloguing of 1841.

Not infrequently, there is no distinction between descriptors (concepts) and identifiers (names): this is most apparent in the Library of Congress scheme.

Indeed, no existing scheme could be described as a logical system that provides sufficient discrimination. Nor are any of them truly able to keep up to date. New terms like World Music appear and may become quickly accepted, yet existing classification schemes are likely to take many years before the term is included, if at all.

Bryant (1985) has useful assessments of existing music information services and classifications, although it is disappointing that the Library of Congress Class M, which was published in 1978, was not assessed in the 1985 edition. Nor does Bryant have computer or online in its short index, which admits to being deficient.

McColvin (1924) believed in the separation of books and scores, with sub-arrangement for the performer rather than the listener. McColvin was the City Librarian for Westminster, and therefore had the Central Music Library (CML) in his domain. He found Dewey unsatisfactory and designed a scheme to replace Dewey 780, advocating the separation of miniature scores from full scores, and scores from books. There are many errors in the scheme itself, and in the typography; some headings such as '783.08 Miscellaneous generalia: polygraphy, collections', and '783.9 Miscellaneous theoretical questions & general practical topics, A-Z' are of doubtful value. Singulars and plurals are inconsistent, and there are duplications. The geographical scheme is disastrous, with Scotland shown as a division of England, and Ireland, Wales and the British Empire being given as divisions of Scotland. Few would agree with his view that viols and violas da gamba are 'obsolete bowed instruments'.

An interesting scheme was developed by Dickinson in 1938 for musical compositions, as a revolt against the inadequacies of the Library of Congress system. Evidently he was unaware of McColvin's work, or ignored it, since he does not mention it. In 1968, Bradley supplemented the work, with a rearranged facsimile of Dickinson's original publication. It is a joy for cryptographers, and very economical on coding. In fact, a design criterion for the codes was the desirability of keeping them short, so that they could more easily be put on the spines of thin volumes. But as Bradley points out, 'the tables are not exhaustive' and reflect the music holdings of Vassar College and/or the State University of New York at Buffalo.

Olding (1954) proposed a new scheme, having found Dewey Decimal Classification (DDC), Universal Decimal Classification (UDC), McColvin, Library of Congress Classification (LC) and Bliss 'most inconsistent in arrangement, and difficult in use'. His scheme, which has only an abridged version in his article, is better in its design that the previous schemes. Bryant does not refer to it.

The *BCM* Classification was prepared by Coates (1960, the first issue being in 1957) and used from 1957 to 1981 for the *British Catalogue of Music*. It was then abandoned by the British Library, in favour of the DDC phoenix scheme.

Line (1963) drew attention to the need to give better attention to the needs of earlier music. Musicologists today would no doubt wish to question the chronological periods he used (for example 1740–1930 for secular vocal music, and for instrumental music), but his scheme does overcome some of the problems in LC, which it is designed to replace. He correctly identified the problem of division by medium, and advocated the separation by historical period, with further division as 'the material demands' – by musical form for earlier material, and by medium for later music.

Melvil's DDC system reversed Bacon's order from history (memory), through poetic literature and fiction (imagination), to science and philosophy (reason), so the result is philosophically unsound. Clews (1975) noted 'the disfavour which all British writers on music librarianship ... have viewed DC class 780', and then proceeded to cremate it. It was a bold step to start the scheme for 780 over again (hence the name 'phoenix'), but the result is still 'constrained by the overall system' and the skeletons of earlier schemes ('do not use') is part of the DDC liturgy, it would seem. The phoenix scheme is now accepted in the twentieth edition of Dewey, and should not therefore be referred to as the phoenix scheme. There are many errors and inconsistencies, including some major ones. Bryant (1985), regrettably, describes the revision as 'done brilliantly'. We would not concur, and draw particular attention to the inadequacy of the classification presented for ensembles in 785, which seems to be designed primarily for popular music, since 55 out of the 70 classes elaborated include either electrophones (which are mostly electric guitars) or percussion, or both.

The UDC, evolved from Dewey, although Dorcas Fellows, Dewey's assistant, opposed the idea. It first appeared in 1905 as an adapted French translation by two Belgians, Paul Otelet and Henri La Fontaine, and was known as the Brussels Classification. It then had more detail than Dewey. From 1927 to 1933, the *Classification décimale universelle* appeared in four volumes, sponsored by the Fédération international de documentation (FID), which had evolved in 1931 from the Institut international de bibliographie (IIB), founded in 1895. For the main part, it is a synthetic scheme, in that components can be assembled, whereas Dewey is an enumerative scheme that lists classes to a sufficient level. Music in UDC has not progressed beyond the medium edition (BSI, 1985), where it has less than 200 classes. Some UDC methodology, such as the use of auxiliary tables and association, is used in *Musaurus*.

Thomas Jefferson's personal library was shelved in a sequence based on Bacon's scheme: it later became the nucleus of the Library of Congress. His 44 subdivisions were maintained until 1901, when it was revised to produce a scheme that did not claim to be philosophically sound, but merely pragmatic. Yet, on pragmatic examination, LC fails not only in the most probable places – as the pragmatist philosopher Peirce predicted – but also at all levels of detail. The Library of Congress itself has been unable to update its published 1978 third edition, with the result that *Additions, Changes & Accumulations* are available for a not inconsiderable sum from Gale Research, Detroit. The many deficiencies of the LC scheme have been noted by many, not least its users. We offer an additional one that does not seem to have drawn comment: Finland is in the same class M1972 as the Soviet Union for student songs, a foolishness almost beyond belief. Librarians need a place to shelve material, but they are not served well by the LC scheme. Nor is it of much value to the browsing scholar.

Bliss (1953) was influenced by Brown (1898), but problems now exist since the latest edition was founded on the *BCM* classification.

The Colon classification of Ranganathan (1960) is not an enumerative scheme, and is excluded from consideration.

Music Index (1949–) is a dictionary catalogue that inter-files authors, names and subjects. The lack of structure means that, unless the user is fortunate, it is unlikely that all relevant material could be found, because of alphabetiasis. The scheme is structurally deficient in that subheadings under a topic are not generally repeated, although the subheading may exist with other entries. There is no coding system for the headings, although an annual list of subject headings provides some amelioration.

The Répertoire internationale de littérature musicale (RILM, 1990), has a classification system outlined by Brook (1989) in the table of contents of RILM's *Abstracts*. The RILM thesaurus was developed to enable indexers to work from the same list of terms. The RILM thesaurus that was issued in 1990 is for 1982 abstracts onwards. The introduction states that:

> RILM's thesaurus is a 'treasury' of English words used in music, a wealth of words gleaned from writing on music and compiled in a systematic manner that reflects the structure of the various areas of the study of music. The thesaurus has two primary purposes: first to provide a standard set of headings and descriptions so that RILM's indexes are consistent in their terminology; second to enable users of RILM's Abstracts to discover which of many words are actually employed as index headings ... . The Thesaurus also serves ... as a rulebook by RILM indexers ...

On examination, little structure can be discerned. There is an alphabetical list of general terms. There are around 520 headings, with 'see', 'sa' (see also) and, very confusing, 'x' and 'xx' *(sic)* references, the former identifying that the related terms that follow are not used (!), whereas the latter informs users that a 'see also' reference has been made from another heading.

There is an alphabetical list of around 470 instruments, which is 'not intended to represent a definitive system of classification'. Finally, there is an alphabetical list of places, with a repetition which alphabetically lists 'places by continent affiliation', with some incorrect affiliations. Northern Ireland is treated ambivalently, both as part of Ireland and of the UK; Finland is said to be part of Scandinavia (instead of the Nordic Countries, which are incorrectly also put as part of Scandinavia); Greenland is given as part of North America, which may be news to the Royal Kingdom of Denmark, in view of their responsibility for Greenland's external relations. Asia is combined with the Pacific Rim, so that Turkey is found with the Philippines, while the USSR is in both Asia/Pacific Rim, without division.

There is no coding system in the RILM thesaurus, although the contents page of RILM's *Abstracts* has 11 unnumbered section headings with allowance for 99 numbered subheadings. The relationship between these headings and the thesaurus is not made clear, and indeed cannot be discerned. The purpose of the RILM Thesaurus is far from clear, particularly as its yet unstructured alphabetical approach prevents code ranging in online retrieval.

There is no satisfactory way of dealing with historical periods in RILM, as Steinberger (1981) admitted. The example that she gave must rank as one of the all-time classics in trying to optimize a search, and all credit to her for the imaginative approach to the problem. She wrote: 'Historical periods prove to be the most difficult to search. Notwithstanding their importance, they can be very cumbersome' (ibid.).

Musaurus design and construction It was clear to us that existing special music subject classifications and thesauri, as well as general schemes that had as their objective the classification of all knowledge, had serious shortcomings in that they were structurally unsound, or incomplete, or both. Most special library classifications have been developed to deal with the deficiencies of general classification systems for sheet music collections. Such schemes have not generally had sufficient sophistication, nor elaboration, to deal adequately with other music materials, as music librarians and scholars are only too aware. We agreed with McKnight (1989) that 'no current list of terms offers comprehensive help to those providing information services to music researchers, since neither RILM nor *Music Index* is applicable to the access of music itself'.

The aim of *Musaurus* was to provide a comprehensive system for indexing the whole field of music, including music scholarship, the music profession and the music industry. *Musaurus* was designed to be suitable for indexing music, books, journal articles, newspaper items, documents, recordings, instruments, brochures, files, artefacts – in fact, anything of musical interest. Initially, only Western art music was treated thoroughly, but the geographical and historical infrastructure, as well as the instrument section, allows for expansion into other fields.

Abandoning reliance on the alphabet as an aid to indexing and retrieval requires the elaboration of better systems – a task perhaps one or two magnitudes greater in difficulty than producing alphabetical lists of terms. However, once such a list has been produced, it is easier to use than a purely alphabetical list. Once a term has been found in the index, homonym problems – same word, different meanings – can easily be resolved. Then, by means of a code, the position in the structured part of the thesaurus is found. The juxtaposition of all related topics then allows an accurate choice to be made as to the proper indexing term, and the code allows this to be recorded efficiently. There is a pedagogical element in such an approach, which is not really achievable in non-structured thesauri.

The principles that were used in the development of *Musaurus* are:

1 Where possible, the development is from abstraction to complexity. Lea (1973) introduced this principle that derives from Bacon's 'Philosophia prima' (*The advancement of learning,* 1606). The application of this principle is seen in the overall arrangement of *Musaurus.*
2 Another general principle is development from generality to specificity: this is seen in the hierarchical arrangement. *Musaurus* at present has up to eight levels in its hierarchy: these are indicated by the level of indenting.
3 The history of development of music is considered from a present-day viewpoint of Western art music.
4 A major consideration is the retrievability of the information. To achieve good relevance and recall, the essential requirements are a hierarchical arrangement,

and a coding system. The coding system is essential for code ranging in computer retrieval – the possibility of including in a search many adjacent categories – for example, all the countries in Asia. If there were no coding system, it would be necessary to enter the name of every country and region. Of course, in the absence of a structured thesaurus, the names needed would not be known and an imperfect retrieval would result.

5   Faceting is used extensively to avoid repetition. *Musaurus* consists of a subject thesaurus, together with history auxiliaries, geography auxiliaries and language auxiliaries.

6   It is desirable to make provision for subjects about which little has been written so far. In this way, the thesaurus is able to encompass material about areas at the forefront of musical scholarship, rather than long after a new discovery, for example.

7   *Musaurus* was devised on the basis of division rather than classification.

8   In devising a coding system, both coding theory and psychology have been taken into consideration. Thus codes are only four characters long – well within the limits of easy memory – and of equal length. It is anticipated that a future version of *Musaurus* will expand the code by adding another digit. The value of shortening the code by suppressing trailing zeros was considered to be less than the processing and presentation convenience of fixed length codes. Previous experience indicates that equal length, concise codes are easier to use, and to remember. The psychological barrier created by codes such as: 789.422162183, 789.4BEEE62183 or AC/D(YH)E(YDB)FD(YC) should not be overestimated. It is extremely difficult to use such coding systems for computerized retrieval, and quite unnecessary to have to resort to complex notation.

9   The subject part of *Musaurus* generally consists of descriptors (concepts) rather than identifiers (names), unless an identifier has given rise to a descriptor, as for example in the case of Gregorian chant and Ars nova.

10 The following terminology is used for *Musaurus*. There are seven subject divisions at present, lettered from A to G. Because the terms are structured by division, the subsections are referred to as subdivisions. Those at the hundreds level are referred to as the primary subdivisions. In many cases the tens level represents secondary subdivisions, and the units level tertiary subdivisions, quaternary subdivisions, and so on. However, to keep the coding reasonably concise, and not sacred, there is an independent system of level codes that is not seen in the published version of *Musaurus,* except as the level of indenting of each term. The auxiliary tables are the history auxiliaries, the geography auxiliaries and the language auxiliaries, each auxiliary table having its primary, secondary and tertiary divisions. Each division has a code and an associated term:

	CODE	TERM
Division C	C000	Musical works
1y subdivision	C600	Ensemble music

2y subdivision	C610	Duets
3y subdivision	C611	Single instrument group
4y subdivision	C612	String duets

11 Any new requirement should be accommodated.

Previous schemes had tended to give excessive emphasis to monophony versus polyphony, and to ignore the historical setting and geographical variability. A different approach is desirable in dealing with Western and non-Western music. It is not a question of sophistication, but more a question of the amount of scholarship, the amount of extant music and the difference in the music of different periods. Terms such as 'pop' and 'classical' are a source of terminological inexactitude: pop music devotees tend to call non-pop music classical, and vice versa.

Some rules were found necessary, since no structure, however carefully designed, could be sufficiently pragmatic and at the same time intellectually rigorous:

1 The repetition of concepts is allowed in different parts of *Musaurus,* particularly where it is desired to distinguish between historical aspects and present-day performance practice. Distinction is made by appropriately qualifying the term.

2 Generally, a term will be elaborated from the general to the particular, with narrower terms considered to be too narrow to index separately following a colon: for example, A134 Vibration amplitude: loudness, volume, intensity, decibels.

3 Where it is necessary to add a clarifying remark, to distinguish homonyms, for example, the term may have to be developed by using parentheses. This distinction from a colon results from the parenthetical comment usually being a broader term: B083 Bone (instrument material) and B614 Bones (jingles).

4 An equals sign is used to separate preferred terms (which are given first), from synonyms, near synonyms, and sometimes translations: B175 Lyric tenor = tenore leggiero; B242 Cembalo d'amore = clavecin d'amour; D643 Radio = wireless broadcasts. In formal thesaurus terminology, one would find: Lyric tenor 'used for' [or UF:]: tenore leggiero. Tenore leggiero 'see' [or USE:] lyric tenor. We believe that our usage is simpler, and avoids unnecessary jargon. 'Used for' is the same as 'includes'.

5 Plurals are used in preference to singulars, where the context allows. The singular is used for processes or properties, such as conducting, silk (as a material in instrument manufacture), and for example, performances like tremolo. The correct plural of the original language is normally preferred to any Anglicized plural, although we find sonate does not find general acceptance, whereas concerti does, or at least to a sufficient extent. This is a little unsatisfactory. (After all, why else does one learn foreign and dead languages? We are rather proud of Eistedfoddau.)

6 Because of the *Musaurus* structure, there is much less need for cross-referencing by means of 'see also' (SA) – which may be expressed as 'related term' (RT).

However, where we feel this might be useful, we have included such references: C130 Sacred vocal unaccompanied music – 'See also' C300 Orthodox liturgy.

7 Where it is useful to elaborate on the use of a term, a 'Note': [elsewhere referred to as scope notes, or SN] may be added below the term: C135 Sacred vocal unaccompanied chamber choir – Note: each person singing a different part.

The definition of chamber music has changed with time. *Musaurus* accepts the most common present-day usage, which is narrower than it was in the seventeenth to nineteenth centuries. Scholes (1970) suggests that chamber music

> excludes (quite logically) music for orchestra, chorus and other large combinations, but it also (more arbitrarily) excludes all vocal music and all instrumental music for one instrument (for example piano sonatas). It includes all seriously intended instrumental music for two or more instruments played with one instrument to a part – and it includes nothing else.

The scheme proposed is the result of a consideration of the possible groupings of instruments (very many, if worked out mathematically), tempered by a study as to the amount and importance of music in each category, and finally rendered into a system that is both practicable and easy to use. In *Musaurus*, the following principles were applied:

1 It is assumed that the most important criterion is the number of instruments.
2 Next in importance is the grouping of instruments.
3 Groups of instruments are given in the sequence: bowed strings, wind, brass and keyboard. These groups are included in the first part of the scheme, because there are many works for such combinations.
4 Plucked strings are treated in the second part of the scheme, which excludes electrophones and percussion. The intention is to allow the separation of lute, mandolin and classical guitar music, without having to incorporate plucked instrumental music in the first part of the scheme, where many theoretical combinations would have no music.
5 The third part of the scheme is for electrophone and percussion combinations. This is the only area that the Dewey phoenix scheme covers reasonably completely, yet even so two possible categories have been missed. Much popular music would of course be included in this part of the scheme.
6 No distinction is made, for example, in the case of a trio for woodwind and brass as to whether there are two woodwind and one brass, or one woodwind and two brass. It is at this level, and lower levels when actual instruments are specified, that we have for the time being drawn a line. Further division could be by a local coding system, using the instrument codes.
7 From sextets onwards, the analysis is less full, since there is less music and the number of combinations increases very considerably.

Examples of the more common instrument combinations are included in the first and second parts of the scheme, but the elaboration is not intended to be complete. A scheme for ensemble music that deserves special mention and praise is that by Holden (1988) of the Guildhall School of Music Library. It has confronted the situation squarely, and devised a sophisticated scheme, using an appropriate computer retrieval approach involving logical operators.

We have used auxiliaries in *Musaurus* to avoid the repetition of identifiers. In the case of language auxiliaries, there are geographical problems because of changing boundaries throughout history. Fortunately, it is not necessary to have a geographical thesaurus for every 100 years or so, because area boundaries are relatively less important musically. The action, so to speak, tended to take place in cities, churches, palaces and populated places where music flourished, rather than along the borders.

The *Musaurus* geography auxiliaries present a complete thesaurus in themselves. Development proceeded by moving around a continent in a logical fashion, either from north to south, or clockwise from the centre, starting in the north-east sector. This makes it possible to keep groups of countries together, and to add physiographical regions where their borders overlap with more than one country as, for example, with the Nordic and Benelux countries, and the Leeward Islands.

In addition, races such as Aborigines have been integrated in the appropriate place. People from a nation are only mentioned specifically if the name is significantly different from the country or region name. For example Lapland is included, but not Lapps. The commonly accepted English name is normally used for a country or region.

In the case of history auxiliaries, having around half a dozen classes to cover at least 6000 years of musical history – as most of the existing schemes do – is grossly unsatisfactory. It has to be admitted, however, that it is not an easy task to devise historical schedules, and only those who have tried to devise tabulations of musical history can know the extreme difficulties that confront the compiler. The fundamental problem is to represent in two dimensions a multidimensional situation where the individual dimensions (such as the geographical boundaries of an area) are themselves changing dynamically. The principal dimensions are the date, major historical events that affect the freedom to compose, musical styles, geographical location, the availability of patrons, instrument makers, composers and, not least, musicians.

Scholars are, of course, well aware of the imprecision of events and the consequent difficulty of attaching precise labels to them, quite apart from differences in the usage of terms between different groups of scholars. A good example of the latter is seen in the use of the term 'Flemish school' by American and British musicologists with Apel's (1969) *Harvard Dictionary of Music* preferring it to be active from 1450 to 1600, but British writers opting for a shorter period, perhaps 1520–60. Our resolution of this particular dilemma is to call the school the Flemish International School, since this seems to be a more accurate description, and to indicate parenthetically the other names, such as Franco-Flemish or Franco-Netherlandish. There are, of course, no fixed boundaries for major periods like the beginning of the Renaissance or the Baroque, and the problems of earlier styles carrying over into later periods is well known. The historical tables are offered as a first step in the development of a more comprehensive scheme.

A rotated index contains every significant word in the *Musaurus* divisions, although numbers have been excluded since they are mostly dates, which are given in historical sequence in the history auxiliaries.

It is to be hoped that bibliographical and factual databases will become more accepted in the music world, and that a yeomanry of users will emerge. The major problem, however, is likely to be the non-use of information (LEA, 1989).

It is our view that a detailed set of rules for the use of *Musaurus* are best developed by the music librarian, to suit both the clientèle and the collection. In this way, any library deciding to adopt *Musaurus* could so with the minimum disruption required to achieve a better arrangement. Detailed rules for the use of *Musaurus* are presented in the full version of the introduction, including some suggestions as to how collections of scores can be accommodated.

Acknowledgements   The authors would like to thank all those who contributed, directly or indirectly, to making *Musaurus* possible. In particular, AH thanks Dr Monica Hall, and GL thanks Dr Neil Saunders for introducing him to musicology.

MusBib

MusBib was a current, bimonthly bibliography that indexed a wide range of music journals, general periodicals and books, as well as news items and reviews from the press. In volume 1 (1991), some 124 serial sources were indexed, with which the authors were pleased as it was the first issue. *MusBib* covered the whole field of music, with the exception of pop, and was arranged in four sections:

1 *Bibliography:* arranged by *Musaurus* divisions. Books are included in the appropriate section for that book; book reviews are included; serial titles are given in full. The authors felt that any other inadequacies appearing in existing bibliographies should be rectified.
2 *Performances:* reviews of concerts, operas and festivals, arranged by date. Instead of the usual headings in each review for orchestra, soloist, conductor, and so on, this section of *MusBib* has interesting symbols – cubes for composer, pointing hand for conductor, and so on.
3 *Recordings:* recordings and reviews are arranged by recording company.
4 *Index:* works, performers, conductors, musicologists, venues, obituaries and biographies, orchestras and ensembles. The 1991 cumulated index contains 28 593 references.

There was serious interest in Music Press publications, including the one of which we are most proud – the Vatican, who thought that the sacred music, particularly the Roman Catholic liturgy, in both publications, was complete. We are indebted to IAML(UK) for the opportunity to exhibit at their conferences, and for word-of-mouth publicity. The legacy of Music Press remains, and it is hoped that at a future date a new edition of *Musaurus* will be published.

References

Adler, M.J (1986), *A Guidebook to Learning*, New York: Macmillan.

Apel, W. (1969), *Harvard Dictionary of Music*, Cambridge, MA: Belknap Press of Harvard University Press.

Bliss, H.E. (1953), *A Bibliographical Classification*, New York: H.W. Wilson.

Bradley, C.J. (1968), *The Dickinson Classification: A Cataloguing and Classification Manual For Music*, Carlisle, PA: Carlisle Books.

Brook, B.S. (1989), The road to RILM, in Mann, A. (ed.), *Modern Music Librarianship*, New York: Pendragon Press, pp. 85–94.

Brown, J. (1898), *Manual of Classification and Shelf Arrangement*, London: Library Supply Company.

Bryant, E. (1985), *Music Librarianship: A Practical Guide*, Metuchen, NJ: Scarecrow Press.

British Standards Institution (BSI) (1985), *Universal Decimal Classification*, London: British Standards Institution.

British Standards Institution (BSI) (1987), *British Standards Guide to the Establishment and Development of Monolingual Thesauri*, London: British Standards Institution.

Buth, O. (1975), 'Scores and recordings', *Library Trends*, **23** (3), January, 427–50.

Clews, J. (1975), ' The revision of DC780 – the phoenix schedule', *Brio*, **12** (1), Spring, 7–14.

Coates E. (1960), *British Catalogue of Music Classification*, London: British Museum.

Dickinson, G.S. (1938), *Classification of Musical Compositions: A Decimal-Symbol System*, New York: Vassar College.

Gilchrist, A. (1971), *The Thesaurus in Retrieval*, London: Aslib.

Holden, P. (1988), 'Indexing and retrieving chamber music', *Brio*, **25** (1), 21–4.

Lea, G. (1973), 'Geological literature', in *Encyclopedia of Library and Information Science*, New York: Marcel Dekker.

Lea, G. (1989), *Non-Users of Information Services*, London: Graham Lea and Partners.

Line, M.B. (1963), 'A classification for music scores on historical principles', *Libri*, **12** (4), 352–63.

McColvin, L.L. (1924), *Music in Public Libraries*, London: Grafton.

McKnight, M. (1989), 'Improving access to music: a report of the MLA Music Thesaurus Project Working Group', *Notes*, **45** (4), June, 714–21.

Music Index (1949–), Detroit: Information Coordinators.

Olding, R.K. (1954), 'A system of classification for music and related materials', *Australian Library Journal*, **3** (1), January, 13–18.

Ranganathan, S.R. (1960): *Colon Classification*, Bombay, Asia Publishing House.

RILM, (1990), *Abstracts of Music Literature, English-Language Thesaurus for Volumes 16–*, New York: RILM.

Scholes, P.A. (1970), 'Chamber music', in *The Oxford Companion to Music*, Oxford: Oxford University Press.

Stebbing, L.S. (1943), *A Modern Elementary Logic,* London: Methuen.
Steinberger, N. (1981), *Selected Problems in Searching the RILM Database: National Online Meeting Proceedings, New York, March 1981,* Medford, NJ: Learned Information.

Chapter 6

'The most intricate bibliographical enigma': understanding George Thomson (1757–1851) and his collections of national airs

Kirsteen McCue

Introduction

Between 1793 and the mid-1840s Edinburgh music publisher George Thomson edited numerous volumes of Scottish, Welsh and Irish folk songs with new lyrics by over 80 contemporary literary men and women, including most importantly Robert Burns, and with new musical arrangements by Pleyel, Kozeluch, Haydn, Beethoven, Carl Maria von Weber and Hummel. Thomson's large coffee-table volumes were lavish products with fine contemporary illustrations and with separate instrumental parts for violin, cello and later for flute.

Information about Thomson and his collections is difficult to come by. There is a biography – *George Thomson: the friend of Burns* – by James Cuthbert Hadden from 1898, and there are a variety of articles connected with Burns's songs, or with the folk-song settings of Haydn, Beethoven and Weber. But even including these, and brief remarks in the small selection of general Scottish musical histories, we are still very much in the dark about Thomson and his master plan to 'collect all our best melodies and songs' and create 'accompaniments to them worthy of their merit', as he stated so clearly in his essay for J. Wilson's *The Land of Burns* published in 1840.

We are even more in the dark when it comes to dealing with the volumes of songs themselves. The problems of following the various issues of the six volumes of Thomson's Scottish Collection – *A Select Collection of Original Scotish Airs* – have confused and frustrated scholars for many years. Even fine music bibliographers Cecil Hopkinson and C.B. Oldman found it a challenge. In their article 'Thomson's collections of national song', published in 1940,[1] they valiantly attempted to find a pathway through numerous volumes of varying dates, so that Beethoven and Haydn scholars might be able to follow the histories of individual musical settings throughout the various volumes. Their article is vital to anyone working on Haydn and Beethoven folk songs, but Hopkinson and Oldman did state clearly that their study related primarily to the settings of these two composers,[2] and there were many aspects of the publications which they deliberately excluded. The single most valuable part of that article – for anyone working more generally on Thomson – is the 'Tabulated list of the different editions'. This is a chronological listing with brief descriptions of the different volumes, and a useful tool for any librarian or scholar. The task of creating such an index, however, was not without its difficulties. In a letter to American collector William Harding in 1964 Hopkinson wrote: 'Now this Thomson enquiry of yours raises the most complicated problems for it is about the most intricate bibliographical enigma that I have ever encountered.'[3] Thomson's Welsh and Irish folio volumes were issued only once and consequently are easy to catalogue,[4] but producing any list of Thomson's Scottish folio volumes is complicated and confusing. The first problem with this collection is that it spanned a period of over 50 years, during which Thomson published various issues of the same six volumes of songs.

My own doctoral research completed in 1993–94 included a new 'Tabulated list of the Scottish volumes', which is more akin to a proper bibliography than a simple list of dates and titles. I, too, had a great deal of difficulty creating it. When I began my work on Thomson's collections I was still under the impression that a bibliography was that list of reference materials at the end of an academic essay. My first year of doctoral work included a variety of postgraduate classes, looking at different approaches to research. The English literature postgraduate students at Oxford were obliged to take a course in bibliography – indeed, they were examined in it at the end of their first year. As a music student I was not compelled to do the examination, but I was thrilled by the course. Had it not been for Don McKenzie's inspirational classes I would have been totally lost in the jungle of Thomson's volumes. McKenzie's lectures on letterpress, copperplate, lithography and paper-making and binding were a revelation, and he gave me a great deal of invaluable help when it came to describing volumes in my 'Tabulated list'. I will come to that process shortly, but it is helpful to know about Thomson's publishing business before tackling the volumes themselves.

Thomson's publishing house

George Thomson (1757–1851) came to Edinburgh in 1774 from the north-east of Scotland. He took up the post of a clerk in the office of a Writer to the Signet and in 1780 got the job of junior clerk to the Board of Trustees for Arts and Manufactures in Scotland, established by an Act of 1726.[5] This institution supported fisheries, manufactures and improvement, and during the second half of the century administered the production and export of flax, hemp and linen.[6] Thomson worked first as their junior and then their senior clerk until his retirement in 1839. His publications were produced quite independently, even if Thomson used connections with the board to facilitate the transportation of composers' manuscripts or the financing of the collections.

Thomson was obsessed from the beginning of his publishing venture with high standards of presentation: the aesthetics of his product relied equally upon its artistic content and its visual beauty. From the outset he wanted to produce top-quality, sophisticated and elegant volumes. Fortunately, Edinburgh's newly found freedom in the publishing trade made this task a simple one. With the exception of large firms such as those run by the Gow or Corri families, or George Walker, who could afford to employ engravers and printers on their premises, smaller businesses were able to produce musical publications by subcontracting to freelance engravers, printers and paper-makers. This was precisely what Thomson did. As Senior Clerk to the Board of Trustees he had limited time to spend on his publications. The establishment of a full-time publishing house was unthinkable, for he had little capital and, at the outset, planned only to produce one or two small books of Scottish songs. Although he found enough time to supervise the artistic content of his volumes – as his letters to and from composers and writers illustrate[7] – he relied, for the practical production of his publications, on a group of individuals who were based in Edinburgh and its surrounding districts, or in London. Thanks to the expansion of the Scottish publishing trade, he was able to find willing engravers, printers and paper-makers who would produce the goods quickly and cheaply. He was also able to choose from a wide range of individuals and companies who were able to create high-quality products which were among the best in Britain. An understanding of the mechanics of this group is an essential tool for following Thomson's activities as a publisher and in understanding the production of his volumes.

Thomson chose to present himself on his title pages, from the first sets of Scottish airs in the 1790s, as 'proprietor' of his publications, but he never appeared as their publisher. While he was undoubtedly the publisher in spirit, it was crucial at the beginning of the venture to find a fully-fledged publisher able to deal with the large-scale production and distribution of the volumes. Thomson followed the general pattern of the bigger non-musical Scottish publishers by having an almost wholly Scottish production line while at the same time forging a strong link with a much bigger London publisher. The main publisher involved from the beginning was Preston of London. John Preston began his business in 1774–75 as a musical-instrument maker, printer, music seller and publisher. In 1789 he purchased the stock and plates of the Scotsman Robert Bremner, and this may have influenced his decision to work with Thomson only four years later. John Preston, and subsequently his son Thomas, dealt with all of Thomson's publications from 1793 until the company's closure in 1834, when they were succeeded by Coventry and Hollier, who published most of Thomson's later volumes. It is impossible to determine the reasons Thomson had for choosing Preston, when he could have selected any number of London publishers. It was no surprise that he veered away from Edinburgh's music publishers – Corri, Urbani, Gow and Johnson – for all of them were producing rival collections. A London publisher removed parochial pressure from the venture and also opened distribution networks for Thomson, who would otherwise have found it difficult to break in upon the monopoly of the main music publishers in London. The Bremner connection most probably attracted Preston to Thomson's proposal, for he acquired many other 'Scottish' publications in 1789.[8] Perhaps William Napier's Haydn arrangements had shown that there was an expanding market for such a publication.[9] As programmes for the musical societies of major towns and cities illustrate, there was something of a British vogue for the 'Scotch Song'.[10]

The problems of defining the term 'publisher' at the turn of the nineteenth century are highlighted by the correspondence between Thomson and Preston. At first glance it may appear that Preston was chiefly concerned with assembling the printed sheets which Thomson shipped to him from Edinburgh.[11] We know that he was responsible for issuing the early folio volumes in a simple paper cover, since they would most likely be bound to order for the customer. By the 1810s the volumes had sturdy, coloured, millboard bindings – pink for the Welsh volumes, green for the Irish and grey for the Scottish. But closer examination of Thomson's letterbooks, particularly his letters concerning paper orders, show that Preston was much more closely involved with the publications and that, in addition to at least two other Edinburgh companies, the firm was responsible for printing many of the volumes. Preston is mentioned in Thomson's earliest correspondence – concerning the publication of Kozeluch's piano sonatas[12] – but the first detailed reference to Preston's printing volumes is not until late in 1812.[13] Preston had written to Thomson with his account of sales of the volumes from July to December 1811, and had also informed him that they had only a small amount of paper left. Thomson replied by asking him to print 100 copies of the fourth volume of the Scottish Collection without delay, and informed him that he had shipped 11 reams of paper on 'The Nimble' the previous day.[14] He also sent a detailed inventory of the volumes which Preston had printed – and the paper he had used – since 23 August 1811, when Thomson had shipped another batch of paper to London (the numbers 50 or 100 refer to the number of copies printed): [15]

Sep 21: 50 Scottish Songs Vol. 2 – 28 quires
 "   28: 50 Scottish Songs Vol. 1 – 28 quires
 "   28: 100 Welsh Songs   Vol. 2 – 40 quires
Oct 5: 50 Welsh Songs   Vol. 1 – 17½ quires
 "   26: 100 Scottish Songs Vol. 4 – 56 quires
Nov 2: 50 Scottish Songs Vol. 3 – 29 quires

This inventory therefore states that between late September and early November 1811 Preston had printed 400 volumes of Scottish and Welsh songs for Thomson, and he was clearly also printing in 1812. Another letter of 11 June 1815 from Thomson to his paper-maker also referred to 20½ reams of heavy paper (for music) which he ordered on behalf of Preston.[16] Such evidence is enough to prove that Preston was far more than a distributor. The appearance of Preston's name on the title page of Thomson's volumes was most probably a result of his printing and distributing in London, and also because he was better known and doubtless better respected than any of Thomson's smaller printers.

Thomson's correspondence with his paper-maker presents most of the information concerning the printing of his volumes. In addition to finding a main publisher for the collections, one of Thomson's initial tasks was to find good quality paper upon which the letterpress for the lyrics and the musical plates could be printed. Unlike the printing, engraving and publishing, which were distributed among many, the paper for Thomson's collections was produced by one firm alone, namely Cowan and Sons of Valleyfield, near Penicuik to the south of Edinburgh. Scotland's rising reputation for paper-making was a natural consequence of the success of her publishing trade at the end of the eighteenth century. The south-west of Scotland, thanks to partnership with a French company, began to produce high-quality white paper, but the mills to the south of Edinburgh nursed the Scottish reputation.[17] Thomson, by all accounts, could not have found better paper than that produced for him by Cowan. Thomson's letters to Cowan outnumber all of his letters to printers, engravers, publishers and illustrators, and provide much of the information of print runs which is missing elsewhere in the correspondence. It is Thomson's letters to Cowan, for example, which show that, in addition to Preston, several Scottish printers – Balbirnie, McLeod, Walker and Lizars – were employed by Thomson. The Cowan correspondence shows that the printing of letterpress usually always exceeded that of music, but also reveals that the print runs of music frequently exceeded 100 in number before the 1820s.[18] Moreover Thomson's letter to Cowan of 11 December 1824 is the only evidence to show that, by this time, Thomson's print runs of music rarely exceeded 100 copies at any given time.[19]

The numbers of volumes being produced, and the details of large print runs of letterpress and music in particular, help to explain Thomson's mixing of sheets between editions. Numerous sheets, particularly the prints from the musical plates, were left unused and were incorporated in later issues of the same volumes.[20]

Thomson was just as fastidious about the thickness, colour and general quality of his paper as he was about the standards of printing or engraving. As his volumes illustrate, he experimented with paper thicknesses earlier in his career, sometimes employing a standard thickness throughout a volume, and often using thicker paper for the musical plates and thinner for the letterpress. The colour of the paper also varied considerably from volume to volume. Orders for different 'dimensions, quality & thickness'[21] of paper correspond with the arrival of more beautiful and sophisticated presentation in Thomson's volumes. In his letter of 10 April 1813 he criticized Cowan's paper for being 'not so good either in colour or free of specks as before' and stated quite clearly that he wanted the Irish volumes to be as elegant as possible.[22] The letter of 1815, mentioned above, was written at the time of the production of the two Irish volumes and the last Welsh volume, which surpassed any earlier volumes in appearance.

While some of Thomson's volumes were printed in the south, many of them were produced in Edinburgh by a small group of printers and engravers. Little is known about John Moir, whose name is frequently found on the colophon of Thomson's volumes. He was originally a partner in the firm of Grant and Moir of Paterson's

Close (1790–93) and set up independently in New Bank Close until he was declared bankrupt in 1825. Thereafter he is said to have worked for D. Stevenson and Co. He was known primarily for his publication of Gaelic and Roman Catholic books and pamphlets, which may well explain his lack of prominence among Scottish publishers of the period, for neither the Gaelic language nor Catholicism were particularly popular in Scotland at this time. Moir was also responsible for producing Anne Grant of Laggan's *Poems on Various Subjects* in 1803,[23] a venture Thomson had encouraged, as Mrs Grant was one of his most important contributors. Indeed Thomson makes reference to this publication in his correspondence.[24] Moir's name is found on many of Thomson's early folio volumes and on those of the octavo edition of 1822–23.[25] A letter from Thomson to his paper-maker of 11 December 1824, in which he ordered 30 reams of single paper for the letterpress of the octavo edition,[26] suggests that Moir was also involved in printing some of the 1825 volumes. After this date, doubtless as a result of his bankruptcy, Moir disappears from Thomson's publications.

By 1825 at least two other names had been mentioned in Thomson's letterbooks in connection with the printing of his volumes. William Balbirnie's name is found on the octavo volumes of the 1820s: 'Eng^d. by W^m. Balbirnie, 105 High St. Edin^r.' appeared at the foot of the first page of music of Vol. I of 1822. Even less is known about Balbirnie than Moir. He is not included in Bushnell's *Scottish Engravers,*[27] or in any lists of publishers such as those of Kidson or Humphries and Smith. Thomson's letter to him of 12 October 1818,[28] however, shows that Balbirnie was both an engraver and a printer to trade. Mention was made in the same letter of another printer, one Mr McLeod, who was probably Peter McLeod, an amateur composer and semi-serious music publisher in Edinburgh.[29] 'Mr McLeod Music Printer' was sent paper for 100 copies of both Vols II and III of the Scottish Collection and one additional volume.[30]

Balbirnie was not the only engraver who undertook two jobs for Thomson. George Walker was associated with Thomson's publications from the 1810s. He began his engraving career in the 1790s and was still in business in 1848. Between 1815 and 1826 he was in partnership with John Anderson, and, based at 42 High Street, they were known equally well as music engravers, printers and publishers. Thomson's letter of 26 October 1818, mentioned above, requested a delivery of 2 reams 15 quires of paper to Walker and Anderson to print 100 copies of Vol. IV of the Scottish Collection. In 1826 Walker and Anderson's partnership dissolved, and Walker set up alone as Walker and Co. In this capacity he continued to work for Thomson, and on 24 August 1826 Thomson asked Walker to print 100 copies of the new Vol. V.[31] It was in this letter that Thomson, still a stickler for excellence, explained the need to produce a high-quality product and faultless impressions: 'The English Public will not look at works imperfectly printed and it is in vain to send any such to London.' He also warned Walker to take particular care over his use of paper. Reference was made to the creasing of paper in the printing of engraved plates, for this produced 'faulty impressions' and Thomson warned Walker that this could lose him the job of printing his music. Walker obviously continued to impress Thomson, for the name Walker and Co. is found on the 1831 volumes of the Scottish Collection.

William Home Lizars (1788–1859) worked for Thomson until the mid-1820s. Unlike Walker, he was not well known as a music engraver but was chiefly concerned with illustrations. There is only one letter from Thomson to Lizars, of 1 August 1825,[32] in which Thomson ordered a print run of 50 copies of the songs of Vol. V and 30 copies of *The Jolly Beggars* – 'in all 63 plates requiring paper'. But Lizars must also have engraved musical plates for Thomson, for his name is found in connection with the song 'Low down in the broom' in the sixth volume of the octavo edition of 1825.[33] Not surprisingly, Lizars also engraved some illustrations for Thomson which were likewise included in the octavo edition. One nameless London engraver is mentioned in Thomson's letter of November 1813 to William Smyth with reference to the song 'Dermot and Shelagh' – included in Vol. I of the Irish Collection.[34] It is therefore possible that Thomson was also employing a London music engraver, though there is no evidence as to who it was. The only London engravers mentioned in the correspondence were those connected with Thomson's illustrations.

Thomson's decision to include illustrations in his volumes resulted in his employment of a completely separate group of artists/engravers. These illustrations, while regarded as an investment – no other similar contemporary Scottish publications included such sophisticated pieces – also stretched Thomson's budget considerably. They were originally offered to subscribers alone, but by 1801 they had become an integral part of the volumes, and they were also sold separately at Preston's shop. Two Scottish artists, David Allan[35] and David Wilkie, and the Englishman R.T. Stothard were approached, and all three accepted Thomson's commission, Allan and Stothard producing by far the greatest number of illustrations included in his volumes, particularly the octavo volumes of the 1820s. Alexander Nasmyth's portrait of Burns (SIV), Sir Joshua Reynolds's depiction of St Cecilia (IrI and SIf), and drawings by W. Hamilton,[36] Robert Smirke,[37] and Thomson's brother, David, also appeared.[38] Allan, Wilkie and Stothard often engraved their own designs, but other engravers were also employed: Paton Thomson, John Thomson, Robert Scott, David Scott, Lizars and Cunego.

So, with the creation of paper, the engraving of musical plates and illustrations, the setting of letterpress and the printing and binding process itself there was, therefore, a large number of individuals and firms employed in Thomson's publishing venture. This information is vital when examining the volumes themselves. The letterpress of Thomson's volumes, for example, is rarely the same from one issue of a volume to the next. On first examination, one automatically assumes that Thomson was obsessed with producing new, more beautiful and presentable publications at every turn. But surely, it was both a waste of time and money to change the letterpress from one print run to the next, especially when nearly all of the songs had the same lyrics from issue to issue of the same volume. Thomson was working with numerous printers. Several of them had small establishments, and some would work with different typefaces. Most of them would be unable to store standing type – they would have to dismantle the type after print runs of the letterpress – and when Thomson approached them with a new order for 300 copies of letterpress they would set the type afresh. This process immediately explains the slight changes in letterpress between volumes, most noticeable in the differences of typeface or in spacing.

The bibliographical process

With this knowledge the process of 'understanding' the volumes becomes a little easier. At least there is a simple practical explanation for some issues – like that of the changing letterpress. Armed with certain answers about the practical assembly of the volumes we can begin to tackle their complex bibliography with a little more confidence.

Thomson's original intention was to produce only two sets (that is, books) of Scottish songs in the 1790s.[39] The First Set of 25 songs appeared in 1793, but Thomson produced three more sets by 1799. These four sets, with some changes, became in 1801 his first two volumes of 'Original Scotish [later 'Scottish'] Airs' and they were followed by third and fourth volumes published in 1802 and 1805, and a fifth volume in 1818. Forty-eight years after his first set of Scottish songs, Thomson's sixth, and last volume, dated 1841, appeared, but he was still dabbling with the volumes in 1845–66, as new settings from that year illustrate (see GB-En Mus. L.l.69). Over and above his folio volumes Thomson issued a set of octavo volumes which have their own quirky bibliographical history, to be discussed later.

Naturally, because of the long periods between the publication of brand new volumes, Thomson was obliged to produce new issues of existing volumes as copies ran out. Copies of Vol. I dated 1814 and Vol. IV dated 1808 and 1812 were probably issued to revitalize stock.[40] Moreover, Thomson decided that whenever a new volume appeared for the first time, the previous volumes should also be newly presented. While each volume was produced quite separately from the others, it was marketed, at the same time, as part of a set of matching volumes. Vol. III of 1802 was issued to match Vols I and II of 1801; Vols I, II and III all dated 1803 were released as a set for which the new Vol. IV of 1805 was also intended;[41] Vols I, II, III and IV produced between 1815 and 1817 were clearly issued as a set to stand alongside the new Vol. V of 1818; Vols I-V, with many new songs incorporated, were presented as a 'new edition' in 1826 and in 1831; and Vols I-V appeared again in 1838, and possibly once more after this, to match the new Vol. VI of 1841. The fact that these volumes were frequently bound together by their purchaser illustrates that Thomson's marketing technique was successful. The only volumes which do not fit into the above scheme were the two issues of Vol. I published in 1809 and 1814, issues of Vols II and III dated 1810 and issues of Vol. IV dated 1808 and 1812. As suggested above, some of these volumes were undoubtedly produced to replenish stocks. The 1809 and 1810 volumes may have been released as a set – Thomson certainly presented Vol. I of 1809 as the first part of a new edition – but the set would have been incomplete unless Vol. IV of 1808 or 1812 was sold alongside them. Another anomaly recently discovered by Dr Marjorie Rycroft of the University of Glasgow, when she was editing the Haydn songs for the new Haydn *Gesamtausgabe,* relates to a volume found in the National Library of Scotland (GB-En Mus. E.1 15 [5 vols]). The title page of this volume states that it is a 'New Edition/With Additions by Beethoven' and is part of a five-volume set. It has a colophon date of 1822, yet the nearest full five-volume set of that time is the 1826 edition also marketed by Thomson as 'New'. Marion Linton, the National Library of Scotland music librarian, corresponded with Cecil Hopkinson of the British Library in 1958, discussing in detail the unique qualities of this particular volume and the others of varying dates in a five volume set she had just purchased for the music collection.

Trying to piece together a reasonable guide through all of these varying volumes, especially when Thomson gaily names them 'new editions' all the time, is complex to say the least. It quickly becomes apparent that taking Thomson's statements at face value will only end in disaster. Don McKenzie, my bibliography guru, gave me sound advice in a letter of 15 November 1992 when he stated:

> I would make two points: The first is that the distinction between what constitutes a new edition and a reissue (with *some* alteration of text) is always to some extent subjective. An alteration of the title page information about date and/or the auspices of publication may only be evidence of a reissue. So too alteration of the text (even up to half of it) may not justify classification of the new product as anything more than a reissue. What then you are in need of is, not an ex-cathedra statement about which label to apply, but a means of being consistent about your own judgements.

He then went on to make his second point:

> I would break down the various collections into their smallest bibliographical units. These may be 'Volumes' 1 to 4, as well as 5 and 6 in due course. And then deal with them individually, not as parts of sets. Then give them your own numbering system.

Finally he made the sage comment:

> Don't worry unduly about not being able to say with certainty whether a particular volume is a new edition or reissue: classify it as one or the other and then simply say by way of qualification that (given the extent of resetting) it might equally be described as …

This advice was music to my ears. Thomson most commonly advertised his sets of volumes as 'new and improved editions', yet the individual volumes of each set have a unique bibliographical description.

For example, the five volumes produced in 1826, which Hopkinson and Oldman termed 'the sixth edition', comprised Vol. I in its seventh issue, Vols II, III and IV in their fifth issue and Vol. V in its second issue. This dual identity of each volume presents an insoluble problem when trying to find the correct bibliographical terminology. Should the second issue of Vol. V dated 1826 be regarded as a second issue, or as the fifth part of a new 'sixth edition'? And what does the bibliographer do with the various forms of the same volume? Vol. I, for example, appeared in nine different forms between 1801 and 1838, but it had also appeared before this as the first two sets of 1793 and 1798. Furthermore, the First Set had been issued twice, in 1793 and 1794. No volume was ever identical from one issue to the next. Numerous issues of a volume appeared, sometimes with exactly the same content as their predecessor, but sometimes with new musical arrangements or lyrics, sometimes with new title pages and prefatory material or different thicknesses of paper, sometimes with different pagination, sometimes with newly engraved musical plates or adjustments to plates, and nearly always with new letterpress. Thomson's volumes were not imposed in gatherings, but were assembled rather from single sheets which were bound together. The music for two songs was printed recto/verso on one sheet of paper and the lyrics for two songs were printed in a similar fashion. Single sheets of music were thus bound alternately with sheets on which the words were printed creating a pattern of music/text/text/music/music/text and so on. The changes between issues of the same volume were inconsistent: often there seems to be no discernible pattern. Naturally new musical settings and new verses required new musical plates or the setting of new letterpress, and when plates became worn then new ones were engraved. The letterpress, however, changes by the issue. Different fonts and spacing can result in a volume which appears to be brand new, even though the content is identical to that of its predecessor.

Unlike Hopkinson and Oldman, I decided not to label the various sets of matching volumes as 'editions'. While Hopkinson and Oldman's 'Tabulated list of the different editions' was the basis of my bibliography, it is important to note that there were significant differences between the two lists. Hopkinson and Oldman stood firmly beside Thomson's descriptions of his volumes and editions, which not surprisingly go against the bibliographer's rules and regulations. Thomson was inconsistent with his own labelling, and although he was happy to call Vol. I of 1809 the first volume of his third edition, he forgot to give the volumes of 1801 a description, or Vols I-III of 1803 a number, thus causing Hopkinson and Oldman nothing but problems. By choosing to examine and list each volume as a separate issue, I managed to avoid this situation. Hopkinson and Oldman also concluded from the prefatory advertisements alone that Thomson must have produced editions of Vols I-IV in 1809, 1811 and 1817.[42] While we can prove that there was indeed a set of Vols I-IV in 1817, complete sets of volumes dated 1809 and 1811 are not, it seems, extant. Thomson was always carried away by his own enthusiasm, ordering far more illustrations than he could hope to publish, and sometimes advertising editions and publications before receiving agreements from his composers.[43] Thomson's advertisement for a new edition or volume was by no means a guarantee of its publication. I have been unable to find volumes dated 1811, although Hopkinson and Oldman clearly found a copy of Vol. II with this date,[44] and only one volume dated 1809 has been found. It is most unlikely that volumes published between 1808 and 1814 were part of any new matching editions, primarily because

Thomson was concerned at this time with the publication of the first and second Welsh volumes (1809 and 1811) and the first Irish volume (1814).

There is an even greater problem with the later volumes of the 1830s. The five-volume set produced in 1831 incorporated a number of changes, particularly relating to the format of individual volumes. These were the first and only volumes in which Thomson shuffled existing songs and gave them different numbers, and they were the only volumes in which Thomson reverted to earlier settings, previously discarded. As Hopkinson and Oldman make clear,[45] there is something of a problem in comparing the first volume of this set with the first volume of the 1838 set, as the title pages of both issues appear to be identical (SIg and SIh). Examination of various volumes indicates that the title pages for the five volumes of 1831 and those of 1838 are often mixed and matched. The information presented and the general format of the title page do not change between 1831 and 1838, although different fonts are often employed. Dates are frequently changed, by hand, on the title pages. Sometimes they will bear the name 'Coventry & Hollier', which dates them to 1838,[46] but more often they still show Preston as publisher. These volumes should not be dated by their title pages, but it is often difficult to date them by anything else.

Thomson's new Appendix of *Twenty Scottish Melodies added in 1838–9...* adds to this confusion. Its title page would suggest that it was actually published after the first issue of his five volumes dated 1838. This is possible, or even probable. The title page for some 1838 volumes, for example, states that many belonged to a six-volume set, and not the regular five volumes, thereby implying that 1838 volumes were reissued, after the publication of the Appendix, to be sold as a set alongside the 1841 Vol. VI. Most of the songs in the Appendix are included in this sixth volume, but Thomson *did* incorporate some of the Appendix songs in other volumes – for example, a copy of Vol. II of 1838 in the National Library of Scotland (GB-En Mus L. l. 51–5). No one has been able to find an 'ideal' copy of the six-volume set supposedly released in 1841. It seems most likely that Thomson simply altered copies of the 1838 set to be reissued with the new Vol. VI. Settings of an even later date suggest that he was dabbling with these 1838 volumes throughout the 1840s. There are three Hogarth settings dated 1843 which appear at the back of some copies of Vol. V of 1838 (see GB-En Mus. L. l. 69), and two G.F. Graham settings of 1846 which often appear in copies of the same volume (see GB-En Mus. L. l. 51–5). There are two new Bishop settings dated 1845 which appear as the last two songs in Vol. VI (GB-En Mus. L. l. 69), and there is the bizarre and well nigh inexplicable appearance of Thomson's new 1850 lyric for 'Maggie Lauder's Nuptials' in at least one copy of Vol. III of 1838 (see no.124 of GB-En Mus. L. 1.68–9).[47] Hopkinson and Oldman concluded that the last publication was a lithographic reprint of the 1838 volumes with Bishop's two 1845 settings added, but copies of Vol. III and Vol. V in the National Library of Scotland (NLS) mentioned above indicate that the publications actually continued until 1846, or even 1850.[48]

After much debate I decided that each volume had to be treated as a separate bibliographical unit. I numbered each volume separately and then listed its different forms chronologically. The number of the volume is always given in Roman numerals and is preceded by a letter which identifies the collection to which it belongs: S = Scottish; W = Welsh and Ir = Irish. For example, Vol. I of the Scottish collection in its first form dated 1801 will be labelled SIa, and its subsequent forms will be identified by the same number but with a different letter attached – SIb for Vol. I of 1803, SIc for Vol. I of 1809, SId for Vol. I of 1814, and so on. Rather than comparing each new issue with its first edition, each volume was compared with its immediate predecessor (that is, Vol. I of 1803 was compared with Vol. I of 1801, then Vol. I of 1809 was compared with Vol. I of 1803, and so on). There is no evidence to suggest that Thomson always returned to the first edition of a volume before making changes; in fact, it appears that his editing process was a progressive one. It was only when he reached the 1830s that he looked back to the earliest issues of his volumes for songs which he had since omitted. I also decided that it was futile to fight with different bibliographical terminology with which to describe the different forms of one volume. There are so many discrepancies between forms of the same volume, that it is difficult to be consistent with the terms 'edition', 'reissue' and 'state'. These volumes are frequently a combination of all three descriptions. As the basic format of the volumes remained unchanged for a 50–year period, and as most of the material included in each volume was static, I decided that one term which covered the majority of changes and inconsistencies would be best. I therefore chose to use the term 'issue'. Each form of a volume was referred to in the list as 'another issue' of its predecessor, and therefore its mother volume. The mother volume was always the first edition of a volume, and full details of the contents (music = m and verses = v) were given for each of these first editions: namely, sets 1–4 (A to D) and Vol. I and II of 1801 (SIa and SIIa), Vol. III of 1802 (SIIIa), Vol. IV of 1805 (SIVa), Vol. V of 1818 (SVa) and Vol. VI of 1841 (SVIa). The titles and contents of the two appendices that Thomson produced were also listed, namely. the *Appendix: Containing Twelve Favourite Melodies* ... of 1826 and *Twenty Scottish Melodies added in 1838– 9...* .

The basic numbering system therefore looks like this:

Sets of Scottish Airs:

A – First set 1793
Aa – First set 1794
B – Second set 1798
C – Third set 1799
D – Fourth set 1799

Scottish volumes (S):

Volume I
SIa – 1801
SIb – 1803

SIc – 1809
SId – 1814
SIe – 1817
SIf – 1826
SIg – 1831
SIh – 1838

Volume II
SIIa – 1801
SIIb – 1803
SIIc – 1810
SIId – 1815
SIIe – 1822
SIIf – 1826
SIIg – 1831
SIIh – 1838

Volume III
SIIIa – 1802
SIIIb – 1803
SIIIc – 1810
SIIId – 1817
SIIIe – 1826
SIIIf – 1831
SIIIg – 1838

Volume IV
SIVa – 1805
SIVb – 1808
SIVc – 1812
SIVd – 1815
SIVe – 1826
SIVf – 1831
SIVg – 1838

Volume V
SVa – 1818
SVb – 1826
SVc – 1831
SVd – 1838

Volume VI
SVIa – 1841

Welsh volumes (W):

WI – 1809
WII – 1811
WIII – 1817

Irish volumes (Ir):

IrI – 1814
IrII – 1816

The numerous changes to the musical settings and to the verses provided for the music needed to be included too, and they were listed by the number of the song. Numbers in brackets referred to quantity (for example, Kozeluch (25) = 25 settings by Kozeluch), whereas numbers without brackets referred to the number of a particular song (for example, Kozeluch, 25 = song no. 25 by Kozeluch). It should be noted that Thomson's volumes were not paginated, but rather numbered by opening. Each opening included the music and the verses for one song and the two pages of the opening shared one number. Occasionally two songs were included on the same plate or printed with the same number – for example, if two settings of the same melody appeared. Only in the later volumes, particularly those of the 1831 set, was the numbering inconsistent.

I also conceived a shorthand for referring to changes to the songs themselves. New musical settings were noted under 'nm' and new verses under 'nv'. In the early volumes (1801 and 1803) some of the original settings were simplified by the composer at Thomson's request (these are noted on the list), and sometimes new settings were published alongside old settings of the same melody (these particular songs were marked with the symbol +). Many of the songs were simply altered or adjusted ('am' or 'av'). Rather than list every difference between issues I listed only transposition and simplification as musical adjustments ('am'). The deletion or addition of single notes to musical plates, and the alteration of tempo markings or inclusion of violino parts on plates are mentioned in passing but are not listed under am. The deletion of an old verse or alterations to particular stanzas were the only changes listed as adjustments to the verses ('av').

The practical problem of examining individual volumes adds to the bibliographical complications. Understandably, no library houses complete sets of Thomson's publications, and some are unable to lend volumes for comparison, or to photocopy relevant volumes if the volume is in bad condition. Between them, The British Library (BL) and the NLS hold almost all of Thomson's volumes, though sometimes issues of a specific date are missing. I based my study on the collections of the above libraries and also on volumes found in the Bodleian Library, Oxford, the Faculty of Music in Oxford, the library of the University of Glasgow, Edinburgh University Library, Aberdeen University Library and the Mitchell Library in Glasgow. I was also able to examine some copies in private collections and also photocopies of material from the Newberry Library in Chicago. It is important to recognize that my bibliography was compiled from study of these volumes alone and as such it cannot be exhaustive, though I have also concluded that no Thomson bibliography will ever be exhaustive or 'correct'.

Sadly, few of the volumes now kept in libraries are found in their original state: most of them were bound by the library, or by the individual who owned them. In normal circumstances this would not be problematic, but in the case of Thomson's volumes it further complicates matters. Volumes of varying dates are bound with title pages, illustrations and prefaces from other volumes, resulting in confusion for any bibliographer. Cataloguers naturally list volumes by their latest date, when often title page, preface and colophon dates conflict hopelessly with one another. Thus the volumes which arrive on the reader's table seldom follow their catalogue description and frequently contradict it. Frontispieces, title pages, prefatory material, illustrations, indices and glossaries are sometimes bound with the volume, but are often missing. Occasionally they appear at the front of the volume, but sometimes at the back. Whoever bound the volumes did so at his or her own discretion and no single description would necessarily correspond with volumes which the reader might be using. Suffice it to say that while this information can certainly help in dating a volume, it can also be misleading. The contents of a volume are the safest method when it comes to dating individual volumes. So my bibliography gave also, whenever possible, full details of the title pages, frontispieces (f), illustrations (i: with designer/engraver) and publisher (p). If the prefatory material presents any problems of dating then such details were also included. I also gave the Stationers' Hall entry (sh). Although it is dangerous to date a volume by its entry date alone, Thomson was scrupulous about entering his material at Stationers' Hall, thinking that it would also give him some copyright control. Because of this, these particular entry dates are safer than some.

So, with all of the above taken into account, a standard bibliographical entry would look something like this:

SIa – Vol. I (1801):

A/ Select Collection of/ ORIGINAL SCOTTISH AIRS/ For the Voice./ With Introductory & Concluding Symphonies/ & Accompaniments for the/ PIANO FORTE, VIOLIN & VIOLONCELLO/ By/ Pleyel, Kozeluch & Haydn/ With/ Select & Characteristic Verses both Scottish and English/ adapted to the Airs, including upwards of One Hundred New Songs by/ BURNS/ [price]/ [vignette]/ [publisher's details]

p: T. Preston, No. 97 Strand
vi: Now see where Caledonia's genius mourns – Stothard/J.Thomson
f: The Birks of Invermay – W. Hamilton/P. Thomson

coverpage:
FIFTY/SCOTTISH SONGS,/WITH/ SYMPHONIES & ACCOMPANIMENTS:/ THE FIRST TWENTY-FIVE BY/Pleyel,/THE OTHER TWENTY-FIVE BY/Kozeluch./ VOL.I ...

Another issue of the first and second sets (Aa + B)
with new title-page, new prefatory material, illustration and new letterpress.
Preface dated 1801 (pp.1–4); Text, nos.1–50

am: 29; 36, 46 (new, simpler settings by Kozeluch requiring new plates)
nv: na, 20: R. B. Sheridan, 5; Mrs Barbauld, 15

note: To be matched with SIIa. The volumes of 1801 comprised two paper
thicknesses – thinner paper for the letterpress and thicker paper for the music.

There are areas of Thomson's publications which I chose to exclude: parts for violino and violoncello up to 1818, and then additional flute parts and harp parts for the Welsh volumes are difficult to come by. They were produced separately, in fine paper covers, to be purchased only if the customer desired. They were not bound into the volumes proper and, consequently, many copies have gone missing. It is impossible to list all the changes made to parts, but it is possible to glean enough information from my bibliography to enable any reader to match a particular instrumental part with its rightful volume, and thus be able to date it.

Happily the new Thomson edition – a long-term research project at the Music Department of the University of Glasgow – will ultimately cover this area as it brings together all the sources and creates new performing editions of all of Thomson's songs. Indeed, the reason why I am not including a copy of the full bibliography with this essay relates to the above Thomson project. My colleagues Dr Marjorie Rycroft and Dr Warwick Edwards and myself have already discovered additional volumes with new dates, like the 1822 copy mentioned earlier, and are finding new materials all the time. It appears from the collection of Thomson material at Aberdeen University Library, for example, that Thomson also sometimes issued separate songs. So the research undertaken over the next couple of years may well result in major additions to my original bibliography.

There is also another area for investigation, which was not included in my earlier work, namely, Thomson's octavo volumes, first produced in 1822–25 and then reissued throughout the 1830s. In order to produce a smaller, more compact and, ultimately, cheaper edition, Thomson decided in the early 1820s to produce a collection in royal octavo which would include songs from all three folio collections.[49] These volumes were produced as an offshoot of the larger collections and demanded far less of Thomson's time, energy and expenditure, primarily because they were smaller and thus cheaper to produce, but also because the majority of the songs included had already been printed in the folio volumes.

The first five volumes appeared in 1822–23 entitled:

The Select Melodies of Scotland/ Interspersed with those of/ Ireland and Wales/ united to the songs of/ Rob'. Burns, Sir Walter Scott Bart./ and other distinguished poets:/ with/ Symphonies & Accompaniments/ For the/ Piano Forte/ by/ Pleyel, Kozeluch, Haydn & Beethoven/.

But when the sixth volume was added in 1825, Thomson also reissued the first five volumes and renamed the collection:

> Thomson's Collection/ of/ the Songs of Burns,/ Sir Walter Scott Bart./ And other eminent lyric poets Ancient & Modern/ united to the/ Select Melodies of Scotland,/ and of Ireland & Wales/ with Symphonies and Accompaniments/ for the/ Piano forte/ by/ Pleyel, Haydn, Beethoven &c..

There were no changes in content between the volumes produced in 1822–3 and those issued in 1825, in fact Hopkinson and Oldman suggested that the same sheets for Vols I-V had been used in 1825. Copies of subsequent issues are always problematic, since they usually brandish several dates. As Hopkinson and Oldman noted,[50] Thomson probably reissued the six volumes in 1828 and 1831, as copies of individual volumes with these dates have been found. The NLS also has a copy of all six volumes, which bear between them the dates 1822, 1824, 1825, 1826, 1829, 1830–31, 1836 and 1838,[51] but it has been concluded that these volumes, regardless of their multifarious dates, are also reprints of the earliest issues. The volumes bearing the date 1838 (usually attached to their illustrations) were, in Thomson's words, a 'new edition'.

The first five octavo volumes were clearly modelled on the first five Scottish folio volumes. With the exception of the second volume (which mysteriously includes 51 songs), each volume included 50 songs[52] and, in general, they were exactly the same as those found in the folio volumes, although some songs were numbered differently and many had new verses. Although the majority of songs printed in the folio volumes appeared in the corresponding octavo volume, some changed place: for example, songs originally found in folio Vol. I were printed in octavo Vols III or IV, and so on. The Welsh or Irish songs were never scattered randomly throughout the new octavo volumes, but usually always appeared at the end of each volume, most often as nos 41–50. Thomson also stated which of his songs were 'Highland' or 'English', which he was not so keen to do in his earlier volumes. Volumes II, IV and V contained one or two choice Highland songs and an English song appeared in Vol. V and Vol. VI.

As the folio Vol. VI did not appear until 1841, the octavo Vol. VI is an unusual addition. It contained only 43 songs, some of which were taken from folio Vols I-V, and some of which were new. Ten of them were settings by Beethoven and Haydn for three voices, which only appeared for the first time in the folio volumes in 1826. Although some settings were unique to the octavo volumes, most of the new settings were included in the folio volumes of 1826, 1831 and 1838. Some of the illustrations which appeared for the first time in the octavo collection were likewise presented in these later volumes. David Allan's illustrations for 'Contented wi' little and canty wi' mair', 'Her mother hastily spake', 'She crept in ayont him', 'Hooly and fairly' and 'O, whistle and I'll come to you my lad' and Stothard's sketches (engraved by Lizars) for 'Blythe and merry' and 'Love's goddess in a myrtle grove' are not found in the folio volumes.

Suffice it to say there is still work needing to be done on the ultimate Thomson bibliography, but the building blocks are certainly well in place. The lessons learnt in understanding Thomson's collections can surely be helpful to anyone dealing with music publications of the eighteenth and nineteenth centuries, though I would hope that no other stories are quite as complex as Thomson's. Don McKenzie's advice to look at each volume, even if it belongs to a set, as a unique object, to aim above all for logical descriptions and never to feel burdened by standard bibliographical terminology is crucial to remember. It is also well worth endeavouring to put the publications in a business context. Without knowledge of Thomson's so-called 'publishing house' some areas of his bibliography would still be a mystery. But, at the end of the day publishers and editors are human beings and will thus forever find themselves fussing and poking when they ought perhaps to leave their volumes well alone!

Notes

1   Hopkinson, C. and Oldman, C.B. (1940), 'Thomson's collections of national song: with special reference to the contribution of Haydn and Beethoven', *Transactions of the Edinburgh Bibliographical Society*, Vol. II, Part 1, 3–64. Amendments to this article were published in the same journal: Vol. III, Part 2, (1954), 123–4.

2   References to Hopkinson and Oldman numbers for individual songs are as follows: for example, for Haydn songs – HO, Hay 87; and for Beethoven songs – HO, Bee 87.

3   Hopkinson's description of Thomson's volumes in a letter of 20 October 1964 to the American collector Walter Harding, now found in the Thomson volumes of the Harding Collection at the Bodleian Library, Oxford.

4   See Hopkinson and Oldman (1940, p. 5). They explain that Thomson noted in IrI that this 1814 volume was a corrected copy of a previous issue. No other copies have been found.

5   Details of the establishment of the Board of Trustees for the Encouragement of Arts and Manufactures, and their records, are held at the Scottish Record Office (SRO): ref. NG.1.

6   Arnot, H. (1779), *The History of Edinburgh*, Edinburgh: W. Creech, p. 541. Arnot stated, 'This institution [the Board] has been of great advantage to the country. It is in consequence of this establishment, and of the bounties granted upon the exportation of linen, that this valuable branch of manufacture has risen to any importance.' Arnot also listed the materials imported and exported to and from the port of Leith. Scotland exported linen products to Denmark, Norway, Spain, Gibraltar, Russia, North America and the West Indies, and woollen products to Norway, Sweden, the Netherlands, North America and the West Indies. Fish was exported only to the Netherlands (salmon) and the West Indies (herring): see Arnot (1779, p. 576).

7   There are 7 letterbooks now housed in the British Library – GB-Lbl Add MS 35263–35269.

8   An Additional Catalogue from 1790 – 'The Late Property of the Eminent Dealer ROBERT BREMNER' – printed by Preston includes copies of Bremner's Scots songs and Scots reels, of his *Curious Collection of Tunes with Variations* and of publications by William McGibbon and Francis Peacock: GB-Lbl Hirsch IV 1113 – 1–13.

9   William Napier, another Scot in London, published his *Selection of Original Scots Songs* in three parts in 1790, 1792 and 1795. Haydn's first settings appeared in 1792, following his first London visit.

10 Fiske, R. (1983), *Scotland in Music: A European Enthusiasm,* Cambridge: Cambridge University Press; chapter 1 is entitled 'The Scotch Song comes to London'.

11 Thomson wrote to Preston, for example, on 27 October 1822 to inform him that he had shipped 20 copies of Vol. IV of his octavo edition along with an extra two copies for Stationers' Hall: GB-Lbl Add. MS 35268/107.

12 GB-Lbl Add. MS 35263/36–7; 54–5; 56–7; 74–5; 86–7.

13 This letter is undated, but must have been after 2 November, as mentioned in the list below.

14 Because of the differing weights and quality of Thomson's paper, the number of sheets in a ream, or quire, would vary. A quire was generally 24 or 25 single sheets, and a ream normally consisted of 20 quires, or 480 or 500 sheets. See Gaskell, P. (1985) *A New Introduction to Bibliography,* Oxford: Clarendon Press, pp. 57–77.

15 GB-Lbl Add. MS 35267/39. Thomson concluded that Preston had used 198$\frac{1}{2}$ quires or 9 reams 18$\frac{1}{2}$ quires of paper and should still have at least 6 reams 7$\frac{1}{2}$ quires remaining.

16 GB-Lbl Add. MS 35267/151.

17 Coleman, D.C. (1958), *The British Paper Industry 1495–1860,* Oxford: Clarendon Press, p. 221. Coleman noted that by the 1840s 'the mills within the Parish of Penicuik paid more duty than did the whole Irish industry'.

18 Thomson to Cowan, 17 February 1815: GB-Lbl Add. MS 35267/138.

19 GB-Lbl Add. MS 35268/135. Thomson ordered 30 reams of paper for the octavo edition. He also stated that the order of 25 reams of heavy paper for the folio volumes is 'only for 100 copies of the music at a time, & I fear will last for a year at the least'. The letter reveals that sales of the folio volumes left much to be desired and illustrates Thomson's desperation in deciding to issue an octavo edition.

20 Hopkinson and Oldman (1940, p. 4). Hopkinson and Oldman noted: 'when ... he [Thomson] ventured on a new edition, he was continually finding himself with sheets of previous editions on his hands, which he was apt to mix indiscriminately with sheets freshly printed for the new edition'.

21 Thomson to Cowan, 12 February 1815: GB-Lbl Add. MS 35267/138. See also Thomson to Cowan, 11 June 1815 (35267/151) in which Thomson asked for different weights of paper. Also Thomson to Cowan, 2 March 1818 (35268/37–8), in which Thomson orders thicker paper for music: 'of the same quality and weight with what I have been used to get lately from you'. The thicker music paper was described by Thomson as 'the soft or music paper' in his letter to Cowan of 11 December 1824 (35268/135).

22 GB-Lbl Add. MS 35267/75.

23 The title page gives Moir as the printer (Royal Bank Close) and also lists the publishers involved, who included, most importantly, Longman and Rees and J. Hatchard both of London. See also Thomson's letter of 22 December 1803 to Anne Grant referring to subscriptions for the above: GB-Lbl Add. MS 35266/20–1.

24 GB-Lbl Add. MS 35266/20–21.

25 Moir's name always appears on the colophon at the foot of the last page of lyrics in Thomson's volumes. Sometimes his name is not included, and so it is probable that on these occasions the reader is dealing with a volume printed by Preston. To my knowledge, Preston's name never appears on the colophon, only on the title page.

26 GB-Lbl Add. MS 35268/135. Thomson wrote: 'for Mr Moir says that only a little is necessary'.

27 Bushnell, G.H. (1949), *Scottish Engravers,* Oxford: Oxford University Press.

28 GB-Lbl Add. MS 35268/27–8.

29 Baptie, D. (1894), *Musical Scotland, Past and Present,* Paisley: J. and R. Parlane, p. 126.

Baptie gives the dates 1797–1859 and states that McLeod's songs are 'at once melodious and vigourous, full of animation in the bolder passages, yet tender and pathetic in other places'. His three collections of *Original Melodies* were published in 1828, 1834 and 1838 respectively.

30   GB-Lbl Add. MS 35268/28.

31   GB-Lbl Add. MS 35268/168. The address for Walker is now 140 Princes Street.

32   GB-Lbl Add. MS 35268/157.

33   'Engraved W.H. Lizars. 3 James's Sq. Edin.' appears at the foot of the page.

34   GB-Lbl Add. MS 35267/86–7. 'Dermot and Shelagh' is found in Vol. I of the Irish Collection – no. 14, p. 35. Smyth's verses were not printed, for the song appears with lyrics by T. Toms.

35   Thomson to Smyth, 28 January 1822: GB-Lbl Add. MS 35268/83–5. Thomson referred to Allan as 'an Artist who had a peculiar talent for the humorous deliniation of Scottish character and costume'. See also Burns to Thomson, November 1794: Burns, R. (1985), *The Letters of Robert Burns,* vol. 2, 1790–1796, ed. J. Ferguson, 2nd edn, ed. G. Roy, Oxford: Clarendon Press, pp. 327–31, n. 647. Burns was delighted with Allan's illustrations for his songs: 'I look on myself to be a kind of brother-brush with him. – "Pride in Poets is nae sin", & I will say it, that I look on Mr Allen [sic] & Mr Burns to be the only genuine & real Painters of Scotish Costume in the world!'

36   'The Birks of Invermay' (SI) and 'The Soldier's Return' (SIII).

37   Robert Smirke (1752–1845) was a book illustrator in London. His father and uncle were architects of the British Museum. See 'The Fortune Teller' (IrII).

38   'Llangollen Vale' and 'Conway castle' (WI and WIII).

39   See Preface to his First Set of 1793.

40   See Thomson's order for Preston in a letter of 1812: BM Add MS 35267/36–7.

41   See Hopkinson and Oldman (1940, p. 6). They refer to these volumes as the '1804 Second Edition' because the launching of the volumes was delayed until 1804. As the date of the preface and the colophon is 1803, I have chosen to use this date instead.

42   See Hopkinson and Oldman (1940, p. 6).

43   The Preface to the First Set of 1793, for example, advertised Pleyel's 'Twelve Sonatas for the piano forte with Accompanyments: in with a variety of favourite airs, both plaintive and sprightly, are introduced as themes or subjects'. In fact, Pleyel only completed six of them, and he had not yet responded to Thomson's commission when this advertisement was published.

44   See Hopkinson and Oldman (1940, p.6).

45   See Hopkinson and Oldman (1940, pp. 9–11).

46   Coventry and Hollier succeeded Preston in 1834, when Preston's company closed, and consequently became Thomson's main London publisher. Any volume produced after 1834 will bear Coventry and Hollier's name as opposed to Preston. Many of the 1838 title pages, however, still have Preston's name.

47   If we are to believe his correspondence, Thomson had sold the property of the Scottish Collection by 1849 to George Wood and Co. of Edinburgh (see Chapter V).

48   The copy of Vol. III which includes the 1850 lyric and the copy of Vol. V which includes G.F. Graham's two 1846 settings are found in the NLS – Mus. L. l. 68–9.

49   Thomson's reasons for the production of an octavo edition are given in a letter to William Smyth of 30 July 1821 – see BM Add MS 35268/52–5.

50   Hopkinson and Oldman (1940, pp. 8–9).

51   NLS – MH. s. 69–71.

52   Although the numbering of the songs continued from one volume to the next in the folio

collections (i.e. Vol. I = 1–50, Vol. II = 51–100, Vol. III = 101–150, and so on), the songs in each octavo volume were numbered 1–50.

Chapter 7

Con *Brio*: a history of the Branch journal

Malcolm Jones

Brio, the journal of the UK and Ireland Branch of IAML, is so much a part c
Branch life that it is, with the *Newsletter,* the only point of contact for some people
It was not always thus, for it was some little while after the foundation of th
Branch, the subject of the present celebrations, before a journal appeared. Howeve
this was not because the topic was overlooked: in October 1953, six months afte
the inaugural meeting, Walter Stock, the indefatigable General Secretary, 'submitte
details of a proposal for a journal of Music Librarianship'. The proposal wa
welcomed by the President, although he added: 'it would require a great deal o
thought'.

The subject then cropped up in meetings of the Branch Committee (later to b
renamed the Executive Committee) for the next few years, but lack of finance, an
of someone to do the work, appeared to have put the dampers on any progress o
this, as on many other worthwhile projects at that time and later.

Meanwhile discussion took place on a number of possible occasiona
publications, including conference papers and a 'selective list of music in print'
both were shelved, not surprisingly in the latter case, one feels. Cecil Hopkinso
argued for a 'Bibliographic Journal', though what exactly he meant is not recorded
Walter Stock returned to the subject of 'the urgent need for a branch magazine' in .
memorandum submitted to the committee on 4 October 1961, proposing that i
should cover the following topics:

1 reports of meetings
2 musical news from public libraries, university libraries, antiquarian and othe
   booksellers as well as interesting British publications and (geographical) are;
   interests
3 major items of bibliography
4 general topics, for example, new libraries
5 articles by members
6 descriptions of British music libraries and collections
7 items that would interest music librarians and which might otherwise be misse(
8 an index of magazine articles
9 reports on work and activity in gramophone record libraries
10 critical articles from various sources.

The proposal was agreed, and allocated £200 for initial costs. The minute also records the suggestion that George Maby (then Librarian at Bristol University) or Roger Crudge (Music Librarian at Bristol City, and later to be Branch President) be invited to become editor. In the event, both declined, and Ruzena Wood of the National Library of Scotland agreed to take up the post.

The title of the journal was to become a vexed question: Ruzena Wood proposed *Staccato,* but this did not find general acceptance with the committee which considered *Allegro* and *Commodo* as well. Clearly, music librarians of the 1960s knew their Italian terms. *Allegro* was settled upon, only for someone at a later meeting to announce that this clashed with some (unspecified) pre-existing title. Then Ruzena, not defeated, proposed *Brio.* And so it was.

The committee was not going to be ridden over, though, and it gave the new editor detailed instructions. The list of topics to be covered, given above, was adopted with the deletion of items 6, 7 and 10. Clearly a very cautious view was still being taken; initially it was intended to produce 200 copies of each issue, but this became 500 before the first issue appeared. This was in April 1964: the Branch had gone just over ten years without a journal, and from then the history seems to fall into ten-year periods, as we shall see.

The committee, maintaining its 'hands-on' approach, now turned to the design of the front cover. Looking at volume 1 number 1 (Spring 1964) now, it does not seem as dated as was argued in the 1980s, when it was changed. Just in case the casual reader missed the music pun in the title, a logo was adopted on the cover, which consisted of a large quaver, with IAML on the notehead and UK on the flag. The front covers have a strangely empty look until volume 6, when the practice of listing the contents there was adopted.

As to the contents, there was an index of articles in selected periodicals, compiled by Christel Wallbaum, personal assistant to the antiquarian dealer Herman Baron, which was a regular feature from the outset, along with a considerable number of reviews of books. There were also several advertisements, mostly from music publishers and retailers. The articles covered a predictable range of topics: matters of professional practice in general, but particularly cataloguing and classification, descriptions of individual libraries or those of an area, some pieces of historical research, especially when based round a collection or a composer, and reports of meetings. This pattern was to continue throughout the next decade, and an interesting overview may be obtained by consulting the index, compiled by David Baker, of these early issues.

It is clear from minutes throughout the first decade of *Brio's* life that the committee took a detailed interest in the contents, appearance and particularly publication schedule, all of which, but particularly the last, were the cause of concern.

By 1971 this had become serious. Not only were issues regularly late in appearing – the printer (in Edinburgh) was late – but the chain of distribution was long and unreliable. The issues were originally dated Spring and Autumn respectively; this became Spring/Summer and Autumn/Winter as members received their copies well into the later seasons. Costs were increasing, and the editor expressed concern over a lack of contributions. In 1972 there was a meeting with the Sound Recordings Group (now Audio Visual Group) of the Library Association to discuss the future of *Brio* in conjunction with that of the *SRG Newsletter*. This was inconclusive. Christel Wallbaum sought to resign as compiler of the index to periodicals, but was persuaded to do one more. The subject came up at the January and April 1973 meetings: at the latter that most English of solutions, the creation of a working party, was agreed. A questionnaire was circulated, asking in particular how far the index was used. The replies were less than one-tenth of the number sent out. Nevertheless the committee still felt that the index was useful. Then the editor, Ruzena Wood, resigned.

The minutes are silent over what happened next, merely recording the startling news, given the history, that Malcolm Jones and Clifford Bartlett were to take over as joint editors. What had happened was that these two, in discussion during the international conference of IAML, which took place in the summer of that year in London (actually in Regent's Park), had found that they both felt that a revitalized journal could be produced more cheaply, even if this meant sacrificing the production standards somewhat. Bartlett was already some way up the learning curve which was to lead him later to set up his own publishing house, King's Music, to produce his own editions. He urged that cheap reprographics, rather than typesetting and letterpress printing, was the solution. Some canvassing of these ideas took place among UK members at the conference, and thus the committee of 18 October 1973 was persuaded to appoint Jones and Bartlett joint editors, and production to continue on a trial basis for a year, after which 'the position would be reviewed'.

The proposed contents were recorded as:

Meetings, bibliographies, theses.
Current events in music publishing.
Book reviews of dictionaries, reference books, general books of interest to music librarians, reprints, new series and collected editions.

Although some misgivings were expressed, the plan for cheaper printing was approved. It was agreed that the index cease forthwith; it was hoped that it could be resurrected, but in the event, other publications took on the task more comprehensively, and it never reappeared. John May agreed to be the advertising agent and, with his excellent connections among the trade and elsewhere (he was a retailer and also managed the Association of British Orchestras), the advertising portfolio was expanded. However, in order to finance continued production, even on this basis, without undue strain on Branch finances, it was felt necessary to increase subscriptions to the Branch, in those days an unusual occurrence, and an extraordinary general meeting was summoned for the purpose. The increase was approved, and the restyled *Brio* duly appeared, approval being given by the committee on 17 January 1974 for 'a 24 page issue, in the cheapest format'.

Looking back, the difference in appearance does not seem so great as the above might suggest, although memory is that it felt different at the time.

After a year, in January 1975 there was duly a discussion on whether or not it should continue. Little is recorded, and indeed no decision was minuted. However, it did continue! Indeed, in October 1975 it increased in increase size by four pages, and it became quite elastic thereafter. Concern was expressed in committee that the Spring 1980 issue ran to 40 pages, the largest up to that time. However, the spring 1981 issue was of 48 pages.

And so the journal settled down. Indeed, the committee seems to have either lost interest in supervising matters of detail, or any discussion did not seem worth recording, for the minute book, up to this point a mine of information on the trials and tribulations of the journal, falls largely silent from here on, with occasional reports from the editor(s) confined mostly to a reassurance that the next issue was imminent, or similar. The position as to joint editorship remained; in fact, the editors arranged matters so that for a given issue, one of them did the lion's share and that person's name appeared on the inside of the front cover of the issue, in discreetly small type, as the editor.

Clifford Bartlett reported that the quality of the Autumn issue of 1980 was less than previously, and he was investigating other printers. Printing came to a firm in London, and it was felt possible to improve the production standards, albeit at greater cost. The joint editors' arrangement became less successful now that printing was in London, as was Bartlett, while Jones was in Birmingham, and so from the 1981 AGM Malcolm Jones stood down and Bartlett continued as sole editor.

In April 1982 Clifford Bartlett reported that printing costs were to double, as a result of returning to a commercial printer. The Executive accepted this, and, such was the increase that was obtained from more advertising, almost all of the increase was covered.

In the mean time Robert Stevens persuaded the committee that a second publication, dealing less with the more scholarly, bibliographic or, at least, professional side of things would improve communication and keep members up to date on the goings-on at the increasing number of meetings that the Branch now sponsored, having replaced the single committee with a number of committees with more specific responsibilities. The first issue of the *Newsletter* appeared in autumn 1981 and it has, like its big sister, appeared twice yearly since. The first two issues contain no clue as to their dates, and it was initially regarded as rather an ephemeral production; as a result, copies of those early issues are quite scarce. The *Newsletter* added interviews, 'Desert Island Choices' and crosswords, as well as personal news, 'hatched, matched and despatched' (as well as translations from one post to another) but at the same time managed to acquire the reports of annual study weekends from *Brio*, since it was possible to get these into circulation more quickly this way. As a result, each journal is now an indispensable part of the Branch's record.

To return to the history of *Brio:* Clifford Bartlett stood down in 1984. He had served a little longer than Ruzena Wood, and longer than any successor is likely to, since a revised constitution of that time set most officers of the Branch, including the *Brio* editor, a maximum of five years in post. At the AGM of 1984 Ian Ledsham was appointed editor. The takeover was not abrupt, and the handover was not entirely smooth: Clifford Bartlett's final editorial, in the Spring/Summer 1985 issue, refers to a difference of opinion between him and the executive on when (not whether) he should finish, and it was, with hindsight, sad that his term should finish thus.

Ledsham's opening 'manifesto' was to place the magazine at the disposal of members for anything of general interest, and to call for papers for publication. He was evidently heeded, for the Spring/Summer 1986 issue was a new record in more than one sense, having 52 pages.

In 1987 the question of an index of articles in journals was considered, but it was decided that this would not be proceeded with; there were several sources covering the subject already. *Brio* was by now a sufficiently solid (in both senses) and established publication by itself: reviews in particular had been expanded. Clifford Bartlett had written most of these himself, and Ian Ledsham was content to leave them with Clifford. The Executive Committee felt that a spread of reviewers would be more appropriate, and a separate post of Reviews Editor was created, Karen McAulay (who was also editing the *Newsletter* for much of this time) agreeing to do the work, which was to become an official post a while later.

The task of collecting and encouraging contributions from advertisers, so important to the financial state of *Brio,* was entrusted to a succession of more-or-less willing members. Distribution had been in the hands of the British Library at Boston Spa, under an arrangement made through the good offices of Tony Reed, the Music Librarian there; it had previously fallen to a (volunteer) Distribution Officer.

At the AGM of 1990 John Wagstaff become editor. Discussion took place about a redesign of the journal, which had looked almost exactly the same (the colour of the card on which the covers were printed, the first two appearing under John Wagstaff's editorship being bright yellow; but nothing else changed) since volume 1 number 1. After some negotiations with the firm of BH Typesetters and Designers, based near Banbury in rural Oxfordshire, a new look was agreed upon, and this has prevailed to the present day. The firm had considerable experience of working with scholarly journals and, as well as setting and printing from then on, they were instrumental in the redesign. At the same time, distribution was placed on a commercial basis. The redesign meant the demise of the quaver symbol, and a new logo was invented, mostly by Malcolm Turner. This consisted of a stave whose lines were formed of the full name of the Branch, the IAML having recently changed its name by the addition of 'Archives and Documentation Centres' to the title. At the left was a treble clef, and in various forms other details followed. This has been widely used to the present day.

There was a kind of 'in joke' in this. The Branch had recently opposed the change of name with some vigour, and refused initially to accept it. This had led to a near constitutional crisis, with the International Secretary, Anders Lönn, flying in from Stockholm to address the AGM, and the Branch President, Malcolm Jones, earning some opprobrium at International Council meetings. The suggestion had been made, in jest, that we could accept the new name, but only if it was never printed in type more that 4 point in size (that is, very tiny). And thus the new logo came about.

John Wagstaff remarked in his first editorial that his predecessor, Ian Ledsham, has consolidated a mix of 'library, trade and bibliographical topics'. He declared his intention, with a passing reference to the contretemps with the International body, of taking *Brio* from the largely parochial (his word, perhaps used somewhat metaphorically, but national, certainly, was the literal meaning) to more international matters, with reports of various activity on the international scene, some of which involved Branch members.

In the latter part of his editorship, John Wagstaff continued this tradition, which, it may be argued, reflected a new interest in international co-operation. Music librarianship in countries of the former Eastern bloc were not merely springing up, but flowering abundantly in some cases. There were visits to study weekends from many countries, and the arrival of the International Congress in Oxford in 1989 had given such matters a boost, and led to many more members than hitherto attending these gatherings. The efforts of Roger Taylor, in particular, had put the word 'outreach' into the Branch lexicon as never before. So by 1995, when the memory of disputes was fading, the journal was reflecting the concerns and affairs of a Branch which was more aware (among the generality of members, as opposed to a few enthusiasts) of its place in the International Association.

The next editor, Paul Andrews, in his opening editorial manifesto (Spring/Summer 1995) gave as his priorities, first, music librarianship and, second, music and librarianship, even if the library connection was tenuous. Some evidence of his own interests, especially the works of Herbert Howells, may be detected, and it has become a noticeable feature, and surely a very good one, that, with shorter fixed terms of office, editors have some freedom to stamp their personality on the journal: it is a source of continuing interest. Paul Andrews saw the journal to the final issue of 1999, and Geoffrey Thomason took up the reins thereafter.

Geoffrey Thomason's opening message, eschewing any discussion of the implications of the new first digit in the year, spoke instead of the music librarian's 'abiding love and understanding of our subject coupled with a desire to use them in the service of others'. This has been true of the journal, as it is of the Branch, and long may it continue!

Editors

Brio editors

Ruzena Wood	1964–73
Clifford Bartlett and Malcolm Jones (jointly)	1973–81
Clifford Bartlett	1981–84

Ian Ledsham   1984–89
John Wagstaff   1990–94
Paul Andrews   1995–99
Geoffrey Thomason   2000–

Brio review editors

Karen McAulay   1990–92
Karen Abbott   1992–95
Christopher Grogan   1996–99
Antonio Rizzo   2000–

Newsletter editors

Bob Stevens   1981–87
K. McAulay (née Manley)   1986–90
Barbara Padjasek   1991–94
John Wagstaff   August 1994 issue only
Kathy Adamson   1995–98
Viv Kuphal   1998–2001
Rupert Ridgewell   2001–

Chapter 8

Making a library for IAML(UK)

John Wagstaff

It is a happy coincidence that, at the same time as this *Festschrift* for IAML(UK)'s fiftieth anniversary is published, the UK Branch's own library will also celebrate a significant, if rather less impressive, anniversary of its own: its tenth. Turning this statement on its head leads one to conclude that the UK Branch managed, apparently perfectly well, *without* a library for its first 40 years, something that may surprise and puzzle some readers of the current chapter and, perhaps, lead them to read further about the present library, its beginnings and its *raison d'être*. Why was it established? Why was it founded in 1993 in particular? And what is its purpose/membership/usage? These are questions that will be dealt with in some depth in what follows. Whether the library will, like IAML(UK), survive to celebrate its own fiftieth anniversary will depend on its continuing to demonstrate its usefulness to the UK Branch and to its members.

The beginning

The basic facts about the genesis of the IAML(UK) library (hereafter 'the Library') are easily stated: it was established in 1993 following a suggestion from the present writer at IAML(UK)'s 1992 Annual Study Weekend in Swansea, and this suggestion led to further discussion, and to action, by the UK Branch's Executive Committee. A small paragraph in *Brio* volume 29 (1992), page 99 reflected the discussions that had taken place up to that time – many aspects of running the collection had yet to be decided, but it was considered important for members to be able to obtain items from the Library either as the result of a personal visit to select items for themselves, or through the requesting of items by post. Donations to the collection were invited, and advice requested on what it should contain. An outline of a justification for the Branch having its own library was attempted in the report's final sentence:

> Having our own collection will ... make useful materials available to libraries whose staff cannot easily obtain professional literature; and will enable IAML(UK) to make more effective and speedy responses to changes proposed by local and central government and by other bodies whose activities have a bearing on our own.

Both these points were amply justified by librarians' previous experience:

material on music librarianship was frequently hard to obtain, and for those outside London almost impossible without a good deal of effort and initiative, because the only significant collection in existence at the time was based at the London headquarters of the Library Association, and even that was apparently under threat (see later in this chapter). As regards the reference to government, it should be noted that IAML(UK) has frequently found itself having to respond to government proposals on library matters, or making representations to funding political and funding bodies – usually public authorities, less often academic institutions – concerning the proposed closure or downgrading of music library posts or service points. Such activity requires ready access to appropriate statistics and to reports that, until the foundation of the Library, were not centrally housed. As the world of lobbying and representation has become more sophisticated, IAML has increasingly been required to back up its position with clear, often statistical, arguments. In the spirit of self-help that is reflected also in its provision to its members of courses and conferences, and, of course, in its Library, IAML(UK) compiled between 1984 and 1999 its own *Annual Survey of Music Libraries,* whose contents must have been used to back up or disprove many an argument over the years. But government-sponsored reports such as Follett[1] and Anderson,[2] plus other material such as Audit Commission data[3] are also required in today's world, and are therefore to be found in the Library. Further examples of this sort of material, also now in the Library, are the Arts Council's *Creating New Notes: a Policy for the Support of New Music in England* (London: Arts Council, 1996), and the manifesto of *Re:source* by the UK Council for Museums, Archives and Libraries (London, 2000). Comedia publications such as *Borrowed Time? The Future of Public Libraries in the UK* (Bournes Green: Comedia, 1993), and François Matarosso's *Learning Development: An Introduction to the Social Impact of Public Libraries* (London: Comedia/British Library Board, 1998) are also there, along with John Howson's *Final Report on the Folk Arts Archive Project for the Arts Council of England and the National Folk Music Fund* (London: Arts Council, 1995).

Today's world is therefore far different from that of 1953, when the UK Branch took its first steps and IAML itself had only been officially established for two years. Libraries at that time were, in general, expanding, and perhaps the biggest question facing many libraries in the UK was whether or not to develop a collection of sound recordings.[4] Discussion of music library topics was, by and large, covered in the general librarianship press,[5] and there was only one journal dedicated specifically to music library issues – *Notes,* the journal of the Music Library Association of America, an institution founded in 1931.[6] IAML(UK)'s own journal, *Brio,* was not to appear until 1964 (see Chapter 7 of this book). But over the succeeding decades, publishing about music libraries and librarianship expanded, just as it did in other fields of library work. Manuals on how to run a music library appeared, and increasing numbers of articles and books on specialized areas of what could now legitimately be called a music library 'profession' were published. User education began to develop a literature of its own, and, during the past couple of decades, *Festschriften* – that is, books honouring distinguished individuals or institutions – for particular music librarians have begun to appear.[7] Much of this material has given the field an increased historical dimension, and the Library reflects this, just as it also tries to reflect current developments in the field.[8]

The proliferation of collectable material on music librarianship, and the requirement for a wide range of this and of related material by IAML(UK) members, made the foundation of IAML(UK)'s own library inevitable. But why 1993 in particular? The principal explanation, although not perhaps the most obvious, lay in the proposed move during the 1990s of the British Library's Information Sciences Service (BLISS) collection from the London headquarters of the UK Library Association (LAHQ) to the new British Library site at St Pancras. Although in the event the new British Library did not open until 1998, the decision to move the BLISS collection to St Pancras had already been taken in the late 1980s. There were several reasons for alarm bells to ring in the minds of UK librarians, including music librarians, for, while the BLISS collection of music librarianship resources was far from good, it was nonetheless the best available resource at the time, and did include a few rare items. Furthermore, with the move of the collection would come the end of the postal loans scheme whereby Library Association members could ask to have material posted to them: this postal loan service had been of considerable benefit to members outside London, and had had the effect of providing all of them, irrespective of geographical location, with an equal service. It was therefore, in the minds of many, a very visible and valuable benefit of Library Association membership and was not something to be abandoned lightly.[9]

In many ways, of course, the British Library could not be criticized for its proposal. There must have been operational sense in moving the BLISS collection to St Pancras, even though wide publicity had been given to the fact that the new library building would be full almost from the day it opened. From the Library Association's point of view it was becoming more difficult to justify housing the collection at its headquarters: statistics reported in 1995 were to show that visits to BLISS had dropped by 50 per cent between 1990–91 and 1994–95, and that loans had decreased by 40 per cent over the same period.[10] The Library Association was also known to be keen to use the space vacated by moving the library for other purposes, although the building of a fourth storey onto LAHQ in 2001–02 suggests that this particular strategy did not solve all its accommodation problems. The Association also knew, however, that the national press would not fail to see the irony of a professional organization representing libraries getting rid of a library collection from its own headquarters, and there was therefore much trepidation about press 'leaks'.

Set against this backdrop, it became obvious that 'self-help' would be IAML(UK)'s best defence against any loss of facilities at LAHQ, and so it came about that serious thought began to be given to the matter in 1992. But the proposal made at the 1992 Annual Study Weekend was successful for several additional reasons. First, it had the strong support of the then President of IAML(UK), Malcolm Lewis, under whose presidency, it is worth recalling, the Branch put in place several other significant and lasting initiatives, including the formulation of the Library and Information Plan for Music (Music LIP), and an early attempt to forge links with Irish music librarians. Secondly, it was strongly backed by the Branch's membership, several of whom made donations of stock, with one member also making a significant and welcome financial donation. Furthermore, space to house and administer the collection was made available at the Oxford University Music Faculty Library, which remains the Library's home. The project thus enjoyed an auspicious start, and quickly built up momentum. Lists of new additions to library stock were regularly published, first in *Brio* and later in the *IAML(UK) Newsletter*, to encourage members to borrow. Once the IAML(UK) web site was established, a catalogue of the library's holdings, arranged by author only, was added to it. (One of the long-term aims of the library is to make available a subject index to the material.) The URL is www.music.ox.ac.uk/library/Iamllib.htm

A decision was taken early on that the library would not confine itself to collecting only English-language material, even though it was recognized that this was likely to be of most benefit to the majority of users. Significant material in foreign languages on music librarianship is also acquired, either by gift or purchase and part of this material consists of the newsletters produced by overseas IAML branches. Some of these newsletters had been collected individually by a few members before the Library was founded, but the Library's establishment has led to more systematic collecting, and the contents of the newsletters often make an appearance in the 'Some Recent Articles on Music Librarianship' column of *Brio*, which helps IAML(UK) members keep up to date with library literature.

An international IAML library?

Given the international collecting policy of the Library, and its comparatively small membership, questions may be asked as to why it is not available to all members of IAML rather than just UK members, and why IAML as a whole does not set up its own library. Interestingly, and proof, if any were needed, that few initiatives are ever totally 'new', IAML did in fact take a decision to set up a library of its own in 1980 and the minutes of its council meeting in Cambridge on 3 August of that year recorded that 'A proposal by the Dutch Branch for the establishment of a IAML Library was discussed and accepted. The Library is to be housed in the Nederlands Bibliotheek en Lektuur Centrum (NBLC), Den Haag'.[11] A steering committee consisting of Anders Lönn (IAML Secretary General 1974–83, and President 1983–86) and the American music librarian Vincent Duckles, was appointed to liaise with the NBLC,[12] and at the beginning of 1982 a description of the Library's aims and objectives was published in *Fontes artis musicae*,[13] together with the announcement that 1982 would be regarded as an experimental period for the library. It was proposed that quarterly lists of new accessions would be supplied to the steering committee, which in turn would submit them for publication in *Fontes*

Unfortunately, only one such list ever appeared in the journal (in *Fontes artis musicae*, 30 (1983), p. 215), and the whole project seems eventually to have come to nothing. One probable reason for this was that Evelyn van Kaam, a leading light in the project, left the NBLC for a position at the public library in The Hague, and was no longer involved. At IAML's conference in Brussels in July 1982 it was reported that the NBLC would be appointing a new officer to oversee the library,[14] but this seems to have been the last published mention of the project before it was wound up in the late 1980s. Activity did, however, continue behind the scenes, as is evident from surviving material in IAML's archives.[15] A typescript report dated 15 November 1982 and entitled 'IAML Library News', written by Diane van der Heyden and Ad Blokland of the NBLC, already noted some problems. Although the library was receiving material, the majority of it was not considered relevant to the collection, and therefore could not be accepted. At the second council meeting of IAML's Washington congress in 1983 it was agreed that the IAML board would set up a committee to study problems in the functioning of the library, but in the event this did not happen and Ad Blokland, as liaison between the NBLC and IAML, instead submitted a report for the Board's attention in summer 1984. His report made the following points:

- The library was still being sent unsuitable material. To help alleviate this problem the report provided a set of guidelines for donations, as it was felt that some people might have misunderstood the library's aims.
- The library had no official budget, and therefore was forced to rely on donations. This was not a good way to build a collection.
- Some people felt that, since many music library schools already had their own collections of music librarianship literature, there was no need for a IAML collection. Since interlibrary loan from some of these collections was possible, such requests were not being submitted to the IAML library.

Blokland concluded that, if the IAML library were to continue, 'the provision of information about the library must be enlarged and improved. Besides that[,] a budget must become available for the library to buy and collect titles on an independent basis in a more directed way'. It was also suggested that the library restrict itself to material in the three official languages of the Association – English, French and German. In the event, the library continued to flounder, and finally closed in 1988.[16]

Contents of the IAML(UK) library

A look back at the Library's first accessions list in *Brio,* volume 30 (1993), pages 64–6 reveals what might most charitably be described as a 'miscellaneous' collection of material. There are newsletters from IAML branches in Denmark, Finland and New Zealand; a report of IAML's first official congress in 1951; an article from 1893 by James Duff Brown on the 'formation of a music library', surely one of the earliest examples of a piece specifically devoted to this topic; and some more general material such as R.C.Alston's *Research in the Humanities and Social Sciences* (London, 1992), F. Bray and C. Turner's *Monitoring the Library and Information Workforce* (London, 1991); Jane Gottlieb's *Guide to the Juilliard School Archives* (New York, 1992) and the consultative document *Towards a National Arts and Media Strategy* (London, 1992). As already noted, much of this was donated by IAML(UK) members, who might previously have been unwilling to dispose of such items but did not have space for them in their own collections. Over the years a large amount of IAML-related material has arrived in this way – papers from particular conferences or congresses, now long past; an almost complete set of IAML(UK) annual reports, and so on. The UK Branch's publications officer regularly deposits copies of Branch publications in the Library. Some users have also generously provided photocopies of articles and chapters that they have used in their own library research, and consequently the Library now has a sizeable collection of offprints and photocopies. The second-hand market for music library material is small, but items when they can be found are relatively cheap to buy, and the second-hand bookshops of Hay-on-Wye have frequently been 'plundered' for useful items. An ephemera file in the Library contains anything and everything, including publicity material and information booklets produced by music libraries, and a file of information about particular librarians, often – alas – including obituaries. The Library obtains elusive material via interlibrary loan, and furthermore holds a copy of essays and dissertations submitted for IAML(UK)'s E.T. Bryant Prize. Having these prize entries allows the Library to keep up to date with current research and, since so many entrants actually use the Library's resources to help them research their entries, a useful sort of symbiosis is created. At the end of 2001 the Library had a total of *circa* 750 items in its collection. These include material from across the spectrum of music librarianship – information on music library acquisitions, cataloguing and conservation; on reader services and technical services; publicity and promotional materials; periodicals issued by particular libraries or by particular branches, IAML and the Music Library Association included; and even some audiovisual material. IAML(UK) continues to provide the bulk of the Library's funding.

Library statistics

Between 50 and 100 items are added to the Library's stock each year. The majority of acquisitions are small in scale, since new books on music library topics are published relatively infrequently (typically, two or three per year internationally). Newsletters and journals arrive at a steady rate, and the Library has several rare examples. Usage of the Library, even after several years, has not settled into any sort of pattern, as is evident from the figures below:

Year	Number of users	Number of loans
1994	24	58
1995	27	61
1996	18	30
1997	11	30
1998	17	66
1999	14	38
2000	21	40
2001	9	107
Totals	141	430

(The Library also receives several requests for information each year that do not require the loan of Library stock.)

Discounting the figures for 2001, which are unusual both for the low number of users and high number of loans, the average number of users per year has been 19, and the average number of loans 46. While these figures may seem low, they should be seen in the context of UK Branch membership as a whole: the Branch's membership directory for 2000 listed 130 personal members, not all of whom were active members of the Branch. This suggests that between 14 per cent and 17 per cent of members *do* use the Library in a 'typical' year, an encouraging figure that one hopes will increase over time.

The future

A traditional strengths/weaknesses/opportunities/threats (SWOT) analysis provides a fair summing up of where the Library is at present, and where it is likely to go in the future. The fact that it is quite a small-scale initiative is probably – possibly surprisingly – a strength rather than a weakness: its funding up to now has by and large been adequate, especially since many items come to the collection by donation, which suggests that it is seen by donors as a worthwhile project. It is also well able to respond to individual members' requests; and it is a very visible benefit of membership of IAML(UK), which must help the Branch in the recruitment and retention of members. Weaknesses include the lack of a subject index to its holdings: members researching a particular project do not want to have to work through its entire catalogue to find the material they require and, in any case, the catalogue does not include details of the *contents* of the journals it holds or of individual chapters in books. Furthermore, the collection is stored in quite cramped conditions that fail to show it to its best advantage. Opportunities for development look quite bright, and one simple but useful initiative might be for new materials in the library to be displayed at IAML(UK) Annual Study Weekends, which are attended by many Branch members. Actually being able to see and examine items is always going to make them more 'real' than simply finding a reference to them on a book list or web site. Library school students continue to show an interest in music topics, and advertising the Library as a benefit of IAML(UK) membership, in conjunction with the UK Branch's reduced subscription rates for students, makes membership more attractive to this class of user. Those who begin using the Library as students will, one hopes, continue to do so once they are in professional posts, especially in these days of continuing professional development. The only real threats on the horizon are that other priorities might prevent the Branch from continuing to offer the Library the generous support it has enjoyed in the past, or that usage might dip to a level where the Branch no longer feels justified in giving funds to the Library: but at the moment all seems healthy. Long may it remain so!

Notes

1   United Kingdom Funding Council's Libraries Review Group (1993), *Report,* Bristol: Higher Education Funding Council for England (HEFCE). This document is known as the 'Follett' report because Sir Brian Follett was Chair of the Review Group.

2   *Joint Funding Council's Library Review: Report of a Group on a National/Regional Strategy for Library Provision for Researchers* (1994–95); published online, and available at http://www.ukoln.ac.uk/services/elib/papers/other/anderson/). Professor Michael Anderson was head of this group, whose aim was to investigate the issues that would be involved in developing a libraries strategy for researchers in the UK.

3   An example is the Audit Commission's report (2001), *North East Lincolnshire Public Library Service: Best Value Inspection, November 2000,* London: Audit Commission Inspection Service.

4   On this topic see, for example, Howes, J.W. (1959), 'Gramophone record library procedure", *Library Association Record* (*LAR*), **61** (1959), 289–94 ; Willmot, L. and Skilling, B. (1959), 'Gramophone record libraries: the second phase', *Library World,* 60 (1959), 176–8; and Burbridge, E. and Audsley, J. (1964), 'Gramophone record libraries: a review article', *LAR,* **66**, 100–104. I am indebted to Malcolm Lewis for bringing these articles to my attention and for depositing them in the Library, along with an unusually early article on the topic, S. Snaith's (1928–29), 'The gramophone in public libraries', *Library World,* **31**, 6–9. H. Currall's (1963), *Gramophone Record Libraries: Their Organization and Practice,* London: Crosby Lockwood, was in some ways the culmination of such literature, and also significant was the setting up of the Library Association's Sound Recordings Group in late 1964: see Howes, J.W. (1965), 'The Sound Recordings Group of the Library Association', *Assistant Librarian,* **58**, 64–5.

5   A.H. King, in his 1952 article on 'The Scope of the Music Research Library', *LAR,* **54**, 126–31, noted that the literature on music libraries at that time was 'admittedly not very extensive'. The IAML(UK) Library has several items that sum up the state of music librarianship work at this period, such as D. Phillips's (1974), *Selected Bibliography of Music Librarianship,* Urbana, IL: University of Illinois, and C. Schutz's (1978), 'Musikbibliothekarische Fachliteratur im deutschen Sprachraum ... ', thesis, Stuttgart, which covers the German-language field from 1945 to 1977. F. Grasberger's *Der Autoren-Katalog der Musikdrucke,* which forms the first volume of IAML's (1957), *Code international de catalogage de la musique,* Frankfurt: Peters, includes a useful bibliography of literature on music catalogues and cataloguing up to that time.

6   The first series of *Notes* was published from 1934 to 1942; a second series began in 1943 and continues to the present. A *Supplement for Members* was published between 1947

and 1964. From 1952 to 1953 IAML produced a small *Bulletin d'information* for its members; but it only really began to have a journal approaching *Notes* in scale and scope once *Fontes artis musicae* commenced publication in 1954.

7   The library holds the following works of this type, presented here in alphabetical order by name of honorand: Leuchtmann, H. and Münster, R. (eds) (1984), *Ars iocundissima: Festschrift für Kurt Dorfmüller zum 60. Geburtstag,* Tutzing: Schneider; Rehm, W. (ed.) (1984), *Musikdokumentation gestern, heute und morgen: Harald Heckmann zum 60. Geburtstag am 6. Dezember 1984,* Kassel: Bärenreiter; Bradley, C.J. and Coover, J.B. (eds) (1987), *Richard S. Hill: Tributes from Friends,* Detroit: Information Coordinators; Neighbour, O. (ed.) (1980), *Music and Bibliography: Essays in Honour of Alec Hyatt King,* London: Bingley; Hunter, D. (ed.) (1994), *Music Publishing and Collecting: Essays in Honor of Donald W. Krummel,* Urbana, IL: Graduate School of Library and Information Science, University of Illinois; Fauquet, J.-M. (ed.) (1988), *Musique-signes-images: liber amicorum François Lesure,* Geneva: Minkoff; Banks, C., Searle, A. and Turner, M. (eds) (1993), *Sundry Sorts of Music Books: Essays on Music in the British Library Collections, Presented to O.W. Neighbour on his 70th Birthday,* London: British Library; Laird, P.R. and Russell, C.H. (eds) (2001), *Res musicae: Essays in Honor of James W. Pruett,* Warren, MI: Harmonie Park Press; Katz, I.J. (ed.) (1991), *Libraries, History, Diplomacy and the Performing Arts: Essays in Honor of Carleton Sprague Smith,* New York: Pendragon; and Mann, A. (ed.) (1989), *Modern Music Librarianship: Essays in Honor of Ruth Watanabe,* Stuyvesant, NY: Pendragon. D.L. Keer's (1991) MSLS thesis, 'Helmut Kallmann: an Account of his Contributions to Music Librarianship and Scholarship in Canada', University of Alberta, honours a significant Canadian music library practitioner, while the founding father and first Secretary General of IAML, V. Fédorov, was honoured by 'Mélanges offerts à Vladimir Fédorov à l'occasion de son soixante-cinquième anniversaire', produced as a special issue in 1966 of *Fontes artis musicae,* **13** (1). Chapters on music libraries appear in Festschriften honouring particular institutions, such as R. Holmes's contribution to Cochrane, P. (ed.) (2001), *Remarkable Occurrences: the National Library of Australia's first 100 Years, 1901–2001,* Canberra: National Library of Australia; K.-H. Köhler's chapter in Dube, W. (ed.) (1965), *Deutsche Staatsbibliothek 1661–1961 ... ,* Berlin: Deutsche Staatsbibliothek; and in G. Brosche's contribution on the music collections of the Austrian national library to Mazal, O. (ed.) (1987), *Ein Weltgebäude der Gedanken: die Österreichische Nationalbibliothek,* Graz: Akademische Druck. Perhaps the most unusual music librarianship Festschrift is Wursten, R.B. (ed.) (1990), *In Celebration of Revised 780,* Canton, MA: Music Library Association, a series of essays issued to coincide with publication of the twentieth version of the Dewey Decimal Classification.

8   A prime mover in the writing of music library history has been C.J. Bradley, several of whose works are in the Library's collection. They include her (1973), *Reader in Music Librarianship,* Washington, DC: Indian Head; *idem* (1978), 'The Genesis of American Music Librarianship, 1902–1942', PhD thesis, Florida State University: and *idem* (1990), *American Music Librarianship: A Biographical and Historical Survey,* New York: Greenwood.

9   The full history of how the British Library came to own the library resources at LAHQ is outside the scope of this chapter, but may be sketched as follows: until 31 March 1974 the material at LAHQ in fact belonged to the Library Association, but the Association was finding it increasingly hard to support it. The LAHQ Library and Information Bureau (LIB), as it was known, had cost £36 400 to run in 1971, £41 768 in 1977 and £45 290 in 1973. The LA did not have the funds to continue its support at this level, and therefore

asked for expressions of interest from outside bodies. The British Library's bid was considered the best, to the extent that it would protect the jobs of the current staff and relieve the LA of the financial burden of the LIB, henceforth named the British Library Library Association Library (BLLAL). A memorandum of understanding was drawn up, and published in the 1973 *LAR,* **75**, 237. By 1988, however, the British Library felt unable to continue on these terms, and a new agreement was made under which the BLLAL became BLISS – the British Library Information Sciences Service. It was made explicit in the new agreement that the BLISS collection would be moved to the British Library's St Pancras site when convenient, and would be made available as an open-access collection; see (1988), *LAR,* **90**, 412–13.

10   [Anon.] (1995), 'How do you want us to keep you informed?', *LAR,* **97**, 440–41.

11   Reported in (1981), *Fontes artis musicae,* **28**, 14.

12   Ibid., p.15.

13   Kaam, E. van (1982), 'IAML Library: a new section of Fontes', *Fontes artis musicae,* **29**, 72–4.

14   See (1983), *Fontes artis musicae,* **30**, 2–3.

15   IAML archives, secretary general's documents, vol. 27 (1983–86). I am grateful to IAML's archivist, Inger Enquist, for making this archival material available to me at short notice.

16   The report of IAML's business meeting in Tokyo on 8 September 1988 (printed in [1989], *Fontes artis musicae,* **36**, 9) notes: 'In 1980 a IAML library was established following a decision made at the General Assembly in Cambridge that year. The library, which is [that is, has been] housed at the NBLC Library in the Hague has received hardly any donations and no requests for lending[,] and Council decided as suggested by Ad Blokland, who has looked after the collection, to close the library down.' The mechanics of closing down the library were probably not complex, as the nexus of its collection had in any case been material already in the NBLC's collection: presumably the few donated items deemed to be of value were taken into the NBLC's ownership after the library's closure, which explains why the IAML library's collection never appeared for sale or dispersal.

Chapter 9

The unique first edition of Byrd's *Gradualia* in York Minster Library

Richard Turbet

It has always been a matter for surprise that the unique surviving copy of the *Gradualia* of 1605 sidled into Byrd criticism without a fanfare. It was only its appearance in the *British Union-Catalogue of Early Music* in 1957[1] that triggered critical attention,[2] yet its existence, if not its significance, had been noted in York Minster Library in each of the preceding centuries.

As early as 1782, page i of looseleaf item [2], compiled by William Mason, inserted into the front of 'Libor continens catalog. libror. musicor. Bibliotheca Cath. Ebor. anno MDCCCXXXVII' (MS Hailstone B7) lists as its first entry 'Tallis & Bird No 1. 24 books of 3 Setts'. The published catalogue of the printed music in the Minster Library[3] lists 25 such 'Books': five partbooks (one missing) of the joint *Cantiones sacrae* composed by Tallis and Byrd (1575); five partbooks each containing, in order, Byrd's first book of *Cantiones sacrae* (1589), the *Gradualia* under discussion, and two publications of sacred music by Dering (shelfmark P 2/1–5 S); six partbooks containing another set of Byrd's first *Cantiones* à5 plus the second *Cantiones* (1591) à6, the sixth partbook consisting of the Sextus part of the latter; four partbooks (one missing) of Byrd's *Psalmes, sonets, and songs* (1588); and five partbooks (one missing) of Byrd's *Psalmes, songs, and sonnets* (1611). As to Mason's wording, the three 'Setts' could be the joint Cantiones, Byrd's own two *Cantiones* (including *Gradualia*) and his *Psalmes;* or all three *Cantiones* (including *Gradualia*) plus two 'Setts' of *Psalmes.* The single numerical discrepancy may be the 1591 Sextus partbook, or mere miscounting.

What is beyond dispute is that 'Byrd (Wm.) Gradualia ac Cantiones Sacrae, 4to, *L., ibid.*, 1605', that is, published in London by Thos. Snodham, is listed on page 78 of *A catalogue of the printed books in the Library of the Dean and Chapter of York* (York: Sampson, 1896) (see Figures 9.1 and 9.2), by James Raine.[4] It is disappointing though predictable that Raine overlooked the import of his entry for Byrd's *Gradualia.* Nevertheless he deserves credit for providing what amounts to an analytical entry; the binding of the volume containing this and its other three items is contemporary, that is, early seventeenth century.[5] Much more disappointing is the fact that no Byrd scholar latched onto this piece of evidence, not even during the heightened publishing activity surrounding Byrd's tercentenary.[6]

A CATALOGUE

OF THE

PRINTED BOOKS

in the Library of the Dean and Chapter of York.

RECORDEMUR OMNI HORA, DILECTISSIMI FRATRES, QUALES
HABUIMUS PATRES ET PROGENITORES, QUAM PRÆCLAROS ET
PIOS, DEO AMABILES, ET OMNI POPULO HONORABILES.   NON
SIMUS DEGENERES ILLORUM NOBILITATE FILII !
[ALCUINI *Ep. ad Fratres Eboracenses*, A.D. 793].

YORK: JOHN SAMPSON.
LONDON : SIMPKIN, MARSHALL, HAMILTON, KENT & CO.

1896.

Figure 9.1   James Raine's catalogue, which as early as 1896 listed the unique first edition of Byrd's *Gradualia*. (Author's collection)

Butler (Chas.) Oratoriæ Libri II, *F. F.* 4to.   *Oxonii,* 1629
——The English Grammar, *F.* 4to.   *Oxford,* 1633
——(Chas.) The History of Bees, 8vo.   *L.,* 1704
——Account of the Confessions of Faith. *Presn. copy to Archdn.*
    Wrangham, C. 8vo.   *L.,* 1816
——(John) Sermon at St. Paul's before the Sons of the Clergy,
    May, 1754, 4to.   *L.,* 1754
——(Joseph, Bp. of Durham) Fifteen Sermons preached at the
    Rolls Chapel, &c., 8vo.   *L.,* 1749
——Primary Charge at Durham, 1751, 4to. *Durham, I. Lane,* 1751
——Id. 2nd ed., with Preface by Bp. Halifax, 8vo.   *L.,* 1786
——The Analogy of Religion, 8vo.   *L.,* 1765
——Id. Abridged by F. Wrangham. *"From the Author." Di.* 8vo.
                                                      Pr. pr., 1820
——Works of, 2 vols., 8vo.   *Oxf.,* 1849
——Some Remains of. Ed. Steere, 8vo.   *L.,* 1853
——Memoir of, by Thos. Bartlett. *Presn. copy to the Bp. of Victoria,*
    8vo.   *L.,* 1839
Butterworth (John) Concordance of the Holy Scriptures. Ed.
    Clarke, 8vo.   *L.,* 1812
Buxtorfius (Gerlacus) Dissertatio Historico-Juridica in XVII priora
    Aureæ Caroli IV Bullæ capita, 4to.   *Basileæ,* 1613
——(Joann.) Synagoga Judaica, *M.* 8vo.   *Hanoviæ,* 1604
——Thesaurus Grammaticus Linguæ Sanctæ Hebraicæ, *F.* 8vo.
                                                     Basileæ, 1629
——Concordantiæ Bibliorum Hebraicæ, &c., *B.* fol.
                                          Basileæ, Lud. König, 1632
——Lexicon Chaldaicum, Talmudicum, et Rabbinicum, *B.* fol.
                                                        ibid., 1639
——Tiberias, sive Commentarius Masorethicus triplex, 4to. *ibid.,* 1665
Byam (Henry) A Returne from Argier : a Sermon at Minehead,
    Somerset, *C.* 4to.   *L.,* 1628
Byfield (N.) The Principles, or, The Patterns of wholesome Words.
    6th ed., 12mo.   *L., J. Dawson,* 1637
Byrd (Wm.) Psalmes, Sonets, and Songs of sadnes and pietie, 4to.
                                               L., T. East, 1588
——Id., 4to.   *L., Thos. Snodham,* 1611
——Liber primus Sacrarum Cantionum, 4to.   *L., ibid.,* 1589
——Liber secundus Sacrarum Cantionum, 4to.   *L., ibid.,* 1591
——Gradualia ac Cantiones Sacræ, 4to.   *L., ibid.,* 1605
——*see* Tallis.
Bythner (Vict.) Lyra Prophetica ; sive Analysis Critico-practica
    Psalmorum, *F.* 4to.   *L.,* 1650
——Id. (*Exors of J. Jarratt, preb. Ebor.,* 1891), 4to. *L.,* 1653
Byzantine Historians.   Byzantinæ Historiæ Scriptores Varii,
    27 vols. in 24, fol.   *Venetiis & Lipsiæ,* 1729-51

C.A. *see* Champnæus, Champney (Anth.)
C.G.B. Plots, Conspiracies and Attempts of Domestick and For-
    raigne Enemies of the Romish Religion, against the Princes...
    of England, Scotland and Ireland, *C.* 4to.   *L.,* 1642

Figure 9.2   Page 78 of Raine's catalogue where the unique first edition of Byrd's
Gradualia **is the twenty-seventh item. (Author's collection)**

Notes

1   Schnapper, E.B. (ed.) (1957), *The British Union-Catalogue of Early Music, Printed before the Year 1801: A Record of Holdings of Over One Hundred Libraries throughout the British Isles,* London: Butterworth.

2   Jackman, J.L. (1963), 'Liturgical aspects of Byrd's Gradualia', *Musical Quarterly,* **49**, 17–37.

3   Griffiths, D. (1977), *A Catalogue of the Printed Music Published before 1850 in York Minster Library,* York: York Minster Library.

4   Raine lists the 1611 set as if it were a subsequent edition of the 1588 *Psalmes* which precedes it in the catalogue. At the end of the entries for Byrd, which do not include the 1575 joint *Cantiones,* he writes '*see* Tallis', but there is no entry for Tallis on either page 415 or 416. James Raine, styled *the younger* in the British Library catalogue to differentiate him from his more prolific father, was chancellor and canon-residentiary of York.

5   Brett, P. (1989), 'Preface', in Byrd, W., *Gradualia I (1605): The Marian Masses,* Byrd edition 5, London: Stainer and Bell, p. xiv.

6   Anon. (1923), 'The Byrd Tercentenary', *Musical Times,* **64**, 545–7.

Chapter 10

Information technology and music libraries*

Julie Crawley

Introduction

The first use of the phrase 'information technology', according to the *Oxford English Dictionary*,[1] was in 1958 in an article by Harold J. Leavitt and Thomas L. Whisler. Writing about 'Management in the 1980s' they described a new technology that had begun to take hold in American business, so new that it was difficult to determine its full significance: 'The new technology does not yet have a single established name. We shall call it *information technology*.'[2] Searching the online databases ERIC and Compendex the phrase does not seem to have generally taken hold until well into the 1980s.[3]

Information technology has meant different things at different times. It has increased from just a small number of applications to influencing most parts of our work and daily lives. Early descriptions of computer assistance involved little more than automated indexing using electronic valve computers. One of the earliest records of using a computer in musicological research was by Bertrand H. Bronson in 1949, who used a computer to assist with the indexing of *The Traditional Tunes of the Child Ballads*.[4] Other early applications in musicology relate to the development of automated encoding systems to identify musical themes or incipits, for example DARMS (1961),[5] and the encoding system by Bernstein and Olive (1969),[6] both of which build on the work of Barlow and Morgenstern's printed *Dictionary of Musical Themes* (1948).[7]

From the early 1960s use of computers in libraries presented a growing number of possibilities applied to different library procedures. Machine readable cataloguing data, which we now know as MARC, was first considered in the early 1960s. From the mid-1960s, online bibliographic databases began to emerge, such as *Index Medicus and Chemical Abstracts*, available via the database hosts DIALOG and BRS. In the late 1960s and early 1970s library procedures, such as circulation and cataloguing began to be automated, at first involving little more than punched cards and paper tape.

Hardware developments at the end of the 1960s changed things further.

Computers known as 'minicomputers', came to be used as satellites of the larger conventional 'mainframe' computers, and this was followed in the early 1970s by the birth of the 'microcomputer', making use of silicon chip technology, beginning a gradual improvement in processing power and miniaturization. The considerable reduction in size and cost meant that computers soon became an attainable reality for many libraries. The hardware developments inspired subsequent growth of software packages, such as Visicalc in 1978,[8] the first spreadsheet package, enabling use of microcomputers to spread from the enthusiast to the generalist. The launch of the IBM Personal Computer in 1981 pushed this development further.

The 1980s saw the launch of the compact disc (1983), followed a few years later by the text-based CD-ROM. This was also an important period in networking for the academic community with the establishment of high-speed network connections, such as JANET[9] in the UK. The library catalogue was one of the first applications to be networked in many academic institutions, obtaining the name online public access catalogue (OPAC). The late 1980s and 1990s saw even greater changes, with the huge networking and Internet explosion and the birth of the World Wide Web. Online bibliographic services became available through academic institutions free at the point of access and many other resources became available electronically, such as journals and digital surrogates of actual documents, along with digitization of sound and image. These developments all brought with them new challenges, meanings and applications of IT to music and libraries, as well as developing higher expectations from users. The 1990s saw a plethora of research projects looking at different ways of implementing the new developments in information technology.[10] Some of these, such as Encore!,[11] realized long sought after dreams, while others, such as Harmonica,[12] looked at ways of using the new technologies to meet the ever changing and growing demands of the user.

In this chapter I attempt to record how all these changes in information technology have influenced developments in music libraries. It is necessary to describe the general developments in information technology in libraries to place the changes affecting music libraries in context but efforts are made to draw out the music examples at all times. Written as a celebration of the last 50 years of IAML(UK) I make particular reference to the work of the UK Branch and, where relevant, to its parent association IAML. I have attempted to draw examples of developments and projects in music from all sectors of the library community but at particularly significant stages the academic community has led the way.

In IAML, the international body of IAML(UK), the first formal mention of information technology was recorded in 1965 at the IAML Congress in Dijon. A round-table discussion was held on the 'Utilization of data-processing techniques in music documentation'.[13] The principal report was given by Barry Brook and one has to admire his optimistic and forward-looking approach. The report makes interesting reading today because amid wild speculations Brook made alarmingly close predictions. At the time, no one (including Brook) could have known just how true the following would become:

The scholar-librarian in this brave new computerized world sits in front of a screen in his office or in his study at home pushing buttons with one hand and holding a vermouth with the other. His special typewriter enables him to hold "conversations" with a computer many miles away. Notetaking is hardly necessary since any page passing before him on the screen can immediately be reproduced in paper form or be recalled at will later.[14]

The MARC format and other early computer applications in libraries

The possibility of producing machine readable cataloguing data was considered as early as 1963 by the Library of Congress (LC) in the USA[15] but it was not until 1966 that the first pilot project transpired. This came to be known as MARC I, involving 16 selected libraries to receive machine readable catalogue records of current books. In 1966 the British National Bibliography began to investigate ways of utilizing machine readable data and discussions began into looking at an international co-operative project, between LC and the Office for Scientific and Technical Information (OSTI), in the Department of Education and Science. From 1967 BNB received grants from OSTI to develop and run experimentally a service providing at weekly intervals on magnetic tape the full bibliographic records of current British books. These records were made available in MARC II, which had become the standard exchange format. The tapes formed the basis for a number of research projects, including BLCMP,[16] which looked at how far these centrally produced records could reduce the amount of time spent cataloguing in local libraries. In 1967 the *Anglo-American Cataloguing Rules* were published.[17] A decision was taken, shortly after publication, to use *AACR* as a basis for MARC. For music, the publication of *AACR* in 1967 was a significant breakthrough. The standard codes prior to 1967 provided only very elementary rules for music, leading to music librarians applying very individual rules and the publication of *AACR* was the first time that music had been included comprehensively in a general code. Miriam Miller concluded: 'These rules (chapter 13 on printed music and chapter 14 on sound recordings) are not perfect, indeed they show rather too clearly the influence of the Library of Congress code from which they sprang, but they are immensely significant.'[18] The earlier Library of Congress rules for descriptive cataloguing of 1949,[19] to which Miller refers, acknowledged the problems of cataloguing materials other than books but gave only very peripheral mention to printed music, and reference to sound recordings was only added later in 1953.[20] The other important feature of *AACR* was the convergence of cataloguing practice between the USA and UK but ironically, it is interesting to note that at the same time, divergence was emerging in developments of the MARC format. In the UK, in the late 1960s OSTI funded many large and small projects to look at computer applications in libraries. *Vine: A Very Informal Newsletter* was set up to share the results of these early projects looking at circulation control and catalogue production at universities such as Newcastle, Cambridge, Southampton and Loughborough.[21] Southampton University Library started to look at the establishment of a computer-assisted circulation system as early as 1966 using punched cards and a machine called a collectadata, recording the transactions on paper tape. At the end of the 1960s, two co-operative ventures received OSTI funding, namely SWULSCP and BLCMP.

The South West University Libraries Systems Co-operation Project (SWULSCP, from 1979 known as SWALCAP) began its life in 1969. It was a major co-operative approach to library automation looking at the feasibility of co-operative automation of acquisitions, cataloguing and circulation across the university libraries of Bath, Bristol, Exeter and University College Cardiff. Its emphasis was on automating general housekeeping procedures as applied to standard book material, and it made important advances in this area.

Birmingham Libraries Co-operative Mechanisation Project (BLCMP) was a co-operative scheme between Aston and Birmingham University Libraries, Birmingham Public Libraries and, for the purpose of discussing the handling of music cataloguing, the Birmingham School of Music Library (now Birmingham Conservatoire). For music, this was the most significant of the early projects because from the outset it was the intention of BLCMP 'to integrate systems to handle all forms of material without obscuring the special requirements of any form'.[22]

BLCMP was set up to investigate the feasibility of utilizing MARC tapes within the group of Birmingham libraries and, later, in terms of developing a regional database. The project led to the design and implementation of an automated shared cataloguing system, using LC and BNB MARC records, as well as original cataloguing from the contributing libraries. The scope of the cataloguing programme included monographs received in the Birmingham libraries from January 1972, all serials held by the libraries, as well as other library materials, for the most part printed music and gramophone records received since the beginning of 1972. To look at the particular requirements of printed music and sound recordings a music group was set up in the early 1970s comprising Malcolm Jones (Birmingham Public Libraries), Kenneth Wilkins (Barber Library, Birmingham University) and Sue Clegg (Birmingham School of Music). The group produced a supplement on music and sound recordings to the BLCMP MARC Manual and, more importantly, showed that it was perfectly possible to use chapters 13 and 14 of *AACR* 1967 as a basis for a machine readable format for music. Peter Stubley summed up the music aspect of BLCMP: 'BLCMP created the first MARC file in the UK containing music and by October 1976 remained the only British music MARC format that had passed the theoretical stage. By June 1976 the union database contained over 15000 titles of printed music.'[23]

Further work was done on a national level and the Music Bibliography Group of IAML(UK), chaired by Malcolm Jones, compiled a proposal outlining the additions required to the British MARC practice by the draft music MARC format and this was submitted to the Bibliographic Services Division of the British Library. Jones summarizes how the British proposal differed from the US proposal in an article 'Printed music and the MARC format'.[24] He notes that the Library of Congress had produced three drafts of a Music MARC format. The first of these was considered by the BLCMP group, and the third and last by the Music Bibliography Group – but the proposal submitted to the British Library differed in a number of ways. A full account of the development of the MARC Music format in the USA is described by Donald Seibert.[25]

The emergence of different MARC formats in the UK and US has been attributed to the different practical requirements of the British National Bibliography and the Library of Congress, and at the time there was no obvious need for the two countries to adopt identical formatting standards. In Australia and Canada AUSMARC and CANMARC emerged, while in the late 1970s UNIMARC[26] was established as a common international exchange format adopted by some European countries. It has been only in the advent of later technological advances that these differences have proved a serious disadvantage and hindrance to the international exchange and retrieval of data, whether for sharing catalogue records or in searching multiple databases via a common interface, using protocol such as Z39.50. While the standardization of cataloguing practice has become more and more important, the need to accommodate metadata standards for digital material has also become an increasing concern.

Efforts to look beyond MARC have been taking place for some time. In 1997 the Performing Arts Data Service (PADS) in the UK held a series of resource discovery workshops, one of which was devoted to music. The aim of the series was to assess how the Dublin Core[27] descriptors could be applied to the needs of different disciplines. The PADS Resource Discovery Workshop for music was held at the University of Warwick 24–25 April 1997, funded by UKOLN[28] and the AHDS.[29] The workshop focused on sound resources but also looked at the needs of printed and manuscript music sources. The talks took the Dublin Core as an alternative descriptive framework to models such as MARC, trying to identify the main concepts necessary for efficient resource discovery in music. The participants were encouraged to break down original conceptions and assumptions and to look at a richer level of content description, more applicable to the special needs of the different music formats, taking into account the new possibilities and applications of the electronic age. A talk by Malcolm Jones mapped MARC onto the Dublin Core, pointing out some of the inadequacies of MARC for printed music. Chris Banks took the core bibliographic record for printed music,[30] and Chris Clark took fields from the National Sound Archive's catalogue Cadensa and mapped them onto the Dublin Core model. While none of the participants saw the Dublin Core as 'the answer' for music, we all believed the workshop was an important stage in looking beyond MARC and welcomed the opportunity to point out the specific needs of music. For sound recordings the Dublin Core actually proved a more successful model than the MARC format, which few sound archives follow.

Recent developments have seen a convergence of MARC standards, in the form of MARC21. This was formed when the National Library of Canada decided to integrate CANMARC into the Library of Congress USMARC in 1999. The decision by the UK to adopt MARC21 was taken the following year. The full implications of this decision are yet to emerge but in the long term, future cataloguing standards can be assessed from a common platform. We can work together in seeking methods of accommodating suitable descriptors for digital material, which will, hopefully, also be more suitable to the special needs of music materials than the original MARC formats.

The online bibliographic database

Today we are familiar with web-based bibliographic databases to search for articles in journals and to survey what dissertations and published monographs have been written in particular subject areas. We can do keyword searches of the title and subject fields, search the abstracts and, even, the full text. The norm is for users independently to search information resources and to want to obtain the document itself online. Gone are the days of mediated searches, when online charges required searches to be executed quickly and efficiently by trained staff, and when the users were bound by what was held in physical form within the library walls.

RILM[31] is a good example of a bibliographic database for music literature, which has moved through several different guises in accordance with changes in technology.[32] First published as a printed index, from 1979 it was available in online form via the database host, DIALOG, then in the early 1990s on CD-ROM, paired with the Library of Congress music catalogue under the name MuSe,[33] and since 1996 through OCLC's First Search service.[34] Initially RILM was only available through First Search via telnet but since the year 2000 it has become available via a web interface.

For international coverage RILM has been an important bibliographic tool since it began publication in 1967. The proposal for RILM was first formally presented at the seventh IAML congress in Dijon in 1965; however, IAML's plans to produce an international listing of articles from music periodicals goes back a lot further. Brook[35] recalled that this was discussed at the Lüneburg Congress in 1950. Alec Hyatt King of the British Library amplified the discussion of the proposed project to include abstracts at the Paris Congress in 1951.[36]

Brook was well aware of the early automated databases around in the USA at the time. In 1961 Luhn of IBM developed programs for generating keyword indexes to the titles of articles appearing in *Chemical Abstracts*.[37] It was also in the 1960s that the National Library of Medicine in the USA investigated using a computer to assist in the production of its printed index to medical literature, *Index Medicus* (the electronic database known today as *Medline*). Both *Index Medicus* and *Chemical Abstracts* aimed to achieve total bibliographic control of current literature in their fields, and it is clear from Brook (1965) that both of these databases were an inspiration for RILM. While periodical coverage was the primary aim of RILM, the secondary aim was to cover theses, books, *Festschriften* and annuals, all of which it covers today.

Database hosts, such as BRS[38] sprang up in 1965 and DIALOG[39] a year later. In the UK, BLAISE-LINE began in1971.[40] From September 1979[41] the RILM database was searchable via the US database host DIALOG. Keller and Lawrence[42] give examples of searches executed on the online version of RILM available through DIALOG. The costs involved meant that researchers needed to have a good reason for using it and have well prepared search strategies before turning to DIALOG for bibliographic assistance.

Currently, File 97, as RILM is known to the Lockheed computer, is available to Dialog subscribers in the continental United States at the rate of $65 per hour for use of the data base, plus $5 per hour for use of the communications network, known to the computer and its attendants as Telenet. Most on-line searches take between ten and twenty minutes and would thus cost between $11.68 and $23.34.[43]

Searching the online databases was costly, the charges were not only calculated by time spent online but also by the number of citations retrieved. Libraries trained specialist staff to search the databases for the users. The search strategies were usually formulated offline according to the users' expressed needs and so then the searches online could be executed quickly and efficiently to keep the costs to a minimum. The rapid technological advances in bibliographic searching also placed an increased pressure on libraries to obtain the documents. F.W. Lancaster noted as early as 1977 the need for similar developments in document delivery:

The rapid technological advances in bibliographic searching have unfortunately not been matched by comparable advances in the document delivery system. We now await the technological breakthroughs that will allow the economical transmission of microimages or digital text from a central store to remote user stations efficiently and cheaply.[44]

Today, progress has been made in the area of electronic journals but dissertations, monographs and printed music scores are also in demand.

CD-technology

The audio CD was launched in 1982 and recording industries quickly predicted the decline of the LP. The CD-format, a 12 cm optical disc read by a laser, was developed jointly by the Philips and Sony corporations. Staffordshire claimed to be the first public library authority in the UK to introduce compact discs for public loan in June 1983. The County Librarian, Louis J. Livesey, wrote: 'Though their cost against vinyl discs seems high for the public, it is extremely economical for libraries. Records may last for 70 issues, but often they are badly worn after only two or three. CD's give the same sound to the 70th borrower as to the first.'[45]

The durability of CDs was provocatively over-promoted by the recording companies and the public soon found ways of scratching them and causing them to jump but compact discs did gradually replace LP collections in public libraries. In contrast many individual collectors and academic libraries with archival collections retained their vinyl discs, recognizing the value of the older recordings, so vinyl never quite went away. A recent[46] revival in LP sales was noted by *The Times,* claiming that LP sales had gone up 40.2 per cent in 1999–2000 in the areas of jazz and dance music.[47]

Text-based information CD-ROMs[48] came onto the scene a few years later. Steve Brown[49] recalls that CD-ROMs were officially launched as a commercial product in 1985, promising a reliable data storage and distribution medium, while conforming to a series of internationally agreed technical standards. Brown wrote: 'From just 12 titles in 1985, there are at least 10,000 available today.'[50]

Moore[51] recalls *Vine* 64 (November 1986) was the first issue to include the mention of a CD-ROM. The announcement was by LA Publishing and SilverPlatter Information Ltd of their plans to launch the full database of *Library and Information Abstracts (LISA)* on CD-ROM. He added: 'Libraries were advised they needed an IBM-compatible micro with at least 512k main memory and a commercial industry standard CD-ROM reader.'[52]

As a stand-alone item the CD-ROM provided good storage of a large amount of data. CD-ROMs also gave users the advantage of being able to search for themselves rather than through a librarian. The cost of the disc and the hardware to run it was borne in advance and so searching could be much freer, without limits due to cost of time online or number of citations downloaded. Users could also make use of keyword and Boolean search techniques, to which they had not been introduced with printed indexes, and this encouraged user interfaces to become more user-friendly. As a consequence, CD-ROM technology raised users' expectations of methods of retrieving information and considerably influenced the future developments for bibliographic searching online.

Brophy[53] recalls how the adoption of CD-ROM databases by academic libraries led very swiftly to the implementation of CD-ROM networks, which were at first stand-alone networks but later became part of the library and then campus network. Bevan[54] describes the technical issues, which arose from CD-ROM networking and elaborates on the networking difficulties.

As early as 1990 McSean and Law wrote a scathing attack on the medium referring to it as destined for oblivion and 'one step on the road to somewhere else'.[55] McSean and Law claimed that very few users spent enough time on any one database to justify the cost. They also claimed that costs should be looked at in terms of cost of the hardware as well as the data, and that true savings were not made unless it involved the cancellation of a printed index. However, their comparisons fell mainly against the printed indexes, rather than the online databases. They did not mention the cost of staff time involved in mediated searches of online databases to be added to the online costs. Nor did they mention the new opportunities and ways of searching offered to users by CD-ROM technology. The realities were that with shrinking budgets, libraries were finding it hard to bear the extra costs of the new technology, which brought with it increased demands and expectations from users. Maybe it was these factors that influenced McSean and Law's scathing attack on CD-ROMs.

For music libraries the use of CD-ROMs took off in the 1990s, several years after they were first introduced. The CD-ROM version of RILM and the Library of

Congress music catalogue was demonstrated at the IAML conference in Helsinki in 1993, under the title MuSe. The *IAML(UK) Newsletter* of August 1995 includes an article entitled 'CD-ROMs – who has what already'. The article lists the holdings of music and the performing arts CD-ROMs in academic, public and other libraries. The two most popular CD-ROMs at that time were CPM Plus (the catalogue of printed music in the British Library) and Music Index. It should be noted that RILM is primarily of interest to the academic community.

For some music libraries and small specialist libraries CD-ROMs still have an important place today and have proved not to be as transient as Law and McSean predicted. They are a small compact means of containing data and they do not rely on a networked infrastructure which, outside academic libraries, has been lacking for public and small specialist libraries. In 1997 the IAML(UK) Annual Study Weekend included a lively session on CD-ROMs, which resulted in reviews of popularly used CD-ROMs in music libraries. The reviews are published in the *IAML(UK) Newsletter* of August 1997.[56] Some music libraries today still access RILM on CD-ROM.

Shared online bibliographic services

Developments in the academic sector took many of the benefits of CD-ROM technology and applied them to shared online bibliographic services, which were made possible by the developments in networking that had taken place during the 1980s. The cumbersome online search systems of the 1960s and 1970s were replaced in the 1990s by services, such as BIDS, EDINA and MIMAS.[57] They offered user-orientated interfaces with easily constructed search strategies, and became available to the user via the JANET network, free at the point of access, the individual institutions paying a fixed annual fee.

The first shared online bibliographic service in the UK was the BIDS, which was launched in 1991 by JISC.[58] It provided access to the *Science Citation Index (SCI), Social Science Citation Index (SSCI), Arts and Humanities Citation Index (AHCI)* and *Index to Science and Technical Proceedings (ISTP),* produced by the Institute for Scientific Information (ISI). Since August 2000 the ISI databases have been available through the Web of Science at MIMAS, based in Manchester. For music, the *AHCI* indexes a variety of music journals, as well as providing useful sources of material in related arts and humanities journals. The popularity of BIDs, from its inception in 1991, is traced in an article by Morrow.[59] At first BIDs was only available via telnet but by the end of the 1990s the web interface had become more popular.

In the USA, the OCLC launched First Search in 1991, containing its WorldCat database as a central reference tool. The OCLC is famous for its online shared cataloguing system, which was introduced as early as 1971. Today it holds catalogue records created by libraries around the world. First Search is also host to Medline ERIC, BIOSIS, ABI/Inform, the Modern Languages Association database, and since July 1996, RILM.[60] RILM became available through a web interface in spring 2000.

In the UK, BIDS played a major role in bibliographic research for the higher education community. The service was designed for the non-expert searcher with a menu-driven interface and widely available printed support material. An email option for delivery of results was introduced at an early stage. Since October 1993 users were able to mark articles and then order copies of the original for delivery by post or fax, paid for online or through an established account. In 1999 this was taken a step further by Ingenta journals providing an electronic option for the full-text. On First Search, some of the databases provide links to an Electronic Collections Online of scholarly journals where the full-text of articles can be retrieved, though RILM does not at present.[61]

The developments in bibliographic searching over the last few decades have been immense. Users connected to an academic institution can now access bibliographic databases from their own home. The librarian's role is no longer to do the searches for the user but to teach them how to use the databases effectively. With the development of the web, library catalogues first issued on CD-ROM are now available via a web interface on the Internet. There is even progress in providing digital surrogates of the documents themselves in the area of electronic journals, via service providers, such as Ingenta, OCLC's First Search Electronic Collections, Elsevier's Science Direct and Academic Press's Ideal Journal Service.

In the mid-1990s free electronic journals began to emerge. In musicology the first of these was *Music Theory Online,*[62] which began publishing in 1993. This was followed by others, such as the *Journal of Seventeenth Century Music*[63] and *Ethnomusicology Online,*[64] which both began publishing in 1995. The success of these gave additional encouragement to commercial publishers to experiment with electronic as well as printed versions of their subscription journals.

A survey was conducted in March 2001 by electronic mail on the IAML(UK) email list looking into the use of full-text electronic journals in music by music libraries.[65] The response was disappointingly small but it revealed an interesting variety of journals available in electronic form used by academic university libraries but according to the survey not by music libraries from any of the other sectors. The replies are recorded in Appendix 1.

In the UK there are future plans to integrate access to online bibliographic services, full-text services and other Internet resources through a series of portals within the over-arching framework of the Distributed National Electronic Resource (DNER), set up by the Joint Information Systems Committee (JISC).[66] This 'joining-up' of the information landscape is described more fully by Breaks and MacLeod.[67] While this can be seen as an attempt to synergize bibliographic searching and document delivery services further, progress still needs to be made in making a greater variety of material available electronically, as Lancaster noted as early as 1977.[68]

Electronic mail

Developments in electronic communication took place during the 1980s and 1990s. In the UK the setting up of Mailbase in 1989 at the University of Newcastle was of crucial importance to later developments. Funded by the UK Higher Education funding bodies and sponsorship, Mailbase was set up as a national service to provide electronic mail list and information sharing facilities for the higher education community. In the library community several small lists were set up, such as lis-info, lis-it, lis-poly and lis-univ but there was considerable overlap among the lists and little traffic. In 1991 it was decided to merge the small lists and to form lis-link, which is today the most widely used email discussion group for academic librarians in the UK. At its formation in May 1991 the list had 600 members but this increased significantly from 1993 onwards, peaking in about 1995. Williamson[69] explains the increase in membership from 1993 (by over 100 per cent in three years) with the explosion in access to the Internet. Prior to 1993 only a limited number of people in academic libraries had access to the JANET network. In March 1995 CTI Music,[70] based at the University of Lancaster, listed 44 dedicated music discussion lists. These included the American Musicological Society list, Early Music, Medieval and Renaissance Music, Middle Eastern Music, the Music Library Association list, Music Performance and Pedagogy, Music Theory Online, Musical Aesthetics, New Music, Society for Music Theory and Thesaurus Musicarum Latinarum.

In the summer of 1994 the IAML(UK) electronic mail list came into being, set up on Mailbase. It was initially set up for members of the Branch only and as a closed list anyone wanting to join had to email the list owner to gain acceptance onto the list. The *IAML(UK) Newsletter* of August 1994 announced the IAML(UK) discussion list to the membership: 'It has been established to provide a forum for discussion of issues, problems or events in music librarianship. It can also be used as an additional channel of communication for Branch news and business.'[71]

The email list was slow to gain membership. Established at the University of Exeter by the author, the first person to be signed up as a member was John Wagstaff at the University of Oxford, followed shortly by Chris Banks at the British Library. Figures from the IAML(UK) annual reports illustrate the very gradual rise in membership:

1996 – 48 members
1997 – 76 members
1998 – 97 members
1999 – 132 members
2000 – 144 members

A questionnaire sent out to academic members before the Annual Meeting of Academic Music Librarians in Birmingham in May 1994 gleaned some information on the use of electronic mail amongst academic music librarians at that time. The responses are summarized in the *IAML(UK) Newsletter* of August 1994.[72] The show only 16 out of 31 members having email addresses. Of those, only three wer members of other music email discussion lists, and these were MLA-L, Med-and Ren and Thesaurus Musicarum Latinarum (TML-L). Unfortunately th questionnaire did not distinguish between members who did not have access t email and those who chose not to use it. There were a number of people in th academic community who held out against using electronic mail at this time.

After the first year of the email list it was opened up to include anyone wh wished to join. The list owner still had the right to remove a member from the lis if it proved necessary but breadth of communication and contribution to discussion was deemed more important than whether someone was a paid-up member of th branch. Since many IAML(UK) events were publicized on the list a non-membe may subsequently decide to join.

Use of the discussion list developed as people gained more confidence. Th volume of traffic on the list for the year 1999 showed an average of 47 messages pe month. For ten months of the year 2000 the average rose to 69.9 messages pe month. Prior to the year 1999, the *Annual Report* for 1998 records, an average o only ten messages per month for the 53 months of the list's existence.[73]

Today, the content of the messages on the list is broad. Music enquiries requirin specialist knowledge, defying the usual sources, are passed over to members on th list gaining replies in minutes. Less experienced music librarians have gaine helpful advice from people on the list, including suggestions of printed sources an web sites to try. Unwanted periodicals, sets of music or monographs have bee advertised and found good homes via the list. Cataloguing problems have been aire and solutions thrashed out. Orchestral and vocal sets have been requested, after th usual sources have drawn a blank. The list is regularly used for announcements o courses, job advertisements, new catalogues on the web, useful web sites and branc news, though commercial advertising is forbidden. Practices and procedures withi different music libraries have been usefully compared via questionnaires circulate electronically by members. Opinions have been sought on government papers an national issues affecting music librarianship, such as the adoption of MARC 21 before a Branch response has been sent by the President to the relevant body. Ou workplaces are supporting fewer urgent phone calls to seek advice on professiona matters, and the Branch no longer has to pay for hasty mailshots to circulate documents to its members. The ease of electronic communication in speed and cos means that the Branch is more able to democratically seek members' opinions o matters requiring an official response, with the majority of members now havin access to electronic mail.

Music librarians have always been scantily distributed over wide geographica areas and electronic mail has helped very many of us in our day-to-day work t share skills and knowledge and provide a better service to our users. The email list which in November 2000 migrated to JISCmail (the successor to Mailbase) wil inevitably remain an important vehicle for communication for some time to come.

Networking and the Internet

Barry Brook's vision cited in the introduction to this chapter was written four years before the first large network was created in the USA.[74] While smaller networks were in existence earlier, it is now well known that it was in 1969 when the US Department of Defense created the first large network, ARPANET,[75] to link computers in different parts of the USA together. The developments that followed were gradual but by the 1990s the networking possibilities had exploded.

The Internet can best be described as a global network of computers, which communicate using the TCP/IP protocol, each with a registered IP number and domain name for identifying their site or location on the network. Transmission Control Protocol/Internet Protocol (TCP/IP) is the Internet standard protocol influencing the way data is exchanged across a communications link. While the Internet appears to the user as one large network, it is in fact many networks joined together.

Developments in the 1980s were led by the academic community, looking at new ways of handling information through networked environments. Stone describes how JANET (the Joint Academic Network) was created on 1 April 1984 by the Computer Board for University and Research Councils in the UK. It was set up 'replacing a variety of networks that had been established over the previous ten years to serve the scientific community'.[76] As well as providing high-speed network connections between all UK universities and polytechnics, JANET also connected a number of other organizations, which included the national libraries, library system and service suppliers and publishers. In the USA, academic institutions were linked by a similar network called BITNET (Because It's Time Network). These non-TCP/IP networks developed gateway connections to allow for the exchange of information. During the 1980s various enhancements and developments were planned, which included providing greater bandwidth for the transfer of data files, graphics and multimedia. In the UK this advanced version was named SuperJANET.

Like ARPANET, both JANET and BITNET were designed for the transmission of text files, programs and data. For the library, this provided the potential for electronic access to information not available locally, as well as greater co-operation between individuals and organizations by means of electronic mail. One of the first applications to be networked in academic institutions was the library catalogue, which became known as the online public access catalogue. The OPACs could be accessed within local networks or by logging into a remote computer via telnet. For library users the library catalogue could be accessed on campus from outside the library building, and librarians could access other university OPACs to check holdings before attempting an interlibrary loan or before advising staff or students to visit collections in other university libraries. A crucial factor in these developments was that the facilities made possible by JANET were without any online charge to the user, the fixed costs being covered centrally by the university.

By the late 1980s remote login via telnet was used to access a growing number of resources, not just library OPACs. Services such as *Uncover* scanning journal tables of contents became popular. In 1990, a BUBL (Bulletin Board for Libraries) was created as an experimental service by the University of Glasgow. In music a number of databases became accessible via telnet, for example the Beethoven Bibliography at the Ira F. Brilliant Center for Beethoven Studies at San Jose State University, the database consisting of books and printed music. Today this is available on the web.[77] Other examples specific to musicology and ethnomusicology are described in *Computing in Musicology.*[78]

File Transfer Protocol (FTP) is used to move files between computers connected to the Internet. It involves logging into a remote computer, executing a simple set of standard commands and transferring documents or software. Anonymous FTP refers to files retrieved from public data archives, which do not require an account. A number of music files became available in this way in the early 1990s, one of the most popular being the Music Archive at the University of Wisconsin, Parkside, which included popular song lyrics.[79] To locate files for FTP, ARCHIE[80] was developed at McGill University in Canada. ARCHIE enabled one to find the location of files on hundreds of FTP sites around the world, consisting of a database of file listings with a simple interface for searching.

Troutman,[81] in an article for academic music librarians in the USA, gave numerous examples of music resources available via telnet and FTP at this time, while providing a practical primer to help demystify the technological advances. The article describes the different network applications of remote login, file transfer and communication (that is, electronic mail), going on to describe advanced resource discovery tools – ARCHIE, WAIS,[82] Gopher and World Wide Web (WWW).[83] In 1994 the WWW was at its very beginning and its rapid advance in popularity and transformation of use of the Internet was unforeseen by most people, therefore it is of no surprise that the description of Gopher receives three times as much space as the WWW. At the IAML(UK) meeting of academic music librarians in 1993 a paper was given by the author on the history of networking,[84] and again, while the WWW was mentioned, Gopher was the prevalent information retrieval system at that time and so received more attention.

Gopher, the forerunner of the World Wide Web, began as a tool to distribute campus information to staff and students at the University of Minnesota. Following the client-server model, it consisted of a series of nested menus linking one Gopher server to another. Picking out menu items you moved up and down the menu hierarchies moving from one Gopher server to another with no perceived change in environment. By 1994 there were over a thousand Gophers, each with dozens of sub-menus. VERONICA (Very Easy Rodent Oriented Internet-wide Computer Archive) was created to deal with some of the problems created by Gophers and provided a means of searching Gopher directories throughout the world.

The World Wide Web originated at CERN,[85] the European Particle Physics Laboratory in Geneva, and like Gopher and WAIS (another forerunner of the WWW), the system was designed for the retrieval of information on the client–server model. However, the WWW contained a number of unique features.

These include the address system, known as the Universal Resource Locator (URL), the network protocol called HyperText Transfer Protocol (HTTP) enabling retrieval of text, hypertext or images and the HyperText Markup Language (HTML) used to create the documents. The popularity of the WWW has been attributed to its multimedia capabilites, its highly interactive nature due to the embedding of hypertext links within documents, and its user-friendliness. The ease of creating documents in HTML has gone some way to account for the proliferation of documents on the web, and the development of web editors towards the end of the 1990s made this still easier. In the future, the move to XML (Extensible Markup Language) may change this pattern, when the code includes information about the content as well as the structure of the web pages.

Many people attribute the sudden expansion in use of the WWW to the release of the first version of Mosaic[86] in mid-1993. Mosaic was easy to use and for a long time was the most popular browser for the WWW. Furner-Hines and Willett illustrate the sudden expansion by the following figures: 'there were 62 registered Web servers in April 1993 but this had risen to no less than 1,248 by May 1994'.[87]

Poulter, looking at the growth of the Internet, notes that the WWW and Mosaic also pushed interest in the Internet beyond the academic community: 'The biggest growth spurt was contemporaneous with the arrival of WWW and the Mosaic WWW client/browser in 1993, which sparked commercial interest in the Internet.'[88] Poulter illustrates the enormity of the growth of the Internet beyond the academic community by adding that by the middle of 1996 nearly 12 million computers were directly linked by the Internet, many of which were in commercial domains.

Like Gopher, the World Wide Web lacked an in-built search engine but while VERONICA was developed for Gopher, a multitude of different search engines were devised to search the WWW. Today, many of these use a type of program called a robot to wander or crawl the WWW, following links between pages. Whenever a page is found it is copied back to the site running the program and it is added to the database for later indexing to create a keyword search engine at that site. The first search engine of this kind was WebCrawler created in April 1994[89] and others quickly followed.

To cope with the ever changing maze of sites, containing information of varying quality, people have been looking at strategies from the beginning of the 1990s. The first web subject directory was The WWW Virtual Library[90] developed at CERN. The WWW Virtual Library presented an alphabetical index of subjects leading to subject resource lists containing links and brief descriptions of the content of the different sites. This set the pattern for other subject directory lists, such as Yahoo.[91] Subject lists for specific subject areas became referred to as subject trees, with or without descriptions attached to the links. For music, the most popular and extensive of these by the mid-1990s were the Music Resources list compiled by the Sibelius Academy in Finland and Music Resources on the Internet compiled by the Indiana University Music Library in the USA.

In 1995 the IAML(UK) web site was created by the author at the University of Exeter, along with links to other music sites on the Internet to form a music subject tree. The site was reported in the *IAML(UK) Annual Report* for 1995 as going live in June of that year:

> It consists of an introduction to IAML(UK), addresses for members of the Executive Committee, lists of members of other Committees and Project Groups, membership information, a list of IAML(UK) publications, information on the 1996 Annual Study Weekend and details on how to apply for the E.T. Bryant Memorial Prize and the C.B. Oldman prize. There are also links to other music sites on the Internet via the Music subject tree created for Exeter University Library's WWW pages in the Arts and Humanities.[92]

Further efforts to improve information retrieval within specific subject areas on the Internet have continued. The idea of subject gateways was explored in the Electronic Libraries Programme (eLib), funded by the Joint Information Systems Committee. The eLib programme was set up as a direct response to the 1993 Libraries Review commissioned by the UK Higher Education Funding Councils. The review saw the need for higher education libraries to look to technology to help alleviate some of the problems caused by declining book funds. Access to shared networked resources was just one of the areas under investigation but resulted in the establishment of the subject gateways, SOSIG,[93] EEVL[94] and OMNI.[95] The gateways were set up to identify specific sites on the Internet, with subject experts assuring quality control. As a continuation, the Resource Discovery Network (RDN) was set up in January 1999, to extend the project to include gateways for all subject areas, to provide end-users with clear and simple pathways through the mass of varying quality information available on the Internet. The gateways already established contain descriptions of Internet resources selected and maintained by subject specialists within the UK academic community, based upon agreed criteria determining relevancy and quality. Now links are being made with international colleagues, who are developing similar gateway projects in the Nordic countries, Australia and the USA.

Music is to be covered under the Arts and Creative Industries hub. A preparatory report and proposal for funding has been completed by CALIM (the Consortium of Academic Libraries in Manchester). A report given on 16 May 2000 recorded that they had undertaken research defining the sector, identifying stakeholders, establishing the demand for the new hub and recommending potential design features and content, together with setting up a business plan and marketing strategy.[96] From the RDN web site[97] you can access the individual hubs already running, in their differing stages of development.

The RDN holds an important place within JISC's wider vision of the DNER, a concept, which emerged during 1999.[98] The DNER is envisaged as an integrated service where information gateways, databases, abstracting services and full text repositories will be available virtually side by side, enabling the user easily to move between them. Some RDN hubs, such as EEVL, have already developed beyond their original gateway remit, to include access to related online bibliographic databases, integrating access to free Internet sites with subscription-based services.

Public libraries and the Internet

While public libraries were involved in early computer applications in libraries, they were slow to address the implications of the Internet. Automated circulation in several public libraries, as in academic libraries, first appeared in the late 1960s and was developed in the 1970s. Batt records that by the end of 1983 more than two-thirds of the 169 library authorities were, or soon would be, operating automated circulation.[99] In the late 1970s several public libraries began to make use of microcomputers to run spreadsheet or database management systems, such as Visicalc and Silicon Office but in the area of online databases very few public libraries became involved. In the 1980s, public libraries increased their range of microcomputer applications but began to be left behind as the academic community made important advances in networking. In 1995 the Library and Information Commission conducted a public library Internet survey.[100] The survey revealed that while 53 per cent of public library authorities had some form of Internet connection, only 3 per cent of individual service points in the UK had an Internet connection. The report went on to say:

> The survey uncovered general low connectedness to the Internet and low use of networked services. However, there was great enthusiasm among respondents about the topic and most very much saw the Internet in some form as an integral part of their future services. Many respondents were keen to talk about their plans for the near future. However, such plans as seemed to exist had limited ambition: typically they were to join the exploratory activity on a low scale, which typifies much of current public library Internet use. There did not seem to be a shared view of how networking might contribute to systemic change, or of how the public library movement should collectively define a future service role for itself in a digital future.[101]

It had become clear that if public libraries were to continue to be effective information providers they had to integrate networking and the Internet into their services. EARL[102] was conceived at the Computers in Libraries Conference of 1994 by people in and close to the public library community looking at the opportunities that the Internet could bring to the public library service. Following a scoping study EARL was officially launched in November 1995, with 33 public library authorities contributing. By the summer of 1996 Dolan[103] records that EARL had become a formal consortium of over 70 library authorities and related organizations. EARL established three core services to assist the public library sector in meeting the opportunities that the Internet offered: EARL Connect, EARL Information and EARL Developments. Within EARL developments a number of task groups were set up to look at developing networks and resources for different topics. The music task group was established in 1996. The founder members of the music group were: Ruth Hellen and Susi Woodhouse (jointly leading the group), Andrew Baker (Staffordshire) and Chris Muncy (Berkshire), with Viv Kuphal joining in early 1997.[104]

In October 1997 the Library and Information Commission published *New*

Library: The People's Network which identified public libraries as the future information hub of the community. The government endorsed this and set a target for all public libraries to be connected to the Internet by the end of 2002. Funding for infrastructure and staff training was made available from the national lottery through the New Opportunities Fund. This allowed public libraries to provide access to electronic information for the public and gave staff the opportunity to use the Internet to answer enquiries. Library staff needed to be able to assist the public in their use of information technology and a massive programme of staff training, centred around the European Driving Licence, was initiated. In addition, specialist courses were devised by several organizations, including IAML(UK), to teach information sources in subject areas. One of the great benefits of the People's Network for librarians working with music was that communication with colleagues in other sectors was now much easier, giving access to many sources of information including email discussion lists and databases, such as Encore! Public libraries had now, in terms of technology, achieved equality with librarians in academic institutions.

Audio and the Internet

The developments in information technology and in particular the Internet, have had far-reaching influences on all media: books, journals, printed music and audio. Traditional methods of marketing, selling, distribution and broadcasting have been questioned in favour of electronic means. E-commerce is in the thoughts of all developing businesses. The convenience of purchasing from one's own home direct from the publisher or recording company is already possible and developments in securing online financial transactions and copyright protection on the Internet are moving fast. In the field of pop music digital distribution is quickly becoming a reality.

Before the Internet, there were many changes to the physical carriers of sound products; vinyl discs were challenged by compact discs in the 1980s, and digital audio tapes (DAT) and mini discs found their respective roles in the market place in the 1990s. But the new means of sound distribution over the Internet has threatened to overturn everything that has gone before, challenging existing copyright law, undermining the present structure of the music industry and posing real challenges for music libraries.

The main advances in sound transmission over the Internet that have taken place during the last decade are streaming technology and MP3. Early downloading techniques involved a considerable amount of time and memory to download just a few minutes of sound. However, during the 1990s streaming technology was developed, enabling delivery of audio from a standard web server, utilizing HTTP over TCP/IP networks. Now data can start to be played before the whole file is received, in a steady and continuous stream. Progressive Networks of Seattle was one of the first to offer this software tool, which they called RealAudio. RealAudio is presently available free of charge from the Real Networks web site. Meanwhile, the company is continuing to develop further software products and services for the transmission of audio, video and other multimedia over the web. Microsoft's Windows Media Player is the only significant rival to have emerged so far.

MP3 (MPEG – Motion Picture Expert Group – audio layer III) is another fast-growing format enabling the downloading of sound on the Internet and strongly influencing future developments in the recording industry. MP3 compresses CD-quality sound by a factor of 12, producing a small file which can be quickly downloaded. To achieve the reduction in file size and yet still maintain the quality of sound, a method of perceptual coding is used. The human ear cannot hear every sound in a particular song, since we can only hear sounds within a certain frequency. Therefore the MPEG encoders read the audio file and determine which sounds are audible and which are not, before encoding the file.

In only a few years MP3 technology began to threaten traditional means of sound distribution for the music industry. The web site MP3.com was launched by Michael Robertson in November 1997 and supplied a list of unsigned artists who agreed to let their material be downloaded. When new software emerged to allow exchange of MP3 files in a more direct manner, people began to find it all too easy to copy CDs onto their hard drive and exchange music with other people on the Internet around the world, without the artists' consent. Web sites, such as Napster and Gnutella[105] soon emerged, using the new technology to bypass traditional means of distribution. Napster, in particular, was responsible for allowing music in copyright to be downloaded free via their web site. Developed by Shawn Fanning, he gave the program his boyhood nickname 'Napster', and on 1 June 1999 sent the program to 30 of his online chat pals. Sherman records: 'In just a few days, 3,000 to 4,000 people had downloaded Napster. Little more than a year later, more than 25 million people had registered to use the program.'[106] In the spring of 2001 Napster was taken to the US Courts where they were found guilty of infringement of copyright and were forced to delete many tracks from the database. However, the huge popularity of Napster encouraged recording industries to investigate ways of offering similar sites with methods of payment for the downloading of copyright material. By August 2001 a deal had been struck between Napster, AOL, Time Warner, EMI and Bertelsman, in which Napster users would have to pay a subscription if they chose to use the facility. Fanning is also said to be designing new software for Napster, which will allow artists, publishers and record companies to receive royalties instantaneously when a track is downloaded. Meanwhile, the other major players in the recording industry are finding means of keeping up with the new demand: SonyWarner Music and BMG Entertainment have reached an agreement with MP3.com and the Universal Music Group have entered into a licensing agreement with the music bank web site.[107]

Throughout history advances in audio technology have pushed the limits of copyright law. In 1908 piano rolls were at issue in the dispute between the White-Smith Publishing Company and Apollo.[108] The defendant Apollo was the victor under the Supreme Court's ruling of 1908 but the judicial denial of protection led to

Congress extending copyright law to accommodate the new technological advances in 1909. In the UK, legislation accommodating piano rolls and the new Edison phonograph came into place in 1911. Today, copyright law has a number of issues to resolve concerning the distribution of sound over the Internet. However, while the music industry is afraid of other unofficial programs equivalent to Napster emerging and so want to tighten copyright law, libraries have been restricted from fully utilizing the new technologies by the already tight constraints of the existing copyright law.

Two library projects that looked at implementing the new audio technologies in the 1990s were Jukebox, to widen access to rare sound archives across Europe, and Patron, to develop better distribution of audio and visual aids for study purposes at the University of Surrey.

Project Jukebox was an early project to make use of the new developments in digital technology, sound compression and telematics. Funded by the EU Telematics for Libraries Programme, the project was set up to improve public access to the audio collections of the major European sound archives. The project created a pilot scheme, where users from remote distances could get online access to the sound archives, as well as associated catalogue data, using the latest technology. Three national sound archives ran the project, the British Library National Sound Archive, the Discoteca Di Stato in Rome, Italy and the State Media Archive in Aarhus, Denmark. The trial of the prototype service ran from 2 October 1995 to the end of December 1995, involving seven libraries in Europe. Two of the libraries trialing the service were in the UK: the Barbican Music Library and the Music Library at Southampton University. The project assessed the service and equipment, the copyright issues and the user demand and requirements for such a service.

The project commenced in February 1993, before the Internet and WWW were commonly used. The network chosen to run the project was ISDN,[109] which was the only publicly available pan-European service at that time. It was also the cheapest means of supporting the type of service required and it guaranteed a continuous transmission rate and good quality sound. For sound compression and encoding MPEG layer III was chosen, again for the quality of sound. The technological developments were advancing rapidly and while using existing technology, the project found that the technology was not always as readily available as expected causing serious delays to the project. Copyright issues also caused problems, the legal conditions for use of the material varying from country to country. It became clear during the project that there was no precedent to the Jukebox concept of digital network transmission of protected musical works across borders and so the legal issues could not be clearly answered by the existing commercial and intellectual property laws.

In the academic sector the new developments in digital technology in the areas of audio and video, involving sound compression and streaming, were put to the test in a project devised at the University of Surrey, under the name of Patron. Receiving funding under the Electronic Libraries Programme,[110] the aim of Patron was to provide better access to the short-loan and restricted access collections in the performing arts. This involved developing a multimedia system to deliver on-demand digital audio, video, scores and text in the areas of music and dance, across broadband networks to the desktop. The maintenance of quality was of prime importance, the music needing to be CD quality and the quality of movement in the dance videos needing accurately to reflect the original performance. As with the Jukebox project, MPEG layer III was used for data compression of the audio components, chosen for its sound quality and as a recognized international standard format.

The project assessed the networking requirements, the copyright and licensing issues and the impact of the new facility on the learning effectiveness of the user. As well as being enthusiastically received by potential users, it also proved the ability to deliver the different types of performing arts materials in good quality on current standard computers and so inspired further research in this area.

Project Jukebox and Patron are two projects which have looked at the practical applications of streaming technology and MP3 in libraries. They are examples of projects which have attempted to use the technological breakthroughs to pioneer ways of delivering the materials to users. They have attempted to bring about advances in document delivery comparable to the huge developments in bibliographic searching in the 1970s and 1980s.[111] As technology develops further and methods of digital encryption improve, the ease and potential of accessing multimedia resources over the Internet in libraries must improve and one can hope that copyright law becomes more accommodating for library purposes. But what does the digital distribution of recordings by the recording industry or the artist themselves mean for public music libraries loaning sound recordings in the future? Will legal equivalents of Napster and Gnutella enable users to download music so easily and cheaply in their own home that it makes the public sound recording library redundant? Will the copyright issues for the music industry be resolved without jeopardizing further the progress of projects, such as Jukebox and Patron?

Conclusion

The speed at which information technology develops seems to escalate over each decade. In 1953 when IAML(UK) was formed, computers were far away from most peoples' lives and they had no direct impact on music librarianship. Today, for many music librarians it is difficult to remember a time when computers did not influence some part of their professional work. Few people would deny that the printed music score, the printed text or the sound recording in its original physical form is just as important today as it ever has been but technology has provided alternative and additional means of accessing content. In an attempt to provide greater access to our cultural heritage digital surrogates of valued documents are being made available across the Internet. In the USA several major collections of American sheet music have been made available in this way, for example the Library of Congress's Music for the Nation collection of digitized sheet music.[112] In the UK, the Bodleian Library has made available a digital image database of its Broadside Ballads collection.[113] This chapter has attempted to illustrate how the technological advances have affected all areas of music librarianship, from the cataloguing and circulation of items, to the searching and retrieval of the items themselves. The challenge to keep up with the possibilities technology provides has directed the course of substantial funding in the last decade, which is illustrated in Appendix 2. While librarians and users are thinking increasingly on global terms, the demands and expectations in all libraries are becoming increasingly more complex and difficult to fulfil. The changes that have taken place over the last 50 years have posed real challenges in all areas of the profession and it is largely due to IAML, and in this country to IAML(UK), that music has been served so well and achieved so much.

Appendix 1: Electronic journals questionnaire

Wed, 14 Mar 2001.
Dear All
I would be really grateful if those of you who dabble with electronic journals would take the time to answer the following questions. Please note I am only interested in MUSIC electronic journals, although something like a Performing Arts Journal with regular, significant, music content would also be of interest.
1. Do you refer your users to any electronic music journals? YES/NO
If answering YES, please name the journal(s) and the service through which they are accessed e.g. publisher's website, Ingenta, Ebsco, Indiana WWW site.
2. If you answered YES to question 1, for each journal could you indicate the category it falls into:
a) Free
b) Available in addition to the printed journal for an additional fee
c) Paid subscription to online version only
3. Has anyone cancelled their subscription to a printed music journal in favour of the electronic journal? YES/NO
If YES, please name journal(s) and service provider(s)
4. If answering YES to question 3, are the individual online journals
a) free
b) cheaper than the printed version
c) Chosen in preference for some other reason.
5. Does your library have:
(Please indicate as many options as apply to your library)
a) a web page with links to the electronic journals
b) links from a web OPAC using the 856 field in MARC
c) printed guides
d) other methods, please list

Wed, 28 Mar 2001.
Four responses were received from academic libraries.

The music e-journals listed by respondents included the following.
Free as part of print subscription:
Computer Music Journal accessed via Catchword
Organised Sound accessed via C.U.P. Journals Online
Plainsong & Medieval Music C.U.P. Journals Online
Popular Music C.U.P. Journals Online
British Journal of Music Education C.U.P. Journals Online
Music Analysis accessed via Ingenta
Notes included in PCI Full Text database
Totally free:
Journal for Seventeenth Century Music (Harvard U.P.)
Music Theory Online
Research Studies in Music Education (University of Southern Queensland)
Echo: a music centred journal
Polish music journal
Questions 3 & 4: No one had cancelled a subscription to a printed music journal in favour of the electronic version.
Question 5:
All 4 libraries that responded access e-journals via a web page with links.
2 of the libraries also have links from the OPAC using the 856 field in MARC
1 of the libraries added the URLs to the OPAC but no direct link
1 thinking about using the 856 field for direct links.

Appendix 2: Projects of the 1990s and onwards

The 1990s saw a plethora of research projects looking at different ways of utilizing the new developments in information technology. Funding for these projects came from a variety of sources. On the European level the Telematic Programme for Library Applications resulted in music projects, such as Jukebox, CANTATE and Harmonica. In the UK, one of the results of the Follett Report (1993) was the formation of FIGIT (the Follett Implementation Group of Information Technology). The remit of FIGIT was to set up a programme of development to enable the exploitation of the potential of information technology. This resulted in the establishment of the Electronic Libraries Programme. Music projects, such as Patron and Music Libraries Online received funding from this source. Another major source of funding at the end of the 1990s arose from the Research Support Libraries Programme (RSLP). Projects receiving RSLP funding included Ensemble. The programme aimed at making resources more widely available and encouraged cross-sectoral bids.

The following pages outline the main aims of the most significant projects related to music libraries during this period.

Project BARM (Building a Regional Music Resource)

This project was undertaken by Berkshire library services to establish a regional music database for the South East's printed music collections. It was hoped to lead towards an efficient music interlending service with the potential to evolve into a national resource. The project looked at enabling wider access and minimum record duplication, as well as working towards attaining bibliographic standards for music.

As local government reorganization was going to increase the number of small authorities co-operation and co-ordination of music resources was essential. Budget restrictions and reduced subject expertise had all contributed to the need for a co-operative approach to dealing with printed music resources.[114] The project evolved from the Access to Vocal Sets Project[115] and was later superseded by Encore!

Cecilia

An attempt to map the variety of music library holdings across the UK on a searchable database, covering public, national, academic and special library collections. Funding from The British Library Co-operation and Partnership Programme, Re:source and the Research Support Libraries Programme was received in 2000. The project will create a portal to assist people in locating music collections and in obtaining contact details for the institutions that hold them. Work is under way to gather collection level descriptions of the variety of music holdings in the UK. Further details can be accessed via the web site.[116]

Encore!

The project Encore!, supported by IAML(UK) in collaboration with the BL Co-operation and Partnership Programme, Norsk Systemutvikling AS, Mikromarc UK, EMRLS,[117] IN,[118] NWRLS[119] and the Library Partnership is the most recent and ongoing project arising from the earlier Access to Vocal Sets Project.

The first phase consisted of producing an online searchable database of orchestral sets records in UK MARC, combining the holdings of four different regional databases (EMRLS, WMRLS,[120] NWRLS and IN). The items that were duplicated between the regions were integrated into the same record. Standardization of bibliographic entries was addressed, as each of the existing databases employed different formats.

The second phase aims to complete a national catalogue of vocal and orchestral sets. It is also hoping to improve co-operation between the different regional library systems regarding the interlending of performance sets. The Encore! database is available via the IAML(UK) web site.[121]

Ensemble

Ensemble is a consortium funded by the Higher Education Funding Councils in the

UK through their Research Support Libraries Programme. It consists of the major music libraries that were already members of the Consortium of University Research Libraries (CURL) and a group of conservatoire libraries.[122] The initial aim is to bring about the retrospective conversion of printed music catalogues, by sharing all records free of charge. By working together the libraries hope to reduce costs and catch up on the enormous backlogs of music cataloguing. The first stage concentrates on the retrospective conversion of catalogue records for printed music from 1850 to 1975. Stage two will broaden these chronological limits to include works published between 1800 and 1850. In common with other such projects common standards and a core bibliographic record had to be established from the outset before records could be exchanged. In the long term it is hoped that the British Library Music Collections will be added to the consortium, particularly the British Library lending collection in Yorkshire. Long-term plans are developed further by Pam Thompson.[123]

Patron

Patron was funded through the eLib programme. The project's aim was to develop a multimedia system to deliver on-demand digital audio, video, scores and text in the areas of music and dance, across broadband networks to the desktop. This would provide better access to short-loan and restricted access collections and create more flexible methods of usage. The project assessed the networking requirements, the copyright and licensing issues and the impact of the new facility on the learning effectiveness of the user. A follow-up project Patron 2[124] is currently in progress looking at the integration of the multimedia resource into the curriculum running on a web browser. Patron Mark is another related project, originating from the Patron project, looking into the practical application of digital watermarking of binary images, audio and video.

Music Libraries Online (MLO)

Phase 3 of the eLib programme (1997) invited funding applications for 'large scale resource discovery' projects. Three of the four successful proposals were regional networks: CAIRNS, RIDING and the M25, but the fourth was MLO, the only subject-based project. The aim of the project was to use the Z39.50 protocol to create a virtual union catalogue for music on the WWW. The project was cross-sectoral but the proposal originated from the conservatoire libraries. It was set up as a prototype for other subject clumps, and to highlight areas which need to be addressed for further development. For further information the MLO database is at www.musiconline.ac.uk.

Project Jukebox

Funded by the European Commission Telematics for Libraries Programme the project was designed to promote wider access to the European cultural heritage for member states using the newly available technology. The two libraries in the UK involved in trailing the service were the Barbican Music Library and the Music Library at Southampton University. The project assessed the service and equipment, the copyright issues and the user demand and requirements for such a service.

Harmonica

Funded by the European Commission Telematics for Libraries Programme, the project ran for three years, from 1997 to 2000. The main aim of the project was to examine ways of improving access through libraries to music collections of different types using the new technology available. The project assessed how music libraries are currently organized and make resources available (literature, printed music and sound recordings), it analysed the changing needs of users from different groups and examined the new technological developments available for access and preservation of music resources. The work was carried out through fora, reports and surveys.

The project confirmed the growing desire to search and retrieve information sources, independently of where they are located. It also noted the importance for all libraries to use internationally recognized standards for cataloguing and indexing if we are to develop shared networks and to search effectively and retrieve resources. For further details the final report has been published on CD-ROM available from the IAML(UK) Library.

CANTATE

CANTATE (Computer Access to Notation and Text in Music Libraries) was funded by the European Commission Telematics for Libraries Programme. Beginning in November 1994 the project was set up to look at digitizing sheet music in Standard Music Description Language (SMDL) and to make it available online. The project conducted a survey to see how much music was already encoded and through which programs. It developed a translator to produce a standard code (SMDL) from the many commercial music encoding systems. The questions of copyright and the collection of royalty payments were addressed, and reactions were sought from libraries and publishers throughout Europe.

Notes

* Please note the body of this chapter was written in spring 2001.
1 *Oxford English Dictionary* – online version, March 2001.
2 Leavitt, H.J. and Whisler, T.L. (1958), 'Management in the 1980s', *Harvard Business Review,* **36** (6), November-December, 41–8.
3 On the Educational Resources Information Center (ERIC) database the first references to 'Information Technology' date from the late 1960s but it is not until the 1980s that

the phrase is frequently used. Similar results were found searching Compendex (a database of engineering literature, which includes many computer science journals).

4   Bronson, B.H. (1949), 'Mechanical help in the study of folk song', *Journal of American Folklore,* **62**, 81–6.

5   Bauer-Mengelberg, S. (1970), 'The Ford-Columbia input language', in Brook, B.S. (ed.), *Musicology and the Computer,* New York: City University of New York Press, pp. 48–52. Known as DARMS (Digital-Alternate Representation of Music Scores).

6   Bernstein, L.F. and Olive, J. (1969), 'Computers and the 16th-century chanson', *Computers and the Humanities,* **3** (3), 153–60.

7   Barlow, H. and Morgenstern, S. (1948), *A Dictionary of Musical Themes,* New York: Crown.

8   Developed by Dan Bricklin and Bob Frankston. Kelly, P. (1989), *The Use of Spreadsheet Software in UK Public Libraries,* MA Occasional Paper no.7, Leeds: Leeds Polytechnic Faculty of Information and Engineering Systems Department of Library and Information Studies.

9   JANET – Joint Academic Network.

10 See Appendix 2.

11 Encore! – an online national catalogue of vocal and orchestral sets.

12 Funded by the EU Telematics for Libraries Programme, the project ran from 1997 to 2000.

13 Brook, B. (1965), 'Utilization of data processing techniques in music documentation', *Fontes Artis Musicae,* **12** (2–3), 112–19.

14 Ibid., 113.

15 Stubley, P. (1988), *BLCMP: A Guide for Librarians and Systems Managers,* Aldershot: Gower, pp. 19–20.

16 BLCMP – Birmingham Libraries Co-operative Mechanisation Project.

17 Sumner Spalding, C. (gen. ed.) (1967), *Anglo-American Cataloguing Rules: British Text,* London: Library Association.

18 Miller, M. (1977), 'Music libraries', in Whatley, H.A. (ed.), *British Librarianship and Information Science 1971–1975,* London: Library Association, pp. 239–45.

19 *Rules for Descriptive Cataloging in the Library of Congress,* Washington: Library of Congress Descriptive Cataloging Division, 1949.

20 Lubetzky, S. (1953), *Cataloging Rules and Principles: A Critique of the A.L.A. Rules for Entry and a Proposed Design for their Revision,* Washington: Processing Department, Library of Congress.

21 More information in Overton, C.M. (1973), 'The OSTI-supported library automation projects' *Program,* October, 181–95.

22 Massil, S.W. (1973), 'Music in an automated cataloguing system using Marc', *Brio,* **10** (1), Spring, 3.

23 Stubley, P. (1988), *BLCMP: A Guide for Librarians and Systems Managers,* Aldershot: Gower, pp. 19–20.

24 Jones, P.M. (1976), 'Printed music and the MARC format', *Program,* **10**, 119–22.

25 Seibert, D. (1982), *The MARC Music Format: From Inception to Publication,* MLA Technical Report no. 13, Philadelphia: Music Library Association.

26 UNIMARC was first published in 1977; 2nd edn, 1981.

27 Dublin Core – a metadata element set, consisting of 15 categories, finalized in December 1996 and named after Dublin, Ohio where the original workshop took place.

28 UKOLN – UK Office for Library Networking.

29 AHDS – Arts and Humanities Data Service.

30 Described in *IAML(UK) Newsletter,* February 1997, 41–5.
31 Répertoire international de littérature musicale.
32 Music Index (1949–) and the International Index to Music Periodicals (IIMP) established in the 1990s, are other significant bibliographic databases of music periodical literature but RILM is singled out because it was conceived by IAML(UK)'s parent association IAML and has been marketed using a variety of technologies.
33 MuSe – Music Search CD-ROM available through NISC.
34 OCLC – the Online Computer Library Center based in Ohio introduced the First Search service in 1991 (see page 149).
35 Brook, B. (1965), 'RILM: deuxième table ronde', *Fontes artis musicae,* **12** (2–3), 120–23.
36 King, A.H. (1951), 'International scheme for publishing summaries of articles in musical periodicals' in V. Fedorov (ed.), (1953), *Troisième Congres International des Bibliotheques Musicales, 22–25 Juillet 1951,* Kassel: Barenreiter, pp. 62–4.
37 Large, A., Tedd, L. and Hartley, R.J. (1999), *Information Seeking in the Online Age,* London: Bowker Saur.
38 Bibliographic Retrieval System (BRS).
39 Dialog Information Retrieval Service of the Lockheed Information Systems.
40 Stone, P. (1990), *JANET: A Report on its Use for Libraries,* BL Research Paper 77, London: British Library Board [for] British Library Research and Development Department.
41 Keller, M.A. and Lawrence, C.A. (1980), 'Music literature indexes in review: RILM abstracts (online) and the Arts and Humanities Citation, Music Therapy, Music Psychology, and Recording Industry Indexes', *Notes,* **36** (3), March, 575–600.
42 Keller and Lawrence (1980).
43 Ibid., p. 591.
44 Lancaster, F.W. (1977), 'On-line information systems', in Kent, A., Lancour, H. and Daily, J. (eds), *Encyclopedia of Library and Information Science,* vol. 20, New York: Dekker, p. 404.
45 Livesey, L.J. (1984), 'Compact discs in Staffordshire', *IAML(UK) Newsletter,* **7**, August, 1.
46 Recent at the time of writing this chapter, spring 2001.
47 Quill, K. (2001), 'Setting the record straight', *The Times: Interface,* 19 February, 2.
48 Compact disc – read only memory.
49 Brown, S. (1995), 'An introduction to CD-ROM networking in libraries', *Vine,* 101, December, 3–5.
50 Ibid.
51 Moore, C. (1995), 'The life and times of a very informal newsletter: a quarter century of Vine', *Vine,* **100**, September, 3–7.
52 Ibid.
53 Brophy, P. (2000), *The Academic Library,* London: Library Association.
54 Bevan, N. (1994), 'Transient technology? The future of CD-ROMs in libraries', *Program,* **28** (1), January, 1–14.
55 McSean, T. and Law, D. (1990), 'Is CD-ROM a transient technology?', *Library Association Record,* **92** (11), November, 837–41.
56 Pp. 23–7.
57 Bath Information Data Service, Edinburgh Data and Information Access and Manchester InforMation and Associated Services.

58 Joint Information Systems Committee.
59 Morrow, T. (1995), 'BIDS – the growth of a networked end-user bibliographic database service', *Program,* **29** (1), January, 31–41. See also: Pinfield, S. (1998), 'The use of BIDS ISI in a research university: a case study of the University of Birmingham', *Program,* **38** (3), July, 225–40.
60 'Forthcoming announcement', *OCLC Newsletter,* (1995), 214, March-April, 33.
61 The *International Index to Music Periodicals* does offer a full-text option to some of the articles it indexes, at an increased subscription.
62 Web site: http://societymusictheory.org/mto/ accessed March 2001
63 Web site: http://www.sscm-jscm.org/jscm/ accessed March 2001
64 Web site: http://research.umbc.edu/eol/ accessed March 2001
65 Crawley, J. (2001), Electronic Journals Survey, IAML(UK) email list 14 March. See Appendix 1.
66 In 2002 the JISC announced that the DNER as an administrative entity no longer exists but the original DNER vision remains and the JISC collections and resources will be made available in more user-focused ways, through subject-based portfolios.
67 Breaks, M. and MacLeod, R. (2001), 'Joining up the academic information landscape', *Library Association Record,* **103** (5), May, 286–9.
68 See note 44.
69 Williamson, A. (1999), 'The history and value of lis-link', *Vine,* **109**, 35–40.
70 Web site: http://www.lancs.ac.uk/users/music/research/musicallists.html (accessed 17 March 1995 for a talk given at the IAML(UK) Annual Study Weekend 1995).
71 Crawley, J. (1994), *IAML(UK) Newsletter,* **27**, August, 5.
72 Crawley, J. (1994) 'Questionnaire responses', *IAML(UK) Newsletter,* **27**, August, 34–7.
73 P. 16.
74 See note 14.
75 Advanced Research Projects Agency Network.
76 Stone, P. (1990).
77 Web site: www.sjsu.edu/depts/beethoven/ (accessed 17 April 2001).
78 Hewlitt, W.B. and Selfridge-Field, E. (eds) (1992), *Computing in Musicology: A Directory of Research,* Menlo Park: Center for Computer Assisted Research in the Humanities.
79 Unfortunately, this later ran into copyright difficulties.
80 ARCHIE was created by Alan Emtage in 1990, while a student at McGill University in Montreal. The author originally planned to call the program 'archives'.
81 Troutman, L. (1994), 'An internet primer for music librarians: tools, sources, current awareness', *Notes,* **51** (1), September, 28.
82 WAIS – Wide Area Information Servers.
83 WAIS, Gopher and World Wide Web were all different methods of navigating the Internet.
84 Crawley, J., *History of Networking* handout. See also: Ledsham, I. (1993), 'The IAML(UK) Academic Librarians' Meeting, 13 May 1993', *Brio,* **30** (2), Autumn-Winter, 93–94.
85 Centre européenne pour la recherche nucléaire.
86 Mosaic – an early Internet browser.
87 Furner-Hines, J. and Willett, P. (1995), 'The use of the World-Wide Web in UK academic libraries', *Aslib Proceedings,* **47** (1), January, 1–32.
88 Poulter, A. (1997), 'The design of WWW search engines: a critical review', *Program,* **31** (2), April, 131–45.

89 Chowdhury, G.G. (1999), 'The Internet and information retrieval research: a brief review', *Journal of Documentation,* **55** (2), March, 209–25.

90 WWW Virtual Library available at http://vlib.org (accessed 17 April 2001).

91 Web site: http://www.yahoo.com (accessed 17 April 2001).

92 Crawley, J. (1995), 'IAML(UK) Home Page', *IAML(UK) Forty-third Annual Report,* 18.

93 Social Science Information Gateway – Social Sciences, Business and Law

94 Edinburgh Engineering Virtual Library – Engineering

95 Organizing Medical Networked Information – Health

96 Crawley, J. (2000), 'The RDN', paper presented at the IAML(UK) Academic Music Librarians Meeting, Birmingham, 16 May.

97 RDN website: http://www.rdn.ac.uk (accessed 17 April 2001).

98 See p. 150.

99 Batt, C. (1985), 'Microcomputers in UK public libraries: a review of current trends', *Program,* **19** (1), January, 39–47.

100 Web site: http://www.ukoln.ac.uk/publib/lic.html (accessed April 2001).

101 Ibid.

102 Electronic Access to Resources in Libraries.

103 Dolan, J. (1997), 'The EARL experience', in Ormes, S. and Dempsey, L. (eds), *The Internet, Networking and the Public Library,* London: Library Association, pp. 91–9.

104 *IAML(UK) Newsletter,* February 1997, 17.

105 Gnutella was introduced on 14 March 2000. Unlike Napster, Gnutella uses no central directory of files. It goes beyond Napster in allowing files of any type to be shared, not only MP3 audio but DVD, text and graphics.

106 Sherman, C. (2000), 'Napster: Copyright killer or distribution hero?', *Online,* **24** (6), November-December, 16–28.

107 Rose, N. and Buchanan, N. (2001), 'Taming the beast: the Napster case', *Multimedia and Information Technology,* **27** (2), August, 240–44.

108 Warner, J. (2000), 'What should we understand by information technology (and some hints at other issues)?', *Aslib Proceedings,* **52** (9), October, 350–70.

109 Integrated Services Digital Network.

110 See Appendix 2 for fuller details about eLib.

111 See note 44.

112 Music for the Nation – American Sheet Music at the Library of Congress: http://memory.loc.gov/ammem/smhtml/smhome.html (accessed 17 April 2001).

113 Bodleian Library Broadside Ballads: http://www.bodley.ox.ac.uk/ballads/ (accessed 17 April 2001).

114 Woodhouse, S. (1997), 'Project BARM: a rationale', *Brio,* **34**(1), 23–5.

115 Warren, G. (1997), *Access to Vocal Sets Project,* Development Funding for Public Libraries 5, Birmingham: West Midlands Regional Library System.

116 Web site: www.cecilia-uk.org (accessed 17 April 2001). See also Chapter 12.

117 East Midlands Regional Library Service.

118 Information North.

119 North West Regional Library Service.

120 West Midlands Regional Library Service.

121 Web site: www.iaml-uk.org (accessed 17 April 2001).

122 The University Libraries of Birmingham, Cambridge, Edinburgh, Glasgow, London, Manchester, Nottingham, Oxford and Southampton and the Conservatoire Libraries of the Royal Academy of Music, Royal College of Music, Royal Northern College of Music and Trinity College of Music.

123 Thompson, P. (2000), 'Ensemble: a vision for music cataloguing cooperation', *Brio*, **37** (2), Autumn–Winter, 24–28.
124 Web site: www.lib.surrey.ac.uk/Patron2/ accessed 17 April 2001.

Chapter 11

Larks ascending: co-operation in music libraries – the last 50 years

Pamela Thompson

Cooperation. This is an aspect of library services, both academic and public, to which lip service is constantly paid, but the practical results have usually been miserably inadequate.[1]

This dismaying summary of the situation E.T. Bryant perceived in 1985 is hardly fitting for a volume celebrating the fiftieth anniversary of IAML(UK) nor for a review of productive co-operation between music libraries, but it does provide a stark reminder of a time unlike the present when co-operation, not just between libraries themselves, but between libraries, archives and museums across all public and academic sectors, was far from the norm. It may also ensure that pauses for thought occur amid this survey of co-operation: to what extent does the co-operation now so constantly exhorted only pay lip service to that principle, how far and how fast does co-operation move from principle to practice, and to what extent has true co-operation between music libraries been achieved?

What E.T. Bryant omitted from his few paragraphs on the subject was any consideration of co-operation outside the formal public and academic library structures and any progress which IAML(UK) as a professional association had made by 1985. By that year there had already been significant calls in high-level library reports for increased co-operation, including that published by the Library and Information Services Council (LISC) in 1982, *The Future Development of Libraries and Information Services,*[2] key recommendations which included references to 'the growth of library co-operation', 'the need to facilitate co-operation across section boundaries ... between institutions funded by local authorities and those funded by central government' and 'the need to co-ordinate international library activities, particularly those concerned with the EEC [European Economic Community]'. Royston Brown, reporting on these developments to IAML(UK)'s Annual Study Weekend in Bangor in April 1985,[3] posed a significant question to members present: 'What influence can music librarians exert on the process of change, and how would you organise yourselves to monitor developments and promote the interests of your clients and staff?' Given the invitation extended to him to speak at the meeting and the collaborative cross-sectoral and international work already successfully undertaken by the IAML Branch in the preceding 32 years, it was not surprising that some resentment clouded members' responses. Equally, it focused members' minds and may well have elicited among them a new sense of purpose and some determination to see IAML(UK)'s achievements recognized and developed.

A review of progress since that time can only bear out that thesis. The 'ostrich-like attitude' against which Royston Brown warned in the same paper can hardly be said to have emerged. In fact, as will be shown, the Branch has proved itself versatile, determined and vibrant, not to mention opportunistic, in ensuring that the very considerable setbacks and, bewilderingly, the equally considerable new initiatives presented to music libraries have almost all been met with positive action. Annual reports of the Branch consistently reflect a degree of current awareness and a range of responses to government papers and library initiatives which may well give the impression that the Branch is a force to be reckoned with. Its most recent achievements certainly confirm that; the truth may, however, be that its pen is often mightier than others' swords and its commitment to its members' and users' needs and to music itself often banishes doubts about its strength, size and influence.

In 2001, the UK Branch of IAML(UK) had 254 members, a mixture of institutional and personal, some with international membership, others national membership. No fewer than 62 individuals were engaged in the association's day-to-day work on committees and project groups, while many others made contributions to publications, participated in the Branch's email list and attended its meetings and courses. Membership is higher than it was in 1995 and 1999, lower than in the years 1996–98.[4] There is no consistent trend beyond a buoyancy which is pleasing and which perhaps brings relief that the enormous changes wrought upon music in libraries in recent decades have not stifled its work and influence. If reductions and changes in music library services thwart its hopes for significant growth, regeneration is nonetheless frequently apparent and most recently witnessed in 2002 by the attendance of 18 new participants at its Annual Study Weekend in Durham. It has grown in a variety of ways and reinvented itself with imagination since its quiet beginnings in 1953.

Early in that year an invitation[5] to join the United Kingdom Branch of IAML, addressed 'to librarians, musicologists and all interested in music libraries', was sent from the Royal Academy of Music Library by Walter Stock. It invited the addressees to a meeting on 23 March 1953 and set out the objectives of the new Branch. These included:

to coordinate all matters concerning music libraries and music librarians and to promote their status; to cooperate in measures aimed at the conservation, protection and preservation of all forms of music; to cooperate with other national and international organisations in the fields of music, musicology, documentation and music library science; to cooperate with the parent body in the provision of a code for the cataloguing and classification of music libraries.

Twelve years later, Jack Dove,[6] describing IAML(UK)'s work, included the three objectives which the Association agreed at its inaugural meeting: 'to provide a platform for the discussion of all matters affecting music libraries, to stimulate interest in music bibliography, and to encourage co-operation in all branches of musical librarianship'. These were indeed the main points of the first constitution of the Branch agreed at that meeting and subsequently reported in July 1953 in Walter Stock's report 'The United Kingdom Branch of A.I.B.M.' in the International Association's *Bulletin d'information.*[7] These purposes have certainly been extended since 1953, but the cornerstones of the Branch's work as laid out in the current constitution in 2002 are still based firmly on co-operation, as these random quotes reveal: 'to bring together all members of the Association', 'to strengthen cooperation among institutions and individuals working in these fields [libraries, archives and documentation centres]', 'to cooperate with other organisations in the fields of librarianship, bibliography, archival science, documentation, music and musicology'.[8]

It is perhaps not so easy 50 years on to re-create the background to the times in which both IAML, our parent body, and the UK Branch itself were established. In the aftermath of the Second World War, during which so many libraries and archives had been destroyed, so many collections dispersed and international and, indeed, national contact between both musicologists and libraries suspended, the desire for reconstruction and reconciliation was overwhelming and a determination to rebuild educational and cultural structures was paramount. As early as 1949, the 'Premier Congrès des bibliothèques musicales'[9] in Florence, attended by some 60 music scholars, librarians and museum curators, considered 'the most urgent task to be that of fostering international links between musicologists and, concomitantly, world-wide co-operation between music libraries'.[10] It was suggested by Friedrich Blume that 'a further international music library congress should be held the following year in Lüneberg'.[11] It took place in 1950 and gave rise to a concrete proposal for the creation of an international association of music libraries.[12] By the following year, the Association became a reality, and by 1953 the UK Branch, as described above, had been created.

In an association like IAML, whose very being arose from a need for co-operation and whose single most focused aim was furtherance of it, any consideration of the co-operation achieved constitutes a very broad subject, for there are few activities of the Association which might not to a greater or lesser extent be considered co-operative. The very fact that IAML(UK) has no paid staff nor officers means that every activity must be undertaken on a voluntary and collaborative basis. Contributions to IAML's journals and newsletters, whether produced by the International Association or by a national branch, almost invariably come from members who collaborate in ensuring the publications' relevance and continuation. The writing of this celebratory volume is itself an act of co-operation, as Richard Turbet, its editor from the University of Aberdeen, pointed out at the Branch's Annual Study Weekend in April 2002. The extensive documentation projects initiated and carried through equally demand collective bibliographical and organizational effort. Meetings of the Association, in this country or abroad, are a joint effort in organization, and the papers given at conferences are mostly contributed by members. The courses run by IAML(UK) depend upon members' freely given time. The very existence of national branches is due to a coming together of members, the committee structures they create and the voluntary endeavours of all involved. Beyond those organized structures, perhaps the most telling contributions to co-operation come at the most basic levels of informal discussion after meetings, networks of colleagues who can be contacted for information or for the exchange or loan of materials and, quite simply, through the friendships which develop. These co-operative benefits cannot be quantified, but are indubitably just as important as the wider, more formal collaborative projects established within IAML at international and national level or the national, regional and local co-operative initiatives established in parallel, beyond the auspices of IAML(UK) although often involving its members.

The varied membership of IAML itself reflects its spirit of equality and non-sectarianism. Members come from every type of music library, from public, national, university, conservatoire, broadcasting or orchestral libraries, and from music information centres and composer archives, and the Association is happy to invite into the fold any others who are interested in and wish to contribute to its work. Indeed, some of its members in the retail and publishing sectors have made significant contributions to IAML's work and frequently offer support to those attending conferences or to the Branch's financial administration and projects. There is a two-way process of contact and advice to the mutual benefit of all involved. There is also a refreshing lack of hierarchy, with members meeting and working together regardless of their positions within their libraries or of the relative standing of those libraries. The experienced may well speak more than they intend at annual meetings, but contributions from and interaction with the newer and younger members present seems to be an unspoken point of principle.

This essence of co-operative enterprise and mutual support was curiously such a given that it was rarely spelt out in the Branch's early days, Even in the earliest years of *Brio,* IAML(UK)'s journal founded in 1964, references to formal co-operative projects were minimal, with the benefits of *international* projects and work stressed much more often than such activities in the UK Branch which seems at least publicly to have limited its collaborative undertakings to questionnaires on the status of music libraries. Such negative evidence is perhaps testimony to IAML(UK)'s underlying ethos, that co-operation is the essence of the Branch. Walter Stock, reporting on the 1965 international congress in Dijon, summed up what for most members of the Branch is its principal value: 'The real value of the congress became apparent when delegates from places as far apart as Sweden and Brazil, America and Finland found an opportunity to exchange views.'[13] This sentiment is so often echoed at IAML(UK)'s Annual Study Weekends, that its currency is beyond doubt, as is that of the value of collaborative projects for the greater good of all music libraries, first conveyed lucidly in print in *Brio* in Robert Vollans's tribute to Lionel McColvin in 1966: 'he encouraged the branch in its efforts to create and foster projects which would be of use to music librarians as a whole.'[14]

Such projects were from the very beginnings of IAML, both internationally and in the UK Branch, fundamental concerns. Within a year of IAML's foundation some of the major projects which were to occupy it for years to come had been initiated, with the active participation of UK members, most prominently Alec Hyatt King of the British Museum who was a Board member. At the meeting of the Association in Utrecht[15] in 1952, just one year after its foundation, it was reported that working commissions had already been set up to further work on RISM (Répertoire international des sources musicales/International Inventory of Musical Sources)[16] jointly with the International Musicological Society and on an international code for the cataloguing of music,[17] one which, as Alec Hyatt King later noted, would be internationally accepted.[18]

While work on RISM continues to exercise the ingenuity of those members of IAML(UK) in research libraries, the task in those early days did not seem quite so daunting. Work was already in progress on *The British Union-Catalogue of Early Music*,[19] which was to record the holdings of music published before 1800 in over 100 British libraries, resulting in some 55 000 entries. This would constitute the bedrock of the UK's research on its own holdings of printed music for transfer to the international inventory, even though omissions continued to be found.[20] Work on the manuscript holdings of the libraries could then be taken forward by a UK RISM commission, chaired by C.B. Oldman. By 1967, thanks to funding by the British Museum, Walter Stock could report[21] that the two cataloguers under the Commission's direction continued to make good progress, with over 50 000 records of the pre-1800 manuscripts of 18 libraries already completed. By the early 1980s, funds were again sought by the RISM (UK) Trust and gained from the British Library to enable further documentation of manuscripts. A more fallow period followed, but work for RISM has now been revitalized with the recent award of a major grant by the Arts and Humanities Research Board (AHRB) to Royal Holloway, University of London, which will enable the creation of over 25 000 more records for manuscripts.[22] This will leave the not inconsiderable task of documenting cathedral holdings of manuscripts and any printed works acquired since the original work was done, unless or until a proposal comes to record nineteenth-century holdings!

Contributions to the next major international joint project, RILM,[23] computerized abstracting service and bibliography of scholarly writings on music throughout the world begun in 1966, were also facilitated by the British Library, with the assistance of volunteer contributors whose work continues to this day. Work on RILM has likewise been refreshed in recent years by a grant from the AHRB, again under the auspices of Royal Holloway.[24] Another joint project, RIPM (Répertoire international de la presse musicale),[25] providing indexes to the musical press of the nineteenth century, also had input from the UK, with six important titles published and a further one *The Musical World* in preparation. The other of IAML's joint projects, RIdIM (Répertoire international d'iconographie musicale), which records iconographical representations of music and musicians, has fared less well. While much work was undertaken at the Royal College of Music some years ago, independent funding and staffing have never been sufficient to make a real impact. Efforts are currently under way to establish RIdIM work on a firmer basis.

Two new areas of international documentation, databases for which are currently being tested at Brigham Young University, will continue to keep IAML(UK) occupied. The first concerns music archives, the second concert programmes, both areas of increasing interest for researchers. Beyond UK involvement in the testing, some practical steps to aid UK participation have been initiated and funded by the Music Libraries Trust. A scoping study of the locations and range of concert programme holdings in UK libraries is already under way and will, according to the publicity leaflet produced by the project's co-ordinator, Rupert Ridgewell of the British Library, produce 'a methodology for a longer-term project, provide estimates of scale and cost, identify cataloguing and IT requirements, evaluate conservation needs and suggest strategies for the discovery of further collections'.[26] A further study towards a register of musicians' papers is planned for later in 2002.

With such intimidating commitments to international projects, it would not have been surprising if IAML(UK) had refused to contemplate any documentation programmes of its own, but as early as 1968 tentative thoughts began to emerge. *Brio's* 'Notes and news' column contained an item on loans of multiple copies of choral, operatic and orchestral scores, in which Walter Stock ventured: 'The Secretary would like to compile a list of such libraries [who offer this service] with a view to assisting other librarians in their quest for such copies'.[27] Thus the seeds of an idea for a union catalogue were sown, but germination and growth took rather longer. The matter had certainly been touched upon again by 1974 when Malcolm Jones of Birmingham Libraries reported: 'The joint working party of IAML(UK) and the AVG (Audio-Visual Group of the Library Association) has proposed initially the production of a national union catalogue of orchestral materials. There is a possibility of the cooperation of the British Library in the project.'[28] By the following year's conference in Aberystwyth, a definite announcement of a national union catalogue of orchestral sets complete with an editor, Sheila Cotton (later Compton), and funding from the Polytechnic of North London, could be made, and all libraries were invited to co-operate.[29] By 1976, 34 500 sets had been identified from questionnaires[30] and further funding awarded by the British Library Lending Division,[31] although at that year's Oxford conference Miriam Miller of the BBC in a contribution, *Trends in Music Librarianship*, remarked, 'The notable thing about all these achievements is that they have been done by groups of music librarians working amongst themselves rather than as a result of any central or official interest'.[32]

Such a promising start was alas thwarted. One year on, the *British Union Catalogue of Orchestral Sets (BUCOS)* was reported to be in difficulty, as the data was held in a British Library computer for which the British Library had other priorities.[33] Only in 1982 could Brian Redfern, then President of IAML, announce at the international conference in Brussels that after ten years' work *BUCOS*[34] had finally been published. He commented: 'The history of the orchestral catalogue would make a very good cautionary tale, as well as providing a good research project for some future students. Perhaps IAML(UK) ought to enforce the fifty year secrecy rule ... .'[35]

It was indeed a cautionary tale, but not one much heeded by the Branch, which had further adventures both in mind and in train. As George Pratt noted in a review,[36] which welcomed the catalogue for both librarians and borrowers, 'the biggest single problem, however, is to keep *BUCOS* up-to-date as borrowers lose irreplaceable parts and libraries acquire new material'. Interestingly, while this did remain a concern, the future of *BUCOS* was less convoluted than he feared, as the British Library in Boston Spa did take the matter of updates under its wing and its indomitable Tony Reed repeatedly whipped recalcitrant reporters from libraries into action. A second edition of *BUCOS* was published in 1989[37] and Tony Reed's successors in Boston Spa continued to note updates until their data was finally subsumed into Encore! (of which more below) in 2001.

The same review of *BUCOS* by George Pratt noted the need for a similar union catalogue for sets of vocal music, reiterating the hopes of Walter Stock in 1967 and, assuredly, of all music librarians thereafter, as Brian Redfern noted in 1982:[38]

> Librarians receive many pleas from users for a similar catalogue for vocal music. In fact the material is much more difficult to deal with. It has been decided therefore to cover this on a regional basis. So far we have had catalogues for London and the South East and the East Midlands.

Vocal music was indeed a format more difficult to handle, the quantities of material being greater and the bibliographic detail more complex. The regional catalogue was a pattern which was to be replicated across the country, with regional catalogues painfully and slowly emerging in the UK regional library systems. Valuable as these were, they quickly went out of date and only some were published, a situation which led to a notable imbalance in the use of collections and more than a little lamentation. This was compounded by the fact that many inexperienced library staff without musical expertise had to handle requests from borrowers, resulting in costly problems in handling requests and obtaining material. As was noted by Tony Reed in an article[39] based on a talk at a Library Association/IAML course in 1983:

> Here in particular we are up against the most important point of all for cooperation between libraries ... it is especially important for sets; since central provision is not possible for these, availability can only be assured by a considerable degree of cooperation in both acquisition and exchange of information. There are increasing signs of cooperation locally, both within the RLBS [*sic* Regional Library Bureaux] and independently. There is very little sign of much cooperation *between* regions, on a national basis ... . It is a truism, which has apparently still to be discovered by many librarians, that cooperation is a two-way business ... . As a result, those libraries that do cooperate are deluged with requests and before long are applying loan restrictions as their own antidote to this. Then a vicious circle sets in, a situation which not only endangers goodwill between libraries, but affects availability even more adversely.

It was a conundrum which ran and ran, despite assistance at various times from the Library Information Cooperation Council and CONARLS (Circle of Officers of National, Academic and Regional Library Systems). Knowing that they lacked the resources at that time to embark on a national union catalogue of vocal sets, IAML(UK) took the pragmatic approach, setting up a working group under the able direction of Malcolm Lewis to produce guidelines which might make the process more efficient and effective. The result was *Sets of Vocal Music: A Librarian's Guide to Inter-Lending Practice*,[40] a best-seller in IAML(UK) terms. The need for a union catalogue continued to be pressed.

The other major union catalogue on which IAML(UK) was working from the mid-1970s was one for music periodicals. As early as 1975 Anthony Hodges (a true begetter of ideas for union catalogues over the years) had suggested 'a cooperative effort in the acquisition of music periodicals, coupled with a union catalogue'.[41] The catalogue was to embrace the holdings of all UK and Irish libraries and, true to form, Hodges embarked on collecting the data in his own time, 'an effort for which he deserves the thanks of every music librarian in the United Kingdom', as Brian Redfern so aptly put it.[42] The course of true devotion ran no more smoothly however. It took until 1985 for the *British Union Catalogue of Music Periodicals (BUCOMP)* to appear,[43] but once it did, its comprehensive coverage marked it out as 'a landmark of musico-bibliographic literature' as Roger Taylor of Somerset County Music Library subsequently observed.[44] Under these circumstances it would be a bold successor who would take on a second edition, but by 1992 a volunteer emerged from the Library of the Faculty of Music in Oxford – John Wagstaff. This time a more sensible arrangement was made with a commercial publisher, a project committee of volunteer assistants was assembled, there had been much progress elsewhere in the documentation of music periodicals which could ease the work, and computers were much more advanced. With a few inevitable delays but with admirable smoothness, publication was achieved in 1998. John Wagstaff would give due credit to his team, but in fact the lion's share of the work was his.

During the gestation period of these major undertakings, IAML(UK) did not relax its other publication programmes. *Brio* continued to appear twice a year, almost always on time, as it has since 1984, but with somewhat less timeliness over the years, the *Annual Survey of Music Libraries*, under a fine succession of editors: Roger Taylor, Celia Prescott, Christopher Bornet and Adrian Dover. Its future is currently under review. Its purpose was to collect statistics on the holdings, staffing and services of all UK music libraries to provide solid evidence for comparative study and further research, an aim which it achieved admirably until pressures of work in recent years for a shrinking band of designated music librarians caused the return of questionnaires to diminish.

It was another publication in 1988 which set in motion further endeavours by IAML(UK) to investigate access to music. This was *The Availability of Printed Music in Great Britain: A Report*, published by IAML(UK) with support from the Arts Council of Great Britain. It explored extensively the relationship between the commercial sector and music libraries, but considered access to music and co-operation between libraries in that broader framework and provoked much thought on what further research was needed.

In parallel, from 1983 onwards the Branch's Trade and Copyright Committee had embarked on a ground-breaking exercise to formulate a numbering system which could become an internationally-accepted standard for the identification of printed music materials.[45] The lack of a control number was already hampering co-operative cataloguing and the exchange of records, while the multiplicity of different versions and forms of the same work made the creation of a unique identifier for each publication highly desirable. For eight years, Malcolm Jones of Birmingham Libraries, Malcolm Lewis of Nottinghamshire County Library and Alan Pope of Blackwell's worked to develop the standard and to gain acceptance for it. Finally in 1992 the Draft International Standard ISO/DIS 10957 for an International Standard Music Number (ISMN) was approved.[46] Since that time, ISMN agencies have been set up around the world, most recently in Turkey and Australia, with the USA soon, it is hoped, to follow. In 1994 the branch made a Special Achievement Award for Outstanding Achievement to all three members who, as Roger Taylor reported, had 'a record of inspiration, frustration, and persistence ... which has brought about one of the greatest achievements of IAML(UK)'.[47] Each recipient was presented with a copy of the first publication to bear an ISMN.

Despite so much co-operation between branch members in carrying through these individual projects, the Branch had long been aware that the multitude of different co-operative schemes of varying kinds in operation around the country – and the lack of them in other places – was hampering the creation of a good national strategy for music libraries. As early as 1976 Miriam Miller had noted that greater co-operation was necessary, between both music libraries and the publishers and booksellers who provided library materials.[48] By 1987, Malcolm Jones was making a plea that 'effort put into the area of developing new technology and adaptations of existing programmes for a particular library need not, and indeed should not, duplicate work being done elsewhere'. The reporter, Rachel Draper, noted that this was something which would demand increased co-operation and communication between libraries.[49]

The growth in the utilization of information technology, which might be expected to aid collaboration, had perhaps paradoxically exacerbated pre-existing difficulties, whether in the public library sector or elsewhere. While regional library systems and individual institutions were investing in ever more expensive computer systems, little was at that stage being done to ensure that they would be compatible and thus adaptable to shared cataloguing and the exchange of records. This was a great enough problem for the cataloguing of monographs, but for printed music, so often included in systems for monographs fundamentally unsuitable for music's and music users' needs, the difficulties were greatly, and in the long term expensively, compounded. Often music's 'difficulties' were viewed as so complex that music collections were simply left aside while vast cataloguing and retrospective conversion projects advanced.

None of this facilitated improvements in the interlibrary lending of music, as regional authorities built up their own systems for regional use which might or might not include holdings of music. In the universities sector there was at least the development of the Consortium of University Research Libraries which took in many of the foremost music collections in universities with policies for shared cataloguing and a common interface for university users. Among the conservatoires, access to technology developed rather more slowly. The BBC embarked on the automation of its own catalogues. But, overall, little attention was paid to national co-operative development.

Progress towards co-operation within regional systems for libraries not unnaturally produced a concomitant development in the music collections their members held. Early in the 1960s the North Western Regional Library System had even begun a scheme for the purchase of multiple copies of vocal scores with both acquisitions and the loan of scores shared among the partner libraries.[50] Such schemes were gradually taken up by many of the regional authorities and where possible central catalogues were developed both for their sets and for their individual scores and recordings. In the South West Region and in Yorkshire an even more centralized approach was taken. In Plymouth a collection of sets to serve the whole South West Regional Library System was developed, and local authorities in Yorkshire agreed to co-operate to establish a centralized music collection in Wakefield, now one of the most extensive in the country with over 500 000 items of music. In London, Westminster Music Library, taking in the collections built up by public libraries in Westminster and by the Central Music Library, an independent trust, has acted as a focal and access point for all the borough and branch libraries in London, its exceptional music collections serving the needs of many generations of musicians, researchers and students in the capital. It remains a collection of immense importance, despite variations in its well-being and funding over the decades.

The success of the schemes for the interlibrary lending of sets was greatly assisted by the special arrangements built up for their transport from library to library. Sets, particularly of vocal music, are bulky and heavy and their delivery by post both complicated and expensive. While recent years have seen a decline in regional transport schemes, much to the dismay of their music users, most authorities have succeeded in finding alternative commercial carriers. The importance of the availability of sets of music for amateur societies and evidence of their significant underpinning of musical activities around the country was amply displayed in a survey of the loan of sets in September and October 1997 conducted by IAML(UK). In just the two months surveyed and the 23 public libraries who supplied information, 6000 sets were loaned, comprising 136 000 individual copies. If only 60 people attended the concerts where these sets were used, then another 360 000 people in the audiences gained enjoyment and benefit.

The major restructuring of local government during the 1990s left many respected music collections, particularly those in the county music libraries, in danger of dispersal and disarray. The issues at stake were extensively laid out by Malcolm Lewis in an article in 1991[51] which included his response to a Department of the Environment consultation paper.[52] A decade on, while all is not universally well, it has been cheering to note that many of the authorities and their librarians have found alternative means of securing their music services through fortitude, consensus-seeking and formal agreements. Good examples are those drawn up between Nottinghamshire and Nottingham City, and Rutland, Leicester City and Leicestershire Libraries, where access both to catalogues and to collections for all local users have been maintained.

But, apart from the use of regional agreements for interlending, both within the regions and to other authorities, and agreements forced upon authorities by local government restructuring, co-operation *between* the regions has advanced very little and any structured partnerships remain to this day largely insignificant or aspirational. Still less was formal co-operation between the authorities and the educational establishments in their catchment areas to the forefront in their strategic planning.

The great exception to a lack of national and regional planning for music library services is the existence of the music collection at the British Library Document Supply Centre (BLDSC) in Boston Spa. The development of the music service and its collections from early in 1975 (when BLDSC was the British Library Lending Division) owed much to the vision of Maurice Line,[53] its Director General, and to the enthusiasm and commitment of its first music librarian, Tony Reed. Its creation provided a lending facility unique in the world, a national resource of printed music encompassing all but sets of orchestral and choral music and available for loan to any UK music library at remarkable speed.[54] The inclusion of notoriously expensive collected editions of music was particularly important, but just as significant was the sheer range of British and foreign publications purchased. It has been used regularly, devotedly and necessarily by libraries from all sectors, not least as budgets have shrunk. There has long been no doubt that it would be used still more if its catalogue were published or accessible online. Technology has already assisted access to its holdings, as the current staff are happy to receive requests as to availability by email, but it must be hoped that the debate which has surrounded the lack of a published catalogue and the periodic threats to the service (engendered in part by use being restricted by the catalogue's unavailability – a classic vicious circle) will soon be stilled. There are other music library projects which hope to ease its catalogue's progression to automated form. It is an invaluable service without which many music libraries would be unable to meet so many of their users' needs. It is also one which IAML(UK) has defended vociferously for several decades, not least because its loss would be a symbol of how 'rationalization' and 'economic reality' can destroy even the unique and the irreplaceable. It is a lesson already learned in too many music libraries around the country.

If provision of the catalogue of a national institution proved difficult, at local level at least, both in automation and other projects, there were attempts to rationalize and to effect more mutually beneficial arrangements. In Birmingham, the Birmingham Libraries Co-operative Mechanisation Project, with a cataloguing programme and agreed cataloguing codes shared between partners from the academic and public library sectors, was upon its inception in 1973 hailed as providing the expectation of great benefits.[55] Much later in 1994, Berkshire Libraries developed Building a Regional Music Resource[56] with assistance from the Public Libraries Development Incentive Scheme, which aimed to create a regional database for music which might ultimately grow to include all the disparate and uncoordinated music collections in the South East Region, including the important collections in Westminster and Kensington and Chelsea. It was not helped in the longer term by local government reorganization in Berkshire, nor rather later by the gradual demise of LASER (the London and South East Region library co-operative), but the potential long-term benefits were outlined very clearly by Susi Woodhouse, by then working for Westminster Education and Leisure Department and well placed to have an up-to-date view on the needs of Westminster's exceptional music collections vis-à-vis co-operation.[57] Initiatives since then for collaboration between those music libraries and for a centralized regional catalogue have not really moved forward.

Over time however more and more links between music libraries at *local* level sprang up, such as that in the Northern Region, where an inter-authority music group was established with a brief 'to discuss cooperative purchase and inter-lending of sets of music'. Alan Hood, who reported on its development at IAML(UK)'s Durham conference in 1983, admitted that progress was a little hampered under conditions where of the nine authorities involved only four had a music librarian.[58] Nonetheless a pattern of regional and local gatherings of music librarians did emerge, with those in many regions meeting at regular intervals, a welcome practice that commends itself to all areas, large or small, to ensure the exchange of local information and experience, to develop shared practices and policies and to seek economies of scale when budgets are pressed. Such meetings do indeed continue, with music librarians still congregating regularly in most areas with significant collections, most particularly in the North West, the South West, the West and the East Midlands, and in Greater London. In Manchester, music librarians from various sectors have joint meetings. A recent welcome development is that music librarians in Scotland, from all sectors, have also begun to meet. Conservatoire librarians now meet twice a year, and IAML(UK) still organizes annual meetings for music librarians in the academic sphere.

Printed music was not, of course, the only commodity of interest to music librarians. Most had also long been developing audio collections, often seen by authorities as a useful source of income generation, but in the London area an innovative scheme had been devised in 1972 for the acquisition and interlending of gramophone records. The Greater London Audio Specialization Scheme (GLASS), had as one of its main objectives 'to ensure that at least one copy of all current domestic issues within the field is purchased and preserved for public lending within the region'.[59] As Miriam Miller noted in 1977:

> The fugitive nature of much recorded material makes this doubly necessary, in a field still regrettably short of reliable reference material, and the GLASS system is yet another example of how music libraries are solving their own problems through co-operating with

one another when their problems are being largely ignored by the national library network.[60]

With each London public library authority concentrating on defined areas of sound recordings, the scheme's overall success has been long-lived, albeit with some snags, as, for example, those outlined by Peter Griffiths of Redbridge Public Libraries in 1993: the early withdrawal of three authorities and the failure to cover popular music and language courses.[61] But, by 1979 approximately 4000 recordings were being supplied through the scheme.[62] This buoyant figure unfortunately declined over the years for a variety of reasons laid out very clearly by Daniel Williams in a 1996 article.[63] Reports by Frank Daniels of Wandsworth and Robert Tucker of the Barbican Library, privately circulated, led to recommendations in a GLASS Performance Report which were eventually ratified by the Association of London Chief Librarians. Essentially, as Williams reports:

> Although the ideal of comprehensive or representative coverage remains, the service will henceforth become request-driven, with one main objective: 'to ensure that at least one copy of each requested item which falls within an authority's allocation is placed on order and purchased for lending via the scheme and subsequently preserved for future lending via the scheme'.[64]

Hopes that the GLASS scheme might be extended to other geographical areas have not yet been realized, and it is doubly surprising that compact discs, videos and digital versatile discs (DVDs), with their more robust constitutions, have not encouraged the development of more interlending schemes for audiovisual materials (one certainly exists in the Birmingham area). The more cynical would suspect this to be connected in some way with a possible loss of income from loans.

Technological developments in sound carriers and the transmission of sound via the Internet have certainly transformed the possibilities for a greater sharing of audiovisual resources not just in the UK but worldwide. An early experiment in the field was collaboration on the project Jukebox in which the National Sound Archive in the UK and the national sound archives in Denmark and Italy in association with the Western Norway Research Institute participated. Jukebox was a project supported by the European Community under its European Library Plan between 1993 and 1996 with the aim of setting up and testing a pilot system for a new library service where library users in remote locations might gain online access to sound recordings in archives in their own and other countries.[65] Its investigations and surveys were wide-ranging and provided ample data for further research, covering as they did the potential for users, the infrastructure of databases, the digitization of sound materials and the legal, technical and functional issues. The project's final report, available online,[66] gave strong indications of the project's value while acknowledging that technology had progressed so fast that many of its achievements were already being superseded. Just how the expansion of computer facilities in public libraries and the amount of music now available for downloading from the Internet will affect audiovisual collections and co-operation in the future remains to be seen.

By 1990, IAML(UK) had become more and more convinced of the need for more co-operation. Self-sufficiency, whether in individual academic or public libraries or in regional authorities, had been increasingly tested and called into question during the 1980s, a trend which shows no signs of retreating. Articles in 1989 by both Malcolm Lewis[67] and John Wagstaff[68] gave a clear outline of the difficulties in public and academic libraries respectively. As Malcolm Lewis wrote:

> the last decade has seen a period of change in which local government, perhaps more than any other aspect of national life, has been subject to continuing government scrutiny and almost unending legislation. Tight control of public expenditure coupled with a policy of forcing local government to test the quality of its services ... have forced a fundamental re-examination of the philosophy and practice of public library provision in this country and this has affected public sector music libraries as much as anyone else ... . The pressures have been intense and show no sign of letting up. Staffing levels have been cut yet opening hours remain the same; funding has been cut yet we are expected to increase the income from our sound recordings and video collections: services are meant to be more sharply targeted towards the consumers who use them and yet more and more time is spent by music library managers in discussing and implementing internal policy reviews which have no direct beneficial effect on the services provided to the public ... . Let us hope that ... at the end of the next decade [music services] have not evolved into being just quasi-commercial centres of income-generating entertainment.

Concerted action to resist cutbacks in music library services and staff had already been a major concern in IAML(UK) for a number of years, as it was widely perceived that music sections, being easily identifiable and expensive in terms of documentation, were receiving disproportionate attention when economies and 'rationalization' were sought. From early in the 1980s Liz Hart, music librarian for Barnet Public Libraries, had been monitoring cuts in music libraries on behalf of the Branch's Executive Committee and alerting them if any library felt that IAML intervention would assist. By 1987 she could report[69] that an 'ActionPack' had been prepared for libraries in difficulty with 'sections covering statements defending the value of music libraries, arguments often used against music library services with answers refuting them, people to approach for support, examples of letters to write, and so on'. A network of regional reporters was also set up. Fifteen years later it is distressing to report that the Executive Committee still hears at almost every meeting of more threats of music library closures or amalgamations with other services, further diminutions in services and further losses of music library posts. The need for specialists and specialist knowledge and handling is still not really appreciated, specialists in general are still viewed as an anachronism, budgets continue to be reduced, and it is music users who suffer and, paradoxically, the very income which is so needed and can be raised from the loan of recordings – if there is anyone knowledgeable to buy the right material and provide good access to it.

It would have been easy to sit back and sulk, but once again IAML(UK)'s devotion to the needs of musicians and recognition of the bewilderment of inexperienced staff led to a pragmatic approach. Basic courses for staff lacking musical knowledge (and entitled 'Everything you wanted to know about music but were afraid to ask') were organized and run where they were requested. 'The course covered many aspects of music provision, including terminology and enquiry techniques. It was very popular and was put on in many locations around the country, but the lack of time and resources eventually took their toll and the course was "rested".'[70] Its resurrection came some years later, as re-structurings and low staff morale were continuing to take their toll, and 'Music for the terrified: a basic course for library staff' was devised by Liz Hart and Ruth Hellen, for immediate use in their own libraries in Barnet and Enfield respectively, before its launch around the country. It continues successfully to this day, now in the company of other courses devised by IAML(UK)'s Courses and Education Committee ('Notes from cyberspace: an intermediate level course for music resources on the internet'; 'Advanced reference sources for music librarians and 40 copies of Messiah please') and of a ring-binder of basic music library information *First Stop for Music,* now due for a reprint.[71] These IAML(UK) courses are now supplemented by those run by Ian Ledsham of Allegro Training and a member of the Executive Committee.

If a true altruism existed in IAML(UK)'s concerns for inexperienced staff while qualified staff were taking early retirement or being moved from music library posts and if it took enormous co-operative effort to address those needs, there was an equal determination to ensure that those training for the profession had access to specialist music library training. There had been no dedicated course in 'music librarianship', as it was formerly known, since the path-leading course at the Polytechnic of North London was discontinued in the 1980s. IAML(UK) offered free input to courses at library and information schools over the years, but the offers were not often accepted (though recent developments are more promising). By the mid-1990s the lack of instruction became acute. The Music Libraries Trust (MLT), and in particular Michael Freegard and Nancy Kenney, took up the challenge, approaching 'library schools' again. A positive response came from the University of Wales, Aberystwyth, suggesting that a music librarianship module might be developed for use in their distance learning course. The MLT gained generous funding from the Britten-Pears Foundation to add to their own contribution and the module was prepared by Ian Ledsham. It has since been developed into a stand-alone course with accompanying CD-ROM for use by any individual or any music library,[72] and serves as a fine example both of the MLT's value and of the long-term collaborative endeavours which can eventually bear fruit.

Librarians may in the last decade have learned to 'play the game' in order to protect their services, but as retrenchment continues inexorably and more and more music services are adversely affected, a re-examination of public library objectives, historically identified by Lewis as 'Education, Information, Culture and Recreation', may be overdue. Recent government reports such as *Culture and Creativity: The Next Ten Years*[73] and *Empowering the Learner*[74] have emphasized the important role which libraries can play in supporting cultural services and their current preoccupations with lifelong learning and social inclusion. While their recommendations include co-operative arrangements (among them library and information plans), cross-sectoral funding arrangements, the need for 'access mapping' and training which includes the development of mutual support, the need to rebuild the stocks which have declined and to train the specialist staff to support their redevelopment and use is yet to be addressed.

But this was still far in the future when in 1986 a major report was produced by the LISC, *The Future Development of Libraries and Information Services: Progress Through Planning and Partnership.*[75] Its basic contention was that 'library and information services are a national heritage and require a conscious effort to maintain them' and it recommended strongly the development of library and information plans, most commonly centred on a region or local area (and interestingly still advocated in the year 2000, as shown above). By 1990 the concept of national library and information plans for *subject* areas was emerging, and IAML(UK) was offered £500 by the Library and Information Co-operation Council (LINC) to develop a proposal for a study of the policies and resources which affect co-operation in the provision of music information, printed music and sound recordings in the UK and the Republic of Ireland. This was the first encouragement at national level of IAML(UK)'s wildest dreams. By 1991 a formal proposal for a Library and Information Plan for Music (Music LIP) had been submitted by the Branch to funding bodies. Funding was secured from LINC, the British Library Research and Development Department, the ERMULI Trust, founded by IAML(UK) to support education and research in music libraries, and from the Office of Arts and Libraries. The plan was to be completed in 18 months.

By the autumn of 1992, as the Music LIP report documented, a steering committee had been established to direct the planning process, provide guidance and oversight, and to facilitate liaison with the music community. Representation on the committee was wide, with members from music publishing and retailing, the recording industry, the British Library, popular music, music library suppliers, broadcasting, amateur music societies and music researchers, as well as music libraries themselves. With the committee chaired by Pamela Thompson from the Royal College of Music who was then Past-President of IAML(UK) the process began with the employment of an information consultant, Royston Brown, and, most importantly, of a Project Officer, Susi Woodhouse. All involved had a very tight deadline to meet and those most closely involved, the above-named and Malcolm Lewis, then IAML(UK) President, embarked on a whistle-stop adventure. Alongside the sending and analysis of 400 detailed questionnaires delivered to every music library and library authority in the UK and Ireland, 27 visits and meetings were accomplished and long hours devoted to polishing the final document, culminating in a week of some stress when Malcolm Lewis made four trips to London from Nottingham and Susi Woodhouse three trips to London from Hove. So many issues relating to the supply of printed music were addressed that many other areas which the project would have liked to consider had to be noted as 'requiring further study'. These included music societies and associations, the commercial sector, other collections, the loss of archives, music literature, music periodicals and discarded items, a list long enough for further major studies.

But the deadline was met and by the summer of 1993 the Music LIP was published.[76] It included 53 recommendations, five of which were formally dedicated to the issues of co-operation, although many others were to require just as much co-operative effort. It contained the most thorough analysis of the issues affecting music libraries that the Branch had ever undertaken and it concluded that work on the plan's development could not be carried through without a national music planning and co-ordination structure – and an officer to see it though. IAML(UK) was beginning to feel exhausted in tackling all the work itself. Various funding mechanisms were proposed; all ultimately came to nothing. While the plan was generally well received, the prevailing climate of retrenchment was not helpful. Unabashed, or almost so, IAML(UK) set up a Music LIP Development Group. Its work, while substantial, went largely unnoticed, and it was feared that this would be yet another report that would gather dust. With the benefit of hindsight, nothing could have been further from the truth and it is indeed surprising how many of its recommendations came to fruition or provided evidence of the need for further work. As Pamela Thompson said at the launch of the Music LIP at the British Museum in 1994, 'It was an unmissable opportunity to put music libraries in the spotlight and to put some sparkle back into glazed eyes'. So it was, though rose-coloured spectacles were needed for a little longer.

Meanwhile, just as depression set in, exciting developments emerged in the higher education sector. The Follett Report[77] on libraries in higher education establishments from the (Higher Education) Joint Funding Council's Libraries Review Group was to change the climate and future in libraries throughout the sector. Its recommendations, which were far-reaching and wide-ranging, contained one crucial element: that, for radical progress to be made, funding should be top-sliced from the whole higher education budget in order to benefit libraries directly. While music libraries could not expect to benefit exceptionally, their very backwardness was in some respects helpful – they were among those which needed most help. Several programmes were quickly established as a result of the report, including one for non-formula funding for special collections in the humanities which provided *inter alia* money for retrospective conversion of catalogues, conservation and improvements in access, which for some music libraries was heaven-sent and finally allowed them to develop automated systems which might aid collaboration in the longer term.

Another was the establishment of the JISC[78] to direct and encourage programmes relating to information technology. The JISC's work was boosted considerably when in 1995 the Anderson report[79] on library provision for researchers gave clear indications that higher education institutions would never have resources to build adequate independent research collections and would have to share resources. It further recommended that 'networks of libraries should be encouraged to develop at national or regional level, which might be discipline based or cover a number of subject areas', and substantial funding of £15 million was allocated to an 'Electronic

Libraries Programme' (eLib) to develop digital and electronic library services. Phase 3 of the eLib programme invited proposals for large-scale resource discovery projects. Possibilities for music conservatoire catalogue co-operation were deciphered from a document full of terminology wholly alien to its conservatoire librarian readers. Only a little deterred, they persevered, and the idea of Music Libraries Online (MLO) was born with a consortium of nine conservatoire libraries and plans to produce a web-based virtual union catalogue of their 'clumps' (as they were informally known) of resources by using the Z39.50 retrieval protocol. The initial consortium included all nine major UK conservatoires: Birmingham Conservatoire, the Guildhall School of Music and Drama, Leeds College of Music, the Royal Academy of Music, the Royal College of Music, the Royal Northern College of Music, the Royal Scottish Academy of Music and Drama, Trinity College of Music and the Welsh College of Music and Drama. The libraries involved were not a little bemused to find their project chosen, the only 'clumps' project with a national rather than a regional remit.[80] Some were even more embarrassed that with relatively few records in their relatively new catalogue systems, there was a danger that if they did not improve their cataloguing targets they would form part of a virtual union catalogue with far too few records and that, if core bibliographic standards were not quickly agreed, chaos could ensue. The technical knowledge required was also daunting.

In the event, the project soon overcame initial difficulties, with direction from Kate Sloss, then Librarian of Trinity College of Music, and with the appointment of Katharine Hogg, formerly of the Royal Academy of Music, as music library consultant and Matthew Dovey of Oxford University as technical consultant, an appointment which provided much relief at the time and much more general advice in the future. The establishment of a steering committee provided a fine opportunity for all the participating conservatoire representatives to meet more regularly than at their usual annual meetings. As the project progressed, libraries from non-conservatoire sectors were invited to join the consortium, resulting in the inclusion of secondary partners from Birmingham University, Huddersfield University, the Faculty of Music in Oxford, the Senate House library of the University of London, Birmingham Central Library and Westminster Library, as well as the British Music Information Centre. It became the first truly cross-sectoral music library initiative and reflected an increasing realization that cross-sectoral work was essential for efficiencies of scale to be achieved. The project's history and the ways in which the technical issues of inter-operability between different systems and the targeting of searches were addressed are carefully documented in an article by Katharine Hogg.[81] Its vision of becoming a gateway to music libraries throughout the UK was spelt out by Marian Hogg, the Project Administrator, at IAML's Edinburgh conference.[82] The MLO continues until funding ends in July 2002, which is already providing an incentive for broader collaboration with some of the other important music projects which, much to music librarians' surprise, followed in its wake.

With many institutions still holding music collections with catalogues only in manual form, the next initiative to emerge in the higher education sector was equally exciting. The Research Support Libraries Programme (RSLP) was established in 1998 to enhance access to research collections, prioritize needs nationally and reduce expenditure and effort. Its documentation not only highlighted the need for the retrospective conversion of catalogues to automated form, but, most fortuitously, also identified music as a subject in need of particular attention. Happily, significant funding opportunities were available. Preliminary meetings of music librarians recognized the opportunities and the possibility that a consortium might at last bring about more shared cataloguing without additional operational charges. With the support (not to mention astute analysis and hard work) of Clive Field, Director of Birmingham University's Library and Information Services and Chair of CURL, a consortium, Ensemble, was born consisting of many of the foremost music libraries in the country: at the universities of Birmingham, Cambridge, Edinburgh, Glasgow, London, Manchester, Nottingham, Oxford and Southampton, and at three conservatoires – the Royal Academy of Music, Royal College of Music and Royal Northern College of Music (Birmingham Conservatoire and Trinity College of Music were to join later). Secondary partners included the British Library, whose lending collection at Boston Spa it was hoped might eventually be included.

The consortium's bid for funding was successful, as was a later supplementary bid. Its primary aim was to bring about the retrospective conversion of printed music catalogues, as it was estimated that the 14 collections in the original consortium contained 1 131 000 items in need of cataloguing in automated form. Items from the period 1850 to 1975 were selected for priority action (although the starting date later moved back to 1800), as it was recognized that most earlier material was already in RISM and that an electronic record might already exist for post-1975 material. Swift retrospective conversion was envisaged by using the good offices of CURL, sharing all records free of charge and reducing (perhaps over-optimistically) the cost of one record to £4.00, much less than the previously common £6.00–£8.00. The project was funded from 1999 to 2002. The tribulations involved in meeting the bibliographic standards required by RSLP were long and difficult, especially for the conservatoires, but they were resolved, as were initial difficulties in recruiting experienced music cataloguers and meeting targets,[83] but the success of the project was undeniable, not only in achieving the targets set, but in bringing together the libraries involved with a shared purpose and sense of vision.

Ensemble did, however, have a longer-term vision: the creation of a distributed national library resource for music through partnerships across the sectors in order to widen public access to the wealth of resources available. It is still seeking funding for its new proposals and for a further project, with few hopes of moving forward before 2003. It will be difficult to keep up momentum for the project and yet more difficult to retain the staff trained at considerable cost in Ensemble's first phase. But a determination to continue, fuelled by continuing need and a vision for the future, remains.

IAML(UK) as a body was not, of course, directly responsible for either Music Libraries Online or Ensemble, but it was about to meet an invigorating new challenge. The achievement which had consistently eluded it was the creation of a national union catalogue of vocal sets. Malcolm Jones, his enthusiasm for national union catalogues undimmed after 25 years of promoting their virtues, had already created an online union catalogue for the West Midlands Regional Library System (WMRLS), having just before his retirement found and rescued data from Birmingham Public Libraries and installed them with their agreement on his personal computer. 'From such an accident', he later reported, 'the modern era of bibliographical control of sets was born'.[84] With funding from the Public Libraries Development Incentive Scheme, the WMRLS project forged ahead and the resulting catalogue was published in 1997.

But Mr Jones had greater ambitions. Liaisons with IAML(UK) colleagues began, starting in the East Midlands where Malcolm Lewis in Nottingham facilitated access to their data and Helen Mason in Lincoln 'undertook the mammoth task of editing the rather minimal entries'.[85] Now working entirely on a voluntary basis but with a rare obsession, Malcolm Jones pursued leads in other areas, tracking down and acquiring material from the North West Region (a mere 6639 entries recorded long before, also largely on a voluntary basis, by Tony Hodges of union catalogue renown at the Royal Northern College of Music), from Information North and from the National Library of Scotland. 'The thought was in several minds that a national database was within grasp'.[86]

Late in 1999 the British Library announced its first Co-operation and Partnership Programme, but the possibility that funding might be granted to a professional association like IAML(UK), rather than to a library or library authority, seemed remote. When the application was not only accepted from IAML(UK) but also funded, there was rejoicing, not just because Malcolm Jones's enormous past efforts were recognized and would at last be recompensed to some degree, but also because the Association was trusted to see the Encore! (as it was named) project through. Encore! is now a reality and is far more than was originally expected. The data on orchestral sets still stored at BLDSC were worked upon and provided by Pat Dye, so that Encore! could encompass all performance sets. All available data on vocal sets from all library regions were collected and in some cases put into electronic form for the first time. The demise of LASER meant that individual libraries in London and the South East had to be approached individually, but their co-operation was splendid. Pragmatic, but faithful to the principles of standardization so long desired, the catalogue uses *AACR2* and UKMARC to a sensible level and permits searching in a number of ways which users will find useful. The catalogue can be accessed through a link on the IAML(UK) web site.[87] Encore! was formally launched at the British Library in London in October 2001 by Baroness Tessa Blackstone, Minister for the Arts, with a further launch in November at Leeds College for Music for members in the north. An irresistible footnote to the voyage towards Encore! over the decades is that Malcolm Jones was able to fulfil a long-cherished ambition and acquire a narrow-boat. He baptized it Encore!

Encouraged by their success in gaining funding, members of the Branch's Executive Committee already had other initiatives in mind, the most important being the development of an online directory of music libraries. Earlier published directories were long out of date and work had already been started by the Branch, in particular by Peter Linnitt of the BBC, on a new and more comprehensive resource. It went by the irresistible but ultimately too humorous working title: MILDRED (*M*usic *I*n *L*ibraries: a *D*irectory for *R*esource *D*iscovery). By the autumn of 2000, MILDRED had metamorphosed into Cecilia, 'the name taken from the patron saint of music rather than having any acronymic derivation'.[88] When in November 2000 funding applications were again invited by the British Library's Co-operation and Partnership Programme, IAML(UK)'s team of ingenious application writers (Chris Banks, Curator of Music Manuscripts at the British Library; Susi Woodhouse, now at Resource, the Council for Libraries, Museums and Archives; and Ruth Hellen from the London Borough of Enfield) leapt into action, completing by the deadline early in January 2001 the application for Cecilia – Mapping the UK music resource.

New times and changing priorities called for a new approach. The need to create synergies between projects, not only in the music library field but across the cultural landscape of museums, libraries and archives, was by now widely recognized. Few projects, however, could have equalled the number of potential synergies which Cecilia's authors found and incorporated. MILDRED's more modest objectives were amplified to include data collection from all music collections, whether in libraries, archives, museums or music information centres, the creation of collection level descriptions not only to inform the music community but also contribute to the RSLP's work on collection level descriptions, and a web interface built to include wide options for searching and links to item-level catalogues. Sustainability beyond the envisaged 15–month period was a central issue to be addressed. The application was approved, with support coming not only from BLCPP but also from RSLP, Resource and the Music Libraries (formerly ERMULI) Trust. For IAML(UK) it seemed a singular triumph and a source of pride: that the Branch could be entrusted by such eminent bodies with so significant a project. By August 2001, Reverend Dr Paul Andrews, formerly both editor of *Brio* and music librarian for Bedford, was appointed as project manager with Susi Woodhouse as project director.

As Paul Andrews revealed to IAML(UK)'s 2002 Annual Study Weekend,[89] Cecilia will be 'an online directory of institutions holding collections of music materials', it will 'provide a web based tool enabling enquirers to search descriptions of collections in music using free-text and structured keywords', will 'include every kind of music and support a broad range of enquiries' and 'will provide a gateway or portal to UK music resources', as enquirers are led to descriptions of collections or to relevant links to online music information and catalogues. It will be an immensely valuable tool for all who seek music materials.

Such a plethora of music library projects were clearly in need of a framework for future development, particularly as by March 2002 funding to achieve the project's continuation was, if only temporarily, elusive. A conference to discuss the issues and achieve a consensus on future action was suggested by Emma Robinson, London University Librarian and by then Chair of Music Libraries Online. Clive Field, now

Director of Scholarship and Collections at the British Library, agreed to host the event and give a keynote address. The conference was also supported by Music Libraries Online, Ensemble, Encore!, Cecilia and IAML(UK). With a good attendance from delegates from the breadth of the country, it represented a significant advance in music library co-ordination. At the end of an excellent day, a consensus drawn together by Clive Field was achieved on four main priorities for the future, reported here in full because of their importance:

- Responsibility for the next stages of planning the strategy for developing the online music resource should lie with IAML(UK) in partnership with the British Library and Resource.
- An advocacy strategy should be developed, communicating music's framework of advantage to amongst others policy-makers, the music industry, and colleagues in archives and museums.
- The 1993 Library and Information Plan for Music should be updated in such a way as to enable the community to develop priorities and phasing for future action, not least in terms of resource discovery, retrospective conversion, national discography, metadata standards, system requirements, staffing, training, interlending (of performance sets and multimedia), public access, digitization and conservation.
- The Cecilia project should be developed as a music portal, integrating where appropriate with the Resource Discovery Network. Cecilia II, seeking UK funding sources, could usefully link in a range of general music sources, a UK national music catalogue, further retrospective conversion, and provide access to existing digitized content (whether sound or images, free or commercial). Cecilia III could usefully extend the scope to continental Europe, with European funding.

It will be interesting to see how these recommendations can now be further developed, how successful they will be, how they will stand the test of time and whether a real vision for the future has been created. IAML(UK) may perhaps be forgiven for feeling that its own vision for international and national cross-sectoral co-operation and national planning, often questioned or sidelined over the years, has finally been vindicated. There is a tacit suspicion that the information community has caught up with principles long advocated by IAML, rather than that IAML has had to espouse new trends and stipulations. The terminology may be impenetrably new, but the philosophy is not.

The need for a wide vision has always been central in IAML's activities, and as globalization affects so many previously stable musical institutions, the need for a vision not just nationally but internationally becomes an ever growing imperative. Music has an international language and is an international resource which can never be seen only in a national context. Many of the projects which IAML(UK) has developed and participated in could well be extended to Europe and beyond and music librarians in the UK may soon find, as did UK members in IAML's early days, that projects elsewhere in the world may be well worth joining or emulating, so that duplication of effort is avoided, standards are internationally agreed, resources are more fully shared and the benefits delivered to the whole music community internationally.

Meanwhile, ideas for new collaborative ventures in the UK itself continue to emerge, while other long-standing projects for which funding or strength have not yet been found are restated. A projects desiderata list, drawn up by the Music Libraries Trust in consultation with IAML(UK) in 2002, lists some old and some new:

- Register of musicians' papers.
- Survey of music publishers' archives with recommendations for a national strategy for their cataloguing and preservation.
- Catalogues of off-air and unreleased sound recordings.
- Catalogue of the holdings of light and popular music collections.
- Catalogues of collections of film music and associated documentation.
- The extension of RISM to include manuscripts and early printed music in cathedrals, churches and other religious orders and in private houses.
- Improving access to the catalogues of hire libraries and ensuring the preservation of unpublished materials.
- Survey of archives of music societies and performance organizations with a related national cataloguing and preservation strategy.
- 'Family tree' of music publishers up to the present.
- Catalogue of musical ephemera falling outside other projects listed.
- Development of recommended standards of service and resource provision for music libraries.
- Histories of major performance organizations which are inadequately documented at presented.
- Catalogue of musicians' letters held by Arts Council/regional arts boards.

It is also worth remembering that there are other long-discussed proposals which IAML(UK) has failed to bring to fruition, in particular national collaboration on indexes for songs in collections, which has remained elusive since Alan Hood first reported work on an index in the Northern Region in 1985[90] and raised the matter again in a letter to *Brio* in 1987.[91] There have been few years since when annual gatherings and the Executive Committee of the Branch have not returned to the subject nor, indeed, attempted to advance it. Suggestions to collect together existing data, lovingly created but duplicated in many libraries, to use the BBC's vast song index as a basis, or to build on a most useful song index now available online from Plymouth Library Services[92] have all come to nought, even though few days pass when most music libraries do not have to battle to track down a song title.

So, even at national level much remains to be done and much more co-operation and opportunistic pursuits of funding will be needed to achieve it. However, the development of a new Music Library and Information Plan, if (or rather when)

IAML(UK) can achieve it, will provide the opportunity to set out once again a national strategy for music collections. The Music LIP was one of the first subject LIPs (the others were for the visual arts and for law) and proved itself invaluable in providing a structure for future development which IAML(UK) could build upon. May the next Music LIP help achieve even more and may the value of subject planning, so long regarded as tangential by most library managements if not by enlightened funding bodies, be once again accepted.

The most recent significant development for IAML(UK) as an association has been a landmark decision at its annual general meeting in Durham in April 2002, when the constitution was changed to enable the expansion of the Branch to include IAML members in the Republic of Ireland. Some Irish members of IAML had indeed been members of the UK branch for many years; others had elected to pay their dues directly to the International Association, but no formal Irish branch had ever existed. Over the previous ten years various meetings had paved the way to a closer relationship, but it was only in 2001, when Irish music librarians met to consider whether their best interests lay in independent development as a branch, in the *status quo* or in a joint branch, that a unanimous decision in favour of a joint branch emerged. Roy Stanley of Trinity College in Dublin, present in Durham, gave an appreciative account of the history of the two countries' interaction over the years. Members in the UK had been consulted, with no dissent to the proposition received, and the constitutional amendments were presented to the meeting. The establishment of the joint branch was unanimously approved and greeted with acclamation. The new United Kingdom and Ireland branch – IAML(UK & Irl) – can now look forward to a much closer partnership, better representation of Irish members within the Branch and indeed in the International Association, and a new era of wider co-operation between the two countries. It is good to see the UK Branch leading the way in internationalism.

At its most basic level IAML(UK)'s single most valuable asset in its striving for co-operation has been its membership. There may now be a sense in which the 'lip service' which E.T. Bryant felt was paid to co-operation has been eradicated, as these are times when co-operation is at the top of the government's agenda. But at grass-roots level, despite the benefits which IAML work must have brought to every music library in the country, 'lip service' does often seem to linger and, though the evidence is partly anecdotal, it is too often based on fact. There are still members who themselves pay to attend annual study weekends as managers will not support their attendance, still committee members who have to take annual leave to attend meetings and work into the night to achieve worthwhile projects, and still only a handful of UK members who can participate in international meetings, even though music and its materials are fundamentally international in nature. There are still major libraries who regard IAML membership as no more than a periodical subscription to *Brio* or who will not even countenance the value of membership, never mind provide a good music service for their users with adequate stock and qualified staff. These are messages on the vital need for co-operation which IAML(UK) for all its efforts has not yet been able to communicate fully enough.

This survey has necessarily been rather introspective and could give the impression that IAML(UK) has worked in isolation. Co-operation with other organizations has been consistent over the years and must continue. The Branch has long been 'an organization in liaison' with the Library Association and for many years held joint meetings with its Audio Visual Group. It is currently affiliated to the Forum for Interlending, the Library Campaign, the National Forum for Information Planning and the National Music Council, and plays an active role in some of these.[93] Contact with music publishers, retailers and recording companies, and with their professional organizations, has been frequent. Liaison with various governmental library authorities over the years has been persistent and often fruitful. Most beneficial of all is the contact members have with all their library users. To record all these would require another chapter.

Harald Heckmann, IAML's Honorary President, is sometimes reminded that members of the IAML Board far back in the association's history used to joke that AIBM, the acronym for IAML used in France and Germany, actually stood for 'Ach, ich bin müde' (Oh, I am tired), a state with which most IAML(UK) activists are well acquainted. Barry Brook, another IAML Past President from the USA whose vision, energy and determination never revealed any inkling that he knew the meaning of the word 'tired' but who single-handedly created RILM and RIdIM among many notable achievements, is widely quoted as saying that 'IAML' stood for the 'International Association of Magnificent Locations', a tribute to the skill of IAML conference organizers in providing beautiful sites for international conferences. The UK Branch's access to exotic climates and locations may be a little less common, but they might well accept 'IAML' in the UK as an acronym for the 'International Association of Marvellous Liaisons'. They have brought about some extraordinary co-operative achievements through commonality of purpose, dedication to music and musicians and, quite simply, long and stimulating friendships. Long may they and their co-operation flourish!

Notes

1   Bryant, E.T. (1985), *Music Librarianship: A Practical Guide,* with the assistance of Guy A. Marco, Metuchen, NJ, and London: Scarecrow, p. 32.
2   Library and Information Services Council (1982), *The Future Development of Libraries and Information Services,* London: LISC.
3   *Brio* (1985), **22** (1), 9–14.
4   IAML(UK) (1995–2001), *Annual Reports.*
5   Invitation preserved in the IAML(UK) Library.
6   McColvin, L.R. and Reeves, H. (1965), *Music Libraries,* vol.1, completely rewritten, revised and extended by Jack Dove, London: Deutsch, p. 23.
7   Association International des Bibliothèques Musicales (1953), *Bulletin d'information,* **2** (1), 7–8.
8   IAML(UK) Constitution, approved by the Annual General Meeting held on 5 April 1992, as amended at the Annual General Meetings held in 1999 and 2000.

9 Sieber, P. (1949), 'Weltkongress der Musikbibliotheken und -Museen in Florenz, 27.-30. Oktober 1949', *Schweizerische Musikzeitung,* **89**, 497–9.

10 Heckmann, H. (2001), 'Half a century', trans. M. Turner, *Fontes artis musicae,* **48** (1), 20.

11 'Entschliessungen des Kongresses/Ordres du jour du congrès/Resolutions of the congress, *Zweiter Weltkongress 1950'* (1951), ed. H. Albrecht, Kassel: Bärenreiter, p. 64.

12 Heckmann (2001), p. 21.

13 Stock, W.H. (1966), 'Some impressions of Dijon', *Brio,* **3** (1), 2–3.

14 Vollans, R.F. (1966) 'Lionel Roy McColvin, C.B.E.', *Brio,* **3** (2), 2–3.

15 Association International des Bibliothèques Musicales (1952), *Bulletin d'information,* 1 (1), 2.

16 Series A and C subsequently published by Bärenreiter in Kassel; Series B by Henle in Munich

17 *Code international de catalogage de la musique* (1957–83), 5 vols, Frankfurt: Peters.

18 King, A.H. (1993), 'Some memories of 1953', *Brio,* **30** (1), 5–7.

19 Schnapper, E.B. (ed.) (1957), *The British Union-Catalogue of Early Music,* London: Butterworth.

20 Redfern, B. (1983), 'Music libraries and research in the United Kingdom', *Fontes artis musicae,* **30** (1–2), 60.

21 Stock, W. (1967), 'Notes and news', *Brio,* 4 (1), 26.

22 Banks, C. (2001), reporting on activities of the Documentation Committee in the *IAML(UK) Annual Report,* 7–8.

23 Based at the City University in New York.

24 Banks (2001), 8.

25 Based at the University of Maryland (USA) and Parma-Colorno (Italy).

26 Ridgewell, R. (2002), *Concert Programmes in the UK and Ireland,* publicity leaflet, London: The Music Libraries Trust.

27 *Brio* (1968), **5** (2), 22.

28 *Brio* (1974), **11** (1), 21.

29 *Brio* (1975), **12** (1), 15.

30 *Brio* (1975), **12** (2), 42.

31 *Brio* (1976), **13** (1), 31.

32 *Brio* (1976), **13** (1), 7.

33 *Brio* (1977), **14** (1), 26.

34 *British Union Catalogue of Orchestral Sets* (1982), comp. S. Compton, ed. M. Simmons, London: IAML(UK)/Polytechnic of North London.

35 Redfern (1983), 61.

36 *Brio* (1983), **20** (1), 15–16.

37 *British Union Catalogue of Orchestral Sets* (1989), 2nd edn, ed. T. Reed, Boston Spa: British Library Document Supply Centre in co-operation with IAML(UK).

38 Redfern (1983), 61.

39 Reed, T. (1983), 'Making music available: the problems of provision and interlending of music scores', *Brio,* **20** (2), 45–52.

40 IAML(UK), (1989), *Sets of Vocal Music: A Librarian's Guide to Interlending Practice,* Boston Spa: IAML(UK).

41 *Brio* (1975), **12** (1), 16.

42 Redfern (1983), 61.

43 Hodges, A. (1985), *British Union Catalogue of Music Periodicals,* ed. R. McGill, London: Library Association in association with IAML(UK).

44 *British Union Catalogue of Music Periodicals,* 2nd edn (1998), ed. J. Wagstaff, preface by R. Taylor, Aldershot: Ashgate.
45 Pope, A. (1989), 'An International Standard Music Number: a proposal', *Fontes artis musicae,* **36** (4), 295–7.
46 Lewis, M. (1992), 'The International Standard Music Number', *Brio,* **29** (2), 78–82.
47 Taylor, R. (1996), 'National report from the United Kingdom 1994', *Fontes artis musicae,* **43** (2), 210.
48 Miller, M. (1976), 'Trends in music librarianship', *Brio,* **13** (1), 7.
49 Draper, R. (1987), 'Annual Study Weekend, St. Andrews University, 3–6 April 1987: Sunday's 'program'!', *Brio,* **24** (1), 10.
50 Bryant (1985), 32.
51 Lewis, M. (1991), 'The restructuring of local government in Great Britain', *Brio,* **28** (2), 65–70.
52 Department of the Environment (1991), *The Structure of Local Government in England: A Consultation Paper,* London: Department of the Environment. (Similar documents were produced by the Welsh Office and the Scottish Office.)
53 Line, M.B. (1975), 'The British Library and the provision of music on inter-library loan', *Brio,* **12** (1), 1–6.
54 Lewis, M. (1989), 'Music services in public libraries in the United Kingdom', *Fontes artis musicae,* **36** (4), 272.
55 *Brio* (1973), **10** (1), 1–4.
56 Muncy, C. and Chambers, K. (1997), 'Building a regional music resource', *Brio,* **34** (1), 19–22.
57 Woodhouse, S. (1997), 'Project BARM – a rationale', *Brio,* **34** (1), 23–5.
58 Hood A. (1983), 'Music cooperation in the Northern Region', *Brio,* **20** (1), 4–8.
59 McColvin, L.R.(1973), *Directory of London Public Libraries,* 2nd edn, London: Association of Chief Librarians.
60 Miller, M. (1977), 'Music libraries', in Whatley, H.A. (ed.), *British Librarianship and Information Science 1971–1975,* London: Library Association.
61 Griffiths, P. (1993), 'I don't mind if I do – topping up GLASS', *Audiovisual Librarian,* **19** (2), 126–8.
62 Pinion, C.F. (1980), *The Interlending and Availability of Audiovisual Materials in the UK: Report of a Survey in 1979,* British Library Research and Development Report no. 5526, London: British Library, p. 4.
63 Williams, D. (1996), 'Making GLASS visible: the effectiveness and future of the Greater London Audio Specialisation Scheme', *Brio,* **33** (1), 3–10.
64 Report of the working party on the future of GLASS, September 1995.
65 *Brio* (1993), **30** (2), 99–100, contained a preliminary note about the project.
66 Web site at: http://www.sb.aau.dk/Jukebox/finalrep.html#5.1
67 Lewis (1989), 275–7.
68 Wagstaff, J. (1989), 'UK academic music libraries: a need for change', *Fontes artis musicae,* **36** (4), 277–80.
69 Hart, L. (1987), 'Cuts in music libraries', *Brio,* **24** (1), 6–7.
70 Hart, L. and Hellen, R. (2000), 'Music for the terrified: basic music courses for library staff', *Fontes artis musicae,* **47** (1), 22–3.
71 IAML(UK) (2001), *Annual Report 2001,* 6–7.
72 Ledsham, I. (2000), *Music Librarianship: The Comprehensive Guide to Music Librarianship,* Aberystwyth: Open Learning Unit, Department of Information and Library Studies, University of Wales, Aberystwyth.

73 Department of Culture, Media and Sport (2000), *Culture and Creativity: The Next Ten Years,* London: DCMS.
74 Library and Information Commission 2000), *Empowering the Learner,* London: LIC.
75 Office of Arts and Libraries (1986), *The Future Development of Library and Information Services – Progress through Planning and Partnership: Report of the Library and Information Services Council,* London: HMSO.
76 IAML(UK), (1993), *Library and Information Plan for Music: Written Statement,* prepared by Susi Woodhouse, Hove: IAML(UK).
77 Full report available on web site at: www.ukoln.ac.uk/services/papers/follett/report/
78 See web site at: www.jisc.ac.uk for full information on JISC's programmes.
79 Anderson Report (1996), *The Joint Funding Council's Review: Report of the Group on a National/Regional Strategy for Library Provision for Researchers.* London: JFC.
80 Sloss, K. and Duffy, C. (1998), 'Music Library Online', *Brio,* **35** (1), 9–12.
81 Hogg, K. (2000), 'Music Libraries Online: a virtual union catalogue for music', *Fontes artis musicae,* **47** (1), 14–21.
82 Hogg, M. (2000), 'Music Libraries Online', *Brio,* **37** (2), 18–23.
83 Thompson, P. (2000), 'Ensemble: a vision for music cataloguing', *Brio,* **37** (2), 24–8.
84 Jones, M. (2001), 'Encore! again: the history and current state of the project', *Brio,* **38** (2), 16.
85 Jones (2001), 17.
86 Jones (2001), 18.
87 Web site at: http://www.iaml-uk.org
88 Linnitt, P. and Andrews, P. (2001), 'The metamorphosis of Mildred or, Hail, bright Cecilia', *Brio,* **38** (2), 10–14.
89 Information taken from documentation supporting Paul Andrews' presentation
90 Smart, A. (1985), 'Report and information session [at the Bangor Annual Study Weekend]', *Brio,* **22** (1), 7.
91 Hood, A. (1987), Letter on computer song indexes, *Brio,* **24** (1), 3.
92 Web site at: http://www.webopac.plymouth.gov.uk
93 IAML(UK) (2001), *Annual Report.*

Chapter 12

Cecilia: towards a map of the music resource of the UK and Ireland

Paul Andrews

Introduction

At first glance, it might seem as if Cecilia is a completely new initiative, without precedent in music information provision. In some ways this is true: a service to map music collections at a high level across libraries, archives and museums in every sector is an ambitious venture that has not hitherto featured in any IAML(UK) programme and although Cecilia goes some way towards realizing a number of the recommendations for action identified by the Music Library and Information Plan Report, no previous project has attempted to be so ambitious in its coverage and scope. However, as this brief survey will show, Cecilia represents a natural extension of the work undertaken by IAML(UK) in promoting co-operation between music libraries over its entire 50-year history, in particular during the last decade, and sets standards for electronic delivery of services that will inform the next generation of work in music and music information provision.

Background to the project

The idea for Cecilia emerged directly from work done by Peter Linnitt on a project provisionally titled MILDRED (Music in Libraries, a Directory for Resource Discovery). This was itself begun as an exercise to revise and mechanize the fourth edition of the printed directory, *Music in British Libraries,* compiled by Barbara Penney and published by the Library Association in 1992. Penney's work consisted principally of a directory of libraries in the UK with holdings of music materials. It contained details, submitted by the libraries themselves, of library names, addresses and contact details, together with a summary, both quantitative and qualitative, of their music holdings. Penney compiled information about services, charges, opening hours, access conditions, staffing, including the name of the music librarian or member of staff with responsibility for music. Much of this is information that dates very quickly; indeed, some of it was out of date by the time the book was published, and the limitations of a directory whose currency steadily diminishes over time hardly need to be enumerated here. Nevertheless, Penney continued to be a very valuable resource throughout the 1990s. There was a further category of information included by Penney, which allowed contributors to provide details of any special collections. This was an optional extra and yielded a predictably varied (and variable) response, but was nevertheless valuable in identifying and locating a number of significant collections. This remained one of the book's more valuable features and foreshadows Cecilia, in which the primary emphasis is on collections and collection description. This will be examined in greater detail below.

The progress of MILDRED and its development into Cecilia has been described by Linnitt and Andrews (2001). Penney's original approach was re-examined and a new questionnaire devised which took into account some of the issues that had arisen in music libraries since her work was done, particularly in the field of automation and online services. The directory information contained in her publication would be updated and stored in an online database, accessible via the World Wide Web, giving users the opportunity to adopt a variety of search strategies, and offering institutions the opportunity to maintain the currency of their information. At this stage the aim of the exercise was still essentially to create a directory of music resources in libraries and the final product would have been what the jargon of the day refers to as a 'motorized book', that is, a service with all the flexibility that an online search offers to the searcher, but providing the same sort of information, allied to a similar structure, that the printed directory had provided.

As the project progressed Linnitt and the Executive Committee of IAML(UK) began to look at the practical ways in which MILDRED could be developed in an online environment, and for possible funding streams. It was at this point that they realized that work, chiefly in academic library circles, by organizations such as the Joint Information Systems Committee (JISC), the Distributed National Electronic Resource (DNER) and the Research Libraries Support Programme (RSLP), an arm of the UK Office for Library Networking (UKOLN) was directly relevant to the creation of an online music resource. A call for applications for funding issued in November 2000 by the British Library Co-operation and Partnership Programme (BLCPP) concentrated their efforts and expanded their thinking towards the development of a project that would maintain the directory function but take the description of collections as its starting point, rather than as a useful but limited adjunct to a simple directory. The bid to BLCPP was successful and further funding was obtained from RSLP and Resource, the Council for Libraries, Museums and Archives. The project was now renamed 'Cecilia: mapping the UK music resource' (after the patron saint of music), to which MILDRED now formed the pre-project scoping study. With the expansion, in April 2002, of IAML(UK) to include libraries in the Republic of Ireland and its subsequent re-branding as IAML(UK & Irl), a small change to the subtitle of the project also became necessary, resulting in 'Cecilia: mapping the music resource of the UK and Ireland'. The funding carried with it the requirement that Cecilia would not be restricted to the libraries domain alone, but would also embrace collections of music and music related materials held in archives and museums. This cross-domain emphasis is in line with current thinking in information work. Libraries, museums and archives are seen as different types of 'memory institutions', containing different materials and describing them differently, but all contributing to a distributed national resource, and all with collections of potential interest to a very wide constituency. In an important sense, they are all engaged in similar work and, to the enquirer looking for material of interest, the professional distinctions between them may not always be apparent or very important. It was clear that a very broad range of institutions would now need to be approached if Cecilia were to achieve a comprehensive coverage of the national music resource. The libraries domain had been identified for the MILDRED exercise, and the forms received from 116 institutions (out of 238 approached) provided a basic body of data from which to work outwards. Further work was required to gather data from those libraries which had not responded, and to identify potential contributors from the museums and archives domains. More than 600 institutions were identified in total, potentially containing a much greater number of collections.

Aims and objectives

The broad aim of Cecilia is, as the project title makes plain, to map the musical landscape of the UK and Ireland. This landscape is defined as the national music resource, consisting of the sum of the collections of or containing music materials in the country's libraries, museums and archives. This is a concept which itself requires some explanation. The idea of a distributed national information resource is one that has gained currency and acceptance, again chiefly in academic circles, over the past few years. To move from a situation in which libraries freely co-operate with one another in the provision of interlibrary loans from their own discrete holdings, chiefly conventional printed materials, to one in which the materials themselves are seen as part of a wider shared collected resource, a wider resource which moreover includes the holdings of museums and archives, is a significant development, but does not, it would appear, require a quantum leap in thinking. It does, however, require the means by which such an idea can be put into effect; a means that can ensure consistent and comprehensive metadata gathering, storage and search strategies, while also ensuring that agreed standards for the creation of metadata are adhered to. During the latter part of the 1990s it became clear that the Internet would provide the technical means by which such a service could be delivered, and the development of international standards for metadata creation, among which MARC, Encoded Archival Description (EAD), the General International Standard for Archival Description (ISAD[G]) and the Dublin Core Metadata Initiative are all relevant to collection description projects such as Cecilia.

There was no doubt that the distributed music collections of the UK and Ireland constituted an uncharted terrain. Music materials in a wide variety of formats are held by an equally wide variety of organizations. Music scores, manuscript and printed, singly or in sets, recordings, videos, DVDs, instruments, artefacts, images, archival documents, ephemeral material all go to make up a rich and diverse resource, but without an overview of the territory enquirers are left to find their way by varied means and, inevitably, even the most careful searching will miss items and collections of importance. The map analogy for this kind of information work is an apt one. A map describes a landscape but does not reproduce it. A map locates features of interest and, depending on its scale, describes them briefly, but does not usually engage in detailed description. It allows the map reader to decide if a particular location has sufficient features of interest to make it worth a visit, but does not offer a surrogate experience of the locality. It uses conventionally agreed text and symbols to show (say) that a hill, lake or church are present, but gives no indication of the fauna on the hill, the colour of the lake or the height of the church tower. A subject-based information mapping exercise performs essentially the same exercise. Metadata about collections are gathered and indexed in sufficient detail, using agreed standards of description, to alert the searcher to materials of interest, without necessarily giving detailed descriptions of what those resources contain. The purpose is not to provide the detailed analysis offered by the library catalogue once the user knows that it contains material of interest, but to provide an all-important first step towards identifying potentially interesting collections. An oft-quoted metaphor from a seminal paper on collection description uses a geographical analogy: 'The scholar is concerned at the initial survey to identify areas rather than specific features – to identify rainforest rather than to retrieve an analysis of the canopy fauna of the Amazon basin' (Powell, Heaney and Dempsey, 2000). This chapter has so far emphasized the importance of Cecilia to the potential end user, but it should be noted that collection-level description also brings significant benefits for collection managers. It enables librarians, archivists and curators to bring their resources to the attention of a wider community, potentially increasing their use, and this in turn can assist in assessing priorities for item-level cataloguing. It also opens up opportunities for collaborative collection management and greater co-operation between institutions. At the most basic level it provides collection administrators and managers with a further descriptive tool to use in their own institutions.

The requirement that Cecilia draw its collections data from archives and museums as well as from libraries, significantly increased both the number of institutions that could potentially be invited to contribute, and the range of materials that their collections might contain. Music libraries have always contained a variety of different formats including manuscript and printed music as well as books and journals, and a variety of audio and multimedia formats. Museums and archives increase that range by including archival papers of many types, personal and corporate records, musical instruments, musical ephemera, concert programmes, paintings, drawings, sculpture, models, costumes and so on. A further requirement of the Resource element of the funding for Cecilia was that the project did not confine itself to resources held in academic institutions, but embraced the broad range of public, academic and national organizations, including details of some private collections where these could be identified and their owners were willing to contribute. This was in accord with the original aims of MILDRED which, following Penney and in line with long-standing IAML(UK) practice, was to be a cross-sectoral resource.

The development and methodology of the project

A condition of the funding from RSLP was that Cecilia would at least seriously examine the Collection Description Schema devised by Andy Powell of UKOLN, together with its prototype web-based tool, with a view to using it as a basis for collecting information for the database. In fact it would have made no sense at all not to draw on the collected experience and expertise of UKOLN, which had set up its CD-Focus group specifically to advise the rapidly expanding number of projects at work on collection description in a variety of subject and geographical areas. Powell's schema, based on a model of collections and their descriptions developed by Heaney (Heaney, 2000), brings together elements from the standards in use in all three domains, mapping closely to EAD, ISAD(G) and Dublin Core, to create simple descriptions of collections of many different types. It is not intended to replace existing standards however, but to complement them by creating a higher level of resource disclosure and discovery:

> The RSLP Collection Description schema provides a basis for creating relatively simple descriptions of collections of many different types. Just as the Dublin Core metadata element set is not intended to replace richer standards for resource description at item level, the RSLP CD schema is not a substitute for existing collection description schemas [such as EAD and ISAD(G)]. Like Dublin Core however, it offers a simple set of attributes with commonly understood semantics which allows resource managers to disclose and exchange information about their collections. (Johnston and Robinson, 2002, p. [3])

In practice it was quite possible to adapt the RSLP schema and its accompanying form to the needs of Cecilia, and to create fields for the music-specific data that the project required, while building in sufficient flexibility to accommodate the requirements of all three domains. This necessitated abandoning questions asked by the MILDRED exercise for information largely of interest to music library professionals. It was essential, considering that this was a project initiated and led by the libraries domain, that the design of the forms was as 'domain neutral' as possible, and that they did not give the impression of being library centred. In this respect, and in common with other cross-domain collection description projects, we have found that the basis of the RSLP schema is sound and works well in practice.

Having identified that the potential number of organizations to which an approach for institution and collection metadata could be made would be in excess of 600, and that the initial lifespan of the project delimited by the available funding would be less than 18 months, it became clear that a strategy for information gathering would rely almost totally on the voluntary submissions of the contributing organizations. This was also the approach adopted by MILDRED but whereas the earlier project had made use of a paper form, mailed out to libraries, it was decided that Cecilia would be an online project from the start and would offer contributors the opportunity of submitting web forms online. A web site was developed with pages devoted to information about the project aimed at potential contributors and future users, together with the institution and collection record forms and guidance notes to help with their completion. Paper copies of the forms and the accompanying documentation were also available on request to those contributors without ready web access. Forms completed online were emailed direct to the Project Manager who was responsible for entering the data received into a database constructed specially for Cecilia by Matthew Dovey of the Libraries Automation Service at the University of Oxford. An agreement was reached early in the project's life with the Performing Arts Data Service (PADS) at the University of Glasgow, to host the completed version of the database on its web server, and support periodic updates. The first version of the database was due to be launched late in 2002.

In order to obtain as comprehensive a response as possible much work went into publicizing the project and promoting it to potential contributors. The Project Manager contributed articles to the *IAML(UK) Newsletter* (Andrews, 2002a) and the *Newsletter* of the Society of Archivists (Andrews, 2002b), and made presentations to the IAML(UK) Annual Study Weekend, the Meeting of Academic Music Librarians and the Annual Meeting of the Cathedral Libraries and Archives Association, among other bodies.

The nature of collections and their description

A comparison of the different ways in which librarians, archivists and museum curators approach the creation and description of collections was made by Johnston and Robinson:

> Although librarians, archivists and curators have all considered the items within their custodianship as forming groups or 'collections' of some form, the criteria by which they define these groupings, and the emphasis placed on the creation and use of descriptions of those groupings, has varied widely. Different ideas about 'collections' have led to different approaches to 'collection description'. For archivists, the individual item is an integral part of a group of items that forms the record of an individual or organisation, and the description of such aggregates forms a fundamental (and standardised) element of descriptive practice. Traditionally, librarians have concentrated on the description of individual items. The notion of the 'collection' is certainly present, with aggregates defined perhaps by various criteria including location, subject, form or use, but the descriptions of these aggregates tend to be more informal and less structured than those of their component items. Museums too employ the concept of the 'collection', and use a range of criteria (form or type of object, subject, the objects donated by an individual benefactor) to delimit the aggregates they describe and manage. (Johnston and Robinson, 2002, p. [1])

It is certainly true that, for a project initiated and led by librarians, the need to grasp, and convince, colleagues of the concept of 'collection' as the unit of description was of primary importance. As Johnston and Robinson point out, for librarians, the unit of description has traditionally been the individual item, and the need to produce catalogue records, sometimes very detailed records indeed, has always been seen as being of central importance, particularly when the needs of scholars have been considered. Behind this view lie a number of presuppositions which may be gently challenged. Perhaps the two most significant of these, both intimately related, are, first, that all researchers know the literature of their subjects, are familiar with the specialist directories in which information about the location of research resources are to be found and are confident in the rigour of their methodology and, secondly, that the location of every significant collection is in fact known to the scholarly community. A further questionable presupposition is that everyone with a serious research interest is part of the higher education community, with access to well-stocked research libraries. From the outset, Cecilia has been designed as a resource for the whole community, a resource for the ordinary music lover as well as the serious researcher. It should be as simple for the enthusiast pursuing a private interest to find out about music resources available locally, as it is for the postgraduate student to locate a collection of primary resources relevant to a specific area of research. Cecilia is designed to address questions at every level of interest.

It should be re-emphasized that collection-level descriptions are not intended to be a substitute for the detailed item-level descriptions which are, and will presumably remain, the backbone of library catalogues. They are a parallel and complementary resource discovery tool that enables the enquirer to gain an overview of the available resources, before undertaking the detailed item-level work that informs all research.

Collection definition and description

At an early stage in the project it was realized that, if Cecilia were to succeed in gathering usable data from what amounts to a very broad constituency indeed, relying on the voluntary contributions of busy professionals, then a considerable degree of flexibility in defining what constitutes a collection and how it might be described would be necessary. The emphasis from the outset was that these decisions are best left to the professionals involved in the day-to-day management of their collections, realizing that they would often be dependent on the amount of time that librarians, archivists and curators could devote to work on the project. As a minimum requirement contributors were asked to complete one institution record for the directory element of the database, and one collection record in which their holdings of music materials could be summarized. In reality, of course, we hoped that many institutions would wish to be much more specific about defining discrete collections of material, and in many cases institutions have submitted several collection descriptions. It was perhaps one of the more controversial decisions of the project, given the emphasis in the literature on the importance of agreed standards, to avoid specifying any particular subject-heading scheme. Instead, we have encouraged contributors to supply simple keywords or concept phrases as subject descriptors in the keyword field on the form. It is a relatively simple matter to ensure consistency in the spelling of proper names, place names, expression of dates and so on, by reference to widely available authorities such as the *New Grove Dictionary of Music and Musicians* (2nd edn, 2001). However there are several subject-heading schemes in use across and within the three domains and the High Level Thesaurus (HILT) project at the University of Stirling confirmed that there is at present no universally acceptable subject-heading scheme for music. Rather than impose a scheme that many contributors might be unfamiliar with, antagonistic towards or simply lack access to, but wishing to retain the ability to search and browse a list of subject terms, we decided to take the responsibility of building a concordance to the terms submitted by our contributors, retaining the editorial right to prefer certain terms over others and add further terms where appropriate or necessary. Similarly, we have not attempted to impose any minimum or maximum size for collections to be eligible for inclusion in Cecilia. Many collections will be large, but it is also conceivable that a collection might consist of only a few items, perhaps, in rare cases, of a single item if it is of musical significance.

Cecilia has encouraged contributors to think creatively when considering how best to identify discrete collections from among their holdings. In particular it was emphasized that it was not necessary for items described together in an online environment actually to be physically located together within the contributing institution. Individual items could, if required, form a part of more than one collection. It can be argued that every time materials are gathered together to answer a particular enquiry, a new collection with a particular subject focus is created. Such collections may contain diverse materials, in several different formats, drawn from different parts of the parent institution, sometimes from different sites.

A further consideration when thinking about the nature of dispersed collections has been the number and variety of locations, even within a single institution, where music materials might be found. Thus a local studies department of a public library may contain concert programmes for the locality and material relating to local musicians, groups and musical activities; a university or college may hold music materials in libraries, archives or museums; religious organizations such as cathedrals or monasteries also maintain libraries and archives frequently containing music materials; local authority archives and records services are another potential source. All this is in addition to the many organizations dedicated to music, or with specialist music sections or departments; all are contributors or potential contributors to Cecilia.

The future

Cecilia is designed to be a living, growing resource. As it develops a presence and a reputation as a web resource, we anticipate that more organizations will wish to contribute to it, and that contributing bodies will continue to improve and add to their existing entries. However, the sustainability of this type of project is never guaranteed. At the time of writing funding for the second phase of the project is being sought. The link with the PADS ensures that Cecilia has a permanent web presence for as long as it remains a viable up-to-date resource. However, the work of updating and improving the database remains with IAML(UK & Irl), a voluntary organization without centralized staff or funding. The considerable achievements of the organization, which this volume rightly celebrates, have very largely been due to the work of volunteers giving up much of their valuable spare time out of loyalty and a sense of vocation. It is hard to see how a resource as important and complex as Cecilia could be maintained on a voluntary basis. The potential is very real for Cecilia to develop into an even wider and deeper resource: links with other music-related projects to contribute to a national music catalogue, and further plans to acquire a European dimension with European Union funding have already been discussed. The future is very bright. It is my hope that continued, sustained funding for Cecilia will be an early achievement in the second half-century of IAML(UK & Irl)'s existence.

References

Andrews, P. (2002a), 'Appearances in visions: an introduction to Cecilia and collection description', *IAML(UK) Newsletter,* **42**, 2–8.

Andrews, P. (2002b), 'Access to resources about music: an introduction to Cecilia', *Newsletter* [of the Society of Archivists], 152, 10–11.

Heaney, M. (2000), 'An analytical model of collections and their catalogues', UKOLN/OCLC, 3rd edn, HTML:<http://www.ukoln.ac.uk/metadata/rslp/model/>

Johnston, P. and Robinson, B. (2002), *Collections and Collection Description,* Briefing Paper 1, Bath: UKOLN Collection Description Focus.

Linnitt, P. and Andrews, P. (2001), 'The metamorphosis of Mildred or Hail, bright Cecilia', *Brio,* **38** (2), 10–14.

Penney, B. (comp. and ed.) (1992), *Music in British Libraries,* 4th edn, London: Library Association.

Powell, A., Heaney, M. and Dempsey, L. (2000), 'RSLP collection description', Dlib 6 (9), HTML:<http://www.dlib.org/dlib/september00/powell/powell09.html>

Chapter 13

Greater than the sum of its parts: towards a national service for music performance material

Malcolm Jones and John Gough

I spent more hundreds of hours in music libraries, whilst I was growing up, than I dare calculate, and all the first concerts that I conducted, both in Liverpool and London, were only made possible by the availability of material in libraries. I should like to express my support for our music libraries and their contribution to the performance of music.[1]

There is nothing new in music and drama librarians extolling the value of their services made available to the participatory arts community. There is, after all, a community of users of music and drama materials estimated at well over a million. Participatory arts in the UK are thriving, and loans of performance materials continue to increase. Many performances depend, sometimes unwittingly, upon printed music and drama scripts loaned by libraries. Society representatives tell us time and time again that they could not survive economically without library provision. Likewise, for those involved in education – curricular and extracurricular – library provision is said to be absolutely essential.

The demands for performance materials are such that many music and drama libraries struggle to obtain and supply material on time for the beginnings of loan periods requested. The start of the rehearsal year in September sees more loans then than probably at any other time, and the summer months beforehand are often periods of frenetic activity as libraries prepare often large and complex consignments for their users.[2]

The phenomenon of 'music sets' in libraries, familiar enough to most of those who work in the field in this country, is a relatively recent one, and also a largely British one. Such performance sets are the lifeblood of community music-making. They are used by the many hundreds of choral, operatic and orchestral societies in the UK, by many schools to support curriculum activities, by students in higher and further education, at the conservatoires and by professional ensembles.[3]

To define our terms: a 'set', as generally understood, is either a vocal set, that is, a number of copies of a vocal work, identical or sufficiently so for practical purposes, or else an orchestral set, that is, a full score (or equivalent) for the conductor, and a set of parts for all the instruments necessary for performance, with sufficient duplicate parts for each string section for the number of desks likely, given the work.

Furthermore, string orchestra seems to be included, but at least until quite recently, wind and other bands are not. Chamber music is not included, being part of the general collection. Sets have been traditionally stored, loaned and even catalogued as a separate, self-contained part of the library.

Very few other countries make such provision as part of the publicly funded library. It seems to have begun with the acquisition of collections by donation in a few major cities, especially Liverpool and Manchester, in the early part of the century. In the immediate post-war period, there was a great expansion in music-making in schools, and several local education authorities (LEAs) built up collections. Since in those days LEAs were responsible, in the rural counties, for libraries, the administration of the collection often devolved upon the library; to this day, some authorities have a 'schools collection' and a 'library collection' side by side, and often virtually indistinguishable.

Metropolitan authorities followed, as did a lively interlibrary loan traffic. The situation developed with the expansion of library services serving the expanding demand for amateur music-making: those who had developed a taste for the choir or orchestra at schools were now looking for similar provision in the community. The university music departments, keen to promote live music-making to counteract an image of dry musicology, were also building collections, and there was also expansion at the conservatoires.

By the end of the twentieth century, there was a highly developed network of libraries of various kinds, offering a service, some still free, others charging, with so much interlibrary loan traffic that it amounted to a national service, delivered through regional outlets. After all, no user cares who actually owns the copy in their hands, and stories abound of conductors driving long distances in the hope of finding a set in a remote library.

By the 1970s the older-established collections were feeling the pressure, and following the presentation of a paper by Tony Hodges, then deputy at the Liverpool Music Library, to the joint conference of IAML(UK) and the LA Sound Recordings Group (as it then was) at Bristol in 1972, a joint committee of the two organizations was set up. Brian Redfern chaired it and its secretary was Malcolm Jones. It met five times, and its conclusions were that a national union catalogue of orchestral material was practicable, but that one of vocal sets was not, and regional library systems were urged to take up the challenge.

In retrospect, both recommendations seem like either great optimism or colossal cheek, but music librarians have never shrunk from either, and was the setting in hand of the *British Union Catalogue of Orchestral Sets (BUCOS)*, published in 1982, edited by Sheila Compton as a research project at the (then) Polytechnic of North London, largely as a result of Brian Redfern's good offices, and published by that body. The British Library Lending Division (at Boston Spa) assumed, through its music department, responsibility for updates, and produced a second edition in 1989 with a supplement to this in 1995.

For vocal sets, many regions, happily, accepted the challenge, and produced catalogues, several of which ran to more than one edition. A common style emerged, due to the indefatigable involvement of Kenneth Anderson, who had been in charge of the collection at Liverpool, before moving to the library school at Loughborough, but was now retired. Thus, his layout, with entries arranged in groupings, such as Opera, Cantata and so on, followed by author and title indexes was to become the *de facto* standard.

Libraries acquired these catalogues avidly, and to this day well-thumbed copies are hanging on to their binding by a thread up and down the land. Coverage was, however, incomplete and many libraries published their own catalogues. As a result of this rather messy situation, staff got into the habit of making extended phone calls to their colleagues, notwithstanding the advice given in *Sets of Vocal Music: A Librarian's Guide to Interlending Practice*,[4] written by Malcolm Lewis and published by IAML(UK) in 1989, which was, and still is, an indispensable *vade mecum* on the subject.

In 1995, the West Midlands Regional Library System (WMRLS, later The Libraries' Partnership, West Midlands) was considering the production of a new edition of its catalogue. There had been an abortive attempt to produce a catalogue on computer using BLCMP[5] (now Talis), and Ian Ledsham, then music librarian at Birmingham University, had done a great deal of work, although he had not had the resources to finish it, and some years had then passed. By one of those happy accidents, the catalogue came to light, just as Birmingham Public Library was setting up a new catalogue on DS Galaxy, and therefore had, for a few months only, both the necessary hardware and a program to convert the data to a form usable on a PC.

From such an accident, it is arguable the modern era of bibliographic control of sets was born. Malcolm Jones, somewhat conveniently, took early retirement from Birmingham soon thereafter, and the WMRLS under the leadership of Geoff Warren, a good friend to music projects, applied for, and obtained a grant under the Public Libraries Development Incentive Scheme to develop a catalogue using the standards of MARC and *AACR2*, as a pilot for a national catalogue. The advent of the PC had made what, 20 years earlier, seemed impossible into a practicable possibility.

The next task for the West Midlands (WM) project was to obtain suitable cataloguing software. The criteria were that it should handle MARC records, and run on a PC, as well as being reasonably priced. There were few contenders, and the Mikromarc system, from Bibliotekenes IT-senter AS of Oslo, Norway, was chosen, largely for its flexibility and the fact that much of the setting up and the output to print (since this was then still the preferred medium) was controllable by the user without the need to have expensive recourse to the supplier for 'modifications'. This was Mikromarc 1, which had also been chosen by the Britten-Pears Library after the firm visited IAML's international conference at Oxford, so it was possible to see it in action in a UK music library. In the course of nine months, the West Midlands database was completely revised and updated, and in spite of Malcolm spending a week in hospital with heart failure (not cause and effect) the catalogue was published on time, in 1997.[6]

Meanwhile the East Midlands (EM) had decided that a new edition of their catalogue was needed. As computer consultant, Malcolm Jones agreed to take the last published East Midlands catalogue and subject it to optical character recognition, and then process the resulting file into a database using dBase 3. This database was demonstrated to staff in the East Midlands, to general approval. A program was then developed to convert the data from dBase 3 into a MARC file; this was then imported into Mikromarc.

From this, Helen Mason undertook the mammoth task of editing the rather minimal entries, without the possibility in general of travelling to see the material. It says much for her knowledge and judgement that the standard of the catalogue was what it was. Given the source, and the lack of sight of the works, it was not practicable to use *AACR2* completely; nevertheless *Music for Choirs* was published, using the same print program as that for the WM, later in 1997.[7]

At about the same time, the North West (NW) Region had agreed to take under its wing a catalogue produced by Tony Hodges (he of the 1972 paper) who was now at the Royal Northern College of Music. This used a mainframe computer and produced a printed catalogue which in its sheer size, of 6639 entries (compared with the WM's 4911 and the EM's 4946), speaks highly for the energy and enthusiasm put into the work, particularly since for much of the time its author was on his own, without sponsor.

Information North also maintained a database, using the proprietary Cardbox software on a PC, with 1414 titles. Although it was never published, Roger Duce, at the National Library of Scotland, was also working on a catalogue, using a word processor, not a database, on an Amstrad PCW. This was later made available to Encore! Meanwhile the catalogues of LASER, (London and South-East Region) and the South Western Regional Library System (SWRLS) remained in the 'Kenneth Anderson' form, on paper.

This, then, was the state of play at the end of the twentieth century. The thought was in several minds that a national database was within grasp. After all, the projected size of such a database (around 50 000 titles) was suitable for a single database, especially since a number of the collections had no computer, let alone computer catalogue. Network solutions such as those using Z39.50 were therefore not possible. Moreover, the CD-ROM had appeared as the suitable medium for such catalogues. (The British Library's *Catalogue of Printed Music*[8] first appeared in 1993, and transformed the bibliographic control of music in the UK overnight.) A national catalogue on paper was not practicable on cost grounds, although microfiche remained a possibility.

For two or three frustrating years, the possibility was discussed in various quarters, but no real progress was made on funding. However, this time was not wasted, since many good friends of the project were made. The Circle of Officers of National and Regional Library Systems (CONARLS) expressed support, as did all the then regions, who, with one exception, made their machine readable data available for evaluation of the technical feasibility of such a project, and later for the project itself.

It was in the latter part of 1999 that the British Library (BL) announced its Co-operation and Partnership Fund. Here, at last, seemed the right body to approach, if any were. After a very constructive informal meeting with Geoffrey Smith of the BL who was managing the fund, it was suggested that some pump-priming money might be available for the sets project immediately, in the 1999–2000 financial year, without prejudice to a formal application for the first year of the fund. In fact, IAML was successful in both applications. The letter of application for the first was written, on a laptop, immediately after the meeting finished, and the file printed and delivered the next morning, The formal application took a good deal more work, and the efforts of Susi Woodhouse and Chris Banks among others, both being particularly expert in the appropriate language for such documents, were invaluable. And so the project began; it needed a name, and Encore! was as good as any.

The project aims were first and foremost to deliver a single catalogue of vocal sets, with the orchestral sets material added to form a single source for performance sets as defined at the head of this article. However, the other tasks were, first, a collection mapping exercise, to try to locate all the relevant collections, and the contacting of them to discover what data was available; secondly, after the database had been put into use, to attempt to codify the strategic implications for the co-ordination of collection development and the planning of service delivery, as well as the vital question of ensuring the sustainability of the catalogue.

The four databases, from the WM, EM, NW and North, were amalgamated, converted into MARC where necessary, and duplicates removed as far as possible. By this time, a repertory of programs to generate output from a proprietary database while adding MARC coding had been developed. The correct field and in many cases sub-field tags were written automatically, as in many cases were indicators. Building on this, and the identification of other collections, much more data was received, in various forms. A major issue was the fact that LASER declared its intention to cease operations and, therefore, would be unable to fulfil its commitment, made along with the other regions at the beginning of the project, to help in the collection of data. Libraries in the South East, including London, had to be dealt with individually. But meanwhile data were coming in.

It is inevitable that every time a substantial data set is added, the quality and consistency of the catalogue deteriorates. As music librarians come together more in co-operative projects, which involve pooled data, the arguments for standardization apply with ever-greater force. However, Encore! is a pragmatic finding tool and was informed by the belief that it is better to make the information available, warts and all, than to wait for the glorious day when all inconsistencies have been removed.

It should be noted that a part of the database is a collection of information about the libraries themselves, including contact information and a statement as to the terms and conditions on which loans may be made. Locations are given in plain English, prefixed by a two-letter code which designates the region, in library region terms, in which a library is located, in geographical, rather than political terms. These will be modified to reflect the new regional structure in libraries and museums.

It is thus possible to limit a search to the holdings of a particular region by using the first two characters only of the location, as well as to the holdings of one library by giving the full location. The library is a public library unless otherwise given: 'Birmingham' therefore refers to the public library, 'Birmingham Conservatoire' and 'Birmingham University' being used as appropriate. The British Library lending codes, though preserved behind the scenes as data, do not appear in the catalogue: they can become quite complex in a national setting, but within a region the simple number was adequate.

Meanwhile, the orchestral sets data was supplied by the Music staff at Boston Spa, and this involved Pat Dye and her colleagues in a good deal of work, for which we all should be grateful. It covered all entries in *BUCOS* (2nd edition)[9] and its supplement, together with additions and amendments notified to the BL up to July 2001. The data were to different bibliographic standards: personal names have been harmonized with the vocal sets data, and the locations changed to the practice described above, but in other respects the records have not been altered, except in a few details, where these improve both searching and filing order.

Returning to vocal sets, the coverage (in April 2002) is as nearly comprehensive as is reasonably possible for all regions apart from the South East, where, as was mentioned earlier, the demise of LASER has caused problems, but the addition of the remaining authorities is a high priority. Plans are also in hand for ensuring the sustainability of the catalogue: the British Library will continue to accept notifications for orchestral material.

Why is the provision and ready availability of these materials so important? It needs to be said at the outset that this is not merely a librarian's view: the users of these materials are generally sophisticated and vocal. This does not of itself entitle them to special treatment; rather the users are acting on behalf of quite large groups of people, and are similar in this respect to teachers, who often receive special treatment in libraries when they are acting on behalf of classes.

It can hardly be overemphasized that the availability of these sets is the lifeblood of community music-making. A single loan of a set of vocal scores has the potential to benefit several hundred people (those who perform the work and those who listen to the performance). Thus, for example, the (estimated) 50 000 vocal sets held in British libraries have the same potential benefit as some *10 million* books. The range of music is from jazz and musicals to symphonies and the operas. It is sometimes alleged that, since this music is, broadly speaking, 'western European art music', the activity is in some way elitist. To anyone who has seen the groupings of people who come from all ages, backgrounds and walks of life, this is clearly far from the truth; indeed, it has been argued that communal music-making has an effect for good on social cohesion.

For example: the Midshire Choral Society wishes to perform Bach's B Minor Mass. They are able to borrow via their local public library a set of 50 vocal scores of the work together with a set of orchestral parts and a conducting score totalling some 60 units as only two single loan transactions. The audience for the performance in the Town Hall is expected to be in excess of 300 people. Thus, some 400 people benefit from these two transactions (those performing and those enjoying the performance). Scaling this up, the (estimated) 60 000 performance sets held in British libraries have the same potential benefit as some 12 million single item issues.

Music and drama sets have been known to be issued in large quantities for many years, yet direct evidence remained anecdotal until the *IAML(UK) Sets Survey*.[10] This survey was conducted to obtain precise evidence of what was being provided, and listed music and drama sets on loan during the two months of September and October 1997. Comprehensive data regarding loans of music sets were submitted by 23 local authorities. The survey was therefore a 'snapshot' of loan patterns recorded by selected local authorities. Almost 6000 sets were listed comprising over 136 000 copies (this notwithstanding the omission of numbers of scores and parts contained in 1720 orchestral sets). Over 117 000 scores of choral works were listed, and over 12 000 vocal scores and libretti of operas, operettas and musicals.

This represents a potential benefit equal to 1.2 million single issues. Set interloan statistics provided by CONARLS also show that in 1996–97 17 905 loans were made: a potential benefit equal to 3.5 million single issues. To put this figure in context, this represents some 10 per cent of all public library issues.[11]

It needs to be said that the 'system', if it may thus be called, operates under several constraints, which render it less than perfect from the user's point of view. Some of these operate at the administrative level, others are questions of policy.

The unit costs of the material are, by library standards, very high and, so, the acquisition costs involved in the maintenance, let alone foundation, of a collection may well be a very heavy burden. The material is also bulky, and its storage costs are therefore commensurately high. It is difficult to see that any form of digitization will alleviate this: in the nature of things, the end users are unlikely to accept digital documents. When it comes to the question of interlibrary loans, the bulk of the material requires that appropriate transport be available. Some end users travel some distance in private cars, but the majority of loans are transported by a carrier used by the library service. Many of the English regions had a transport scheme, operated by the regional library system, but this broke down in the face of rising costs, and generally, a commercial carrier is used.

The loan procedures involve booking in advance and use of interlibrary loan, as well as a careful check of the material before it goes out and on return – losses can be very expensive. The handling of initial enquiries in particular requires specialist musical knowledge.

A couple of examples may help: orchestral parts are often named only by the name of the instrument in Italian, and musicians, although not claiming any knowledge of that language, pick up the essential vocabulary in their early years.

Thus the parts for trumpet in a score, published by the English firm of Novello, of Elgar's *Falstaff,* about as quintessentially English an edition as may be imagined, may well be headed 'tromba' and the unwary have been known to believe this to mean trombone. Even worse, perhaps, the distinction between parts (for a single instrument) and scores (all the parts, printed above one another so that the whole ensemble may be read), might be clear. But in German (and much music is published in Germany) score is 'Partitur', and this is commonly abbreviated as 'Part', leading to the precise opposite of what was wanted being supplied. It may also be that something that is obvious to a person who reads music is not at all obvious to a person who does not. It is generally expected of library staff that they read text; why then should music library staff not read music?

However, it is a fact that the place of the subject specialist in library work has been downgraded in recent years, and many such posts in music abolished. Interlibrary loan of such materials is often handled by general interlibrary loan departments. Although a few have made efforts to acquire the necessary skills, the end result is a poorer service, with the wrong material being offered through a failure to appreciate the pitfalls.

The truth is, of course, that the provision of such staff is relatively expensive, and leads to a loss of flexibility in staff deployment. The cost problems are local; at a national level, there is a huge gain in the provision of this material.

These various costs have led to a variety of practices in which the library seeks to recoup some costs from their end users. Moreover, there is often a distinction between the costs a library requires directly from the end user, and the costs, in cash or kind, levied to other libraries for interlibrary loans.

Some libraries still provide a service to end users free at the point of delivery, while others charge from a small amount to quite large sums. Charge, in this sense, excludes the charges generally made in library services for reservations, interlibrary loan administration and the return of materials late or in a damaged condition. Of the libraries that charge, some will only lend direct to the end user, while some only lend via interlibrary loan, while yet others will do both. In a few cases, libraries will only lend to those with an address in their local authority area, or lend on differential charges to those within that area and those not.

Charges between libraries are often covered by the voucher scheme operated for loans generally by the British Library DSC at Boston Spa. Here again practices vary: some libraries ask for two or more vouchers for each set loan. The vouchers, originally purchased from the BL in booklet form, have now largely been replaced by an electronic equivalent. But many loan transactions for sets are not conducted using the electronic means available.

All this leads to a situation where the various processes are greatly more complicated than they should be. It also creates some difficult situations; many libraries who do not charge refuse to deal with those who do, often in either direction, since to lend stock from a 'free' collection to a library that is known to charge its user for this set, irrespective of its origin, is widely regarded as unfair. Moreover, since the availability of the Encore! online database on the World Wide

Web, the end user can discover not only where material needed may be found, but also the terms and conditions on which it may be loaned, or hired from each library. This has led, not surprisingly, to some shift in business towards the free supplier.

Table 13.1 **Survey of borrowers 'in person' at the Music Library, Birmingham Central Library, January–December 2000**

Authority	Borrowers	% of whole	Works: total issues	% of whole	Copies: total vocal scores	% of whole
Birmingham	443	50.1	754	46.2	9 239	48.4
Cambridgeshire	1	0.1	1	0.1	0	0.0
Cheshire	1	0.1	1	0.1	0	0.0
Derbyshire	18	2.0	34	2.1	216	1.1
Dudley	57	6.4	113	6.9	1 514	7.9
Durham County	1	0.1	1	0.1	0	0.0
Gloucestershire	2	0.2	2	0.1	95	0.5
Hampshire	1	0.1	5	0.3	0	0.0
Herefordshire	5	0.6	16	1.0	0	0.0
Hertfordshire	3	0.3	10	0.6	0	0.0
Kent	1	0.1	3	0.2	0	0.0
Leicestershire	5	0.6	14	0.9	220	1.2
London	3	0.3	20	1.2	3	0.0
Oxfordshire	3	0.3	4	0.2	58	0.3
Sandwell	29	3.3	46	2.8	613	3.2
Shropshire	14	1.6	26	1.6	322	1.7
Solihull	68	7.7	115	7.0	3 101	16.2
Staffordshire	42	4.8	75	4.6	1 012	5.3
Wales	2	0.2	8	0.5	0	0.0
Walsall	47	5.3	92	5.6	731	3.8
Warwickshire	43	4.9	84	5.1	816	4.3
Wolverhampton	18	2.0	44	2.7	296	1.6
Worcestershire	77	8.7	164	10.0	852	4.5
Totals	884	100.0	1 632	100.0	19 088	100.0

Some of these practices are justified by reference to the 'fact' that the owning authority bought the material; however, the majority of local government funding has come from national sources for many years now.

There is a real tension between national and local aspects of this provision, and is the more surprising in the light of recent policy trends both to build up the position of the regions in arts provision (the regional library systems having been subsumed in the new regional arts boards) on the one hand, and the desire for all public services to exhibit 'joined-up' thinking on the other. We have here what is effectively a national service, operated through local outlets. In the interests of providing the best and most cost-efficient service, let alone of giving 'best value', the days of local authority empire building must surely be put behind us and artificial barriers to co-operation removed. The basic question of whether libraries should be free is a political one and, since 1948 at least, it has not been left to local determination but enacted in national law. The situation for music sets is not a political question, but rather one of discrimination against music as a subject and as a pursuit. Library councils, who would not dream of making value judgements between, say, the reading of Charles Dickens against Monica Dickens, are making value judgements, whether or not they realize it, between reading and singing as a legitimate pursuit.

That said, it is necessary to turn more positively to the kind of provision that one might envisage. There are some things which could be taken forward, either within the Branch's existing machinery, or elsewhere. These include co-operation over collection development and acquisition in detail. There is also the question of the transport of material loaned: the library regions had, in many cases, schemes for the carriage of material from around the region, but these have been disappearing, or coming under pressure. In the longer term it is already clear that the availability of the Encore! catalogue is changing the way libraries go about this part of their work, with gratifying reports of efficiency savings from many quarters and, more slowly, changing patterns of use as the end users themselves learn to use the catalogue.

In the longer term, the wide variety of terms and conditions which are found at present must surely make life more difficult for the musician, as well as the librarian. The thorny question of charging, and even more the restrictive practices of a number of libraries are, at the present, primarily matters for local determination. However, the comparison which Encore! makes possible, and the fact that this may lead users to 'vote with their feet', will force these issues forward. Since the result will be increased pressure on the 'good boys', there may well be serious problems. The attempt to set up arrangements of credit and debit via tokens of some sort, which works well in other interlending contexts, has not succeeded for sets, since many holding libraries opt out. It is to be hoped that, with the improvement in information about holdings of sets, a similar improvement in the practical logistics will, in due course, come about. This can only be to the good of much music-making, and this, we would do well to remind ourselves, is what it is all about.

Notes

1 Sir Simon Rattle in a letter to John Gough, October 1997, in support of National Library Week.
2 Taylor, R. (ed.), (1998), *IAML(UK) Sets Survey: Sets of Music and Drama on Loan during September/October 1997*, London: IAML(UK).

3 Jones, M. (2001), 'Encore again: the history and current state of the project', *Brio*, **38** (2), Autumn-Winter, 15–23.

4 Lewis, M. (1989) *Sets of Vocal Music: A Librarian's Guide to Interlending Practice*, Boston Spa: IAML(UK).

5 Birmingham Libraries Co-operative Mechanisation Project.

6 Jones, M. (ed.), (1997). *Vocal Sets in West Midlands Libraries*. Birmingham: West Midlands Regional Library Services.

7 Mason, A.H. (ed.) (1997), *Music for Choirs*, 2nd edn, Matlock: East Midlands Regional Library System.

8 British Library (1993), *CPM Plus*. (Catalogue of printed music in the British Library to 1990 on CD-ROM.)

9 Reed, A. (ed.) (1989), *British Union Catalogue of Orchestral Sets*, 2nd edn. Boston Spa: British Library Document Supply Centre and IAML(UK).

10 Taylor (1998).

11 Creaser, C., Maynard, S. and White, S. (2001), *LISU Annual Library Statistics: Featuring Trend Analysis of UK Public and Academic Libraries 1990–2000*, Loughborough: Library and Information Statistics Unit.

Chapter 14

International outreach: fireworks of the 1990s?

Roger Taylor

The UK has long felt itself an island apart. At least that used to be its image and for some still a political reality. Yet cliffs are crumbling and our island barriers are falling away. We are now linked to Europe by the Channel Tunnel, our pets have their own passports and we may soon be spending euros. Of course we music librarians feel differently despite any perception of insularity born of our parallel national-international IAML Branch membership structure. From the inception of IAML, UK members have been deeply involved with its international work. Their participation and commitment have dispelled any image of professional insularity.

As the focus of a Commonwealth of independent nations, the UK has long regarded itself as still an active player on a world stage. Professionally, some IAML(UK) members feel that we may not have devoted sufficient energies towards our 'New Commonwealth' colleagues. Geographically disparate, sheer distances from the UK have prevented any systematic explorations such as have followed elsewhere in more recent years. Correspondence during the 1990s involved colleagues in Kenya, Tanzania and Zimbabwe, but it has been impossible to follow up such contacts by personal visits and systematic explorative analysis. IAML(UK) members themselves have received individual communication from those who had the initiative to write, and individually they may have responded. This was true of an approach from Katerina Gosh in Albania to the Royal Academy of Music Library in London, a year before I undertook systematic research prior to my first exploratory visit. Likewise there was an appeal for assistance from the librarian of a Cambodian music conservatoire in Phnom Penh. Such contacts however seem always to have been *ad hoc* without any strategic UK Branch involvement *per se*.

Since its inception, of course, IAML has sought to be as globally all-embracing as possible. More than 20 years on, however, Harald Heckmann, speaking as General Secretary (immediately prior to assuming the IAML Presidency) at the Jerusalem conference in 1974, alluded to a continuing Western preponderance of Association membership.[1] In 1987, Association President, Maria Calderisi Bryce, reported to the Amsterdam Council meeting 'the action of the Board of offering complimentary subscriptions of *Fontes* to one designated institution in each of ten countries where there are no members of IAML ... . The countries are: Argentina, Cuba, Ghana, Greece, India, Indonesia, Iraq, Kenya, Peru, and Romania'.[2]

Internationally, therefore, there had been a conscious awareness of the need for international outreach well before the end of the 1980s. It was then, however, perhaps more than any time before, that 'outreach' emerged as a proactive international concept, a reaction to the collapse of European communism and a desire to establish direct contact with those newly able to operate within the democratic structure of the 'New Europe'. This applied particularly to the newly independent nations of the former Soviet Union. After all, many of the 'Eastern bloc' countries had been active within IAML for many years, benefiting from generous state funding if sacrificing freedoms of travel and expression. The collapse of such state funding is regarded inevitably by many in Eastern Europe as a very expensive price to pay for the notion of Western 'freedoms' – wherefore the freedom to travel or to develop your services if the resources with which to do so are withdrawn? Nonetheless, the concept of 'outreach' did assume a new understanding particularly following the IAML conferences at Frankfurt (1992) and Helsinki (1993). Estonian participation at the Finnish conference, for example, became talismatic of new organizational and participatory freedoms, and the benefits resulting from Finnish Branch assistance to its Estonian neighbours were seen as a model of explorative sectoral outreach. Those of us who that summer took the opportunity to cross the Baltic Sea to Tallinn experienced an almost tangible atmosphere of vibrancy and excitement borne of newfound national independence and identity. The warmth of welcome offered by Aurika Gergeleñiu and her Estonian IAML colleagues, too, rendered this experience revelatory.

IAML(UK) had by then already followed the international lead and had begun offering its journal, *Brio,* as a complimentary gesture of interest and support. By 1997, 17 copies were donated to IAML colleagues and institutional members in 16 countries (Albania, Bulgaria, the Czech Republic [two copies], Estonia, Hungary, India, Macedonia, Mexico, Moldova, Poland, Romania, Russia, Slovakia, Spain, Tanzania and Thailand). It was as a direct reaction to the clarion call of IAML Vice-President Hugh Cobbe at a plenary outreach session at the Helsinki conference that, in 1994, IAML(UK) created a new Branch officership of Outreach Liaison Officer. From that time, we sought to strategize our efforts and adopt more proactive policies.

It was very much a matter of economic pragmatism that we decided to concentrate our efforts within Europe, particularly the countries of Eastern Europe and the former Soviet Union. We sought to avoid ploughing a furrowed field, yet it was surprising that the Estonia-Finland relationship had been replicated so little elsewhere. It was very much as a personal indulgence of curiosity that in 1994 I ventured towards Albania. Three years after the collapse of by far the most extreme and paranoid of European communist regimes, I found that there had been no outreach initiatives by anyone from the West regarding any aspect of library provision, that the land needed desperately to be tilled much more deeply than by just my sectoral plough.

Since 1994, further explorative visits have been undertaken by Margaret Brandram, Ruth Hellen, Pam Thompson and myself to Bulgaria, Croatia, Hungary,

Lithuania, Macedonia, Russia and Slovenia. These individually have been described in detail elsewhere and need not be recounted here.[3] Collectively, in retrospect, certain lessons have been learned which probably confirm prior suspicions.

1 Each country is unique with its own strengths, weaknesses, needs, priorities. It is entirely wrong to apply 'off-the-peg' solutions, and our experiences have confirmed my doubts about the wisdom of major international funders (for example, UNESCO) who decry single-country projects. Collaborative schemes may seem cost-effective, but there are limited circumstances where they do not risk becoming at least partially irrelevant to local needs.

2 No 'assistance' by the well-meaning can substitute for proper and effective national governmental resourcing within a country. For example, in Albania and Bulgaria we have arranged substantial programmes of donations. Such gestures however are rendered somewhat pyrrhic by virtue of costs of consignment. Donations are random, and can induce donor-dependency. Materials are very often purchasable within a country (although Albania is still very much an exception to this rule as far as music and sound recordings are concerned), so that resources devoted to consignment costs might have been used more effectively as a locally organized and properly targeted investment. Random requests for donations from potential recipients can be symptomatic of old command methods. Potential funders would be more impressed by properly structured, targeted and costed bids, professionally more effective than the receptive serendipity of donated 'lucky dips'.

3 Funders do exist who sometimes command resources far in excess of those at the disposal of national governments. Of course, such funding agencies are very often oversubscribed and queues form consisting of representatives with missions varying from the revelatory to the absurd. In Tiranë, Open Society Foundation offices now exist within the city centre, but it was incongruous when, a few years ago, high barbed-wire fences and armed security guards protected the then out-of-town premises in ironic denial of an 'open society'. Such agencies often have their own agendas which may or may not recognize library provision as appropriate. The British Council once described music librarianship as 'remote from our priorities' (at least these were the words used by its Belgrade officer, British Council supervision of Albanian and Macedonian activities being administered at that time – the mid-1990s – from its Yugoslav office). This was a view not shared by other more enlightened (and frankly better resourced) government-funded development agencies (such as those associated with Austria and Switzerland). Furthermore, it has been reported that agencies staffed indigenously have sometimes recruited those who may be blessed by experience gained as senior functionaries of past and discredited regimes. In such circumstances, newly appointed sectoral leaders may be greatly discomforted to find that those controlling such funding resources (well beyond those of the local Ministries of Culture or Education) may be those whom they replaced. Their agendas may then become subject to some measure of suspicion – resources for

example used to re-create reading rooms stocked with permitted periodical literature, rather than converting libraries to open-access browsing. This is not a universal problem, but how does one find out without going there, meeting them and forming one's own opinion? Notwithstanding such local interpersonal incongruities, it is very difficult for either our local colleagues or ourselves to join queues of funding supplicants and expect *eureka* receptions. It is necessary to cultivate such contacts, to sow seeds which may germinate in the future and with unpredictable benefits. Equally, having voyaged great distances and with limited time, one needs sometimes to suspend modesty and persevere *in extremis*. In Tiranë I once camped for hours in the premises of one well-guarded agency whose representative seemed oddly reluctant to meet, rendered still more surreal when we did meet, after dark, during a power blackout, by torchlight.

4 Where national governments are overwhelmed by economic and political crises, local colleagues often have great difficulty in achieving recognition for library – and more so music library – developments within contexts of all-embracing infrastructural programmes. In Bulgaria in 1996, for example, a newly appointed government minister had in former life been a librarian and many professional benefits had been expected. There had been promises of funding for revenue requirements as well as the resources with which to effect a well-developed nation-wide library development strategy. Yet such expectations had not been rewarded, funding was still not forthcoming and senior professional representatives were unable even to arrange meetings with political holders of government purse strings. If outreach visits can achieve any publicity beyond our parochial communities, then they may become facilitating conduits catalystically enabling our colleagues to establish contacts at senior government levels hitherto denied to them. We need to eschew our often ingrained sectoral modesties and promote positively and vigorously the benefits of effective music library provision. IAML has never lacked evangelists for its cause. Sometimes our new-found and perhaps remote colleagues need to experience our enthusiasm at first hand and witness the benefits of effective, professional and sectoral self-promotion.

5 No benefit will accrue without proper and detailed enquiry and research. Guilt of assumption is borne by many well-intentioned donor agencies throughout the world which do not research, assess, prioritize and strategize their work. The world is full of garbage dumps of so-called 'aid' funded and supplied with well-intentioned emotion. Albania, for example, has been awash with unusable second-hand clothing. Hospitals have been embarrassed by supplies of out-of-date and frankly dangerous medications which the country can neither use nor dispose of safely. There was even a classic example of well-intentioned but profoundly misplaced library assistance. In Pogradec, Eastern Albania, overlooking Lake Ochrid, I visited in 1995 a one-time cultural centre which had become known as 'The American Library'. An East Coast expatriate Albanian community had purchased intact two American public libraries – libraries which had closed to the public in America some years before – and arranged for

consignment and relocation in Pogradec. What I saw in 1995 was a museum of American library provision from the 1970s. The task had been enormous in conveying this vast quantity of books, shelving, catalogue cabinets, and all the other detritus of downtown library provision by sea to Greece, overland into Albania and re-created for the ostensible benefit of the good citizens of Pogradec. There was no continuation resourcing for staffing or supplementary book stock. It was in 1995 already an anomaly, a perfect example of well-intentioned but entirely misplaced altruism, the object of quite appropriate derision from professional Albanian librarians, and now destroyed without regret amid the civil chaos of Albanian unrest in 1997. One wonders what resources were spent on this frankly crazy madcap scheme which (notwithstanding further craziness of subsequent home-made orgies of Albanian self-destruction) would better have been devoted to improving the pre-existent, still existing but modest Pogradec public library.

6   We are fortunate in the world of library provision, and particularly within our sectoral world, that there are colleagues of tremendous energy and commitment whose only crime is that they lack the resources with which to realize their plans. Another trap into which many donors have fallen is to assume that poverty equates with ignorance. Such donors have often lapsed into a form of imperialist assistance ('we know best ... '). Professionally, this is witnessed by so-called experts descending momentarily to bestow received wisdom. There is here, quite frankly, an international scandal of mammoth proportions involving fees paid to those who neither know nor care for those who become the lucky recipients of their wisdom. In my travels I have met those who enjoyed the fruits of such expertise, abandoned like gardeners in the Sahara Desert told to plant an oak tree. For myself it was never difficult to portray myself convincingly as something less than an expert. My entirely convincing professional modesty has, I have reason to believe, borne fruits of sympathetic reception and enhanced credibility. Almost as a standard preamble, introducing myself as having no money and no answers, I sought to learn, observe and discuss. I have been saddened that such pragmatic attitudes have been regarded as more the exception than the rule. To the contrary, I was never less than impressed by the professional standards and achievements of colleagues working in conditions which humble those of us from comfortable Western environments.

7   We are all the richer for learning about the resources of others. Certainly there are many of our colleagues who are woefully underresourced. Yet, although they may be consumed by entirely understandable frustrations of professional and personal economies, they are custodians of wonderful collections of often unique local material which needs desperately to be preserved and managed effectively. There is also nothing better than actually meeting colleagues and proving to them *in situ* that there is an international community of like-minded professionals who share their interests, are interested in their local circumstances, and who would benefit by their involvement and participation at international professional fora.

A very commonly encountered need is for specialized professional education. IAML conferences of course are major educational opportunities, but likewise are the Annual Study Weekends long arranged by the UK Branch. Since 1994 we have advertised these throughout Eastern Europe and have consequently welcomed delegates from Albania, Bulgaria, Croatia, the Czech Republic, Estonia, Latvia, Macedonia, Moldova, Poland, Russia, Slovakia and Tajikistan. They are funded sometimes by their own employers, more often by funding agencies such as the British Council and Open Society Foundations. In return for simply the cost of postage, we have benefited by the attendance of these delegates, some of whom have given papers, as much as they have. This has proved to be a very successful and supremely cost-effective outreach achievement.

Our systematic outreach efforts since 1994 brought further indirect and unforeseen rewards of international involvement and participation. Correspondence with the Council of Europe resulted in an invitation for IAML(UK) to contribute to an international seminar at Vukovar, Eastern Slavonia, in December 1996. This was immediately prior to the return of Vukovar from United Nations (UN) mandate to Croatian national authority.[4] In May 1998 I was invited to contribute the concept of music librarianship to a conference in Budapest by, jointly, the Council of Europe and the Open Society Institute.[5] Nearer home, in September 1998 I attended a conference organized by the International Group of the UK Library Association ('Disaster and After: The Practicalities of Information Service in Times of War and Other Catastrophes').[6] Each of these opportunities have provided benefits of new contacts with colleagues from for example Belarus, Bosnia and Herzegovina, and Tajikistan, for whom IAML had been hitherto unknown and who were equally unknown to us.

Apart from personal rewards of international contact, further lessons have been learned from these encounters. Not least is that there is a danger of over-involvement beyond one's own resources of time and finance. There are vast fiscal resources available to be tapped but the preliminary investment of time and effort is considerable. Such resources also feed a plethora of other barracudan organizations far better resourced than ourselves, acting as we do out of professional concern as an international organization plus national branches all without paid secretariats. There is much knowledge published but mostly at some (sometimes substantial) subscription cost. Internationally, any sectoral aspirations for music can be placed within an overall cultural context by, for example, the Zagreb-published *Culturelink: Network of Networks for Research and Cooperation in Cultural Development*.[7]

Without adequate resourcing, there is a real danger of overextension, a whirlpool vortex into which one finds oneself irrevocably trapped. The work of IAML(UK) in Albania during the 1990s had many rewards, but there are also aspects which with wisdom of hindsight may be regarded as cautionary.

Until 1993 my personal interest in Albania had remained hitherto only academic – an enigma of mystery, inaccessibility and self-distance. At the 1993 IAML conference in Helsinki, the plenary session on international outreach included an address by a Czech colleague who listed at length all the countries of Eastern Europe and the former Soviet Union but curiously omitted any mention of Albania. Challenged afterwards, she replied that Albania had simply been 'forgotten', indicative of the irrelevance of the extreme Hoxha defence measures against even his onetime allies of the Warsaw Pact. My curiosity was stirred and that autumn I started to research what little literature existed about Albanian library provision and particularly its music libraries. June Emerson (the UK specialist wind music supplier and instigator of the Albanian Musicians' Trust) had enthused about its musical wealth and her personal experiences from the 1980s.[8] June, however, is first and foremost a musician and a publisher. Although many of her donations were destined for libraries in specialist music schools, she did not by her own admission know anything about the structures of library provision in national, public and academic sectors. Albanian music library provision was a total unknown.

Early in 1994 I corresponded with Valdete Sala of the Open Society Foundation and previously head of the National Library. She strongly encouraged me to come to Albania and learn at first hand. I also established contact with Katerina Gosh, then head of the library of the Academy of Fine Arts, Tiranë, who was equally supportive and provided a professional focus in music librarianship. My first visit in June 1994 to Tiranë, Durrës, Elbasan and Berat was a revelation. Subsequent visits took me to Skhodër, Pogradec, Korçe and Sarandë. In December 1994 the Albanian Library Association formed a specialist music group, Katerina Gosh organized an inaugural meeting, and IAML awarded complimentary membership to her library. IAML(UK) organized a targeted donation of music materials to libraries throughout Albania. In the spring of 1995, Katerina and another music library colleague, accompanied by an interpreter, undertook a month-long study tour of UK music libraries including attendance at the IAML(UK) Annual Study Weekend.

The prime impressions from my first visit were of dedicated staff responding to the needs of their library users as best they could with woefully inadequate collections. Stock inadequacies comprised limited repertoire (indicative of previous repertoire restrictions), physical dilapidation (from overuse of ageing materials), and chronic shortage of funds with which to replace worn-out stock and expand repertoires. Dedicated staff existed at all the music schools I visited, but it was only at the Institute of Fine Arts that there was a nucleus of professional music librarians. All libraries visited were wholly inadequate as library premises. None was openly accessible to users (staff, pupils, students, public), indicative of long-standing state-inspired constraints upon users to select freely from open-access shelves.

There was a common perception among those I met during my first visits to Albania that anyone coming from 'the West' was bound to be rich. Undoubtedly there was a minority who did doubt (quite correctly) the supposed superiority of anything and everyone 'Western'. Sometimes this was borne of political prejudice and sentimentality for the lost era of Communist authority, less by any means of objective assessment. There was however a very common inability to appreciate that everything in 'the West' was not perfect, that we had our own financial difficulties (albeit of different proportions) and that resources were simply not there for the asking. I was therefore mindful to promise nothing that I knew could not be delivered and avoid wherever possible any raising of false expectations. Consignment costs for donations, for example, could be paid from the recently established IAML Outreach Fund designed specially for that purpose. My own exploratory visits were part-funded by the UK organizations the Albanian Musicians' Trust, Charity Know How, Friends of Albania and the Music Libraries Trust, and by personal funds. The month-long study tour of UK music libraries by Albanian colleagues was funded mainly by Charity Know How with generous in-kind contributions from IAML(UK) and many of its members, personal and institutional. Out of this however, and despite my best intentions, all our expectations were suddenly raised.

My correspondence with Charity Know How came to the attention of the UK Officer of the European Union development funding agency Phare.[9] At a subsequent meeting attended by IAML(UK) and the Music Libraries Trust, we were told that, at that time (Autumn 1994), Phare had three spending priorities – Albania, libraries and music – and that we seemed to combine all three. We were encouraged to devise a development programme to be submitted to Phare far in excess of anything which either we had until then envisaged or we could realistically resource ourselves. We were enthused by having been approached by Phare – it was not our original idea but theirs – and flattered by this apparent opportunity to demonstrate our professional abilities to initiate and supervise a major EU cultural development programme in the European country which was, and remains, that of greatest economic need.

Nothing in the European Union (EU) is simple and straightforward. The complexities of the application formula itself were daunting, quite apart from the details of any proposed project. My initial two-week exploratory visit in June had not provided the detailed local knowledge necessary for an Albania-based programme, nor at that time had we anticipated such an in-depth opportunity. I therefore returned to Tiranë during the exceedingly frosty December of 1994 to discuss with colleagues this new situation. Some rather ambitious expectations were thus unavoidably raised. A threefold plan was agreed:

1 Renovation of the library of the Institute of Fine Arts. I drafted a detailed ground plan of the premises and devised a strategy whereby it could be transformed into a modern open-access, electronically secured, browsable collection with enhanced equipment and stock.
2 A national programme of professional training for music librarians in Tiranë and the music schools throughout Albania.
3 Creation of an Albanian Music Information Centre (MIC).

Even during my initial two-week visit in June, I had come to recognize the need for an agency systematically to conserve, document and promote Albanian music. As an archive – essentially a new library – it could be equipped and organized to such modern standards as to represent an example for general library development of significance beyond its sectoral dedication to music. Catalogues would be necessary in order to appreciate the full breadth of Albanian music from past and present. Promotion would bring all types of Albanian music to wider attention both abroad and within Albania. It could publish a regular journal or newsletter. A studio could be equipped with synthesizer facilities for experimental use by composers. A modern computerized music software system could fulfil a particular need for an Albanian music publishing facility. From sales of published music and subscriptions, it could earn income both within Albania and, more importantly, as foreign-currency income, thereby providing at least an element of financial self-sustainability. It could organize events and initiate new recordings. It could in a small way represent a huge success for Albanian national identity.

Imaginations were caught, and I was encouraged by two particular expressions of support. The first was professionally from the Albanian Library Association. The second was politically from the then Albanian Minister of Culture, Dr Teodor Laço. In fact, everyone involved with music for Albania seemed to appreciate and enthuse about the value of what we were trying to achieve.

We were working against the clock in so far as a project outline had to be submitted by the end of December 1994 with a final document submitted by the end of March (1995). This we managed, conforming exactly to the labyrinthine application document. We satisfied the requirement for one local Albanian partner (the Albanian Library Association) plus two EU member-state partners (IAML [UK] and the Music Libraries Trust in the UK, plus the Contemporary Music Centre, Dublin – the Irish MIC). There remained one small difficulty – money. Without delving too deeply into financial complexities, Phare offered 60 per cent of a total project cost (to be calculated in ecus). Twenty per cent could be offered 'in kind', representing the costed value of time and materials contributed *gratis* by partner organizations. The remaining 20 per cent, however, had to be provided by secured finance. In broad terms, for a total project cost of US$225 000, we needed to find $45 000 in order to secure Phare funding of US$135 000. The deadline passed. We were unable to muster the necessary US$45 000. Phare, through its London office, continued to offer encouragement to us to reapply next time round.

Surely, we felt, we could gather together US$45 000 during the next 12 months. This, however, suddenly became an academic dream when Phare changed its terms of eligibility. From 1995, it required all aspects of future Phare projects to include an element of self-sustainability. In other words, it required a means of earning income. This effectively disqualified the first two aspects of the original plan. Library development represented enhanced service delivery but without any income-earning potential. This left the MIC with its proposed music publishing facility.

At the same time, Phare improved its financial criteria in favour of potential bidders in so far as it now offered up to 80 per cent of total project cost, with just 10 per cent required respectively as in-kind and secured funding. I returned to Tiranë in October 1995 with an outline of a revised, smaller project to establish an Albanian MIC. It was pleasing that we continued to enjoy the support and involvement of the Contemporary Music Centre, Dublin – the Irish MIC – which served also as a informational conduit to our colleagues in the International Association of Music Information Centres (IAMIC) for whom it could be argued the creation of an Albanian MIC was more relevant even than for ourselves in IAML.

Following extensive discussions with all those interested, a comprehensively described and fully costed proposal was submitted to Phare in March 1996. We had succeeded with promises of contributory funding, from the Swiss-based Solon Foundation and the Budapest-based Soros-funded Open Society Institute. A total project cost of US$207 323 comprised no less than 18.7 per cent in-kind contributions valued at US$38 763, plus an impressive 21.3 per cent promised contributory funding at US$44 165. The balance of US$124 395 was to be sought from Phare, at 60 per cent of total project cost, well and impressively within the revised 80 per cent maximum now permitted.

During the summer of 1996, while applications were being evaluated by Phare, the Swiss Pro Helvetia organization expressed considerable interest and offered more financial support if we were successful.

The project included:

- The cost of all equipment, including computer hardware for office use, library database, electronic stock security system, composers' audio-experimentation studio, and music publishing system.
- Professional expertise in UK, Ireland, and elsewhere in Europe regarding library technology and MIC development, to be delivered both within Albania and abroad.
- A comprehensive training programme for an Albanian manager of the MIC both within Albania and at scheduled training sessions in UK, Ireland and elsewhere in Europe.
- Salaries (generous by Albanian standards of the time) for the manager and an assistant for the project duration (18 months).
- A proposed structure involving a Board of Management comprising representatives of Albanian organizations who, working with the MIC Manager, would devise policies and set priorities for the MIC as a new and independent organization.
- A development strategy over 18 months involving an independent local finance monitor plus comprehensive locally negotiated insurance for the project duration.
- A written guarantee of continuation funding upon project completion by the Albanian government, and the offer of free and renovated MIC accommodation at the Opera House – the most central Tiranë location imaginable.

I strove with all possible sincerity to ensure that the project description was not too prescriptive. Training programmes and travel opportunities would ensure that the future direction of the MIC would be decided by Albanians in Albania, by the

Board of Management working with the Albanian MIC Manager, and not as some prepared package of supposed wisdom and instant solutions from those of us abroad. For example, by visiting a number of European MICs, the Albanian MIC Manager would become well qualified to assess the best ways forward and make informed recommendations to the Management Board. The Board of Management in turn would comprise the widest possible representation of Albanian views and seek to ensure that the MIC developed as a truly independent facility.

In short, we had a fully costed project with pledges of all contributory and in-kind contributions required by Phare criteria, fully strategized and totally achievable. All looked good, and we all became excited despite trying to resist succumbing to false expectations. In October 1996, rejection by Phare came as a bitter blow.

Phare explained clearly in its literature that it achieved its decisions confidentially and was unable to explain the reasons for project acceptance or rejection. We had, it must be confessed, succumbed to false expectations raised by virtue of having had the project initiated and repeatedly encouraged by a London-based Phare officer. As professional associations in Albania, Ireland and UK, we had invested huge amounts of time and incurred costs we knew would not be reimbursed. We had researched, prepared, printed and disseminated the project application – for example, 30 copies of the final 150–page document had been circulated in Albania alone. The depth of disappointment among all involved and interested was such that I did spend the best part of the next year trying – and failing – to discover exactly why we had been rejected.

The project had been shortlisted, so evidently it had been assessed as meeting all technical Phare criteria. Perhaps the project description was not sufficiently prescriptive. Rumours suggested (but could of course never be proved) that we were among the victims of discrimination against UK-originated projects as a reaction to the anti-EU policies of British Prime Minister, John Major, during 1996 (the UK Officer of Phare advised that the autumn 1996 Brussels meeting approved the smallest ever proportion of UK-originated projects). Subsequent enquiries by colleagues in Albania suggested that there had been little awareness of our project proposal within the Albanian government beyond the Ministry of Culture. Certainly I knew that it had received no support from British diplomatic sources in Albania, being regarded as too low a priority for Albanian infrastructural development. We had in 1996 failed to attract any British government interest or support such as Know How Funding, even though the Know How Fund *had* offered some funding towards the original March 1995 submission – and without at that time having actually seen what we were proposing to do! It had been the British Council regional officer based in Belgrade, again in 1995, who had dismissed our concerns for music and librarianship as 'remote from our priorities'. There was some irony indeed in that our promises of funding came instead from the USA, Hungary and Switzerland. Advice from contacts working with other EU projects in Brussels suggested that our application had lacked sufficient (any?) lobbying of Phare at official government levels, whether British, Irish or Albanian. Phare itself would admit only that it always received more eligible applications than its funding permitted it to accept, and that it was for this reason that, for every project accepted, four were rejected. So could we resubmit our project for reconsideration yet again next time round?

Within one week of the October 1996 rejection, Phare published its call for that next round of funding applications in 1997. However, its revised criteria now specifically excluded any cultural projects. It was very difficult to accept that our project might have been rejected in anticipation of imminent changes of terms of eligibility instead of being assessed in accordance with the current published criteria which we had met in total. We were indeed advised by European Members of Parliament that there seemed to be a *prima facie* case for consideration by the (then newly created) European Ombudsman. This, we felt, would be impossible to prove, and we had neither the time nor resources to invest still further costs in an exercise of probable futility.

The irony as far as Albania and EU funding is concerned is that Phare appeared to have removed cultural projects from its subsequent agenda on an understanding that they were covered by other EU development programmes such as Ariane, Kaleidoscope and Raphael but for which Albania was not a signatory. In the years following Phare rejection we failed to identify any international development agency still active in Albania which does not exclude cultural development as too low a priority among all of Albania's many infrastructural requirements. As time went by, the Contemporary Music Centre, Dublin, advised that due to the demands of its own development and expansion it could no longer offer participatory support for an EU project. Thus we lost the involvement of a second EU state at a time when EU development programmes demanded multi-nation (four or more EU member states) participation in their projects.

It is extremely difficult as professional music librarians to accept that our objectives are 'remote from the priorities' of such development agencies. It has been particularly disappointing that we seem to have failed to prove the importance of our work as an essential pillar of support for music. Music itself is so essential an ingredient of civilized society that we must not abandon our objectives. Music assumes a still greater importance in a society riven by economic and geographical strife. Nigel Osborne spoke of exactly this at the IAML Conference 2000 in Edinburgh.[10] The needs for development of existing music library provision and an Albanian MIC remain as great now as at any time.

As far as the MIC is concerned, there has never been any doubt about the ability of our Albanian colleagues to devise and maintain a sustainable facility. There might be a need for professional advice and training to internationally accepted standards so that decisions taken locally are based upon best possible informed opinion. Certainly Albania needs all the assistance it can find so that an MIC is appropriately equipped and resourced to join the international MIC community on equal terms. Albanian music needs to be conserved, documented and promoted as a jewel in its national crown. The publication within Albania of the journal *Albanian Music Information* by the Pan-Albanian Union of Music Professionals (the Albanian section of the International Society for Contemporary Music – ISCM) is a significant step towards the creation of an Albanian MIC. Moreover it has been initiated and achieved by Albanians with Albanian expertise and dedication. It is a tangible manifestation that achievements can be made locally without waiting for the uncertain benefits of exterior motivation.

There may be more. A general email from Vasil Tole in September 2000 announced the Albanian Music Information Agency (AMIA). Furthermore, in a personal email received from Tiranë in March 2001, Dr Sokol Shupo announced plans for an Albanian Music Documentation Centre. Funding was being sought from a range of sources including the European Cultural Foundation, the Gaudeamus Foundation and the Soros Foundation, plus support from the Danish MIC. My reply to Dr Shupo summarized the history of our involvement and hopes for the future:

> My professional association of music librarians, IAML(UK) devised a plan in collaboration with Albanian colleagues. This was in response to an invitation from Phare to submit a proposal that combined three elements: 1, Albania. 2, librarianship. 3, music. The plan we devised was very detailed and comprehensive, and also was costed in great detail. It involved advice and expertise from UK, Ireland and elsewhere in Europe, but was intended – and this was very important – to be undertaken and implemented by Albanians in Albania. It received support from the Albanian Government in the form of guaranteed premises to accommodate an Albanian Music Information Centre at the Opera House in Tiranë plus continuation funding to pay for staff beyond the period of proposed project funding.
>
> The reason why the project did not proceed was that, having invited its submission, Phare then rejected it! We have never been able to discover the reasons for its rejection, nor have we been able in the years since to find any alternative source of international funding. The lack of funding was the *only* reason why we could not proceed.
>
> I have remained convinced that it was an excellent idea, that it would have been greatly beneficial for all types and sectors of Albanian music, and that together we could have achieved a 'centre of excellence' which would have set an example for library and archive development in Albania as a whole beyond its own sectoral concentration upon music. It has therefore been extremely disappointing and frustrating that our funding application was rejected by the very EU organisation – Phare – that suggested it in the first place.
>
> IAML(UK) deliberately did not place a copyright upon the published proposal. We believe that the details it contained were good. They were relevant and achievable. We would be delighted if they can be realised with the support of anyone else who can provide the necessary investments. We believed then, and we still believe, that essentially it had to be created by Albanians for Albania and its music.[11]

If both these initiatives can be effected and sustained, then more testimony to Albanian initiative. The UK outreach report published by IAML in *Fontes artis musicae* upon which this chapter is based concluded with what in hindsight seems rather declaratory and defiant:

> For IAML(UK) the 'Albanian Experience' has achieved the allegorical qualities of a parable. It would be quite understandable if we licked our wounds of failed expectation

and frustrated ambition and retired wounded to our island eyrie. Yet at the outset I observed that UK members have been deeply involved with the international work of IAML since its inception and that our participation and commitment have surely dispelled any image of professional insularity. We will certainly not allow our commitment to be jeopardised by mirages of EU funding as real pots of gold at the ends of English rainbows. The benefits of outreach are universal. 'Exploring the Unknown' will continue.[12]

Before this be set to 'Land of Hope and Glory', it must be admitted that the 'Albanian Experience' does seem in retrospect to have something in common with a firework. It burned impressively for its short life but bequeathed only a singed odour of spectacular combustion, soon dispelled upon the winds of time. Certainly our awareness of some hitherto unknown colleagues in scarcely imagined locations has been enhanced by personal encounter. Munira Shahidi introduced us memorably to the music of her homeland and the difficult circumstances in Tajikistan when she spoke at the 1999 IAML(UK) Annual Study Weekend (at the University College of Ripon and York St John). Yet this is a country where 'teachers' salaries have fallen to $5 a month', described as 'a forlorn and wintry country in Central Asia ... trapped in time', where a citizen is quoted as saying 'We are living in the 17th century ... blocked in every sphere. Democracy is here, but without money how can we practice it?'[13] This is a country from which, as Munira explained, it is impossible to correspond by mail because there is no funding for postage stamps ('thank goodness for e-mail'). One is left in awe that libraries and librarians still function at all, and almost in despair of our inability of undertaking anything sectorally that will meaningfully impinge upon numbing poverty.

It was in 1994 that IAML(UK) created its Branch Officership of Outreach Liaison Officer. We sought to strategize our efforts and adopt more proactive policies. Experience, however, has reminded us that our own resources are finite. It is extremely difficult for members' time to be invested in appropriate levels of research and preparation prior to effective exploratory missions to the far- (and not so far-) flung outposts of music librarianship. It is time-consuming simply to seek and obtain necessary funding to undertake a journey, let alone delve into a background sufficiently to avoid the obvious traps of an innocent abroad. Taken to extremes, we see the absurdities of 'the American Library' in Pogradec. Nor can we trust our innocent and sincerely held motives to be received and judged accurately in a world riven by self-interest and altruistic ignorance. Ultimately there have to be personal and organizational commitments if we are to continue proactively beyond the relative latency of issuing invitations to our conferences and training opportunities. Perhaps that is the finest legacy of what now seems 'several years of sometimes frenetic activity'.[14] It has proved impossible to maintain the momentum of those systematic and strategized efforts during the 1990s. Fatigue and frustrations caused by thwarted funding applications cannot fail to condition our ambitions, compounded by the lack of volunteers to commit time and energies for further exploratory visits or even provide the co-ordination of the IAML(UK) Branch Outreach Liaison Officership for two years until assumed anew by Roger Firman (May 2001). Roger's dynamism bodes well for the future and we can confidently look forward to newly revitalized direction and impetus; perhaps also to some learning from the past. Were we really seduced by prospects of gold at ends of those English rainbows? Lest foundations become mere mysteries of future professional archaeology, it is essential that our philosophies of internationalism continue to be realized. Otherwise, images of professional insularity will prove difficult to erase.

Notes

1 Heckmann, H. (1975), *Fontes artis musicae*, **22**, 16.
2 Bryce, M.C. (1988), *Fontes artis musicae*, **35**, 12.
3 General information on IAML(UK) outreach work has appeared in Branch *Annual Reports*. More detailed reports of visits to Albania, Bulgaria, Croatia, Hungary and Macedonia have been published in *Brio* and the *IAML(UK) Newsletter*:

IAML(UK) Annual Reports
1994, 12–13 'Outreach: the Albanian initiative'.
1995, 11–14 'Outreach'.
1996, 11–14 'Outreach: Albania, Croatia, Bulgaria, Macedonia'.
1997, 21–23 'Outreach: Albania, Bulgaria, Croatia, Romania'.
1998, 12–14 'Outreach'.
1999, 10–11 'Outreach'.
2000, 13 'Outreach'.

Albania
Taylor, R. (1994), 'Flight for the eagle? A music librarian's research trip to Albania', *Brio*, **31** (2), Autumn-Winter, 79–85.
Taylor, R. (1995), 'Twice to Tiranë', *IAML(UK) Newsletter*, **28**, February, 16–19.
Taylor, R. (1996), 'Albania: a third visit', *IAML(UK) Newsletter*, **30**, February, 21–24.
Taylor, R. (1997), 'Project: establishment of an Albanian music information centre', *IAML(UK) Newsletter*, **32**, February, 27–9.

Bulgaria, Macedonia
Taylor, R. (1997), 'A Balkan journey: an outreach exploration to Bulgaria and Macedonia', *Brio*, **34** (1), Spring-Summer, 1–18.
Taylor, R. (1997), 'A Balkan journey: an outreach exploration to Bulgaria and Macedonia: supplement', *IAML(UK) Newsletter*, **33**, August, 14–17.

Croatia
Brandram, M. (1996), 'Margaret Brandram, music libraries and Croatia', *IAML(UK) Newsletter*, **31**, August, 29–30.
Brandram, M. (1997), 'Croatia, part 2', *IAML(UK) Newsletter*, **32**, February, 25–6.
Taylor, R. (1998), 'Croatia [3]: rabbits, vine trees and a library', *IAML(UK) Newsletter*, **34**, February, 15–18.
Brandram, M. (1998), 'Croatia [4]', *IAML(UK) Newsletter*, **34**, February, 19.
Taylor, R. (1998), 'Croatia [5]: more travels of an endangered species', *IAML(UK) Newsletter*, **35**, August, 2–5.

Hungary
Taylor, R. (1998), *IAML(UK) Newsletter,* **35**, August, 2–5.
Russia
Thompson, P. (1998), 'Mimoletnosti/visions fugitives, a fleeting look at Russian music libraries', *Brio,* **35** (2), Autumn-Winter, 101–4.
Slovenia
Taylor, R. (1998), *IAML(UK) Newsletter,* **35**, August, 5.

4   Taylor, R. (1998), *IAML(UK) Newsletter,* **34**, February, 15–18.
5   *IAML(UK) Newsletter,* **35**, August, 5–6. Proceedings published as, 'Twenty-first century information society: the role of library associations. Proceedings of the Conference (Budapest, 10–13 May 1998)'; includes Roger Taylor, 'Mating pandas, or continuing education for music librarians', 119–25.
6   Proceedings published as, Sturges, P. and Rosenberg, D. (eds) (1999), *Disaster and After,* London: Taylor Graham.
7   Quarterly subscription journal, ISSN 1016–1082.
8   Emerson, J. (1994), *Albania: The Search for the Eagle's Song,* Ampleforth: Emerson Edition.
9   In December 1989, the Council of Ministers of the European Union decided to assist Poland and Hungary with the sweeping changes taking place in their countries. The Phare Programme was established by Council Regulation (EEC) No. 3906/89 of 18 December 1989 (OJ No. L 375, 23.12.1989) on economic aid to the Republic of Hungary and the Polish People's Republic. Thus, Phare is the acronym of the Programme's original name: '**P**oland and **H**ungary: **A**ction for the **R**estructuring of the **E**conomy'. By 1996 there were 13 Phare partner countries – Albania, Bosnia and Herzegovina, Bulgaria, the Czech Republic, Estonia, Hungary, Latvia, Lithuania, Macedonia, Poland, Romania, Slovakia and Slovenia. Croatia, originally the fourteenth partner country, was suspended from the Phare Programme in August 1995.
10 Osborne, N. (2000),'Music as therapy in war-torn areas of the Balkans', paper presented at the IAML conference, Tuesday 9 August, University of Edinburgh, 'Music and disability: plenary session II'.
11 Email from Roger Taylor to Dr Sokol Shupo, 1 March 2001.
12 Taylor, R. (1999), 'Outreach from a participant's perspective', *Fontes artis musicae,* **46** (1–2), 122–34.
13 Constable, P. (2001), 'Tajikistan struggles in post-Soviet poverty', *Washington Post,* reprinted in *Guardian Weekly,* 8–14 March, 33.
14 Taylor, R. (1998), 'Outreach', *IAML(UK) Annual Report,* 12.

Chapter 15

Things to come – or, ignorance is not Bliss so don't shoot the messenger!

Eric Cooper

When commencing to put thoughts to paper, confronting a blank page is far more unsettling than the sensation experienced by an artist facing a blank canvas. The painter will depict an idea, or an emotion, frozen in time, and the image can be worked over and altered. The writer faces a succession of blank pages and, although part of a continuing narrative, each one brings with it new challenges. The aim of this piece is to try to excavate a few memories and ideas from a long life that may open a door to the future. This is not, in part, an historical account of IAML(UK) as that is set down elsewhere in this volume. Rather it is a recall of past and future hopes for our profession, combined with suggestions to set off thoughts in the minds of those who will be active in the years ahead. No group of individuals remembers events in the same way nor do they interpret them in like fashion. This is a truism, of course, and so what follows will arouse considerable dissension. Good! If it is an honest and open response, it will show a proper level of concern about the paths our profession has travelled and where we are heading in the future. Picking over the past is always difficult. Bertrand Russell (1921), in his book *The Analysis of Mind,* suggests the world was created moments ago and we remember an illusory part. There is my escape clause in these attempts to recall events of the past 50 years. They may, after all, be no more than gossamer. Looking beyond to the future makes for an entirely different set of difficulties that arise when peering through the dark glass of conjecture. This, too, can be equally illusory in its peculiarity. With those caveats I will open my submission.

In the late 1940s, like most institutions in the UK, libraries of every kind were working hard to recover from the effects of six years of war. Most commodities were in short supply and music libraries were experiencing difficulty obtaining scores and books to repair the ravages of the war years. Peace brought an increase in demand for a better standard of living, which was only to be expected after so much deprivation and sacrifice. But resources were scarce and the time became known as an 'age of austerity'. In public libraries, staff realized sound recordings were readily available and saw them as one way of improving and adding gloss to a depleted service. It was in this way gramophone records began to be lent in these islands, as libraries in America and Europe had been for years before 1939. In the UK the innovation was not one that met with unqualified approval. Good British

236

bookmen tended to regard sound recordings in libraries as a diversion and a waste of money. Recorded music was viewed as lightweight entertainment having no place in libraries. Libraries equalled books – end of discussion. The Luddite attitude of the profession to non-print information carriers took root at this time and was to impede the involvement of librarianship into the information age for many years. Librarians called upon to organize gramophone record lending services were held to be, along with music librarians, a lesser breed whose status was confirmed by lower salary scales. Handling printed scores and books about music was a small saving grace allowing one a place at the professional table, but always well below the salt. Even now, the attitude continues, as can be observed in times of financial stringency, when non-print media and music are the first elements to be cut in unavailing attempts to protect 'core' services.

The decline in librarianship, particularly public libraries, must also be attributed to a deep unease the British have about most aspects of public service. This can be seen to have increased markedly in the past 30 years until we have arrived at a point where public service is regarded at inefficient and costly, and private enterprise as the only sensible alternative. We all live in hope of a free lunch without realizing that every attractive alternative will be reflected in the cost of a pound of butter. Current dogma conveniently overlooks this fact while failing to deliver and, at the same time, devaluing public service in all its forms. Librarianship has fared poorly while politicians have performed shamelessly in seeking public approval of short-termism. Citizens have not responded with the imagination and energy necessary to counter predatory assaults on the worthier aspects of public service. The public sector should have received the same freedom from political interference accorded to private enterprise to enable the appropriate development of an entrepreneurial ethos and economic management. But over a period of 30 years or more the anti-public lobby grew unchecked. Librarianship found itself in this situation at a time when it was facing the greatest changes in communication since the invention of the printing press. 'The times they are a-changin'' as Bob Dylan sang while good bookmen everywhere hoped for a comfortable *status quo*. At about this period chief librarians spotted a loophole in the Public Libraries Act enabling them to make charges for non-book materials and services. The majority jumped on the bandwagon with unseemly haste, shamelessly putting the monies into book provision the while. At a Library Association conference in the early 1970s I suggested they were opening a door to a situation that would lead inevitably to the end of the net book agreement, public lending right and, perhaps, even the principle of free public lending. My remarks were met with heated derision. It was as though one had announced to a Presbyterian congregation in the 1870s that God was dead. Here was a profession that did not understand the changes taking place in the world and failed to appreciate their day-to-day decision could affect the future of the profession. What they did know was that change could not possibly affect libraries. Now, with the increase of IT in all aspects of life, we are getting there just as I suggested.

But all was not gloom for music librarians in post-war years. The founding of the UK Branch of IAML was a ground-breaking event. Those who were present that evening in 1953 at Duke's Hall in the Royal Academy of Music are a dwindling number now, but everyone knew it to be a significant moment. For the first time there was to be an organization designed to meet the needs of music librarianship. For those at the cutting edge it signalled the end of isolation. We now had a forum to promote the separate identity of music librarianship that would sustain its members in the years to come. Here was cause for jubilation and optimism.

In 1954 the Branch held its first conference in Bristol providing the first major opportunity to meet colleagues and exchange ideas and information. I met E.T. 'Bill' Bryant and John Davies for the first time and established important friendships that endured to the ends of their lives. At one session I raised the need to address attention to the question of music sound recordings and other information carriers, such as tapes, as library materials. The intervention went down like a lead balloon. Agendas had already been established by a founding committee consisting of representatives from academic and research libraries and, to them, the question appeared irrelevant. Indeed, at this distance in time, it may be doubted they understood the question, steeped as they were in the disciplines of a time-honoured profession. However, Bryant, with his passionate love of recorded music, and Davies, with his wide knowledge of broadcasting, both understood the significance of the intervention. At the close of the session they contacted me separately, agreeing the subject was important enough to persevere with, thus repairing damaged enthusiasm.

It is difficult to understand today how the subject of non-book materials had little importance to senior members of the profession totally absorbed in a world dominated by printed information. The problems faced by a new generation of public music librarians in charge of intensively used collections of sound recordings were quite low down in the scale of subjects needing attention. This could hardly be otherwise if one were not directly involved. It was not a case for criticism, but it did lead to considerable frustration. Although we sat at table, so to speak, we were, like Jeremy Bentham, present but not voting. Persistence bore fruit however, and within two years, with the support of Bryant, Davies and others, a small group was chosen to produce a handbook covering the organization of record libraries. Within a fairly short period of time the Branch published the first comprehensive British book *Gramophone Record Libraries: Their Organisation and Practice* edited by Henry Currall (1970). Though not wishing to cavil, the committee saw it as a means to contribute to Branch coffers and less of a work of significance to music librarianship. It sold well and ran to a second enlarged edition. Though the UK Branch maintained a close relationship with the British Institute of Recorded Sound, as it was then called, there was no desire to establish a sound recordings group for members. The way was paved to the Library Association who undertook to establish a specialist section to be called the Sound Recordings Group. It was a protracted negotiation in that no party was really keen to take action. But the scale of developments in libraries overtook resistance.

In the 1950s and 1960s the Library Association's attention was focused on education. In those times many influential librarians had qualified through part-time study and very few had attended any full-time library instruction. A librarian who also possessed a degree was a rarity outside university and research libraries. In a profession that felt itself to be inextricably linked to the arts and scholarship its members saw themselves to be disadvantaged. Those concerned about the status of the qualification devoted maximum time and effort in establishing full-time courses of two and three years' duration. Degree status was the goal. The aim was laudable, but the education deemed essential for the latter half of the twentieth century was nineteenth-century in content. They failed to take account of new technology already transforming industry, commerce and everyday life. The 'movers and shakers' sought to perpetuate an idea that librarians were inseparable from the creative world of the arts and sciences, and one where bibliophilists coexisted with authors, scientists and artists hopefully on equal terms. Image came before substance and they did not understand the world had changed to an information society employing new technology. The new syllabuses needed to contain elements on information management and computer science, along with a broad examination of all non-print information carriers. Traditional studies should by then have become optional papers for students wishing to take them. But the opportunity was missed and courses were organized elsewhere as parts of other professional studies for commerce and so on. The philosophy of information technology was centred in our universities. The library profession should have made itself the central body for qualification in information technology, but obsessive bookmanship stood in the way. This failure has proved a severe setback leaving all sectors of librarianship playing catch-up for years to come.

This sad state of affairs did not have to happen. It was not as if change was sudden and everyone was taken unaware. There had been endless signs of what was coming. From Wells to Aldous Huxley and Orwell, writers had been warning about the future. By 1959 Huxley said much of what he had forecast in *Brave New World* had already come to pass and he expected more to follow. Science-fiction writers had fantasized about communication, travel, warfare and other matters that, with the passage of time, proved to be uncannily accurate. One might speculate whether young scientists were avid readers of futuristic fiction and American comic papers in the 1920s and 1930s, or whether the fantasists were more aware of the directions of scientific research than they cared to admit. It could prove an interesting area for some young student to research. It is certain fiction writers were fishing in well-stocked waters and netting a lot of material from the shoals of early twentieth-century research. They had many connections with researchers and used their acquired knowledge to entertain and inform. Preliminary nuclear research was the stuff of history and Einstein's theories on space and time were being taught in secondary schools. Herbert Marshall McLuhan began his doctoral thesis (McLuhan, 1943) on the future of communication and the printed word in 1938. In 1942, in his native Canada, he became a friend of the Vorticist artist and writer Percy Wyndham Lewis who, shortly after the war, explored the possibilities of McLuhan's work in novels and essays published in Britain. The future options for our profession were being indicated but ignored. One must assume librarians did not read as widely as they professed to do or, perhaps they did not understand the subject matter. Relevant articles in scientific journals of the day should have been the bedrock of future planning for information storage, particularly after the experience gained in the war years.

In 1935, the British scientist and mathematician Alan Turing, the pioneer of computer theory, was studying mathematical logic and, in 1936–37, published a paper 'On computable numbers with an application to the Entscheidungs problem' along with a description of a universal computer. He was awarded a PhD for his research while at Princeton, where he associated with fellow researchers including McLuhan. He returned to the UK to do brilliant work during the war and there, in 1945, built ACE, the first electronic computer, thus completing the work of Charles Babbage (1792–1871). Turing continued work at the University of Manchester Institute of Science and Technology (UMIST) where, between 1945 and his early death in 1954, using patterns of living organisms, he carried forward his research into artificial intelligence. The future of IT was soundly established outside of the realms of fiction. By 1955 J.B. Lyons were using computers to organize every aspect of their restaurant and catering empire and selling surplus capacity to government departments including the Treasury and Inland Revenue.

If, dear reader, you have read this far, and wonder where it is leading, perhaps it is time to pull the strands together. During the inter-war years and after 1945, all the varied media formats were clearly heralding a new information age. The changes were apparent for all to see if they were involved or in any way interested. It was not difficult. There were endless discussions about the social effects of film, television and radio. After 1945, with the advent of transistors and solid state circuitry allied to magnetic tape recording, the pace of change and discussion moved up several gears. Despite ground-breaking changes taking place all around, our profession remained aloof. The signals raised by Huxley and, later, Lawrence Durrell in his novel *Nunquam* published in 1970 raised hardly a ripple. All serious looks at the future course of new technology passed by our captains at the helm. Rather, one suspects, if they read at all, they subscribed to the writings of gurus like Rachel Carson, finding her demonization of new technology more comforting. This kind of stuff had a marked effect on the chattering classes for a decade or more. They doubtless saw themselves as literary tribunes manning barricades against the onslaughts of disruption. Librarians took refuge in a sort of 'bibliolatry' as a comfort blanket. For the smaller number who appreciated what was happening, it was not in their power to influence pragmatic decision-making.

By 1971 electronic mails were being sent. Industrial communication was taking place through a growing worldwide network of fibre optic cables and satellites. Industry, commerce and areas of higher education were embracing new communications technology at an ever-increasing pace. At about this time the Library Association held the annual conference on the South Bank, scheduling a session on new technology, in the Purcell Room. With very little notice it was decided to relocate the session to a small room, in favour of a more traditional topic, despite the invitation to a distinguished panel of speakers. Perhaps the decision was correct, for, although the room was full to overflowing, the delegates in the main showed as much comprehension of the business in hand as nineteenth-century ostlers faced with the growth of railways. The questions from the floor were, in many cases, banal and laced with indignation at the idea that the session supported the end of printing. From that time forward I began to reduce my role in audiovisual proselytism and turned more to IAML where there was a clearer appreciation about the future, particularly at the international conferences. Discussion with the International Association of Sound Archives (IASA), the International Federation of Library Associations (IFLA) and similar organizations were ongoing and covering interesting ground. On the whole, it was a negative scene in the UK, and dispiriting to witness the activities of those librarians who regarded IT as a vehicle to create a reputation. It requires more than vanity to meaningfully progress a movement. Couple this to the adverse conditions created by politicians and their financial advisers, and one can appreciate how imagination and initiative have been stifled in a profession already unsure of its wider role. Partnership initiatives and all those trendy jaunts now being explored are placebos and sticking plasters to cure years of political interference and underfunding.

If this reads like a stream of consciousness hitting the page, I am sorry. It is the way I have always written and in my eighth decade it is difficult to change. Despite the passing of the years I am ever more acutely aware of the changes our profession will have to face. The greatest discoveries of the past 100 years have nearly all taken place in the field of communications, and the range of possibilities continues to increase. We are moving ever further from the age of Gutenburg printing where the journey can be said to have started. It is a nice touch though, that we can now examine that first printed Bible on the web, courtesy of the British Library. The way humankind has developed communication in the past century is greater than any other activity in the whole of human existence. The changes will continue at an ever-increasing pace. Pessimists aver we are sacrificing our intellectual heritage to technology. That is plain nonsense. The logical conclusion of following that line of thought would have us all back in caves listening to jongleurs and storytellers. Humanity fails if it remains shackled to outmoded lifestyles. Librarianship has often been held back from progress by strong, deep-seated desires for a quiet unchanging profession. Without the courage and imagination to embrace change it will not have a future. It must adapt or languish. Surviving on the outer edge of events rather than at the counter is not an option.

Looking to the future and examining elementary conditions in most types of libraries, one sees, due to insufficient staffing levels, returned books often no longer shelved in strict classified and alphabetical order. Busy clients from all walks of life have little time to search randomly for information and are turning increasingly to computers and the web for reference information. It is easier and often more interesting than searching through files of books in your local library and, anyway, printed extracts are more easily retained.

Dependence on cable may, for some users of PCs, be an inconvenience. But there are alternatives. Though fibre optic cables have been available for 40 years, moves are afoot to enable users to be free from the need of online connection. A new generation of miniature computers are already in current use that interact with any database, operating within a reasonable distance, without cable. By the end of 2004 the industry expects to have sold 200 million of these new units worldwide. It is, of course, a matter for concern throughout the industry, when one realizes no program will be secure and it will be impossible to know when material has been invaded and downloaded. New and secure methods of protecting information will have to be developed, but will be extremely expensive to install. It is reasonable to assume, because of cost, that most data banks will not be secure and therefore will be open to copying. If computer buffs are amused or offended by my simple, non-technical language, I am writing up basic information for ordinary mortals to understand.

The avid reader will soon be able to carry a small library with him/her in a pocket-sized unit incorporating a read-off screen the size of the average paperback. It will have the capacity to store 50 average-length books. Individual books may be cancelled and replaced by new ones at anytime, anywhere; no need for choosing a favourite book for a desert island. Take a small library operated by solar power instead. Within a few years all new equipment will translate programs into any language, removing at long last the final barrier in everyday communication.

It is only a matter of time before telephone technology will be as obsolete as semaphore or Morse code. Eventually individuals will be given a code number at birth to operate with PCs the size of signet rings operating on voice or iris recognition. The individual will be online everywhere, 24 hours a day, able to interact with all sources of information. Each person will carry social, medical, educational and professional information with them at all times. Discussion about the identity card will be in the distant past. Beyond what is regarded as moral today, research goes ahead on 'skin phones'. As with present-day identity microchips injected into pets, 'skin phones' might be injected at birth and programmed for every conceivable aspect of information and communication. Such an innovation would be unacceptable today with questions of infringement of liberty and confidentiality, but future generations may well accept them without those reservations. If the world population is set to double as some forecast, new methods of documentation and record-keeping may be essential and the rest could follow in short order.

Many will wonder what kind of screen will be required as miniaturization reaches towards the ultimate. Already flat screens are arriving in high street shops. The next step will be foldable fabric screens incorporating interwoven microcircuitry to interface with miniature PCs or even 'skin phones'. The QWERTY keyboard will be long gone and replaced by direct vocal communication.

The anxious thoughts these possibilities, inevitabilities perhaps, will arouse are natural reactions involving as they do questions of liberty and freedom. But such forecasts are tomorrow's reality and future generations will be faced with many compromises as these come to pass. With the growth of the world community and economy in the next 100 years, society will change beyond recognition.

Today writers, composers and artists are trying to keep up with market options.

Artists are using computers as an alternative to paint. Writers (not this one) work straight to computers and all are seeking ways of using technology to make direct contact with client groups to maximize income. The romantic vision of composers sitting at pianos with pencils and paper is out of date. Many now work with synthesizers direct to disc. The music industry has had to adapt to enormous changes and the technical options in printing, recording and distributing product broaden day by day. Eventually all authenticated written and recorded music, along with written and spoken word, will be available from data banks. Traditional methods of publishing will play a diminishing role as time passes and they become less economic to maintain.

Attending a recent concert of early and baroque music, one could not help but notice how the spontaneity was hindered on the occasions sheet music came into play. Music stands of the future will consist of flat video screens linked to the performer's repertoire data bank, each page on call, edited and marked for performance, at the touch of a switch or foot pedal. No score-sorting, page-turning, mislaid parts or indecipherable cues. The catalogue of works of publishing houses and research collections will increasingly be available online. Archives, expensive to maintain and too precious to handle will, like the Gutenberg Bible and other great treasures, be available for study by everyone. A great deal of this work has already been completed and is available.

And what of copyright? I am not a seer and write only of what I know. The question is too involved to deal with here, although I have suggested above the cost of rights as understood now may become too expensive and ponderous to maintain. The deliberations of interested parties such as the Copyright Licensing Agency (CLA) and the UniversitiesUK (UUK) are running behind the pace of events and, by the time these groups reach any conclusions, the realities will be elsewhere. The stance of some groups, such as 'Wipout' perhaps, are too absolutist and distant from the real world and human nature to be viable. The market will decide the course of events where international companies will purchase copyright materials for one-off payments. It is already happening in the field of illustration and advertising at work. The incentives to forego rights for large single fees will become commonplace and will be simpler than continuing the present fragile system. There will be an exponential rise in costs causing problems needing solutions if social inequality is to be avoided.

The precise nature of the world to come is incalculable. The driving force behind information technology is the achievement of the highest possible return on capital investment. This is achieved, in part, through the obsolescence factor. The market always operates well behind the technical possibilities of product design. This produces a deliberate trickle effect where tomorrow's world is always next year's spending capacity away and this year's purchase will be out of date before the bank clears the payment. Cynical? Well yes, but largely true! Today, as always, consumers cannot avoid being Kings of Sipylus. Though aware of the stratagems of sales people, we are largely incapable of resisting their blandishments to buy the 'very latest' package on offer. There is no escape from a system that drives the world economy.

As to the new world of shorter working time, greater leisure and full employment promised by the gurus of new technology 70 years ago, human greed put an end to that dream. For good or ill we must live with the consequences. Please don't shoot me, I'm only the messenger. Now, while there is still time – where did I put my library ticket?

Bibliography

Currall, Henry H.J. (1970), *Gramophone Record Libraries: Their Organisation and Practice*, 2nd edn (first published 1963), London: Crosby Lockwood.

Durrell, L. (1970), *Numquam: A Novel*, London: Faber.

Huxley, A. (1932), *Brave New World: A Novel*, London: Chatto and Windus.

Huxley, A. (1959), *Brave New World Revisited*, London: Chatto and Windus.

McLuhan, H.M. (1943), 'The place of Thomas Nashe in the learning of his time', unpublished PhD thesis, University of Cambridge.

Russell, B. (1921), *The Analysis of Mind*, London: Allen and Unwin.

Turing, A. (1936–37), 'On computable numbers with an application to the Entscheidungs problem', *Proceeding of the London Mathematical Society*, series 2, **42**, 230–65.

Index

Aberdeen libraries 23
Aberdeen University Library 114
Aberdeen University Press 85
Aberystwyth, training in librarianship at 75,
    78–82, 186
academic staff's involvement with
    information skills 65–6
academic study of librarianship 75–7
Adams, W.G.S. 31–2
Airdrie Library 22
Albania 222–33
Allan, David 105, 115
Allan, Jean 2, 38–9
Allegro Training 82
American Library Association 86
Anderson, John 104
Anderson, Kenneth 7, 211
Anderson Report (1996) 188
Andrews, Paul 7, 125, 192; *author of*
    Chapter 12
Anglo-American Cataloguing Rules 6–7, 143
Annual Survey of Music Libraries 9, 128,
    179
Apel, W. 95
ARCHIE 154
Arts and Humanities Research Board 176
Arts Council 10, 48, 179
Aston Free Library 21–2
Aston Manor 27
Atholl Collection 38
audio and the Internet 158–61
Axon, William 19–20

Bacon, Francis 91
Baker, Andrew 157
Baker, David 121
Balbirnie, William 104
Banks, Chris 145, 151, 192, 213
Banks, Paul 79

Banner, Barbara 2
Barbican Music Library 160
Bartlett, Clifford 5, 7, 122–5
Bateman, R. 46
Bath Information Data Service (BIDS)
    149–50
Batt, C. 157
BBC *see* British Broadcasting Corporation
Beckenham libraries 44
Beethoven Bibliography 154
Berkshire libraries 183
Bevan, N. 148
bibliographic databases 149–50
Biographical Dictionary of Musicians 24
Birmingham libraries 20–21
    Co-operative Mechanisation Project 144,
        182–3
    Central Music Library survey of
        borrowers 217
BITNET 153
Blackboard™ 69
Blackstone, Tessa 14, 191
blind people, services for 19
Bliss, H.E. 89
Blokland, Ad 131
Bluck, R. 57
Blume, Friedrich 174
Bodleian Library 161–2
Bolton libraries 30
Booth collection 44
Bornet, Christopher 179
Bournemouth libraries 29–30
Bradford libraries 38, 44
Bradley, C.J. 88
Bragg, John 26–7
Brandram, Margaret 221
Brigham Young University 177
Brio xiii, 4–6, 120–25, 127–31, 175, 177,
    179, 194–5, 221

Briscoe, J. Potter 22
Bristol City Library 37
British Broadcasting Corporation (BBC) 7,
     181
     Music Library 75, 194
British Catalogue of Music (BCM) 3–4, 88
British Council 3, 222, 225, 230–31
British Library 9, 13, 88, 112, 124, 144–5,
     176, 178
     Catalogue of Printed Music 212
     Co-operation and Partnership
          Programme 14, 191–2, 201, 213
     Information Sciences Service (BLISS)
          129
     Lending Division (Document and
          Supply Centre) 49, 177, 182, 211,
          216
     Research and Development Department
          187
British Museum 2
British National Bibliography 143, 145
British Phonographic Industry (BPI) 10, 12
British Standards 85
British Union-Catalogue of Early Music
     176
*British Union Catalogue of Music
     Periodicals* (BUCOMP) 9, 179
British Union Catalogue of Orchestral Sets
     (BUCOS) 7, 9, 177–8, 210, 214
Britten-Pears Foundation 79, 186
Britten-Pears Library 211–12
Bronson, Bertrand H. 141
Brook, B. 90, 142, 146, 153, 196
Brophy, P. 148
Brown, James Duff 23–6, 30, 131
Brown, Royston 172–3, 187
Brown, Steve 148
Bryant, E.T. 6, 12, 41, 87–9, 172, 195, 238
Bryce, Maria Calderisi 220
Buckingham Palace Road Library 48–9
Bulgaria 222–3
Bulletin Board for Libraries (BUBL) 154
Burnley libraries 33
Bury libraries 33
Byrd, William: *Gradualia* 137–9

CALIM (Consortium of Academic Libraries
     in Manchester) 156
Callander, T.E. 47

Camberwell libraries 26
Camm Music Library 29
Cardiff libraries 30, 37
Carnegie, Andrew 31
Carnegie Trust 31–3
Carnell, E.J. 36
Carson, Rachel 240
Castleford libraries 49
cataloguing systems 86–90
CD-ROM 147–9
Cecilia project 192–3, 200–208
Central Music Library (company) 48–9,
     181
chamber music, definition of 94
charges for library services 216–18, 237
Charity Know How 227
Chelsea libraries 26
Cheltenham libraries 37
Chemical Abstracts 146
Chingford libraries 45
Christie Moor, Winifred 48
Chubb, Leonard 41
Cipkin, Christopher *author of Chapter 3*
Clark, Chris 145
Clegg, Susan 7, 144
Clerkenwell libraries 23–5
Clews, J. 89
Coates, E. 4, 88
Cobbe, Hugh 79, 221
Collinson, R.C.W. 2
Colne libraries 49
Colon classification 89
compact disc (CD) technology 147–9
Compton, Sheila 7, 177, 210; *see also*
     Cotton, Sheila
computer usage in libraries 141–2, 146
CONARLS (Circle of Officers of National,
     Academic and Regional Library
     Systems) 179, 213, 215
Consortium of University Research
     Libraries 181
Contemporary Music Centre, Dublin 228–9,
     231
Cooper, Eric 6; *author of Chapter 15*
Cooper, Gerald M. 48
co-operation between music libraries
     172–96, 200, 218
copyright protection 11–12, 14, 159–61,
     243

Corbett, Edmund 42
Cottesmore Village Library 23
Cotton, Sheila *see* Compton, Sheila
Council of Europe 225
Coventry libraries 41
Cowan and Sons 103
Cowell, Peter 19, 27
Crawley, Julie 12–13; *author of Chapter 10*
Crotch, William 44
Crudge, Roger 9–10
CTI Music 151
Cudworth, Charles 2
Cumberland libraries 33
Currall, Henry 6, 238

Daniels, Frank 184
Davies, Sir Henry Walford 33, 35
Davies, John 2, 5, 238
Davies, Sir Peter Maxwell 14
Davies, Ruth 7
DDC cataloguing system *see* Dewey
       decimal classification
Dent, E.J. 48
Derby libraries 26
Dewey decimal classification 40, 87–9, 94
Dickinson, G.S. 88
Dixon, William 38
DNER (Distributed National Electronic
       Resource) 150, 156
Dolan, J. 157
Dove, Jack 174
Dover, Adrian 179
Dovey, Matthew 189, 205
Draper, Rachel 180
Dublin Core 145, 202, 204
Duce, Roger 212
Duck, Leonard 2, 28
Duckles, Vincent 130
Dundee libraries 23
Durrell, Lawrence 240
Dye, Pat 191, 214
Dymond, Freddie 6

Ealing libraries 43
Ealing Polytechnic 75
EARL (Electronic Access to Resources in
       Libraries) 157
Edinburgh libraries 29, 39–40, 44
Edwards, Warwick 114

electronic mail 151–3, 240
eLib (Electronic Libraries) programme 156,
       189
Emerson, June 226
Encore! catalogue 14, 178, 191, 213,
       216–18
enquiry work by libraries 68
Ensemble project 14, 190
Erith libraries 42–3
ERMULI Trust 9, 187, 192
Estonia 221
European Library Plan 184
European Union 230–31; *see also Phare*
       programme
Evans, Edwin 48
expenditure cuts affecting music libraries
       185
extension work of libraries 36, 41–2

faceted classification 4
Fanning, Shawn 159
Farr, Henry 32
Fearnside, Kate 33
Fellows, Dorcas 89
Field, Clive 190, 192–3
Finsbury libraries 30
Finzi Collection 64
Firman, Roger 233–4
First Search 149–50
Firth, Samuel 37
Follett Report 188
Freegard, Michael 78, 186
Fulham libraries 47
Fuller Maitland, J.A. 38
Furner-Hines, J. 155

Gale Research 89
Galpin Society 4
Gardner, George 37
Garratt, Morris 5
Gergeleñiu, Aurika 221
Germany 1
Glasgow libraries 31, 37
Glasgow University Music Department 114
Gopher 154
Gosh, Katerina 220, 226
Gough, John *co-author of Chapter 13*
graduate diplomas in librarianship 76–7
Gramophone Record Libraries handbook 6

Gray, Duncan 32
Greater London Audio Specialization
    Scheme (GLASS) 183–4
Greville, Lilian 23
Griffiths, Peter 184

Hadden, James Cuthbert 99
Hadow, Sir William Henry 48
Hall, C.J. 29
Hampstead libraries 27, 30
Handsworth libraries 21–2, 26–7
Hargreaves Trust 29
Harrold, Ann *co-author of Chapter 5*
Hart, Elizabeth 7, 9, 13, 185–6
Harvard Dictionary of Music 95
Haxby, R. 26
Hayward, J.D. 44
Heaney, M. 204
Heckmann, Harald 5, 196, 220
Hellen, Ruth 157, 186, 192, 221; *co-author
    of Chapter 1*
Henry Watson Music Library, Manchester
    1, 4, 27–30, 33, 38
Herefordshire libraries 43
Hickling, Jean 47
Hinrichsen, Max 4
Hinton, E. Austin 41
Hodges, Tony 7, 9, 179, 191, 210, 212
Hodgson, Julian 7
Hoey, Bailie 31
Hogg, Katharine 189
Hogg, Marian 189
Holborn Central Library 45, 47–8
Holden, P. 95
Holst, Imogen xii, xiv
Hood, Alan 183, 194
Hopkinson, Cecil 2–3, 99–100, 107–9, 115,
    120
Hornchurch libraries 45
Horrocks, S.H. 47
Hoxton library 36
Huddersfield libraries 37
Hughes, Anselm 2
Huxley, Aldous 239–40
HyperText Markup Language (HTML)
    155

Information North 212
information skills 57–69

information technology applied in libraries
    141–62, 180–81, 188, 240, 243
International Association of Music
    Information Centres (IAMIC) 229
International Association of Music Libraries
    1–12, 77–9, 142, 144, 162, 172–96
    passim, 200–201, 204, 208, 213,
    237–8
electronic mail list 151
expansion of UK Branch to cover
    Ireland 195
international outreach by UK Branch
    130–31, 220–34, 241
library of UK Branch 11, 127–34
membership of UK Branch 175
newsletter of UK Branch 8, 123–4, 130,
    152, 205
objectives of UK Branch 173–4
training courses offered by 186
web site 155–6
International Standard Music Number
    (ISMN) system 9, 180
International Standards Organization 85
Internet resources 13, 67, 69, 150–56,
    184–5, 202
for audio 158–61
in public libraries 157–8
Ipswich libraries 36
Islington libraries 35
ISMN Agency 11

JANET (Joint Academic Network) 153
Jefferson, Thomas 89
Johnston, P. 205–6
Joint Information Systems Committee 188
Jolliffe, Harold 36
Jones, Herbert 31
Jones, Malcolm 5, 7, 10–11, 14, 122–4,
    144–5, 177, 180, 191, 209–12; *author
    of Chapter 7 and co-author of
    Chapter 13*
journals, electronic 150
Jukebox project 160–61, 184

Kaam, Evelyn van 131
Keller, M.A. 146–7
Kelly, T. 38, 45
Kenny, Nancy 78, 186
Kensington and Chelsea libraries 183

Kent libraries 33
Kenyon Committee 37
Kidson, Frank 37–8
King, Alec Hyatt 2–3, 5, 12–13, 146, 176
Kuphal, Viv 157

La Fontaine, Henri 89
Laço, Teodor 228
Lambeth libraries 47
Lancaster, F.W. 147
Lancaster Library 38
LASER (London and South East Region)
    cooperation scheme 191, 213–14
Law, D. 148–9
Law, William 34–5
Lawrence, C.A. 146–7
Lea, Graham 91; *co-author of Chapter 5*
Leavitt, Harold J. 141
lectures in libraries 26
Ledsham, Ian 13, 124–5, 186, 211; *author
    of Chapter 4*
Leeds College of Commerce 75
Leeds libraries 26, 29–30, 37
Leicester and Leicestershire libraries 182
Lewis, Malcolm 10–11, 129–30, 179–82,
    185, 187, 191, 211; *author of Chapter
    2*
librarianship, decline in 237–41
Library Association 2, 6, 8, 10, 12, 24–5,
    44, 49, 75, 82, 128–9, 177, 196, 200,
    225, 238; *see also* American Library
    Association
Library of Congress 87–9, 143–5, 148–9,
    161
Library and Information Commission 11,
    157–8
Library and Information Cooperation
    Council (LINC) 179, 187
Library and Information Services Council
    (LISC) 172, 187
library loan patterns, statistics on 215
Lindsey and Holland libraries 44
Line, M. 88, 182
Linnitt, Peter 192, 200–201
Linton, Marion 107
lis-link discussion group 151
Liverpool libraries 18–19, 27, 38, 44, 75,
    210
    Central Music Library 1

Liverpool Philharmonic Society 38
Livesey, Louis J. 147
Lizars, William Home 105
Llanelli library 36
Lloyd Webber, Julian 11
local education authorities 210
Long, Maureen 6
Long Report (1972) 6
Lönn, Anders 6, 124, 130
Lyons (company) 240

McAulay, Karen 124
McColvin, Lionel 2, 7, 33–6, 40–41, 44–5,
    48–9, 88, 175–6
McCue, Kirsteen *author of Chapter 6*
McKenzie, Don 100, 107, 116
McKillop, John 32
MacKnight, M. 91
Mackworth Collection 37
McLeod, Peter 104
McLuhan, Marshall 239–40
McSean, T. 148–9
Manchester libraries 18–20, 27, 75, 183,
    210; *see also* Henry Watson Music
    Library
Mann, Arthur Henry 44
MARC formats 141–5
Marr, Robert A. 29
Marsh, John Fitchett 17–18
Mason, Helen 191, 212
Massey, Edward Stocks 33
Matthews, E.R. Norris 26
May, John 5–9, 13, 122
Medline database 146
metadata 203
Middlesex libraries 33, 38
MILDRED project 192, 201–5; *see also
    Cecilia* project
Miller, Miriam 7, 143, 177, 180, 183–4
Mills, Patrick 7
Mitcham libraries 42
Mitchell Library 37–8
Moir, John 103–4
Moody Manners collection 38
Moore, C. 148
Morgan, Richard Bonner 37
Mosaic browser 155
MP3 format 158–9
Muncy, Chris 157

Musaurus xii, 84, 91–6
MusBib xii, 84, 96–7
Music Index dictionary catalogue 89–91
Music Libraries Online (MLO) 13, 189
Music Libraries Trust 9, 177, 186, 194, 227–8
Music Library Association of America 128
Music LIP (Library and Information Plan for Music) 129–30, 187–8, 193–5
Music LIP Development Group 188
music performances in libraries 22–3, 34–6, 41–4, 47–8
Music Press 84, 87, 97
Music Publishers' Association 3, 7–8, 14
Music Resources list 155
Music for the Terrified course 13, 78–9, 186
Myres, J.N.L. 23

Napster 159
National Library of Scotland 112
National Music and Disability Information Service 12
National Music Council 14
National Sound Archive 184
networking 142, 148, 153
Nicholson, F. Bentley 28
North London Gramophone and Phonograph Society 35
North London Polytechnic 75, 77, 186
North Western Polytechnic (NWP) Library School 6
North Western Regional Library System 181
Norwich libraries 44
Nottingham and Nottinghamshire libraries 38, 182

Office of Arts and Libraries 187
Olding, R.K. 88
Oldman, C.B. 10, 99–100, 107–9, 115, 176
online public access catalogues (OPACs) 153
open learning 79–80
Open Society Institute 225, 229
Orwell, George 239
Osborne, Nigel 231
Otelet, Paul 89
Overton, C.D. 45–6
Oxford City libraries 22

Oxford University Music Faculty Library 130

paper-making 103
Parr, R.T.L. 31
Patron project 160–61
Peirce, Charles 89
Penge libraries 45
Penney, Barbara 200–201, 204
Performing Arts Data Service (PADS) 145, 205, 208
Perth libraries 38
Phare programme 227–31
piano rolls 159–60
Piper, A. Cecil 30–31
Plymouth libraries 194
Pope, Alan 11, 180
Poulter, A. 155
Powell, Andy 204
Pratt, George 178
Prescott, Celia 179
Preston, John 101–2
problem-based learning 58–9
public libraries
    Internet resources in 157–8
    music provision in 17–50
Public Libraries Development Incentive Scheme 183, 191

qualifications in librarianship 75–7, 238–9

Raine, James 137–9
Ranganathan, S.R. 89
Rattle, Sir Simon 209
Reading University Music Library 57–69
RealAudio 158–9
record libraries 34–7, 43–7, 50, 183–4, 236–8
Redfern, Brian 8, 75, 77, 177–9, 210; *co-author of Chapter 1*
Reed, Tony 124, 178, 182.
Reeves, Harold 41
reference libraries 37–40
Research Support Libraries Programme (RSLP) 190, 192; *see also* ERMULI Trust
Resource Discovery Network (RDN) 156, 193
Riddle, Charles 29–30

Ridgewell, Rupert 177
RIdIM (*Répertoire international
    d'iconographie musicale*) project 176–7
RILM (*Répertoire international de
    littérature musicale*) project 90–91,
    146–50
RIPM (*Répertoire international de la presse
    musicale*) project 176
Riseley, George 37
RISM (*Répertoire international des sources
    musicales*) project 176
Roberts, Sir S.C. 4
Robertson, Michael 159
Robinson, B. 205–6
Robinson, Emma 192
Roulston, Robert William 19
Royal College of Music 177
Royal Holloway College 176
Rugby libraries 43
rural libraries 32–3
Russell, Bertrand 236
Rycroft, Marjorie 107, 114

St Marylebone Central Library 43
St Pancras Library 45
Sala, Valdete 226
Sandeman Public Library, Perth 38
Savage, Ernest 39–40
Scholes, P.A. 94
searching of databases 147–8
Selkirk County Library 36
sets, definition of 209–10
Seven Pillars Model 58–9
Shahidi, Munira 233
shared online bibliographic services 149–50
Sheard, Ernest 5
Sherman, C. 159
Short, Michael 5, 7
Shupo, Sokol 232
Sidwell, L.H. 47–8
Sloss, Kate 189
Smith, Geoffrey 213
Smith, Stanley 36
Solon Foundation 229
Sopher, Alan 5, 7
Sound Sense 12
South West Regional Library System 181
South West University Libraries Systems
    Co-operation Project 144

Southampton University Library 143, 160
Staffordshire libraries 147
Stanley, Roy 195
Steinberger, N. 90–91
Stepney libraries 47
Stevens, Robert 8, 123
Stewart Murray, Lady Dorothea 38
Stock, Walter 2–3, 5, 11, 120, 173–8
Stone, Bayford 44
Stothard, R.T. 105
streaming technology 158–61
Stubley, Peter 144
Surbiton libraries 41–2
Surrey Performing Arts Library 14
Sutton, Charles W. 19
Sutton Coldfield libraries 45
Swindon libraries 44, 47
synonym dictionaries 85

Tajikistan 233
Taphouse Collection 29
Tapley-Soper, H. 33
Taylor, Roger 9, 12–14, 125, 179, 209;
    author of Chapter 14
thesauri 84–7
Thomas, Clare 78
Thomason, Geoffrey 125
Thompson, Pam 11, 13, 187–8, 221; *author
    of Chapter 11*
Thomson, George 99–116
Tole, Vasile 232
training in music librarianship 74–83, 186
Troutman, L. 154
Tucker, Robert 184
Turbet, Richard 174; *editor, and author of
    Introduction and Chapter 9*
Turing, Alan 240
Turner, Malcolm 124
tutorials on information skills 66–7

Vaughan Williams, Ralph 48, 50
Vaughan Williams Trust 6
Village and Country Town Concerts Fund
    33
virtual learning environments 69
Vollans, Robert 175–6

Wagstaff, John 9, 11, 124–5, 151, 179, 185;
    author of Chapter 8

Walker, A. Dennis 4–5
Walker, George 104–5
Walker, James 23
Wallbaum, Christel 121–2
Walthamstow libraries 45–6
Wandsworth libraries 23
Warner, John 30
Warren, Geoff 211
Warrington libraries 17, 30
Warwickshire libraries 33
Waterloo-with-Seaforth library 34
Watson, Henry 27–8
WebCrawler 155
Wells, H.G. 239
West Ham libraries 44
West Midlands Regional Library System 191, 211–12
Westminster libraries 1, 45–9, 75, 181, 183
Whisler, Thomas L. 141

Wighton, Andrew 23
Wilkie, David 105
Wilkins, Kenneth 144
Willett, P. 155
Williams, Daniel 184
Williamson, A. 151
Wolverhampton libraries 26
Wood, Ruzena 4–5, 121–2
Woodhouse, Susi 11, 157, 183, 187, 192, 213; *author of Foreword*
Wright, A. Shaw 43
WWW Virtual Library 155
Wyndham Lewis, Percy 239

York Minster Library 137
Yorkshire West Riding libraries 44

Zanetti, C. 30